Judicial Politics
in the United States

Judicial Politics in the United States

Mark C. Miller

CLARK UNIVERSITY

WESTVIEW
PRESS

A Member of the Perseus Books Group

Westview Press was founded in 1975 in Boulder, Colorado, by notable publisher and intellectual Fred Praeger. Westview Press continues to publish scholarly titles and high-quality undergraduate- and graduate-level textbooks in core social science disciplines. With books developed, written, and edited with the needs of serious nonfiction readers, professors, and students in mind, Westview Press honors its long history of publishing books that matter.

Find us on the World Wide Web at www.westviewpress.com.

Every effort has been made to secure required permissions for all text, images, maps, and other art reprinted in this volume.

Westview Press books are available at special discounts for bulk purchases in the United States by corporations, institutions, and other organizations. For more information, please contact the Special Markets Department at the Perseus Books Group, 2300 Chestnut Street, Suite 200, Philadelphia, PA 19103, or call (800) 810-4145, ext. 5000, or e-mail special.markets@perseusbooks.com.

Set in 10 point Minion Pro by the Perseus Books Group

Library of Congress Cataloging-in-Publication Data

Miller, Mark C. (Mark Carlton), 1958–
   Judicial politics in the United States / Mark C. Miller.
      pages   cm
   Includes bibliographical references and index.
   ISBN 978-0-8133-4679-3 (paperback) — ISBN 978-0-8133-4680-9 (e-book)
1. Political questions and judicial power—United States. 2. Courts—United States.
3. Judicial process—United States. 4. United States—Politics and government.
I. Title.
KF5130.M53 2014
347.73—dc23   2014011388

10 9 8 7 6 5 4 3 2 1

CONTENTS

ACKNOWLEDGMENTS

Like most projects of this type, this book has been a long time in the making. I first developed my interest in judicial politics when I worked as a legislative assistant/staff attorney in the office of the late U.S. Representative John F. Seiberling (D-Ohio). Congressman Seiberling was a lawyer's lawyer, who could easily find drafting errors in a two-hundred-page piece of legislation. He taught me to love the courts and the law, all from a political perspective.

After the congressman announced his retirement from Congress, I went to graduate school in political science at The Ohio State University. At Ohio State, I was able to teach an undergraduate course on U.S. judicial politics as a graduate student. I also learned a great deal about the study of judicial politics from Professors Larry Baum, Elliot Slotnick, and Greg Caldeira. I owe them all a great deal of gratitude for all their help over the years. Larry Baum has been willing to write many letters of recommendation for me over the years, and I truly appreciate his generosity.

My first full-time teaching job after graduate school was at Clark University in Worcester, Massachusetts, where I remain today. At Clark, I was able to found Clark's Law and Society Program, which is an interdisciplinary minor that helps students study law-related issues from a liberal arts perspective. I have also had the opportunity to teach U.S. judicial politics courses on our Worcester campus and comparative judicial politics in our study-abroad program in Luxembourg. I want to thank all of my students at Clark, who have always asked good questions and made life much more interesting. I also want to thank our excellent staff of reference librarians at the Goddard Library at Clark. They have always helped me find answers to my most obscure questions, and they have provided outstanding assistance to my undergraduate students during their many research endeavors.

I would also like to thank my political science colleagues at Clark, who have given me enormous personal and institutional support over the years. I would like especially to thank my Law and Society colleagues at Clark, who come from many departments all over campus, with special thanks to Professors Patty Ewick in sociology and Judi DeCew in philosophy. I have greatly enjoyed our legally based and pedagogical conversations. I also want to thank Professor Kent Rissmiller at Worcester Polytechnic Institute, who has occasionally allowed me to teach judicial politics courses at WPI to their much more natural-science-focused students. The Clark and WPI students are very different in many ways, but I have learned a great deal from both groups.

Clark University has also allowed me to have a variety of stimulating sabbatical and other experiences. For example, I was able to teach law-related courses in the American Studies Program at Leiden University in the Netherlands through the Fulbright program. My friends and colleagues at Leiden deserve a great deal of thanks for all of their help and assistance. I especially want to thank my colleagues in the U.S. Supreme Court Judicial Fellows Alumni Association. Serving as a Judicial Fellow at the Supreme Court of the United States has certainly enhanced my understanding of judicial politics. I also want to thank all the high school students whom I have taught over the years through the Junior Statesmen of America program. These talented high school students have taken a college-level law-related course from me during the JSA summer school programs held at Northwestern, Yale, Georgetown, and Stanford Universities.

I would like to thank Ada Fung at Westview Press for all her help in guiding this undertaking to its successful completion. Thanks to my project editor, Cisca L. Schreefel, and copyeditor, Sue Warga, for their work on this book. I would also like to thank the peer reviewers for their thoughtful and detailed comments on the manuscript, including: Sara Benesh (University of Wisconsin, Milwaukee), Paul Chen (Western Washington University), John Hermann (Trinity University), Karen Hult (Virginia Polytechnic Institute and State University), Paul Lermack (Bradley University), Lydia Tiede (University of Houston), Tammy Sarrer (Benedictine University), Eric Waltenburg (Purdue University), and the others who wished to remain anonymous.

Finally, I must thank my parents for all their love and support over the years. While they may not read all the books I have written, they certainly display them proudly on the bookshelves that my father has lovingly made by hand. My mother makes sure that my books are arranged in just the right order. They were both educators before they retired, and they tolerate my grading of papers and exams while watching sporting events with them during my end-of-semester visits.

LIST OF FIGURES

1

Functions of Courts, Basics of Legal Analysis, and Sources of Law

The study of American judicial politics involves examining how courts, judges, and other judicial actors function and interact in the U.S. political system. For a long time, scholars studying the courts tended to treat them as a unique branch of the government, and judicial scholars tended to focus solely on the judiciary. Today, however, more and more scholars are studying the courts not as isolated institutions but instead as vital parts of the larger integrated political system. Scholars are now looking at how judges and courts interact with the other branches of government and with the general public. They are also studying how American judges interact with their colleagues abroad. Thus, courts are now seen as a part of the broader system of government in a world transformed by globalization.

Courts are generally becoming more important and increasing their power around the globe.[1] After World War II, many countries created new constitutional courts or greatly strengthened existing ones.[2] For example, the European Court of Justice became a highly activist court interpreting and enforcing European law throughout the member states of the European Union.[3] However, American courts have remained some of the most powerful courts in the world. Summing up the views of most judicial politics scholars around the globe, Martin Shapiro, a prominent political scientist, wrote, "If any nation is the peculiar home of the expansion of judicial power, it is the United States."[4] Therefore, it seems natural that the study of judicial politics started with the political study of courts and law in the United States before spreading into the study of judicial systems around the world. This book will focus on judicial politics in the United States, although it will make comparisons to other countries when appropriate.

JUDICIAL POLITICS DEFINED

Before we define judicial politics, we should start at the beginning—with a definition of **law**. *Black's Law Dictionary* states that laws are "rules promulgated by government as a means to an ordered society." (Note that terms in **bold** are defined in the Glossary, found at the end of the book.) Another standard dictionary definition states that laws are "the principles and regulations established by a government or other authority and applicable to a people, whether by legislation or by custom, enforced by judicial decision." Some political scientists define law as "[t]he presence of a centralized authority capable of exacting coercive penalties for violations of legal rules."[5] And according to many sociologists, "[l]aws are rules that are enforced and sanctioned by the authority of government."[6] In short, law is a system of ideas and rules, while the U.S. courts are the human and political institutions that interpret the law. Thus, courts use the law in order to do justice. Obviously, the rule of law and the role of courts go hand in hand.

The law is often described as having its own language and its own analytical approach. Since law is a closed system of rules, legal reasoning in part means understanding, and carefully using, the unique meaning of words in the law, which can differ greatly from their meaning in regular English usage. One of the keys to legal reasoning is "thinking like a lawyer," which means speaking, writing, and reading like a lawyer or a judge.[7] Legal reasoning is an analytical approach that pays special attention to the specific legal use of language as well as to the rules of society. Therefore, the law is in large part the language that lawyers and judges use when they resolve human conflicts using the official rules made by the government.[8]

Laws usually also reflect the norms of a particular society or group. **Norms** are less official than laws and can be defined as "shared rules of conduct that specify how people ought to think and act."[9] The violation of social norms may cause some discomfort for an individual, but the violation of laws may lead to formal legal penalties imposed by the judiciary as representatives of the society. Therefore, law is an approach to dispute resolution that works to preserve social peace and order, and it incorporates both the legal rules and the collective norms of a society.[10]

Next, we need a definition of politics. **Politics** is generally the allocation of power and resources in a society. According to Harold Lasswell, a famous political scientist, "Politics is who gets what, when, and how."[11] Politics obviously deals with the workings of government and includes issues concerning how priorities, costs, and benefits are distributed in a society. As David Easton, another political scientist, argued, "Politics is the authoritative allocation of values."[12] Politics can involve individuals, interest groups, and political parties, and all of these are important in their relationship to the courts. Laws are the end product of politics and are "the prize over which many political struggles have been waged."[13] Thus, law and politics are closely related.

The academic study of the combination of law and politics is known as **judicial politics**, which is often defined as "the political process by which courts are constituted and legal decisions are made and implemented."[14] Sociolegal scholars come from a variety of academic disciplines, but most scholars of judicial politics have their home in the field of political science. Political scientists tend to study the courts as a political institution as well as a legal institution.

Notice that the term *judicial politics* assumes that judges in the United States are both legal and political actors at the same time, making their decisions in part based on legal reasoning and legal analysis and in part based on ideology and other political factors. In the United States, courts are policy makers, just like legislative and executive officials. This is how one group of political scientists describes the intersection of law and politics: "Modern political systems rely on law as one of *the* chief instruments, if not *the* chief instrument, to carry out national objectives and distribute rights and duties. Thus courts and judges, insofar as they help to determine and apply 'the law,' are inevitably participants in the political processes."[15]

The study of judicial politics also includes how courts and judges interact with other political actors and institutions, including interest groups, the media, Congress, the president, the federal bureaucracy, and of course the general public. This book will explore all of these aspects of judicial politics in the United States.

Scholars might argue that, in many parts of the world, law and politics are two distinct realms and ideas, although most political scientists feel that the separation between these two concepts is an artificial one, even abroad.[16] But in the United States, law and politics have clearly been closely intertwined since our nation's founding.[17] It was no accident that lawyers were very influential among the writers of the Declaration of Independence of 1776 and the Constitution of 1789. A little less than half of the signers of the Declaration of Independence were lawyers, and lawyers constituted more than half of the attendees at the Constitutional Convention. Lawyers also dominated the state conventions called to ratify the U.S. Constitution and the conventions called to write the original state constitutions after the American Revolution.[18] It is no accident that the

United States has historically had one of the highest proportions of lawyer-legislators in the world.[19] Lawyers are also elected in large numbers to be presidents of the United States and governors of the fifty states.[20] John Adams was the first of many lawyer-presidents, and he always felt that law should be thought of in combination with other great ideas, including politics, philosophy, and jurisprudence.[21]

In the United States, courts make legal decisions, but they also create public policy in a wide variety of areas, including free speech rights, abortion rights, the rights of criminal defendants, rules for drawing the lines of legislative districts, and the issue of spoken prayer in public schools, among many others. In most other societies, these public policy decisions would be made by the national legislative body or by the bureaucracy.[22] However, in the United States law has never been isolated from political considerations.

Alexis de Tocqueville, a French philosopher, traveled to the United States in the early 1800s in order to compare American society and politics to the European models with which he was most familiar, in particular those of France and England. Tocqueville was fascinated with the role of lawyers and judges in the United States, arguing among other things that lawyers constituted the American aristocracy and noting that American judges were more powerful than jurists anywhere else in the world. He also observed that in America all legal issues eventually become political ones and all political issues eventually become legal ones. As Tocqueville wrote in his book *Democracy in America*, "The judicial organization of the United States is the hardest thing there for a foreigner to understand. He finds judicial authority invoked in almost every political context, and from that he naturally concludes that the judge is one of the most important political powers in the United States."[23]

OUR COMMON LAW ROOTS

The mixture of law and politics in the United States has roots in our historical connections to Great Britain. When the British founded the American colonies that eventually became the United States, they brought their notion of law and legal reasoning with them. Therefore, American courts and the broader American judicial system are part of the international Anglo-American common law family of legal systems. The **common law** family of legal systems originated in England and is based on judge-made court decisions and legal **precedent**, or the articulation of legal principles in a historical succession of judicial decisions, rather than on codified written laws, as in some other legal traditions. In short, in the United States, a court's ruling today is based in large part on the rulings of past judges on similar legal issues. The precedent of prior judicial rulings, referred to with the Latin term ***stare decisis*** (almost literally "let the ruling stand"), is quite fundamental in common law countries.

Anglo-American judges decide current cases and disputes using the reasoning of prior similar cases as their foundation. In addition, judges on lower courts must follow the precedents of higher courts in our legal system. This concept is often called **binding precedent**, which means that the lower court judges must follow the rulings of higher courts in their court hierarchy. By contrast, **persuasive precedent** means that judges may, but are not required to, borrow the reasoning used by judges on roughly equivalent courts. Another way to put this is that binding precedent is a vertical type of precedent, while persuasive precedent is a horizontal type of precedent. For example, persuasive precedent often occurs when one state supreme court borrows the approach of another state supreme court, even though it is not required to do so.

The Anglo-American common law approach clearly has its roots in the English legal tradition. The English developed a system of professionalized judges very early after the Norman Conquest in 1066, and the king sent these professional judges out into the countryside to make legal decisions in his name. These judges helped resolve disputes that the king did not have the time or the desire to adjudicate. They often incorporated local norms into their decisions, but not all local or regional customs became commonly accepted throughout the kingdom. In order to remember why they had ruled as they did in prior cases, the king's judges began to write down the reasoning for their decisions. The written collective reasoning and rulings of these professional judges (precedent) thus eventually became the common law of the English kingdom. Common law rules evolved as judges used precedent from other judges' decisions blended with local customs as the foundations for their judicial rulings.[24] Thus, the Anglo-American common law principles evolved over time, instead of being enacted in a single comprehensive legal code written by legal experts, as happened in ancient Rome or in Napoleon's France, for example. The common law is thus often considered judge-made law. The judge's job in a common law system is to do justice in the particular case before him or her.

Today, common law judges are drawn strictly from the legal profession, and thus judges must first work as lawyers before they can be elevated to the bench. In many other societies, lawyers and judges are seen as two distinct professions with separate educational requirements, and individuals are unable to move from one profession to the other. In the common law world, however, judging and lawyering are closely linked, with relatively frequent movement between the two spheres of what is really considered a single profession. Because professional judges come from the ranks of attorneys and are trained to use precedent as the foundation for their decision making, in the common law tradition only one judge is needed per case at the trial level. However, in the appellate courts, panels of multiple judges hear appeals in this legal system.

DIFFERENCES BETWEEN THE COMMON LAW AND CIVIL LAW TRADITIONS

The common law tradition developed first in England soon after the Norman Conquest and later spread throughout the entire English-speaking world. This tradition is much different from the **civil law** family of legal systems of Continental Europe that are based on the Roman and Napoleonic written legal codes, with France, Spain, and Germany probably being the most notable contemporary models.[25] These civil law legal systems have spread into Japan, Latin America, Eastern Europe, and parts of Asia, among other places.[26] This section will compare various aspects of the common law legal systems with those in the civil law tradition.

One of the key differences between the two legal traditions is that in the common law tradition, judges are aided by an **adversary system**, that is, a system where lawyers protect the interests of their clients and present their clients' best case to the court. From the clash of these two opposing sides in the adversary system, the judge or jury should be able to determine the just result in any particular case. Common law courts worry much more about doing justice than they do about finding the one right legal answer or even the truth in a specific case. On the other hand, in an inquisitorial civil law system, the lawyers, judges, and prosecutors in theory all work together to find the singular truth. As mentioned earlier in the chapter, the law in the common law world is constantly evolving as judges face new situations and must apply the law to ever changing social realities. However, changes in the law in the civil law tradition come only from the national legislatures. Judges in the civil law world merely apply the legal code to the facts before them, but they never make law in the way common law judges can and often do. In the civil law systems, law is generally created by legal experts who write a nation's detailed comprehensive legal code. These complex legal codes with their interlocking rules are then enacted into law by the country's national legislative bodies. These codes are comprehensive, and in theory civil law judges cannot add to the codes or fill in the gaps—they merely apply the code to the specific set of facts before them.

In the civil law tradition, law should be uniform throughout the nation. In the common law world, however, local variations in the law are much more acceptable and happen fairly often. This is in large part because the common law legal systems do not employ a single comprehensive legal code; instead, common law judges use multiple sources of law such as constitutional provisions, statutes, bureaucratic decisions, and perhaps multiple judicial precedents in order to find a just result in any given case. In fact, in many countries that are part of the common law tradition, it was well into the nineteenth century before their national parliaments began enacting statutes that dealt with the everyday lives of common citizens.[27]

In civil law countries, judges do not normally use the concept of precedent. They would merely apply the national code to the case at hand, without examining prior judicial decisions.[28] Because of the fear that a single judge might apply the legal code incorrectly, trial courts in the civil law tradition almost always use at least three judges to hear a case. Very few civil law countries use juries in their trials, but lay trial juries are quite prevalent in the common law world. The sole purpose of civil law appellate courts is to correct any errors committed at trial. Also, appeals courts are much more likely to hear a case *de novo* (starting over from the beginning, almost like a second trial) in civil law countries than they are in common law nations. In common law systems, appeals courts tend to focus as much on creating the right precedent as they do on correcting errors.

In the common law world, law can be seen as an art, where different judges may come to different conclusions on what is a just result in any given case. This is in part because judges must utilize and interpret multiple sources of law and perhaps multiple precedents. In the civil law world, one may think of law as a science, where the job of the judge is to find the one right answer using a single source of law (the legal code). While the key figure in the common law world is the creative and innovative judge in search of justice, in the civil law world the primary source of law is the careful and diligent legal scholar who writes the lucid, detailed, and all-encompassing legal codes that are then enacted into law by the national legislature.[29]

GENERAL THEORIES OF LAW

In our common law system, there are several general theories of law that judges might use in their decision making. These theories reflect the fact that there are basically two views of the law among legal scholars in our country. Some believe that the law is inherently based on some underlying and universal moral standard, while others hold that it is merely the product of social construction.[30] These two approaches can be called natural law theories and positive law theories, respectively.

Natural law theories propose that there are universal rules and norms that supersede laws created by individuals. Since natural law is a higher form of law, lesser human-made laws must yield to the dictates of natural law.[31] Another way of stating this is that natural law looks to "unquestioned universal principles" that inspire and yet subsume legal texts written by human individuals.[32] Some have argued that Justice Clarence Thomas retains elements of natural law theory in many of his judicial opinions.[33]

There are generally three streams of natural law theory: religious, rational, and historical. The religious stream of natural law argues that law is divinely given by God or other higher being. In particular, Catholic natural law theories often find their roots in the thinking of St. Thomas Aquinas, a theologian and philosopher from the thirteenth century. The rational stream of natural law stresses that there are universal rules for human behavior that only rational thought can discover. Influenced by seventeenth- and eighteenth-century Enlightenment thinkers who stressed the importance of observation and experiment in arriving at reliable and demonstrable universal truths, rationalist secular natural law elevates the capacity of the human intellect over the spiritual authority of religion. The third approach, the historical stream, relies on the customs and traditions of civilized societies in order to establish universal rules of behavior. According to these thinkers, law must be made to conform to the well-established but usually unwritten customs, traditions, and experiences that have evolved over the course of history.

In contrast to these natural law theories, **positive law theories** often argue that law should reflect the will of a majority in a society. Thus, the law should be whatever the majority of citizens say it is, as determined through majoritarian democratic processes. Moral concerns play no role in positive theories of the law.

A third approach to the law is more sociological. **Sociological theories of law** often argue that law "represents a reflection of the values, mores, and culture of the society that produces it."[34] As a society changes, the law will change as well. Political scientists tend to study the political effects of law because they usually see law and politics as inherently intertwined. Thus, political scientists tend to adopt the thinking that laws are whatever the majority of a society enacts through the political and governmental processes.

SOURCES OF LAW IN THE UNITED STATES

Like all common law courts, courts in the United States interpret a variety of sources of law. In the United States, there is a clear hierarchy of sources of law that judges can use. Figure 1.1 lists the American sources of law in order of

FIGURE 1.1 Hierarchy of Sources of Law in the United States

1. U.S. Constitution
   ↓
2. Federal statutes, joint resolutions, and treaties
   ↓
3. Presidential executive orders
   ↓
4. Federal agency rules and regulations
   ↓
5. Federal agency adjudication decisions
   ↓
6. State constitutions
   ↓
7. State statutes
   ↓
8. Gubernatorial executive orders
   ↓
9. State agency decisions
   ↓
10. Local ordinances
    ↓
11. Common law rulings

hierarchy. Anything higher in the hierarchy can generally overrule any lower source of law. At the top of the hierarchy is the highest source of law in the United States, the U.S. Constitution, which the courts interpret through their power of judicial review (defined in more detail on page 14). The next category of sources of law includes federal statutes, joint resolutions, and treaties. **Federal statutes** are laws enacted by the U.S. Congress and either signed into law by the president or under certain circumstances allowed to become law without his signature. If the president vetoes a proposed law passed by Congress, it nevertheless becomes a statute if two-thirds of both houses of Congress vote to override the president's veto. In some limited circumstances, joint resolutions serve the same function as bills in Congress. Federal **treaties** are agreements between nations that are negotiated by the president and ratified by a two-thirds vote of the U.S. Senate. Many societies consider treaties as superior to their national constitutions (for example, the member states of the European Union do this), but in the United States treaties are treated as inferior to the U.S. Constitution.

However, treaties are usually considered on the same level as federal statutes because normally the U.S. Congress must enact a variety of measures in order to implement any given treaty.

The next source of law is **presidential executive orders**, usually directed at executive branch agencies in the permanent federal bureaucracy.[35] The president has the power to issue executive orders to the agencies, directing them to do, or refrain from doing, certain things.[36] Following this are **federal agency rules and regulations**, which are the adjudicatory decisions an agency uses to enforce its regulations against various actors within the agency's jurisdiction. Federal agency rules and regulations have the force of law, and they often fill in the details of federal statutes.

All of these sources of law are replicated at the state level, and many states give local governments some limited law making powers as well. Local laws are often called **ordinances**. In general, the U.S. Constitution's **Supremacy Clause** makes the federal sources of law superior to the state sources of law, but state supreme courts generally have the last word on issues of pure state law where there is no federal constitutional question. For example, when in *Goodridge v. Department of Public Health* (2003) the Massachusetts Supreme Judicial Court interpreted its state constitution to require that the state allow same-sex marriages, the state supreme court was the last word on this issue, which was purely a matter of state law. Or when many states interpreted their state constitutions to require that the state legislature equalize funding among public school districts in the state, there was no federal issue presented and the state supreme courts were the last stop for these cases. States were able to do this because the U.S. Supreme Court previously ruled that there is no federal right to an education in *San Antonio Independent School District v. Rodriguez* (1973).

If there is no specific source of law in a particular case, judges many nevertheless make a decision in the name of justice. This last type of judicial decision is often referred to as **common law judicial rulings**. These judicial decisions are not based on a specific written source of law but nevertheless have the force of law themselves. For example, in the late 1800s, there were no statutes or agency administrative regulations covering most consumer products. Despite being unable to cite a specific source of law, judges made a variety of common law rulings that said that consumer products must be safe for their intended purposes. Thus, judges in the United States can and do interpret all of these sources of law in the hierarchy, and, unlike their colleagues in the civil law family of legal systems, they can make a decision even when no specific source of law is directly on point for the case at hand.

LEGAL REASONING AND LEGAL ANALYSIS

The key difference between decision making in the courts and in other political institutions in the United States is the fact that judges must rely on legal analysis and legal reasoning in their decision-making process in addition to any political or ideological influences.[37] Courts are like other institutions of government because they make political and public-policy-based decisions. However, courts are different from other governmental actors because they are separate from the other institutions of government and because courts, or at least the federal courts, are seen as outside the mainstream of pure politics.[38] As Herman Pritchett, one of the fathers of the study of judicial politics, noted, "Political scientists who have done so much to put the 'political' in 'political jurisprudence' need to emphasize that it is still 'jurisprudence.' It is judging in a political context, but it is still judging; and judging is something different from legislating or administering."[39]

Legal reasoning involves viewing disputes through a neutral, analytical, and unemotional lens. Although the courts are clearly political institutions in our society, judges' use of legal reasoning and legal analysis mean that the courts are very different decision makers from the other institutions of government. Justice Anthony M. Kennedy, for instance, has noted that the Supreme Court was "set apart from other branches of government because it speaks a different language from the political branches."[40]

Thinking Like a Lawyer

Although judges do think and act politically, they must also think like lawyers instead of just thinking like politicians. Politicians do not always need to explain their decisions, but judges must always justify their rulings in terms of the rule of law and legal reasoning. In common law countries, all of a judge's rulings must be stated in such a way that they appear to be based on rules, principles, and doctrines external to the judge.[41] Or in other words, legal reasoning justifications for judicial decisions are necessary in our society, even if different judges would have different opinions in any given case due to a variety of political considerations. The notion that judges are constrained in their decision making by legal reasoning makes judges very different from politicians as decision makers.

Formality is very important in the law and legal reasoning. The courts must follow formal procedures, and they must apply formal rules to the facts before them. Their decisions are also delivered in a very formal fashion.[42] It is the job of lawyers and judges to understand the formal law and its language. The rules of the law focus more on form and authority rather than on morality and social context.[43] Thus, legal reasoning and legal analysis are quite rule oriented. As Frederick Schauer, a legal scholar, noted, "Reasoning with *rules* is perhaps the most common image of what lawyers and judges do."[44]

In addition to the careful use of language and a very specific analytical approach to problem solving, legal reasoning also requires the use of a certain process or procedure. That is, *how* decisions are made is often as important as *what* decisions are made. Legal analysis also includes a great deal of reasoning by analogy. And because American legal reasoning takes place in a common law legal system, the legal rules are often discovered by analyzing the precedents of appropriate appellate courts. Since judges are lawyers first, it is no accident that judges learn to "think like lawyers" in law school.[45] In addition, they must also learn to "think like judges," which means learning to act as a neutral arbiter between lawyers who are advocating for the interests of their clients. Therefore, legal reasoning involves careful use of language in a rule- and process-oriented analytical framework. (Chapter 4 covers law school and the legal profession in more detail.)

Decision Making According to the Law

American courts are independent decision makers. In part, this means that other political actors cannot dictate the legal rulings of judges. Justice Stephen G. Breyer, among others, has argued that judicial independence has its foundation in decision making according to the law, meaning that judges must follow specific sources of law and legal procedures when they make their decisions.[46] As mentioned earlier in the chapter, one key aspect of legal reasoning is the reliance on precedent. So although our federal courts are extremely independent and thus free from almost all forms of political control, they still must use legal analysis and the precedents of higher courts. In other words, judges are really only constrained in their decision making by legal reasoning and legal analysis.

The more Americans learn about the unique form of legal reasoning used by the courts, the more public support for the judiciary increases. One study argues that the general public increases their support for the courts when the judges anchor their decisions in legal values and symbols rather than in political ones.[47] Knowledge of how the courts make their decisions produces an understanding of the distinctive role of the judiciary in the American political system, reinforcing the view that courts are different. This study concludes, "[Courts] are different, and they are special, and they are therefore worthy of esteem."[48]

TYPES OF COURT CASES

Now that we have established a broad understanding of the roots of our judicial system, its position within the larger political landscape, and how our judges make decisions, let us take a look at the types of disputes that our courts typically handle. These disputes can be divided into several categories: criminal cases, civil cases, constitutional cases, and administrative law cases.

A **crime** is a wrong against society. In our country, the courts are the only institution with the power to punish criminals. These punishments can include, among other things, fines paid to the government, a prison sentence, or even death in certain cases. In a criminal court case, the **prosecutor** is the lawyer who represents the interests of society and argues against the defendant, who is represented by his or her own lawyer. The **criminal defendant** is the individual accused of the crime. The prosecutor must prove the defendant's guilt beyond a reasonable doubt. The way criminal cases are named—for example, *People v. Defendant, State v. Defendant, Commonwealth v. Defendant, United States v. Defendant*—indicate that the defendant is accused of breaking society's legal rules. The vast majority of crimes in the United States are based on state law, but there are also a smaller number of crimes that fall under laws enacted by the U.S. Congress. Both state and federal statutes spell out the specifics of a crime in our society and provide a range of possible punishments, but only judges can actually impose a criminal sentence on a particular defendant. The only exception is that the death penalty must be imposed by a jury. Under most circumstances, the prosecutor cannot appeal a trial court's finding that the defendant is not guilty. (For more about the criminal process in the United States, see Chapter 5.)

Civil cases in the United States involve wrongs between individuals broadly defined. The **plaintiff** is the one who files the civil lawsuit, while the **defendant** must defend it. Thus, a civil case could be *Smith v. Smith* (perhaps a divorce case), *Smith v. Jones* (perhaps a real property dispute), *Smith v. the U.S. Postal Service* (perhaps for a car accident with a postal truck), or *Smith v. Multinational Corporation* (perhaps a contract dispute or even an employment lawsuit). The case could also be *Netscape v. Microsoft* (perhaps an anti-trust case or a patent dispute). Some of these civil cases, such as divorces or probating a will, require a judge's signature in order to finalize the case. For other civil suits, the courts are available to help settle the dispute when alternatives fail. Courts also provide a neutral judge trained in the law who can help find the most just remedy to the dispute. Generally the plaintiff must prove a civil case by a preponderance of the evidence or perhaps by a higher standard known as clear and convincing evidence. If one were to use the scales of justice as a metaphor, a preponderance of evidence would tip the scales just a little in one direction, while clear and convincing evidence would tip the scales further. However, both burdens of proof used in civil cases are much less difficult to meet than the standard of guilt beyond a reasonable doubt, which prosecutors must prove in a criminal case. (See Chapter 6 for more on civil lawsuits.)

Administrative law cases require the courts to review the decisions made by governmental bureaucratic agencies to make sure that these decisions follow the proper processes and procedures. The interactions between courts and bureaucratic agencies in the executive branch of government will be discussed in more detail in Chapter 12. **Constitutional** interpretation are those in which the courts interpret the U.S. Constitution or the various state constitutions. The United States does not have separate courts for constitutional cases, as do the French and the Germans; rather, constitutional issues can arise in criminal, civil, and administrative law disputes handled by the regular courts in the United States.

PURPOSES OF COURTS IN THE UNITED STATES

The prior discussion of the various types of cases hinted at some of the purposes of the courts in our nation. American courts can resolve disputes among individuals or groups, modify behavior, protect the rights of individuals, and make public policy. Courts can punish crimes. They can also serve as umpires in the disputes between Congress and the president, or between the federal government and the states. In general, courts resolve disputes in our society through their interpretations of multiple sources of law. Donald Kommers, a judicial politics scholar, nicely summed up the roles that courts play in the United States by noting, "From the nation's founding until today, courts have been a mainstay of American democracy. They settle legal conflicts between private parties, protect the legal rights of citizens generally, and supervise the administration of ordinary law."[49] Courts therefore serve a variety of purposes in our nation.

Courts as Policy Makers

One clear function of the courts in the United States is to make public policy, which renders them different from courts in many societies. This is often done through the courts' use of their power of judicial review. **Judicial review** is the power of the courts to determine the constitutionality of the actions of other political actors such as Congress, the president, the bureaucracy, or the states. By interpreting the U.S. Constitution and other sources of law, courts in the United States make many public policies that would be made legislatively or bureaucratically in other nations. For example, using its power of judicial review, the U.S. Supreme Court has handed down a variety of decisions that result in a specific public policy outcome, such as the right of women to choose to have an abortion (*Roe v. Wade,* 1973) or the principle that legislative districts must be almost precisely equal in population (*Baker v. Carr,* 1962). The U.S. Supreme Court has declared that there is an individual right to privacy that the government cannot infringe upon (*Griswold v. Connecticut,* 1965) and decreed that burning the American flag as a form of political protest cannot be criminalized (*Texas v. Johnson,* 1989). The U.S. Supreme Court outlawed discrimination by race in our public schools through its power of judicial review (*Brown v. Board of Education,* 1954), while state supreme courts in Massachusetts and Iowa, among others, have interpreted their state constitutions to require that same-sex marriages be allowed. In addition to making public policy, some also argue that the courts should protect the interests of political minorities that cannot or will not be protected in the more majoritarian institutions of government such as the legislative and executive branches.

In some ways this power of judicial review is uniquely American, although courts in other societies are beginning to exercise this great power with increasing frequency.[50] Technically courts in the United Kingdom and New Zealand do not have the power of judicial review at all,[51] and courts in Canada only formally received this power with the enactment of the Charter of Rights and Freedoms in 1982. However, since that date the Canadian courts have been quite activist in using their power of judicial review.[52] The noticeable difference between judicial review in Canada and the United States is that legislative bodies in Canada can vote to maintain a statute in effect even if the courts have declared it to be unconstitutional.[53] The Canadians refer to this as the "notwithstanding" power of the provinces. The German Constitutional Court also utilizes a form of judicial review,[54] as do constitutional courts in various other societies.[55] Almost no courts elsewhere in the world have used their power of judicial review and its resulting policy-making ability to the extent that they are utilized in the United States. While American judges certainly make public policy to a greater degree than most of their international colleagues, they must nevertheless do so through the lens of legal reasoning and legal analysis. When considering the power of judicial review, most Americans think only of the decisions of the U.S. Supreme Court. But the fact is that all regular courts in the United States can exercise the power of judicial review. For example, after voters in California outlawed same-sex marriage in Proposition 8, a federal trial court in California declared that action to be unconstitutional. For complex procedural reasons, the U.S. Supreme Court allowed the trial court's decision to become law in California. Same sex-marriages resumed in that state in 2013.

Dispute Resolution and Behavior Modification

Trial court decisions may illustrate other purposes of the courts. All changes in legal status must have a judge's order for the change to be implemented. For example, one cannot get a divorce without a judge's decree, nor can one change the status of a child's legal custody or an individual change his or her legal name without a court order. Changes in property ownership after a person's death or changes in real property boundaries also require a judge's order. Most other civil disputes do not require a judge to settle the dispute, although the courts are available when alternative dispute resolution mechanisms do not resolve the conflict. Courts also serve as institutions that encourage behavior modification for the parties involved and/or for the broader American public. Punitive damages awarded in civil cases often have the effect of modifying the behavior of similar parties in the future.

Civil cases serve a variety of other purposes as well. For example, no capitalist society can function without clear and consistent rules of contract law. Courts must decide which contracts are enforceable and what legal remedies are available when contract bargains are breached. Courts also must protect the public from potential bargains that violate public policy and are thus considered unenforceable.[56] In addition, inventors need predictable patent and other intellectual property rules. Buyers and sellers of real estate need predictable real property laws. Civil cases can also be key tools for modernizing rules and procedures within bureaucratic agencies such as local police forces or municipal agencies that install and maintain playground equipment in local parks.[57] Occasionally when Congress and the state legislatures refuse to enact legislation on a specific topic because their members see it as being politically unpopular, the problem gets passed on to the courts, where judges find ways to solve the issue on a case-by-case basis.[58] For example, when anti-smoking activists could not convince Congress to pass tough anti-tobacco laws, they turned instead to a series of civil lawsuits to get rulings that they felt would better protect public health.[59]

The outcome of a particular civil case is important to the parties to the lawsuit, but the collective decisions in these civil cases can create important public policy results and can even help inform legislators what changes need to be made to various laws. In other words, "the accumulation of similar individual decisions defines policy just as much as one major decision [does]."[60] Civil cases help settle individual disputes, but, taken together, rulings in civil cases are another way that American courts make important public policy decisions.

Judges as Umpires Among Institutions

Another purpose of the courts is to serve as a referee between the other institutions of government, thus preventing any single political actor from gaining too much power in our nation. Some constitutionally based court decisions fall into this category. This judicial role of umpire is part of the separation of powers theory in the United States.[61] The concept of **separation of powers** means that governmental power is divided into distinct and separate functions, known as the executive, legislative, and judicial branches of government. Under the traditional notion of separation of powers, each branch of government has its own particular job to do. Our system of government is further complicated by the fact that we are a federal system, with distinct state and federal governments. **Federalism** is the division of power between the national government and the regional governments (in the United States, these are states), with the national government being supreme. In short, the United States has both a federal court system and fifty-one state court systems sharing the same geographical space, and it has separation of powers at both the federal and state levels. (I say that there are fifty-one state court systems because the local courts in the District of Columbia function just like a state court system for these purposes.)

One of the major duties of the judiciary is to help settle disputes between the legislative and executive branches of the federal government and between different levels of government, including disputes between the federal government and the states.[62] Because courts use legal reasoning in their decision-making process, judges carry out a special function in our democracy, often acting as a counterbalance to other governmental actors.[63] In order to serve as an umpire in these potential conflicts between other institutions of government, the courts must remain free from the control of any political actors. This is known as **judicial independence**, meaning that courts must be able to make their decisions without interference by the other branches and without fear that other political actors will directly retaliate against the judges because of their legal decisions. A competing value is **judicial accountability**, meaning that the courts and judges should be accountable to the voters. In general, our federal court system promotes the value of judicial independence, while most state court judicial selection systems promote the principle of judicial accountability. More details about the concepts of judicial independence and judicial accountability can be found in the discussion of judicial selection methods in Chapter 3.

The role of the courts in these institutional disputes can sometimes get quite messy, even though the courts are an independent third branch of government charged in part with serving as the umpire in these inter-institutional conflicts. The day-to-day workings of the separation of powers concept in the United States are not simplistic or clear-cut.[64] Instead of a simple and straightforward separation of powers, we in the United States have "separated institutions sharing powers."[65] In addition, federalism issues in our nation can become extremely complex.[66] We even fought the bloody Civil War in part over competing notions of federalism. Thus, the courts often come into conflict with other political actors in their role as umpire of separation of powers and federalism cases.

Some would argue, however, that these almost constant institutional conflicts are beneficial for our society in the long run. Robert Katzmann, a former professor who is now a federal judge on the U.S. Court of Appeals for the Second Circuit, spent a great deal of his academic career examining the interactions between the courts and the other branches. Katzmann argues, "Governance in the United States is a process of interaction among institutions—legislative, executive, and judicial—with separate and sometimes clashing structures, purposes, and interests. The Founders envisioned that constructive tension among those institutions would not only preserve liberty but would also promote the public good."[67]

FURTHER THOUGHTS ON THE POWER OF JUDICIAL REVIEW

As mentioned earlier in the chapter, judicial review means the power of the courts to determine the constitutionality of the actions of other political actors, including Congress, the president, the federal bureaucracy, and the states. In interpreting the Constitution, the courts also serve as a check on the power of other political actors. In addition to being part of the common law family of legal systems, all the regular American courts have the tool of judicial review at their disposal, thus making our courts very powerful indeed. As Tocqueville noted, "Restricted within its limits, the power granted to American courts to pronounce on the constitutionality of laws is yet one of the most powerful barriers ever erected against the tyranny of political assemblies."[68]

Although the U.S. Constitution is silent on which body should interpret its provisions, in *Marbury v. Madison* (1803) the Supreme Court of the United States decided that it should be the primary interpreter of the Constitution, adopting the power of judicial review. The Court's decision in *Marbury* is consistent with Alexander Hamilton's views as he stated them in Federalist No. 78.

The **Federalist Papers** were written by Alexander Hamilton, James Madison, and John Jay to persuade the states to ratify the U.S. Constitution. Federalist No. 78 argues that the new federal courts would have the power of judicial review. In arguing for the ratification of the new Constitution, Hamilton wrote, "No legislative act, therefore, contrary to the Constitution can be valid. . . . The interpretation of the laws is the proper and peculiar province of the courts. A constitution is, in fact, and must be regarded by the judges as a fundamental law." Certainly almost all Americans agree today that all of the regular courts in the country have the power to determine the constitutionality of the actions of other political actors, including Congress, the president, the bureaucracy, and the states.

Originalism or a Living Constitution

However, scholars and judges often disagree about how the Constitution should be interpreted when courts exercise their power of judicial review. One clear debate is between those who advocate for an originalist approach to constitutional interpretation and those who see the Constitution as a living document whose interpretation must change as the society evolves. A third group is the pragmatists, who utilize more of a case-by-case approach to constitutional interpretation.

Originalism is the belief that the Constitution should be interpreted as the Framers intended. It is somewhat similar to an approach that says that the words of the Constitution should be read literally. These approaches are often collectively called *strict constructionism* or *literalism*.[69] That is, the meaning of the Constitution is fixed by the intent of the Framers.[70] Originalists therefore see the Constitution as a binding contract whose principles can be changed only by constitutional amendment, not through judicial interpretation. One of the founders of the current originalism movement was Edwin Meese III, the U.S. attorney general during the Reagan Administration. In advocating an originalist or literalist interpretation of the Constitution, Attorney General Meese stated, "We know that those who framed the Constitution chose their words carefully. They debated at great length the minutest points. The language they chose meant something."[71] The core of originalism is the belief that fidelity to the original understanding of the Constitution should constrain contemporary judges. Originalists claim that judges need neutral, objective criteria in order to make legitimate decisions that the people will respect, and that the Framers' intent provides those neutral criteria. As Meese explained, "The great genius of the constitutional blueprint is found in its creation and respect for spheres of authority and the limits it places on governmental power."[72] For originalists, the main way to promote the rule of law is to prevent judges from reading into the

Constitution their own personal political philosophies. As Steven Calabresi, the co-founder of the Federalist Society (a group of conservative judges, law professors, law students, and others who promote originalism), wrote, "There is no liberal or conservative meaning of the text of the Constitution; there is only a right meaning and a wrong meaning."[73] Originalism, according to its advocates, ensures that judges choose the right meaning of the Constitution.

Justice Antonin Scalia has often been considered one of the leading proponents of originalism, even though he claims his approach is more nuanced than that of most originalists and he openly rejects the literalist label. Justice Scalia has written, "Twenty years ago, when I joined the Supreme Court, I was the only originalist among its members."[74] Today, most commentators would count at least four originalists on the Court. Justice Scalia has often said that the Constitution is dead—that is, its meaning cannot change over time.[75] In arguing for originalism, Justice Scalia wrote, "Our manner of interpreting the Constitution is to begin with the text, and to give that text the meaning that it bore when it was adopted by the people."[76] Thus, in the eyes of Justice Scalia and other originalists, the original intent of the Framers is almost sacred. Justice Scalia argues that, unless courts interpret the Constitution according to the intent of the Framers, unelected federal judges will improperly impose their own personal policy preferences on our society.[77] And this is exactly what has happened, according to Justice Scalia. He notes, "So it is literally true, and I don't think this is an exaggeration, that the Court has essentially liberated itself from the text of the Constitution, from the text, and even from the traditions of the American people."[78] For originalists, the cure for this constitutional ill is originalism. As Justice Scalia has stated, "Originalism seems to me more compatible with the nature and purpose of a Constitution in a democratic system."[79] In short, originalists want to restrain the power and influence of federal judges, who are appointed for life, and prevent them from imposing their own values and ideologies on the American public through judicial fiat, or decree.

Justices William J. Brennan and Thurgood Marshall were among the chief proponents of a competing approach, often known as the **living Constitution theory**, which holds that the Constitution is a living and changing document that judges should interpret and reinterpret with a modern eye. That is, constitutional interpretation must evolve as the society evolves. They believed that current judges cannot know the intent of the Framers, in part, because a collective group cannot have a single intent. They also argued that judges should use their expertise to produce justice in a particular case, regardless of how the Constitution had been interpreted in the past. Justice Brennan was a strong critic of originalism, and of it he said:

In truth it is little more than arrogance cloaked as humility. It is arrogant to pretend that from our vantage we can gauge accurately the intent of the Framers on application of principle to specific, contemporary questions. [. . .] For the genius of the Constitution rests not in any static meaning it might have had in a world that is dead and gone, but in the adaptability of its great principles to cope with current problems and current needs. What the constitutional fundamentals meant to the wisdom of other times cannot be their measure to the vision of our time.[80]

Justice Marshall took a similar approach. Being the first African American to serve on the Supreme Court, he was especially sensitive to how the Framers treated people of color. He did not approve of the way the original Constitution handled the issues of slavery and constitutional rights for people of African descent. In a 1987 speech, Justice Marshall declared, "I do not believe that the meaning of the Constitution was forever 'fixed' at the Philadelphia Convention. Nor do I find the wisdom, foresight, and sense of justice exhibited by the framers particularly profound."[81] Justices Brennan and Marshall believed that the Constitution should be interpreted in such a way as to protect the most vulnerable in our society.

One of the contemporary examples of the living Constitution concept is when the Supreme Court uses the term "evolving standards of decency" to interpret the Eighth Amendment's ban on cruel and unusual punishments. The phrase was first used in *Trop v. Dulles* (1958), where the Court ruled that it was unconstitutional for the government to revoke the citizenship of a U.S. citizen as a punishment for a crime. In that case, the majority opinion stated that "the words of the [Eighth] Amendment are not precise, and that their scope is not static. The Amendment must draw its meaning from the evolving standards of decency that mark the progress of a maturing society."[82] The Court again used the phrase "evolving standards of decency" in *Atkins v. Virginia* (2002), where it declared that the mentally disabled cannot be executed under the Eighth Amendment.[83] This phrase was also used in *Roper v. Simmons* (2005), where the Supreme Court declared it unconstitutional to execute defendants who were juveniles when they committed the crime.[84] An even stronger statement of the living Constitution doctrine came in Justice John Paul Stevens's concurrence in *Roper*. He wrote:

Perhaps even more important than our specific holding today is our reaffirmation of the basic principle that informs the Court's interpretation of the *Eighth Amendment*. If the meaning of that Amendment had been frozen when it was originally drafted, it would impose no impediment to the execution of 7-year-old children today. The evolving standards of decency that have driven our construction of this critically important part of the Bill of Rights foreclose any such reading of the Amendment. In the best tradition of the common law, the pace of that evolution is a matter for continuing debate; but that our understanding of the Constitution does change from time to time has been settled since John Marshall breathed life into its text. If great lawyers of his day—Alexander Hamilton, for example—were sitting with us today, I would expect them to join Justice Kennedy's opinion for the Court.[85]

In a similar fashion to the Living Constitutionalists, but promoting a third approach, Justice Stephen Breyer argues that judges should be pragmatic in their interpretations of the Constitution: "The Court should reject approaches to interpreting the Constitution that consider the document's scope and application as fixed at the moment of framing. Rather, the Court should regard the Constitution as containing unwavering values that must be applied flexibly to ever-changing circumstances."[86] Thus, Justice Breyer advocates a pragmatic judicial approach that "hesitates to rely on any single theory or grand view of law, of interpretation, or of the Constitution."[87] Judge Richard Posner of the U.S. Court of Appeals for the Seventh Circuit is a prolific writer and commentator on the law, as well as being a judge. Although he is much more conservative than Justice Breyer, Judge Posner also advocates a pragmatic approach to legal questions, stating, "The word that best describes the average American judge at all levels of our judicial hierarchies and yields the greatest insight into his behavior is 'pragmatist.'"[88] Scholars who promote a more pragmatic reading of the Constitution are usually critical of originalism. They often note that the literal wording of the Constitution or the intent of the Framers provides very little guidance about how to decide particular cases.[89] Many contemporary judges are pragmatists because they routinely consider policy, the principles behind the law, and the law's consequences in their decisions.[90]

In this debate, we should be cautious about several things. First, among the justices who claim that they are properly interpreting the intent of the Framers are many who strongly disagree with one another about what that intent might be. For example, in *District of Columbia v. Heller* (2008), both the majority opinion and the dissent forcefully claimed that they were properly interpreting the intent of the Framers in writing the Second Amendment. This case involved the District of Columbia's very tough gun control law, which the majority declared unconstitutional because it violated an individual's right to bear arms. The dissenting justices would have upheld the gun control law because they believed the

Framers intended the Second Amendment to protect only the state's collective right to have an armed militia (known today as a national guard).

Second, many judges who use the rhetoric of originalism are in fact acting and voting in the manner of a judicial activist, a concept discussed in more detail below.[91] This often occurs when judges use the language of original intent to declare a statute or a government official's action unconstitutional. Third, ideological considerations may often outweigh a justice's preferred philosophy of decision making. In fact, several studies[92] have found that for many justices, "commitment to an ideological direction was far stronger than commitment to a mode of constitutional interpretation."[93] Thus, we must look beyond the words of judges to see how they are actually using their power of judicial review.

Judicial Activism Versus Judicial Restraint

Although there is widespread agreement that American courts now have the power of judicial review, there is far less agreement on how judges should use this immense power. There are two main competing judicial philosophies that judges use to help guide them in their use of their power of judicial review—judicial activism and judicial restraint. There is a great deal of debate in the academic community on the precise definitions of these philosophies. Although the dispute between originalism and the concept of a living Constitution forms part of the basis for these competing judicial philosophies, the debate between judicial activists and judicial restraintists is much broader than that more narrow interpretive approach.

Judicial activism is especially hard to define analytically because many people attach the label to any court decisions with which they disagree.[94] Thus, *judicial activism* can be a loaded term that has multiple meanings and politicized connotations, especially as used by politicians.[95] This book, however, will use the terms *judicial activism* and *judicial restraint* in a more analytical and academic sense, which can and often does differ from the way the terms may be used in broader political debates. While some would argue that the definition of judicial activism should include situations where the Supreme Court and other appellate judges overturn existing precedent, I think we should instead define these terms according to the relationship between the courts and other actors. Therefore, I think judicial activism and restraint should be defined not according to what judges say, but in terms of what they actually do.

There are three parts to our definition of **judicial activism**. First, activist judges tend to interpret the U.S. Constitution as a living and changing document that needs to be reinterpreted as society evolves. While they might use the language of originalism, their actions in updating the meaning of the Constitution speak louder than their rhetoric. Second, judicial activists see making public policy as a natural part of the purpose of the courts in our nation. Third, activist judges tend to be quite willing to declare the actions of other political actors to be unconstitutional. Thus, judicial activism typically occurs when judges make decisions that promote justice in alignment with a changing society, and when a court declares something to be unconstitutional.

Although activists can be either liberal or conservative, most commentators today first think of liberal judicial activism. Examples of famous liberal activist decisions include *Brown v. Board of Education* (1954), which declared racial segregation in public schools to be unconstitutional; *Miranda v. Arizona* (1966), which requires police to read criminal defendants their rights at the point of arrest; *Roe v. Wade* (1973), which declared unconstitutional fifty state abortion laws; and *Texas v. Johnson* (1989), which declared unconstitutional laws prohibiting the burning of the American flag as a form of political protest.

Judicial restraint, on the other hand, uses the opposite approach. Restraintists are uncomfortable with judges' immense power of judicial review. They want to restrict the circumstances under which judges may actually use this power. Thus, restraintists tend to believe that the Constitution should be interpreted only as the Framers intended. Second, judicial restraintists believe that the courts should not be policy makers but instead should make only purely legal decisions, much like the courts in the United Kingdom. Finally, restraintists do not often exercise their power of judicial review, instead deferring to the decisions of the elected branches of government. Therefore, judicial restraint occurs whenever a court upholds the constitutionality of the actions of other governmental actors. Some recent examples of judicial restraint are *Bowers v. Hardwick* (1986), where the Supreme Court refused to declare Georgia's anti-sodomy law to be unconstitutional, and *Gonzales v. Carhart* (2007), where the Supreme Court upheld a federal law banning the use of a late-term abortion technique known by its opponents as partial-birth abortion. Another example of judicial restraint was *National Federation of Independent Business v. Sebelius* (2012), where the Supreme Court upheld as constitutional most of President Obama's Affordable Care Act (see Chapter 10 for more details about this case).

As mentioned earlier, the differences between judicial activism and judicial restraint do not break along strictly ideological lines. From the late 1800s until 1936, the Supreme Court was dominated by conservative judicial activists, who prevented most regulation of economic activities in the United States by reading an unyielding right to contract into the Fourteenth Amendment.[96] The Warren Court of the 1950s and 1960s was clearly dominated by liberal judicial activists, who saw the role of the Supreme Court as protecting the most vulnerable political minorities in our society.[97] Today, the Supreme Court hands down both liberal activist decisions and conservative activist ones, depending on the issue.[98] As one influential scholar has argued, the Supreme Court under Chief Justice William Rehnquist in the 1990s and early 2000s was the most activist Court in history because it issued many liberal activist decisions and many conservative activist decisions.[99]

Today, even some conservatives—specifically those who want courts to have a smaller role in deciding controversial national issues—are upset by the recent trend of conservative judicial activism on the Supreme Court.[100] Many of Justice Scalia's critics, for example, believe that his voting behavior in reality reflects conservative activism despite his rhetoric in favor of originalism.[101] The Tea Party movement in the United States seems to advocate for an extreme version of judicial restraint. As scholars Theda Skocpol and Vanessa Williamson have written, "A tour of Tea Party websites around the country quickly reveals widespread determination to restore twenty-first century U.S. government to the Constitutional principles articulated by the eighteenth-century Founding Fathers."[102] These scholars continue, "A persistent refrain in Tea Party circles is the scorn for politicians who fail to show suitable reverence for, and detailed mastery of, America's founding documents."[103] Examples of recent liberal activist decisions include *Lawrence v. Texas* (2003), which declared the Texas anti-sodomy statute unconstitutional and overturned the Court's previous decision in *Bowers,* and *Miller v. Alabama* (2012), which declared unconstitutional mandatory life sentences without parole for juvenile offenders. Some examples of recent conservative activist decisions include *Citizens United v. Federal Election Commission* (2010), which declared unconstitutional federal statutory limits on the amount of money corporations and unions could spend on political campaigns, and *District of Columbia v. Heller* (2008), which declared unconstitutional the gun control laws in D.C. because the majority decided that the Second Amendment provides for an individual right to own guns.

Governance as Dialogue

The concepts of judicial review, judicial activism, and judicial restraint all lead to the question of what the proper role of the Supreme Court in the American political system should be. The **Governance as Dialogue movement** argues that the Supreme Court is not the last word on interpreting the Constitution but instead is part of a continuing inter-institutional conversation. Therefore, the meaning of the Constitution is eventually determined by a continuing discussion among various political actors and institutions. As one research study concluded, "American political institutions by design are inextricably linked in a continuing dialogue."[104] Some scholars have argued that public policy making in this country is a "dynamic process" in which "issues recur."[105] Justice Ruth Bader Ginsburg has stated that constitutional interpretation often requires courts to enter into "a continuing dialogue with other branches of government, the States, or the private sector."[106] As Justice Robert H. Jackson argued more than fifty years ago, "No sound assessment of our Supreme Court can treat it as an isolated, self-sustaining, or self-sufficient institution. It is a unit of a complex, interdependent scheme of government from which it cannot be severed."[107] Thus, the Governance as Dialogue movement looks at how all the institutions of government interact and negotiate the meaning of the Constitution. As one member of Congress told me in an interview, "The relationship between Congress and the courts involves a continuous back and forth between us and the courts. In other words, it is a complex dialogue among equal branches always jockeying for power."[108]

Unlike the other political actors taking part in the continuing conversation or dialogue about the meaning of the Constitution, the courts bring a unique voice to the table because judges must justify their decisions using legal reasoning and legal analysis. Therefore, the Supreme Court should be part of this continuing inter-institutional dialogue about the meaning of the Constitution. This book is written very much in the spirit of the Governance as Dialogue approach.

OUTLINE OF THE REMAINDER OF THE BOOK

This first chapter of this text has examined the functions and purposes of courts in American society, our common law roots, the sources of law our judges use, and the basics of legal analysis. It has also presented some basic vocabulary that is essential to an understanding of judicial politics. Chapter 2 is devoted to exploring the structure of American courts. The next section of the book, Chapters 3 and 4, will examine in more detail the role of lawyers and judges, who are crucial players in the judicial system, as well as both the state and federal judicial selection processes. Chapters 5 and 6 will look at the role of trial courts, first in criminal cases and then in civil cases. Chapters 7 and 8 will consider the policy-making role of appellate courts and how political scientists study judicial decision making on these courts.

The last half of the book will examine the interactions between courts and other political actors, beginning in Chapter 9 with the interactions between the courts and interest groups, the media, and the general public. Chapters 10, 11, and 12 look at the interactions between courts and legislatures, courts and presidents or governors, and courts and bureaucratic agencies. The final chapter examines the interactions between courts in the United States with courts abroad. The goal of the entire book is to give the reader a better understanding of judicial politics in the United States.

For Further Reading

Breyer, Stephen. 2010. *Making Our Democracy Work: A Judge's View.* New York: Alfred A. Knopf.

Carter, Lief H., and Thomas F. Burke. 2010. *Reason in Law.* 8th ed. New York: Longman.

Keck, Thomas. 2004. *The Most Activist Supreme Court in History: The Road to Modern Judicial Conservatism.* Chicago: University of Chicago Press.

Lindquist, Stefanie A., and Frank B. Cross. 2009. *Measuring Judicial Activism.* New York: Oxford University Press.

Scalia, Antonin. 1997. *A Matter of Interpretation: Federal Courts and the Law.* Princeton, NJ: Princeton University Press.

Schauer, Frederick. 2009. *Thinking Like a Lawyer: A New Introduction to Legal Reasoning.* Cambridge, MA: Harvard University Press.

Silverstein, Gordon. 2009. *Law's Allure: How Law Shapes, Constrains, Saves, and Kills Politics.* New York: Cambridge University Press.

Tate, C. Neal, and Torbjorn Vallinder, eds. 1995. *The Global Expansion of Judicial Power.* New York: New York University Press.

Vandevelde, Kenneth J. 2010. *Thinking Like a Lawyer: An Introduction to Legal Reasoning.* 2nd ed. Boulder, CO: Westview.

Van Geel, T. R. 2009. *Understanding Supreme Court Opinions.* 6th ed. New York: Pearson Longman.

2

Structure of Courts in the United States

This chapter will examine the structure of the third branch of government at both the federal and state levels in the United States. The federal court and state court systems have overlapping jurisdictions and share the same geographical space, though of course the state courts are really fifty-one separate court systems defined by individual state constitutions and state statutes (the District of Columbia courts function like a state court system for these purposes, even though the District is not a state with all of the concomitant rights and privileges). We begin with a discussion of the general differences between trial courts and appellate courts. Then we will turn to a discussion of some of the differences between the structure of the federal courts and the state courts. The chapter will conclude with a discussion of the limits of federal jurisdiction because the state courts can, and do, hear many more cases than the federal courts.

Before we dive into the differences between trial courts and appellate courts, we should start with a discussion of the concept of jurisdiction. In this context, **jurisdiction** means the power or authority of a court to hear a certain type of case. Jurisdiction can be vertical, meaning that a lower court must decide a case before a higher court can review that decision. Jurisdiction can also be horizontal, meaning that some courts can only hear cases regarding certain subject matters. These are often referred to as **limited jurisdiction courts**. For example, in some states, housing courts can only hear cases regarding landlord-tenant issues. Juvenile courts in most states can only hear cases regarding delinquency, neglect and abuse of children, or child custody issues. At the federal level, the U.S. Court of Federal Claims will only hear monetary claims against the federal government, the U.S. Tax Court only hears certain federal tax cases, and the Foreign Intelligence Surveillance Court will only grant warrants for intelligence surveillance.

General jurisdiction courts can hear a wide variety of criminal, civil, and administrative law cases. All of the regular federal courts and many state courts are courts of general jurisdiction.

Jurisdiction can also be geographical, meaning that courts can only hear cases within a certain geographical boundary. For example, the Municipal Court of Boston can only hear certain types of disputes arising within the city limits. Thus, the term *jurisdiction* can also be used as a synonym for **venue**, meaning the geographical area over which the court has the authority to hear cases. The state court systems generally have open jurisdiction, meaning that almost all cases can be filed in some specific court in the state, while the jurisdiction for federal courts is limited by federal statutes. Only cases that meet at least one of the four current tests for federal jurisdiction can be heard in federal trial courts; this will be addressed in more detail toward the end of the chapter. Jurisdiction questions clearly affect whether a certain case can be heard in a federal court, in a state court, or in either court system.

TRIAL COURTS VERSUS APPELLATE COURTS

In this section, we will discuss the specific characteristics of trial courts and appellate courts, as well as the differences between the two. Figure 2.1 shows the general organization of the contemporary federal and state court systems, as well as the relationship between those two systems. Because each state structures its own court system according to its own constitution and statutes, Figure 2.1 assumes a simplified generic state court system organization, consisting of state supreme courts at the top, followed by state appellate courts, and then state trial courts. Some states have very complicated court systems, while others are quite simple in their organization, as will be discussed in more detail later in this chapter. The U.S. district courts, the U.S. courts of appeals, and the U.S. Supreme Court are the three courts in the federal court system.

Trial Courts and Questions of Fact

Cases and litigants enter all the court systems through the **trial courts**. In Figure 2.1, the trial courts are the bottom row on both the federal and state sides of the chart (federal trial courts are known as U.S. district courts). In many parts of the world these trial courts are called "courts of first instance." American trials are public events, open to the press and to the general public. In the United States, trial courts in both the federal and state systems usually use a single judge to hear a case. In rare circumstances, a U.S. district court may use a three-judge

FIGURE 2.1 The State and Federal Court Systems in the United States

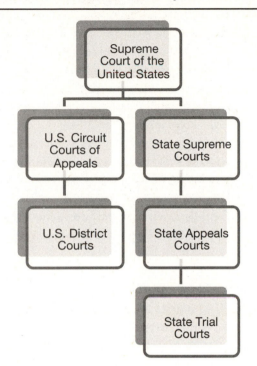

Note: While state supreme courts are the highest interpreters of pure issues of state law, these state courts must follow the precedents handed down by the U.S. Supreme Court. Thus, the state supreme courts are listed below the U.S. Supreme Court because they are considered lower courts for precedential purposes.

panel to hear a case if such a panel is required by a federal statute for a specific type of lawsuit, such as certain civil rights cases.[1]

At a civil or criminal trial, each party is represented by its own attorneys. The lawyers examine witnesses and present evidence in order to assist the court in determining the facts of the dispute or crime. The lawyers present the facts in the most favorable light for their clients, and the jury (if there is one) determines whose presentation of the facts is most correct. If there is no jury, then the judge hands down the **verdict** in the case, that is, the decision of which side's presentation of facts serves as the legal outcome for the dispute. In other words, the verdict announces who wins and who loses, based on the facts the jury or the judge believe to be true. In a criminal case, after a guilty verdict the judge also hands down the sentence because criminal sentencing is a matter of law handled by the judge in almost all criminal cases except capital punishment cases. In a capital punishment case, the jury first decides the verdict, and then, after hearing more evidence relevant to the sentencing phase, the jury determines if the convicted defendant should receive the death penalty or life imprisonment.[2] (See Chapter 5 for more on the criminal justice system.)

The main purpose of trial courts, therefore, is to determine **questions of fact**. The judge is responsible for determining any questions of law (defined below), as well as questions of fact if there is no jury. But if there is a jury present, then it is solely the jury's responsibility to determine questions of fact. In most states, the judge gives the jury instructions that limit the jurors' deliberations to the facts of the case.[3] When focusing on questions of fact, trial courts are only concerned about the specific case before them. The loser at trial has the right to appeal the decision to a first-level appellate court. The only exception is that the prosecutor in a criminal case generally cannot appeal a finding of not guilty.

Appellate Courts and Questions of Law

Appellate courts are where appeals are filed. In Figure 2.1, the trial courts are at the bottom of both sides of the chart. All the courts above the trial courts in the chart are appellate courts. There may be multiple appellate courts in any given court system.

Lawyers communicate their appeals in writing to appellate courts, and appellate courts issue their decisions in written opinions. In three-tier court systems, the loser at the lower appellate court can then appeal to a higher appellate court. Some appellate courts have a **mandatory docket**, meaning that they must hear every appeal filed with them. This is true of all first-level appellate courts, including the U.S. courts of appeals and many state intermediate appeals courts. The U.S. Supreme Court, however, has a **discretionary docket**, meaning that it decides which appeals to hear and which ones to reject. Some state supreme courts also have a discretionary docket. The U.S. Supreme Court is the highest appellate court in the country, and its decisions serve as binding precedent for all lower federal and state courts. The U.S. Supreme Court only accepts about 2 percent of the more than ten thousand appeals presented to it each year for full argument.

The state supreme courts are the highest interpreters of state constitutions and of matters that are purely issues of state law. For example, when the Massachusetts Supreme Judicial Court declared that the state constitution provided the right of same-sex marriage, that case was not heard by the U.S. Supreme Court because there was deemed to be no federal issue in that case. Thus, the Massachusetts Supreme Judicial Court was the last word on the issue of same-sex marriage under its state constitutional provisions. (See Chapter 7 for more details about the appellate court process.)

Appellate courts serve a variety of purposes. One purpose of all appellate courts in the United States is to correct errors of law at trial.[4] Although appellate courts in the United States generally accept the facts as determined at the trial in the lower-level trial courts, they review the legal rulings made by the trial courts to determine if the trial judges have correctly applied the law to the facts of the case.[5] In other words, the appellate courts make sure that the trial judge did not misinterpret the law. Every litigant has the right to at least one appeal in order to make sure that there were no legal errors at trial. The error correction function of appellate courts also ensures that the law is being applied consistently across all courts and judges.

A second purpose of appellate courts is to answer questions of law. **Questions of law** are much broader than questions of fact and are issues that will arise in other future cases. In order to answer the questions of law before them, appellate courts must interpret multiple sources of law, such as constitutions, statutes, and agency decisions. The court's answer to a question of law, and especially the reasoning for that answer, is what is known as **precedent** (a concept you might recall from Chapter 1). When appellate courts answer questions of law, they set precedent for all future cases in the courts below them.

Let us look at an example of questions of fact and questions of law that occurred in the same case. In the original O. J. Simpson criminal trial in California in 1995, the main question of fact in the case was whether or not Simpson had actually killed his former wife and her boyfriend. Part of the evidence in the case involved a bloody glove that was thought to have been used during the murders. The police and prosecutors argued that Simpson left the bloody glove at the crime scene. The question of fact here was fairly simple—did the glove actually belong to Simpson? In the words of Simpson's defense lawyer, Johnnie L. Cochran, "If it doesn't fit, then you must acquit."

The questions of law were more complicated in this case, regarding in part whether DNA evidence should be admissible in any court. The question of law was whether technology had advanced to the point where DNA evidence was trustworthy and reliable enough for use at trial. The Simpson trial was interrupted because the law regarding this issue was unclear at the time. The Supreme Court of California then decided that DNA evidence was scientifically reliable and therefore could be used as evidence at trial. This is a question of law because the decision of the California Supreme Court was binding precedent for all lower courts in the state and applied to all future cases, including the O. J. Simpson murder trial. Although the California Supreme Court's decision was not binding precedent for other courts in other jurisdictions, almost every state and federal court soon followed the California court's decision that DNA evidence is trustworthy enough to be admitted as evidence at trial. This is an example of persuasive precedent, a concept introduced in Chapter 1. After the decision of the California Supreme Court on this question of law, the trial of O. J. Simpson resumed. Simpson was acquitted of these murders, although he did eventually lose a wrongful-death civil suit brought by the relatives of the murdered individuals. Recall that the burden of proof in civil cases is much lower than it is in criminal trials.

Appellate Court Opinions

Appellate courts issue their rulings in writing. An appellate court decision has two parts: the outcome of the case and the reasoning. The outcome means who wins the case and who loses, and so is most important to the parties involved, but the reasoning of the majority becomes binding precedent for all lower courts in the judicial hierarchy because it answers the specific question of law in the case.

There are several types of appellate opinions. Recall that all appellate courts have multiple judges hearing the case. The **majority opinion** reflects the majority outcome and the majority reasoning. In other words, the majority opinion is the one that receives the majority of the votes on the appellate court. On the U.S. Supreme Court, for example, the majority opinion gets at least five votes among the nine justices. The majority opinion states who wins and who loses, and the reasoning behind the majority opinion becomes the precedent from the case ruling. The **holding** in a case is the legal doctrine that the majority opinion articulates, a concise statement of the precedent the ruling has created. A **concurrence** agrees with the majority outcome, but for different reasons. The **dissenting opinion** is the minority's preferred outcome and the minority's reasoning for that outcome. On the U.S. Supreme Court, for example, a dissent gets four or fewer votes among the nine justices. On a three-judge panel on the U.S. courts of appeals, a majority opinion would get two votes, while the dissent would get one vote.

A **plurality opinion** does not get a majority vote on the court but may become the controlling precedent under certain circumstances, such as if the opinion gets some combination of five votes in the U.S. Supreme Court. For example, in *Regents of the University of California v. Bakke* (1978), Justice Lewis F. Powell's plurality opinion became the controlling precedent for the Supreme Court in affirmative action cases. While Justice Powell was the lone justice to sign on to his opinion in its entirety, he did get five votes for each part of the opinion, making it the opinion of the Court. In his opinion, Justice Powell said that race and sex quotas are unconstitutional in the absence of a finding of past intentional discrimination by the specific university or employer in question. This part of Powell's opinion received the votes of four conservative justices plus his own. But the other half of the opinion, where Justice Powell said that race and sex could be considered among other factors in educational admissions and employment, received the votes of four liberal justices plus his own. While the whole of Powell's plurality opinion technically only got one vote, it nevertheless became the opinion of the Court because he got five votes for each portion of his decision.

FEDERALISM AND THE AMERICAN COURT SYSTEMS: A HISTORICAL OVERVIEW

This chapter will now turn to the differences between the state and federal court systems. Recall that there are really fifty-one different state court systems, but for convenience this section will compare the federal court system with a generic state court system. Every state has both a federal court system and a state court system within its borders, with overlapping jurisdictions. We have both state and federal court systems in our country because state courts existed well before the U.S. Constitution of 1789 called for the creation of the federal court system. In many ways, the federal courts were superimposed upon the existing state court structures. The organization and structure of the court systems in the United States are extremely complicated in part because of our unique system of federalism. Most other federalist governments around the world have chosen to have one unified court system, like the one in Canada, instead of having two separate court systems, as we have in the United States.

At this point, a general definition of federalism would be helpful. To understand federalism, we must compare it with other approaches used around the world. There are three basic choices about how to structure the relationship between the national government and regional governments: unitary, federal, and confederal. **Federalism** is the division of power between the national government and the regional governments (in the United States, these are the states). In a federal system, the national government is supreme over the regional governments, although the regional governments retain certain powers. Article VI of the U.S. Constitution contains a **Supremacy Clause**, which, when read in conjunction with the Fourteenth Amendment, clearly indicates that we have a federal system in which the states are legally inferior to the national government. The British Empire at the time of the American Revolution was a **unitary system**, where all power was centralized in the national government in London. **Confederal systems** mean that there is a division of power between the national government and the regional governments, with the regional governments being supreme. Confederal systems will be discussed in more detail later in this chapter. The U.S. Constitution and various federal statutes spell out the structure of the federal court system, while the state constitutions and state statutes generally establish the structure of the state courts.

The Articles of Confederation

The existing state court systems were first created in colonial times. Because the original thirteen states were founded as British colonies, the colonists brought the English common law notions of law and courts with them. Each colony set up its own court system with its own rules and procedures. After the American Revolution, the state court systems remained much as they had been prior to independence.

After the Declaration of Independence in 1776, the national government of the United States first functioned under the **Articles of Confederation**. This confederal system of government divided power between the national government and the states, but the states were considered supreme, with limited power given to the central government. Note that under the Articles of Confederation we did not have a president or a Supreme Court. Congress was the only institution of the central government. Each state maintained its own state court system under the Articles of Confederation, and there were no national or federal courts at all during this period. The state constitutions determined the jurisdiction and procedures to be followed in each state judicial system, including the number and levels of courts available to the state's citizens.

During the Civil War, the southern states experimented with another confederal system, known as the Confederate States of America. The state courts remained intact during the Civil War and most of Reconstruction, although the judges during Reconstruction were mostly unionists loyal to the north.[6] There were great variations among the colonial court systems, the state court systems that existed right after the Revolution, and the post–Civil War courts. These differences among the state courts continue today.

The U.S. Constitution of 1789

The Articles of Confederation proved unworkable, and the Constitutional Convention created a new system of government that included federalism as a key component. The new Constitution created a national executive (the president), a new bicameral legislature (the U.S. Congress), and a new Supreme Court of the

United States. Article III of the U.S. Constitution stated that a Supreme Court of the United States would be created and left it to Congress to determine how to structure the remaining parts of the new federal court system.

Note that Article III of the Constitution of 1789 is silent about the state court systems. The existing state court systems are mentioned only indirectly in the Constitution's Article IV, where the Full Faith and Credit Clause states that "Full Faith and Credit shall be given in each State to the public Acts, Records, and judicial proceedings of every other State." Some scholars also argue that Article IV's Guarantee Clause, which requires that the states have a republican form of government, also implies that the states should have separate court systems. Thus, when the states ratified the U.S. Constitution of 1789, they did not give up their separate and unique state judicial systems. These court systems continued to be defined by the state constitutions and state statutes. The new Constitution merely superimposed a new layer of federal courts on the existing state courts.

In the Judiciary Act of 1789, Congress established the basics of the federal court system that still exist today. Today, the federal courts have a three-tier structure, with the U.S. Supreme Court at the top of the judicial pyramid. The decisions of the U.S. Supreme Court are binding precedent for all the lower federal courts and under most circumstances for all the state courts. In *Fletcher v. Peck* (1810), the Supreme Court ruled that its power of judicial review extended to determining the constitutionality of state laws. In *Cooper v. Aaron* (1958), the U.S. Supreme Court reaffirmed that it is the final arbiter of the U.S. Constitution under the Supremacy Clause.

Some have argued that one of the greatest responsibilities of the U.S. Supreme Court under the U.S. Constitution of 1789 is to protect the federal government from the states. After giving itself the power of judicial review in its decision in *Marbury v. Madison* (1803), the Supreme Court worked hard to consolidate federal power at the expense of the states. For example, in *McCulloch v. Maryland* (1819), the Court declared that the states had no power to tax the newly created national bank, because the power to tax was the power to destroy. The Civil War was fought in part over issues of federalism. Originally, the Bill of Rights applied only against the power of the federal government. However, after World War II, the U.S. Supreme Court began using the Fourteenth Amendment to apply most of the Bill of Rights to the states in a process known as **incorporation**. Incorporation was done in a piecemeal fashion by the U.S. Supreme Court over an extended period of time, and, by today, most of the elements of the Bill of Rights limit state power as well as federal power. Over time, many justices have been concerned about the states improperly encroaching on federal power. Justice Oliver Wendell Holmes supported this idea of protecting the federal government from the states when he wrote, "I do not think the United States would come to an end if we lost our power to declare an Act of Congress void. I do think the Union would be imperiled if we could not make that declaration as to the law of the several States."[7] Issues of federalism remain a great concern for the U.S. Supreme Court as it tries to figure out when the national government can overrule the states and when the states should retain powers of their own.

THE FEDERAL COURT SYSTEM

This next section will examine in more detail the workings of the federal court system. We will first look at the U.S. district courts, followed by the U.S. court of appeals, and then the U.S. Supreme Court. We will also discuss specialized federal courts and federal judicial agencies.

Federal Trial Courts: The U.S. District Courts

Unlike the great variation found in the state court systems, the federal courts are quite uniform in their structure. The federal trial court is called the U.S. district court, and there are ninety-four federal districts in the United States today. Almost all federal cases begin in the U.S. district courts. Every state has at least one U.S. district court, and the larger states may include several districts. Puerto Rico, the District of Columbia, and several of the U.S. territories also have their own U.S. district courts. A few districts have only one or two judges, but some have as many as thirty. Congress decides how many judges will serve in any given district; in 2013 there were 677 judges authorized to sit on the various U.S. district courts around the country. Just like their counterparts on the U.S. courts of appeals and the U.S. Supreme Court, judges on the U.S. district courts are appointed by the president and confirmed by the U.S. Senate for life terms. Many U.S. district courts also have **federal magistrate judges**, selected by a majority vote by the regular judges assigned to the district. These magistrate judges serve an eight-year term and assist the regular federal judges, mostly with highly complex litigation.

U.S. Circuit Courts of Appeals

The U.S. circuit courts of appeals are the intermediate appellate courts in the federal system. Figure 2.2 shows the current boundaries of the U.S. circuit courts of appeals. There are twelve regional circuit courts of appeals, plus the Court of Appeals for the Federal Circuit. The Court of Appeals for the Federal Circuit has nationwide jurisdiction to hear appeals in specialized cases, such as those

FIGURE 2.2 Map of the U.S. Circuit Courts of Appeals

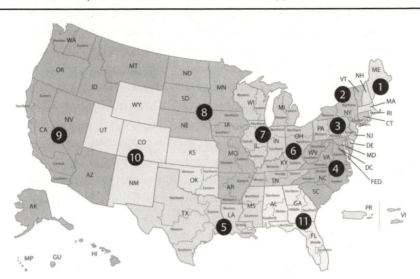

Source: Administrative Office of the United States Courts.

involving patent laws and cases decided by the Court of International Trade and
the Court of Federal Claims. The smallest circuits (the Second, Fifth, Seventh,
and Eleventh Circuits) include three states, while the largest circuit court, the
Ninth Circuit, includes nine states plus several federal territories. In 1997, the
circuit courts heard a total of more than fifty thousand cases; in 2004 they received more than fifty-six thousand appeals,[8] and in 2005 they heard more than
sixty-eight thousand cases.[9] There were a total of 179 judgeships authorized for
these courts in 2013. The smallest circuit, the First Circuit, has six judges, while
the largest circuit, the Ninth Circuit, has twenty-eight judges. Like all other regular federal judges, judges on the U.S. courts of appeals are appointed by the president and confirmed by the U.S. Senate for life terms. The types of cases that the
circuit courts hear vary by region—for example, the Second, Fifth, and Ninth
Circuits tend to hear many immigration appeals, given the large number of immigrants in the areas serviced by those courts.[10]

The existing U.S. courts of appeals system was created in 1891, although the
U.S. Congress has changed the boundaries for some of the circuits on various
occasions since then. For example, in 1980, for both political and management
reasons Congress split the old Fifth Circuit into two new circuits—the current
Fifth Circuit includes the states of Texas, Louisiana, and Mississippi, while the
new Eleventh Circuit covers the states of Florida, Georgia, and Alabama.[11]

These federal appellate courts have a mandatory docket, meaning that they must hear all appeals that come to them.[12] The U.S. circuit courts of appeals hear appeals from the U.S. district courts and from many federal administrative agencies.[13] These courts use panels of three randomly selected judges to hear most cases, although it is possible for a losing party to request that the entire court (or a subset of fifteen judges on large circuits such as the Ninth Circuit) rehear a case, in what is known as an *en banc* review, after the three-judge panel has rendered its decision.[14] In order for an *en banc* hearing to occur, a regular judge on the circuit must first endorse the litigant's request, and then a majority of the regular judges on the circuit must vote for the *en banc* review.[15] Because the Supreme Court hears so few cases each year, the U.S. courts of appeals serve as the last word on many federal law questions. These courts also correct errors of law made by federal trial judges and administrative agencies.[16]

These intermediate federal appellate courts have undergone several name changes over their history, as well as changes in their basic makeup and structure. Originally the U.S. circuit courts were composed of a combination of judges from the U.S. district courts and the U.S. Supreme Court. These borrowed judges rode circuit, meaning that they literally traveled around the states in the circuit, hearing appeals from the lower federal courts as well as having some trial jurisdiction. The Judiciary Act of 1891, however, created the current system of freestanding U.S. courts of appeals with their own judges. The old circuit courts were finally abolished in 1911, though we continue to use *circuit courts* as a colloquial name for the U.S. courts of appeals.[17] Traditionally, researchers did not pay as much attention to the judicial decision making on the U.S. courts of appeals as they did to the U.S. Supreme Court, but more and more scholars are now studying these intermediate federal appellate courts.[18]

The Supreme Court of the United States

The highest court in the United States is of course the Supreme Court of the United States. This court today has nine justices, who are appointed by the president and confirmed by the U.S. Senate for life terms. The exact number of justices on the Supreme Court is determined by Congress, not by the U.S. Constitution. In the nineteenth century the number of justices varied over time, but Congress eventually settled on nine in 1869, during Reconstruction. In what is known as his court-packing plan, President Franklin D. Roosevelt unsuccessfully proposed almost doubling the size of the Supreme Court when the Court kept declaring his New Deal programs to be unconstitutional.[19] This was one of the few votes in Congress that FDR lost in his many years in office. Today, having nine justices on the Supreme Court seems to be constitutionally enshrined in the minds of Americans even though that number does not appear in the Constitution itself.

The chief justice of the United States, often referred to as the first among equals,[20] is appointed by the president and confirmed by the Senate whenever that specific seat is vacant. Only rarely does a president nominate someone already sitting on the Supreme Court for this position, although Chief Justice Rehnquist was an associate justice when President Reagan elevated him to the chief justice position.[21] There is no requirement that the president appoint someone to the U.S. Supreme Court who has previously served as a judge on any court. For example, prior to being appointed as chief justice, Earl Warren served as governor of California. Justice Elena Kagan served as the U.S. solicitor general and before that as the dean of Harvard Law School, but she had never held a judgeship before being appointed to the Supreme Court.

As mentioned earlier, the U.S. Supreme Court creates binding precedent that all the other lower courts in both the state and federal court systems must follow. The U.S. Supreme Court also has administrative responsibilities over all other federal courts, overseeing many of the day-to-day activities of the lower courts.[22] The Judiciary Act of 1925 repealed most of the mandatory jurisdiction of the Supreme Court, thus almost completely allowing it to control its own caseload. With its discretionary docket, today's U.S. Supreme Court refuses to hear about 98 percent of the cases brought to it.[23] The power of judicial review allows appellate courts and especially the U.S. Supreme Court to declare the actions of other political actors to be unconstitutional. Taken together, the ability of appellate courts to make precedent and their power of judicial review makes American appellate courts very strong policy makers.

Specialized Federal Courts

In addition to the regular district courts, there are several other types of specialized federal trial courts. Each district has special **bankruptcy courts**, which are separate units of the district courts. Unlike most other types of disputes, bankruptcy cases cannot be heard in the state courts. They must be heard only in special bankruptcy courts attached to the regular U.S. district courts, and in 2008 and 2009 more than a million bankruptcy cases were filed each year.[24] **Bankruptcy judges** are appointed by the majority of the regular federal judges who sit on the U.S. district court, and they serve fourteen-year terms. There are now more than three hundred federal bankruptcy judges in the United States.

The Court of International Trade has jurisdiction over cases involving international trade and customs issues, and the United States Court of Federal Claims has jurisdiction over most claims for money damages against the United States, disputes over federal contracts, and unlawful takings of private property by the federal government, among a variety of other claims against the U.S. government. There is also a special U.S. Tax Court that hears cases involving the Internal Revenue Service, although this special court does not have a monopoly over these disputes because they are often heard in other federal trial courts as well.[25] Most of the judges on these courts are so-called **Article II judges**, because they do not have the life terms enjoyed by their regular judicial colleagues. Life-term judges are referred to as **Article III judges**.

Another specialized federal court is the Foreign Intelligence Surveillance Court, which approves warrants for federal law enforcement and intelligence personnel conducting investigations into suspected terrorism and other illegal activities occurring on U.S. soil. Its judges are borrowed from the regular U.S. district courts and serve only part-time on this court.[26] The military justice system has its own appeals court, known as the United States Court of Appeals for the Armed Forces, and its own rules of procedure. This court exercises worldwide appellate jurisdiction over members of the armed forces on active duty and other individuals subject to the Uniform Code of Military Justice. It is composed of five civilian judges appointed for fifteen-year terms by the president with the advice and consent of the Senate.[27]

Federal Judicial Agencies

Another important aspect about the structure of the federal courts is the existence of federal judicial agencies of various types. These agencies and bodies generally serve the needs of the federal judiciary and provide necessary assistance to the federal courts. The **Judicial Conference of the United States** (not to be confused with the private meetings of the justices at the Supreme Court discussed in Chapter 7) is the committee that voices the collective views of the federal judiciary to the outside world—in other words, it is the policy-making arm for all federal courts. The U.S. Judicial Conference often presents the positions of the federal judiciary to Congress on legislative matters including budgets, security for judges, courthouse construction issues, and judicial workload crises caused when there are many judicial vacancies because the U.S. Senate is slow in confirming new federal judges. Within the judiciary, this group also produces recommendations that the lower federal courts must follow in order to standardize and thus improve judicial administration throughout the nation. The Judicial Conference was first created in 1922 at the urging of Chief Justice William Howard Taft, and Congress changed its name to the current one in 1948. The chief justice of the United States is the head of the U.S. Judicial Conference, and its members include federal judges from both the U.S. courts of appeals and the U.S. district courts.

Founded in 1939, the **Administrative Office of the United States Courts** (AO) serves as staff for the Judicial Conference. The Administrative Office also provides research, administrative, legal, financial, management, program, and information technology services to the federal judiciary. The AO communicates the views of the judiciary to the president and Congress, thus serving an unofficial lobbying function for federal judges collectively. The Administrative Office employs lawyers, public administrators, accountants, systems engineers, analysts, architects, statisticians, and other types of professional individuals.

Another federal judicial agency is the **Federal Judicial Center** (FJC). This agency provides training and research for the federal judiciary in a wide range of areas, including court administration, case management, budget and finance, human resources, and court technology. In the United States, all judges are drawn from the legal profession, and, because there is no "judge school" like there is in a number of European countries, many of them have no experience with the day-to-day problems and issues that judges face. Thus, the FJC attempts to fill this gap, both for new judges and for long-serving members of the federal judiciary. The FJC also provides assistance and training to judges from around the world who want to learn more about the U.S. legal system. This work of the FJC is discussed in more detail in Chapter 13.

The final federal judiciary agency, the **United States Sentencing Commission**, is somewhat of a hybrid agency. One of the major purposes of the Sentencing Commission is to recommend federal sentencing guidelines to Congress, which must then enact these suggestions into law. The Sentencing Commission also advises Congress and the executive branch about effective and efficient crime policy in general, and the agency collects and analyzes a broad range of information on federal crime and sentencing issues. The U.S. Sentencing Commission is treated as an independent agency housed in the judicial branch of government, but it serves the needs both of Congress and of the federal courts. Currently the Sentencing Commission has seven members who are appointed by the president and confirmed by the Senate for six-year terms. At least three of the commissioners must be federal judges, and no more than four may belong to the same political party.

Congress first created the U.S. Sentencing Commission in the Sentencing Reform Act of 1984, in order to limit the discretion of federal judges in their criminal sentencing decisions, and the first set of federal sentencing guidelines was put into place in 1987. Congress was concerned that federal criminal sentences were not uniform across the decisions made by a single judge, judges serving on the same court, or courts across the country. Congress was also concerned about appearing to be tougher on crime. Thus, the federal sentencing guidelines system was designed to eliminate disparities in federal criminal sentences. Although the Supreme Court had found the federal sentencing guidelines to be constitutional in *Mistretta v. United States* (1989), later in *United States v. Booker* (2005) the Court ruled that these guidelines were merely advisory and could not be treated as mandatory restrictions on the discretion of federal judges. More details about the criminal trial process can be found in Chapter 5.

THE STATE COURT SYSTEM

We will now turn to an examination of the various state courts. When Americans encounter a court firsthand, usually as a juror or as a litigant, it is almost always a state trial court in a state judicial system. Over 98 percent of all legal cases today are heard in the state courts. There are more than sixteen thousand courts in the state judicial systems, and they process approximately a hundred million cases per year. The state courts employ more than thirty thousand judicial officers (including judges and others) and many more support staff. Through its state constitution and other laws, each state can decide how to structure its own court system, including how many types of courts the system will have and which courts will have the jurisdiction to hear what types of cases.[28]

Once a case begins in either a state court system or the federal court system, it usually stays in that system unless a federal trial court grants a writ of habeas corpus (discussed in more detail in Chapter 5) or the U.S. Supreme Court eventually agrees to hear the case. The states employ a variety of selection methods for their judges, although most states use some type of election system. These different state judicial selection processes will be explored in more detail in Chapter 3.

The Structure of State Courts

Some states employ a very simple structure for their state courts, while other states have a very complex system. Figure 2.3 shows a generic state court structure, one that is fairly straightforward in organization. Note that this three-tier system is quite similar to the federal court structure. During the nineteenth century, almost no states had a three-tier state court system, but by the twentieth century most states had added new intermediate courts of appeals to help reduce the caseload of the state supreme courts. This change allowed state supreme courts to focus more on cases that involved important public policy issues, while the intermediate courts of appeals handled the more routine error correction functions of appellate courts.[29] California is a state that follows a simple federal-style three-tier court structure, as shown in Figure 2.4. The one exception to this is that death penalty cases skip the courts of appeals and go directly to the California Supreme Court after the death penalty is imposed by a jury in a trial court. On the other hand, some states have chosen to have a more complicated court structure for their state courts. Figure 2.5 illustrates the extremely complex state court structure in Massachusetts. In the Bay State, there is the traditional three-tier system, but it is complicated by the fact that the Superior Court is the court of first instance (initial trial court) for some cases. Other cases start in one of the other trial courts and are then referred to the Superior Court after a preliminary hearing; in these cases, the Superior Court acts more like an appellate court. At times, two different trial courts could simultaneously have jurisdiction over a case, resulting in judges having to take the time to sort out whether a case actually belongs before their bench. The Massachusetts structure can be confusing even for lawyers with some experience in this extremely complicated state court system.

Because each state has its own court structure, state trial courts can have a variety of names and jurisdictions. Some of these courts hear only major cases, while other courts hear both major and minor disputes. Some of these trial courts hear a broad range of cases, while others hear only very specialized ones.[30]

FIGURE 2.3 A Generic State Court Structure

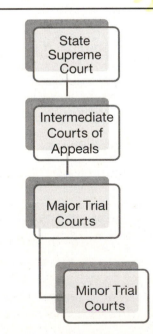

FIGURE 2.4 Structure of California State Courts

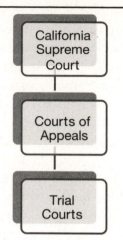

Note: All death penalty cases go directly from the trial courts to the California Supreme Court.

FIGURE 2.5 Structure of the Massachusetts State Court System

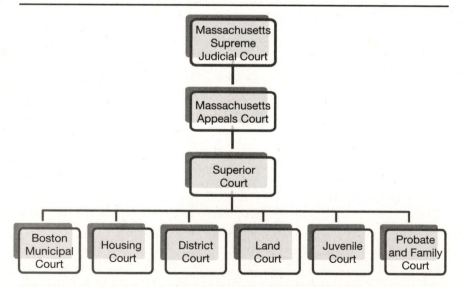

Note: For some major cases the Superior Court is the entry-level initial trial court, and for some cases the Superior Court serves as a review court after preliminary hearings are held in other trial courts.

States might also have both trial courts of general jurisdiction and courts of limited jurisdiction. Depending on the state, these courts may carry such names as *municipal courts, district courts, superior courts, county courts, juvenile courts, probate courts, family courts, housing courts,* or even *drug courts.* In the state of New York some of the trial courts are called *supreme courts,* which is very confusing because in almost every other state the supreme court is at the top of the judicial pyramid, not at its bottom or entry point. The original *Law and Order* TV series was set in New York City and therefore used New York nomenclature, setting its fictional trials in the "supreme courts" of New York City.

Although each state court system is unique, based on the state's own constitution and statutes, there is a certain similarity in the structures of many regular state court systems, which is not surprising given that states frequently borrow ideas from each other. Nevertheless, even though the states may have formal statewide rules on how to administer the courts, local judges often follow their own norms and practices in overseeing their courtrooms. Thus, even where there is a centralized judicial administration, local judges have considerable freedom to run their own courts as they see fit.[31]

The American Bar Association and others have recommended that states simplify their court structures.[32] Part of the court unification movement involved putting state court administration in the hands of professionals supervised by the state supreme courts. The idea was to promote efficiency and to protect the independence of state courts from undue legislative control.[33] This court unification movement failed in many states. For example, in Massachusetts traditionally clerk magistrates who worked for the judges obtained their jobs through a patronage system, and individual clerks were hired by legislators or by the governor instead of by the judges for whom they worked. Most of the clerk magistrates kept their jobs for life because the judges had no right to dismiss them.[34] Even after a patronage scandal erupted in Massachusetts in 2012, when a number of probation officials were indicted for racketeering, bribery, and mail fraud because they created a deceptive hiring system that allowed them to give jobs to their friends, relatives, and political supporters, the state has yet to change dramatically the system for hiring these clerk magistrates.[35]

One category of specialized state trial courts is worth mentioning in more depth. **Juvenile courts** are special courts designed to handle issues of juvenile delinquency and neglect, and they are structured much differently than courts for adults. First created in Chicago in 1899, these courts serve multiple purposes.[36] In most states, the juvenile courts deal with issues of juvenile delinquency as well as problems of neglect and abuse of children. They may also deal with issues of child custody. These courts tend to close their proceedings to the public in order to protect the children's privacy and the confidentiality of the matters at hand, and they usually do not follow the same rules of procedure as the regular courts. One of the most important U.S. Supreme Court decisions in the area of juvenile justice is *In re Gault* (1967). In this case, the Court ruled that while some flexibility in procedures was necessary in juvenile courts, minors still had a number of due process rights in these courts, including the right to an attorney in many situations.[37] The standard in this court even in juvenile delinquency cases is the best interests of the child. As one expert on juvenile justice concludes, "The general purpose of juvenile court acts is to ensure the welfare of the juveniles while protecting their constitutional rights in such a way that removal from the family unit is accomplished only for a reasonable cause and in the best interests of the juvenile and society."[38] Thus, most juvenile courts are more concerned with rehabilitation goals than are most judges in so-called adult courts.

State Appellate Courts

Most states have two levels of appellate courts, an intermediate court of appeals and a state supreme court. In many states, the first-level court of appeals is regional and may be referred to as an intermediate appeals court, while the state supreme court is the top court in the state, hearing appeals from the various regional courts of appeals. In eleven states, cases still go immediately from the trial courts to the state supreme court because the state does not have an intermediate appeals court.[39]

Most state intermediate-level appellate courts hear cases in panels of three judges, while most state supreme courts have seven judges who all sit for every case the court hears, though some states use five and a few use nine. Texas and Oklahoma each have two supreme courts, one for criminal appeals and another for appeals in civil cases. The top courts in the states of Maryland and New York are called the "court of appeals," while every other state calls their court of last resort the "supreme court." The National Center for State Courts, headquartered in Williamsburg, Virginia, coordinates a great deal of research and data dealing with the various state court systems.

There are some issues that bypass the state trial courts and go directly to state appellate courts or, more commonly, to the state supreme courts as part of their original jurisdiction. For example, cases involving disciplining of judges and attorneys often go directly to the state supreme courts after initial administrative proceedings by a bar disciplinary board. For states that allow advisory opinions, that is, opinions on the constitutionality of legislation before it goes into effect, these requests come from the state legislature or the governor and go directly to the state supreme court. Some state supreme courts also have original jurisdiction over certain types of writs.[40]

The state supreme courts are the final interpreters of the state constitutions and the courts of last resort under state law. In *Hortonville Joint School District No. 1. v. Hortonville Education Association* (1976), the U.S. Supreme Court clearly stated, "We are, of course, bound to accept the interpretation of [state] law by the highest court of the State."[41] Even though the state supreme courts are the last word on state law, the truth is that only a minuscule number of cases from state appeals courts are ever reviewed by state supreme courts, and only a tiny fraction of rulings by state supreme courts are ever heard by the U.S. Supreme Court.[42] Thus, state appellate courts retain a certain amount of decisional autonomy.

The state supreme courts have the last word on questions of state law because the U.S. Supreme Court will hear only cases that involve a federal issue of some sort.[43] The U.S. Supreme Court will not review a decision of a state supreme court if the ruling is based on adequate and independent state law grounds. In other words, if a case raises both state and federal law issues, the U.S. Supreme Court will not hear the case if the state law issues are adequate to settle the dispute. For example, *Fox Film Corp. v. Muller* (1935) involved a contract dispute between a filmmaker and an individual who had promised to show one of the company's films. The U.S. Supreme Court refused to hear the suit because the case could be decided based purely on state law. Even though Fox Film Corporation asked the Court to review the case based on both federal and state law claims, the Court ruled that it would not hear the case because the state law issues were an adequate and independent ground for ending the dispute. However, in *Michigan v. Long* (1983), a case dealing with the police finding drugs in the defendant's car, the U.S. Supreme Court took the case because it ruled that the Michigan Supreme Court was in reality exclusively using federal law and federal precedents in its decision and not basing its ruling on purely state law grounds. This case clarified the somewhat confusing doctrine of adequate and independent state grounds for deciding cases. As Alan Tarr, a judicial scholar, has described the effects of the adequate and independent state law doctrine, "State rulings based on state statutes, the common law, or state constitutions are altogether immune from federal judicial scrutiny, unless a 'federal question' is raised or unless the case falls within the federal courts' diversity jurisdiction."[44]

The state supreme courts hear many constitutionally based cases each year. State supreme courts vary a great deal in how they interpret their state constitutions, in part because state constitutions range in size from eight thousand words (similar to the size of the U.S. Constitution) to two hundred thousand words.[45] State supreme courts collectively hear around two thousand constitutional cases each year, while the U.S. Supreme Court hears on average only about thirty. Many argue that scholars have not paid enough attention to the importance of the state supreme courts in shaping American law. According to Neal Devins and Nicole Mansker, experts on state constitutional law, "State supreme courts have eclipsed the U.S. Supreme Court in shaping the meaning of constitutional values."[46]

State supreme courts and state laws are free to provide more protection to individual rights and liberties than is found in the U.S. Constitution because the U.S. Constitution only provides a minimum, or floor, level of such rights.[47] Starting in the early 1970s, many state courts became much more liberal than their federal counterparts. Many civil liberties and social reform interest groups started bringing cases in state courts because they felt that the state courts would provide various constitutional protections that the more conservative federal courts would not.[48] For example, the states can bar discrimination on the basis of sexual orientation even though there are no federal laws prohibiting such discrimination. The state courts were also the forum for rulings that required the states to equalize their funding for public schools across the state. The U.S. Supreme Court had ruled in *San Antonio Independent School District v. Rodriguez* (1973) that, since there is no federal right to an education, it would not hear cases asking for equalized funding for public schools. Thus, the state supreme courts can provide a greater level of constitutional protection on various issues by interpreting their state constitutions more broadly than the U.S. Supreme Court interprets the U.S. Constitution. This is especially true today in some states in the areas of abortion, gay rights, takings, school financing, religious liberty, tort reform, and some criminal procedure protections.[49]

The state supreme courts also have a much harder time avoiding more controversial decisions because they generally do not have the various technical avoidance techniques available to the federal courts.[50] Of course, since the U.S. Supreme Court only hears about 2 percent of the requests for appeals each year, in many cases the decision of the state supreme court is the last word even if there might be a federal issue in the case.

LIMITATIONS OF THE FEDERAL COURT SYSTEM

In this section, we discuss some of the limitations of the federal justice system, including federal jurisdiction requirements and case and controversy restrictions.

Federal Jurisdiction

Unlike the state courts, which generally have open jurisdiction and have some courts that can hear almost any case, the jurisdiction of the federal courts is limited, which is why federal courts hear many fewer cases than state courts. Congress determines the jurisdiction of the federal courts, and for a case to be heard in a federal court it must meet at least one of the four current tests for **federal jurisdiction**:

1. If the U.S. government is a party to the case, then the case must be heard in the federal courts. This means that all federal crimes are tried in the federal courts (the U.S. government is the prosecutor), and all civil cases involving the federal government must be heard in federal court. Bankruptcy cases must also be heard in federal courts. The U.S. government does not appear in state courts.

2. If there is a federal issue in the case involving a federal source of law (e.g., the U.S. Constitution, federal statutes, a presidential executive order, or a federal agency decision), then the plaintiff has the choice of whether to file the case in the federal courts or in state courts. If a state judge hears the case, then he or she must apply federal precedents.

3. In a so-called diversity case, where there are parties from different states in a civil case worth more than $75,000, then the plaintiff has the choice of filing the case in state courts or in the federal courts. If a federal judge hears the case, it is quite likely that he or she will be applying state precedents to the dispute.

4. The Class Action Fairness Act of 2005 created another test for federal jurisdiction. When the parties are from different states and the total amount in controversy exceeds $5 million, then the federal courts may consolidate various individual cases into a single federal class action lawsuit. This new legislation was sought by large nationwide corporate interests, such as drug manufacturers, who felt that they were not being treated fairly when they faced large numbers of lawsuits in numerous state courts concerning a common issue or dispute. Thus, they wanted their cases to be heard only in federal courts.

Since Congress has created these four tests for federal jurisdiction, it is an open question whether Congress can also refuse to allow the federal courts to hear certain types of cases. That controversy will be discussed in more detail in Chapter 10.

Cases and Controversies

In addition to the federal jurisdiction requirements discussed above, federal cases must meet the requirements of having an actual case and controversy, as required by Article III of the Constitution. In some ways, these requirements are internal checks on the courts' power of judicial review. Very early in our constitutional history, the U.S. Supreme Court ruled that it and the other federal courts would never provide advisory opinions. An **advisory opinion** is an opinion on the constitutionality of legislation before that legislation goes into effect. This is the main way for a case to reach the constitutional court of France, for example. In Canada, these are called reference cases. One of the most famous reference cases in Canada came after the national parliament asked the Supreme Court of Canada to decide whether Quebec could secede from the confederation. The Canadian Supreme Court spelled out what must be negotiated before the province could secede.[51] Opponents of advisory opinions often argue that the advisory opinion procedure subordinates the courts to the legislature or to the executive because, even though the courts cannot usually refuse to issue an advisory opinion, the other branches are under no obligation to follow the court's advice.[52]

Some state supreme courts do offer advisory opinions to their legislative or executive branches. Of the ten states that currently have advisory opinion procedures in place, six were among the original thirteen British colonies.[53] For example, after the Massachusetts Supreme Judicial Court ruled in *Goodridge v. Department of Public Health* (2003) that same-sex couples had the same right to marry as opposite-sex couples, the Massachusetts legislature asked the court for an advisory opinion about whether civil unions, then in use in Vermont, would satisfy the court's ruling. The Massachusetts Supreme Court responded by saying that separate was never equal, thus clarifying that, when the court said same-sex couples had the right to marry, marriage meant marriage, and civil unions would not be sufficient.

As part of its case and controversy doctrines, the Supreme Court of the United States has ruled that cases filed in federal courts must also meet certain other threshold requirements in order to abide by the Constitution's Article III case and controversy requirement. The lawsuit must be filed in the right place, known as the proper **venue**, and in the right court with the proper jurisdiction. First, the Court will not allow the federal courts to hear cases that are **collusive**, where there is no actual dispute. *Muskrat v. United States* (1911) can be considered such a case. In this case, the U.S. Congress passed legislation that authorized certain Native Americans to bring a lawsuit to determine the constitutionality of specific laws allocating tribal lands. However, when David Muskrat and J. Henry

Dick did just that, the Supreme Court ruled that there was no real controversy in the case and disallowed the suit. The parties to the case heard in federal court must have **standing**, meaning that the party filing the case suffered an actual harm from the dispute. In other words, standing means that the case is filed by the right party. In *Frothingham v. Mellon* (1923), the U.S. Supreme Court ruled that taxpayers do not have standing to challenge federal spending decisions. This rigid prohibition on taxpayer standing was eased somewhat by the Court in *Flast v. Cohen* (1968), when the Court ruled that taxpayers might have standing in certain narrow circumstances such as challenges under the First Amendment's Establishment Clause. However, the Court seemed to return to a highly restricted view of taxpayer standing in *Arizona Christian School Tuition Organization v. Winn* (2011), when the Court refused to allow taxpayers to challenge an Arizona tax credit program that provides tax credits for contributions to tuition even at religious schools. At times, Congress can give plaintiffs standing to sue, such as when it allowed environmental groups to sue on behalf of the spotted owl and other endangered species.

The timing of the case must also be correct for the case to be heard in federal court. If the controversy is already resolved, then the dispute is **moot**, because the courts will not hear hypothetical cases. However, at times this doctrine is treated as flexible. For example, the Supreme Court in *Roe v. Wade* (1973) ruled that the question of whether or not a woman could choose to have an abortion was not moot, despite the fact that the plaintiff in the case had already had the baby, because she could get pregnant again and the issue would recur for other women who could not get their cases heard during the nine months of a pregnancy. If the case is not **ripe**, it means that it has been filed too early. Often in administrative law cases, the court will require that all administrative proceedings be exhausted before a federal court can hear the case.

Another threshold doctrine is somewhat more complicated and harder to define. The Supreme Court has said that the federal courts should not hear **political questions**. This generally means that the courts should not settle disputes that are better handled by a different branch of government. Many foreign policy issues have been determined to be political questions, better handled by the other branches of government. This doctrine can also be quite flexible. In *Baker v. Carr* (1962), and to a lesser degree in *Reynolds v. Sims* (1964), the Supreme Court held that legislative redistricting issues were not political questions because only courts could grant relief to voters who felt that the legislative district lines in place at the time were violating their equal protection rights by giving urban representatives many more constituents than rural representatives had. In other words, because the legislatures would not handle the redistricting themselves, only the courts could change the current system, and so the issue was not a political question.

CHAPTER SUMMARY

This chapter examined the basic structure of the courts in the United States. It began with a discussion of the broad differences between trial courts and appellate courts, as well as the differences between questions of fact and questions of law. The chapter then turned to a deeper examination of the federal courts and the state courts, looking at the specifics of the organizations and jurisdictions of trial courts and appellate courts in both systems. The chapter also defined the work of the federal judicial agencies, which assist federal judges in their work. The chapter ended with a discussion of the limitations of federal courts, from federal jurisdiction requirements to case and controversy requirements. Both types of requirements, often referred to as threshold requirements, must be met before a federal court will hear a case.

For Further Reading

Baum, Lawrence. 2011. *Specializing the Courts.* Chicago: University of Chicago Press.

Bernard, Thomas J. 1992. *The Cycle of Juvenile Justice.* New York: Oxford University Press.

Klarman, Michael J. 2004. *From Jim Crow to Civil Rights: The Supreme Court and the Struggle for Racial Equality.* New York: Oxford University Press.

Langer, Laura. 2002. *Judicial Review in State Supreme Courts: A Comparative Study.* Albany: State University of New York Press.

O'Brien, David M. 2011. *Storm Center: The Supreme Court in American Politics.* 9th edition. New York: W. W. Norton.

Powe, Lucas A., Jr. 2000. *The Warren Court and American Politics.* Cambridge, MA: Belknap Press.

Rosenberg, Gerald N. 1991. *The Hollow Hope: Can Courts Bring About Social Change?* Chicago: University of Chicago Press.

Rowland, C. K., and Robert A. Carp. 1996. *Politics and Judgment in Federal District Courts.* Lawrence: University Press of Kansas.

Sunstein, Cass R. 2009. *A Constitution of Many Minds: Why the Founding Document Doesn't Mean What It Meant Before.* Princeton, NJ: Princeton University Press.

Tushnet, Mark. 2003. *The New Constitutional Order.* Princeton, NJ: Princeton University Press.

3

Judicial Selection

This chapter will examine the judicial selection processes employed at both the federal and state levels. There are three key questions concerning any judicial selection system: (1) how and why judges are initially selected, (2) how judges retain their seats on the bench, and (3) what are the term lengths for judges. The federal courts and the fifty-one state judicial systems (including the District of Columbia) have chosen different answers to these three critical questions. The chapter will compare the federal judicial selection process with the six different models used by the states to select state judges.

The federal selection system promotes the greatest degree of judicial independence. Federal judges on the U.S. district courts, the U.S. courts of appeals, and the U.S. Supreme Court are all appointed by the president and confirmed by the U.S. Senate for life terms. To promote judicial independence even further, the U.S. Constitution prohibits Congress from reducing the salaries of federal judges, although there is nothing in the Constitution guaranteeing any annual salary increases or budgets for staff, computers, air-conditioning, and so on. Although this judicial selection process is quite straightforward on the surface, this chapter will explore how specific presidents have differed in their approaches to selecting lower federal judicial nominees. The chapter will also look at difficulties faced by certain U.S. Supreme Court nominees in recent history.

JUDICIAL INDEPENDENCE VERSUS
JUDICIAL ACCOUNTABILITY

We will begin with an examination of two crucial concepts in judicial selection: judicial independence and judicial accountability. **Judicial independence** means that judges are protected from any undue outside political influences that could affect their substantive decisions. Keeping judges free from the ambitions, agendas, and priorities of the other branches helps ensure that the courts will be able to interpret the Constitution impartially.[1] As Alexander Hamilton stated in Federalist No. 78, giving federal judges life terms and preventing Congress from reducing their salaries were mechanisms designed to promote judicial independence. Federal judges are appointed through a political process, but, once they are confirmed, judicial independence allows judges to make their decisions free from political controls.

Judicial independence is furthered by the American tradition of not impeaching federal judges or removing other judges from office merely because politicians disagree with their decisions.[2] The U.S. Constitution provides that federal judges can be removed from office when a majority of the U.S. House of Representatives votes for articles of **impeachment**. If that occurs, the U.S. Senate holds a trial, but it still takes a two-thirds vote of the Senate to remove the judge from office. In 1804, Judge John Pickering of the U.S. District Court in New Hampshire was impeached and then removed from office because he was a severe alcoholic and probably insane. The Jeffersonians had just taken control of Congress and the presidency in the elections of 1800, and the trial was a highly partisan affair.[3] Because the Jeffersonians were quite angry with the Federalist judges who then dominated the federal judiciary, they turned their energy toward impeaching Justice Samuel Chase of the U.S. Supreme Court, merely because the Jeffersonians perceived Chase's decisions to be based purely on partisan concerns. The House voted to bring articles of impeachment against Justice Chase in 1804, and the Senate held its removal trial in 1805. However, the Jeffersonians could not get the necessary two-thirds of the Senate to agree to remove Justice Chase from office.[4] It was widely assumed that, if the Jeffersonians had been successful in removing Justice Chase from office, then they would have impeached Chief Justice John Marshall next.[5] The failure of the Chase impeachment efforts would have long-term implications, preventing the impeachment and removal of federal judges merely because politicians disliked their decisions. No federal judges have ever been removed from office simply because of the political implications of their rulings.[6]

Although our federal judges clearly enjoy a great deal of judicial independence, a competing value in the American governmental system is judicial accountability. **Judicial accountability** means that the judges' decisions should reflect the will of the people because courts are making important public policy decisions. Thus, judges should be accountable to the people, either directly or through the other branches of government. Most state judges serve relatively short terms, which also help to promote the principle of judicial accountability. If a judge delivers a ruling that goes against public opinion, then the people or their elected representatives should be able to remove that judge from office in some fashion. Some states directly elect their state judges, while others require that judges face retention elections every so often in order to retain their judgeships. Some states allow the legislative branch to remove judges from office fairly easily.[7] Most state judges also serve limited terms of office, with only a very few New England states allowing judges to effectively serve life terms until they reach a mandatory retirement age, typically seventy or seventy-five.

The United States is unique in its stress on the value of judicial accountability because most societies stress judicial competence instead. Judicial competence means that judges are chosen on the basis of merit, not politics, and retain their seats based on the quality of their decisions. For example, in the civil law world, most judges are selected because of their test scores in judge school, not because of their political connections. Only Japan, Switzerland, and the United States allow elections for at least some types of judges.[8]

According to one study, more than 85 percent of all state judges in the United States today must win voter approval to keep their seats on the bench.[9] Thus, the vast majority of state judges in the United States face limited terms and some sort of election mechanism to retain their judgeships. While the federal courts are designed to promote the notion of judicial independence, most state judicial selection systems instead promote the concept of judicial accountability. The details of the six different models of state judicial selection will be discussed in more detail later in this chapter.

THE SELECTION PROCESS FOR FEDERAL LOWER COURT NOMINEES

As mentioned earlier in this chapter, the U.S. Constitution provides a rather simple process for selecting federal judges. At all three levels of the federal courts, judge candidates are nominated by the president and confirmed by the U.S. Senate for life terms. Technically, the presidential nominees are subject to the advice and consent of the Senate. There is no requirement that a judge have prior judicial experience before being nominated to any of the three levels of federal courts, although by tradition all federal judges are drawn from the legal profession, meaning that they must be lawyers before they can become federal judges. Not surprisingly, there is a fairly vast academic literature on the nomination and confirmation of justices for the U.S. Supreme Court. There is a smaller but growing scholarly literature on the selection process for lower federal court judges.

Although all presidents have the responsibility of nominating federal judges, individual presidents approach this duty differently.

The Presidential Screening Process for Judicial Nominees

Before the president announces the names of any nominees to any federal court, the candidates are usually first vetted by White House staff or by staff in the U.S. Department of Justice, depending on the preferences of the specific president then in office. The Federal Bureau of Investigation (FBI) also runs a background check on any individuals the president is considering nominating, including getting information from the Internal Revenue Service (IRS) about their past tax returns. This process often takes several months to complete.[10]

The president may also send the names of the potential nominees to the American Bar Association (ABA) for its review. The ABA has evaluated prospective judicial nominees since 1946, and it established its Standing Committee on the Federal Judiciary for this very purpose in 1949.[11] Since 1987, the Standing Committee has had fifteen members.[12] Starting with President Dwight Eisenhower, all presidents except President George W. Bush have sent their lists of potential lower court and even Supreme Court nominees to the ABA for its review before the names become public. The Standing Committee on the Federal Judiciary is charged with evaluating the nominee's professional competence, integrity, and judicial temperament. Since the administration of President Jimmy Carter, the committee has interpreted these criteria to mean that a nominee must have at least twelve years of experience in the practice of law before his or her nomination to the federal bench.[13] Today, the ABA rates nominees as well qualified, qualified, or not qualified. The ABA review generally takes about six weeks.[14]

The role of the ABA in the federal judicial selection process has been highly controversial. President George W. Bush did not send the names of his potential nominees to the ABA because he felt that the ABA rating process was ideologically driven and biased against conservatives.[15] By contrast, from the 1950s until at least the 1970s, the ABA was widely perceived to prefer conservative judicial candidates.[16] President Richard Nixon, however, felt that the ABA ratings of his Supreme Court nominees were not fair because of the liberal bias that he perceived in the ABA process, even though most observers at the time still thought of the ABA as a conservative organization.[17] But the reputation of the ABA has changed. At least since the Reagan years, and perhaps even earlier, conservatives have generally viewed the ABA as a liberal organization.[18] Although President George W. Bush did not submit the names of his potential nominees to the ABA, the Senate Judiciary Committee nevertheless forwarded those names to the ABA after it received them from the White House. President Barack Obama has returned to the traditional practice of submitting the names of potential nominees to the ABA before they are released to the public. As of November 2011, the ABA had rated a surprisingly high proportion of the potential Obama nominees (14 of the roughly 185) to be not qualified, and nearly all of the prospects given poor ratings were women or members of a minority group, according to published accounts. The Obama Administration refused to nominate anyone rated as not qualified by the ABA, and this process was among the reasons for the long delays faced by many potential Obama nominees for the lower federal courts.[19]

The Senate Judiciary Committee

After the president makes the judicial nominations public, the names are then sent to the Senate Judiciary Committee for review. Since 1950, all nominees have faced confirmation hearings held by the committee.[20] During its investigation, the Senate Judiciary Committee gathers a variety of information about each nominee. Generally the senators review the full FBI and IRS reports, as well as summaries of the ABA reviews of the nominees. President George H. W. Bush tried to send the committee only a summary of the FBI reports, but the senators on the committee objected.[21] The committee staff members also gather other information about the nominees. For example, each nominee must complete a questionnaire provided by the committee staff and must supply copies of many of their prior judicial decisions.[22]

The Senate Judiciary Committee then holds confirmation hearings on each nominee, the timing and scheduling of which are controlled by the chair of the committee.[23] By tradition, only one circuit court nominee appears at any hearing, although it is common for up to six nominees to the U.S. district courts to testify at one hearing.[24] If the president nominates many potential judges at the same time, there may be a delay in holding all of the confirmation hearings. At the hearings, the nominees testify, and the committee hears testimony from others who are interested in the nomination. The committee chair also determines when the committee will vote on a specific nominee, though any individual senator may request that the vote be delayed until the next meeting of the committee.[25] Therefore, committee confirmation votes can experience substantial delays if senators from the minority party object to a given nominee.

In the Senate Judiciary Committee, judicial nominations may be subject to the Senate tradition of **senatorial courtesy**, meaning that the senators from the nominee's home state must approve the nomination before other senators will vote for that person.[26] Because of this tradition, sometimes presidents have directly asked senators to suggest nominees to the federal courts for their states. Historically, presidents extended senatorial courtesy only to senators from their own party,[27] and then perhaps only to the most senior senator.[28] Since U.S. district courts only have authority within a specific state's boundaries, certainly senatorial courtesy applies to the nominees to these courts. Senatorial courtesy may also apply, however, to many nominees for the U.S. circuit courts of appeals because most of these seats are traditionally "assigned" to a specific state.[29] The exceptions to this rule are seats on the U.S. Court of Appeals for the District of Columbia and U.S. Court of Appeals for the Federal Circuit, because these two circuit courts, which deal with issues of national importance, have no seats assigned to any given state.

The Senate Judiciary Committee has institutionalized the norm of senatorial courtesy in its **blue slip** procedures. When a judicial nominee's name is sent to the Senate Judiciary Committee, the chairman automatically sends a blue sheet of paper to the home state senators asking for their endorsement of the candidate. If a home state senator fails to return the blue slip, then traditionally the chairman will not schedule confirmation hearings for that nominee. This effectively kills the nomination, thus giving the home state senators de facto veto power over U.S. district court nominees for their states and over U.S. court of appeals nominees who are seeking seats "assigned" to their state.

Historically, very few senators refused to return the blue slips.[30] In recent years, however, the confirmation process for lower court nominees has become more contentious and more polarized along partisan lines. More and more senators are refusing to return the blue slips for a variety of reasons, including fights with the president over issues unrelated to the judicial nominees.[31] And it seems that the chairs of the Judiciary Committee are more likely to defer to the wishes of senators from their own party who refuse to return blue slips.[32] The blue slip practice has been controversial in the past, and it remains so today.[33]

Whether or not the failure to return a blue slip means that an individual home state senator can veto a judicial nominee has varied throughout the years, depending on who is the chair of the Senate Judiciary Committee and whether his or her party also controls the White House. When Ted Kennedy (D-Mass.) became chair of the Senate Judiciary Committee in 1979, he stated that he would not allow the refusal of a home state senator to return the blue slip to serve as a secret veto over the nomination.[34] When Senator Orrin Hatch (R-Utah) became chair in 1994, the Republican returned to the traditional practice of letting a single home state senator veto a judicial nomination, but Senator Hatch changed his mind when his party took control of both the Senate and the presidency in 2001.[35] When Senator Patrick Leahy (D-Vt.) became chair of the committee in

2007, he followed the practice of allowing a single blue slip to prevent a confirmation hearing on a nominee regardless of the party of the objecting senator.[36]

Confirmation by the Full Senate

If the Judiciary Committee approves the nomination by a majority vote in a meeting scheduled at the discretion of the committee chair, it then moves to the full Senate. Lower court nominations are the largest group of nominees that the Senate must confirm each year.[37] The majority leader of the Senate controls scheduling of the floor vote on the nominations, and the nominee must receive a majority vote on the floor of the Senate to be confirmed. Any senator can place a hold on the nomination, and this can be done anonymously.[38] By tradition, the majority leader will not schedule a vote when there is a hold.[39] Although there are ways to force a vote on a nominee who is being blocked by a hold, most Senate leaders will not do so. As Congressional Research Service scholars Richard Beth and Stanley Bach have noted, "Recent majority leaders have accordingly tended to honor holds, both as a courtesy to their colleagues, and in recognition that if they choose not to do so, they may well confront filibusters that they prefer to avoid."[40] These holds have contributed to the gradual change in the Senate from a norm of reciprocity to a norm of individualism and eventually a norm of partisan polarization.[41]

In recent years, the minority party in the Senate has frequently filibustered judicial nominations from a president in the opposing party, thus forcing the nominee to receive sixty votes in the Senate in order to break the filibuster. In a **filibuster**, unhappy senators can talk a bill or a nomination to death. Under current Senate rules, it takes sixty votes to invoke **cloture** and end debate on the nomination. Because the Senate majority leader controls the calendar in the Senate, he or she is usually the one to file a cloture motion in order to end a filibuster on any given nomination.[42]

One of the first modern filibusters of a judicial nominee occurred in 1968, when conservatives blocked the nomination of Associate Justice Abe Fortas of the U.S. Supreme Court to become chief justice. Filibusters became much more common in the 1990s and 2000s. There were filibusters of a few of President Bill Clinton's nominees to the lower courts, and, during George W. Bush's presidency, liberals filibustered a variety of Bush nominees to the U.S. circuit courts and even to the U.S. district courts, in part because of the increased involvement of interest groups in nomination fights over lower court appointments. The Republicans threatened to eliminate the filibuster option altogether, but eventually a bipartisan group of fourteen moderate senators prevailed on their colleagues and the filibusters ended.[43] Filibusters returned when President Obama came into office, and they were often accompanied by other delaying tactics.[44] The difficulties continued into the president's second term.[45] In January 2013, the Senate changed its rules to make filibusters more difficult for nominees to the U.S. district courts, but the rule change did not affect nominations to the U.S. courts of appeals or to the U.S. Supreme Court.[46] Throughout 2013, Senate Republicans continued to filibuster all of President Obama's nominees to the U.S. Court of Appeals for the District of Columbia and many of his nominees to other federal courts. In November 2013, over strong Republican objections and with a simple majority vote, Democrats changed Senate rules to eliminate filibusters for all executive branch nominations and for all nominees to the U.S. district courts and the U.S. courts of appeals. Filibusters will still be allowed for nominees to the U.S. Supreme Court. This dramatic change in Senate practices has been called the "nuclear option" because it takes away a great deal of power from the minority party in the chamber.[47] There will be more discussion of the Senate's advice and consent role regarding judicial nominees later in this chapter.

Judicial Vacancies

Another issue in the federal lower court appointment process involves judicial vacancies and how numerous vacancies in our courts can hamper the effectiveness of the judicial branch. President Obama became the first president in recent history to have more judicial vacancies at the end of his first term than when it started.[48] There were fifty-five judicial vacancies when President Obama first took office,[49] but, by December 2, 2012, there were eighty-three empty district and circuit court judge seats, with thirty-three of them considered "judicial emergencies."[50] The lame-duck session of the Senate in late December 2012 did approve a few of Obama's judicial appointments, but nevertheless the president began his second term with seventy-five empty seats on the federal courts.

Obama also had far fewer judicial nominees confirmed in total by the Senate than did his predecessors. While Clinton had 200 confirmed nominees and George W. Bush had 205 at the end of their first terms, respectively, Barack Obama only had 160 confirmed appointments to the bench by early December 2012. President Obama's nominations also took far longer to reach the floor of the Senate. It took an average of 30 days for Clinton's nominees to get a floor vote after being approved by the Senate Judiciary Committee and 54 days for George W. Bush's appointees. In President Obama's first term, it took on average over 139 days for nominees approved by the Judiciary Committee to get a floor vote in the Senate.[51]

At the beginning of his second term, President Obama greatly increased the pace of his judicial nominations.[52] In fact, he quickly renominated thirty-three individuals who had been previously nominated for the federal courts but did not receive an up-or-down vote in the Senate the first time around.[53] It appeared that Obama was willing to invest more political capital in getting his nominees confirmed in his second term than he had in his first term.[54] Unfortunately, the pace of Senate confirmation of Obama judicial appointees remained very slow.

In his State of the Judiciary Report, released on December 31, 2012, Chief Justice John Roberts complained about the large number of judicial vacancies on the federal courts.[55] He wrote:

A significant and prolonged shortfall in judicial funding would inevitably result in the delay or denial of justice for the people the courts serve. I therefore encourage the President and Congress to be especially attentive to the needs of the Judicial Branch and provide the resources necessary for its operations. Those vital resource needs include the appointment of an adequate number of judges to keep current on pending cases. . . . I urge the Executive and Legislative Branches to act diligently in nominating and confirming highly qualified candidates to fill those vacancies.[56]

Various newspapers such as the *New York Times* also complained about the large number of judicial vacancies at the end of President Obama's first term.[57] Even some of the associate justices on the Supreme Court entered the discussion. Referring to the large number of judicial vacancies, Justice Ruth Bader Ginsburg told a group of lawyers in February 2013, "I'm hoping there will be members of Congress who will say enough. We are destroying the United States' reputation in the world as a beacon of democracy."[58] Some argue that President Obama's unwillingness to make judicial appointments a priority of his administration is due to his skepticism that the courts can produce true social change in our society.[59]

Judicial vacancies became a severe problem for some particular courts. In his first term, President Obama became the first president in sixty-five years to have no nominees confirmed to the prestigious U.S. Court of Appeals for the District of Columbia, which handles many administrative law issues and other questions vital to the federal government.[60] This court is often referred to as the second most important court in the country.[61] As of March 2013, there were only seven judges sitting on the court, meaning there were four vacancies. This was the worst vacancy rate in the court's history and a far higher vacancy rate than in any other U.S. Court of Appeals at the time.[62] As one journalist described the situation, "The U.S. Court of Appeals for the District of Columbia is fundamentally broken in ways that are rippling across Washington and the country."[63] In April 2013, the U.S. Judicial Conference, the policy-making arm of the federal courts and the entity representing all federal judges throughout the nation, urged the Senate Judiciary Committee to confirm appointees to the D.C. Circuit Court to bring the court back to its full allotment of eleven regular judges.[64]

In fact, no new judges were confirmed to the U.S. Court of Appeals for the District of Columbia from 2006 until May 2013. This is the same court on which Ruth Bader Ginsburg, Robert Bork, Antonin Scalia, Clarence Thomas, and John Roberts once sat. Four of these individuals became justices on the Supreme Court of the United States, while Bork's nomination to that court was rejected by the U.S. Senate. In March 2013, President Obama withdrew his nomination of Caitlin Halligan to this court because Republicans in the Senate who felt that she was too liberal and too activist in her views filibustered the nomination.[65] President Obama did push hard to get his next nominee confirmed.[66] After several lengthy delays, Sri Srinivasan was finally confirmed by a unanimous vote in the Senate in late May 2013 and became the first South Asian to sit on that court.[67] In early June 2013, President Obama simultaneously announced three new nominees to this court.[68] However, some Republicans then proposed reducing the size of the court and transferring the judgeships to other circuits in order to prevent the U.S. Court of Appeals for the District of Columbia from having a majority of judges appointed by Democratic presidents.[69] When the three Obama nominations to this court were brought to the Senate floor, Republicans filibustered all of them. As mentioned earlier, fights over Obama's nominations to this court led Senate Democrats to eliminate the filibuster entirely for all executive branch and most judicial branch nominees in November 2013.[70] In December 2013, the Senate confirmed two more Obama nominees to this court, thus for the first time in many decades giving it a majority of judges appointed by Democratic presidents. The partisan fight over appointments to this court shows just how important this court is to both parties.

PRESIDENTIAL APPROACHES TO APPOINTING LOWER COURT JUDGES

Although on the surface the selection process for all lower federal court judges looks remarkably uniform, any individual president may emphasize different values in his or her approach to judicial nominations. This section will explore some of the ways that presidents have differed in their approach to judicial selection issues.

The Patronage Approach

Many presidents have seen judicial appointments as an opportunity for patronage. In this context, **patronage** means that presidents and home state senators can reward loyal supporters by appointing them to the bench. In practice, this meant that home state senators would submit their patronage choices to the president, who then would almost automatically nominate these individuals to serve on the lower federal courts. Until the late 1960s, patronage was the primary motivating factor in presidential judicial nominations for the lower federal courts. As former attorney general Robert F. Kennedy once described the process, district court nominations amounted to "senatorial appointment with the advice and consent of the Senate."[71]

One study found that senators fully expected to have a strong role in the nomination process for judges from their states.[72] Traditionally, senators had a much greater role and voice in choosing nominees for the U.S. district courts in their states than they did for the U.S. courts of appeals.[73] Presidents including Dwight Eisenhower, Harry Truman, and John F. Kennedy used the patronage model to reward senators from their own party and to encourage the senators to vote with them on other issues.[74] Presidents such as Franklin D. Roosevelt and Lyndon B. Johnson were highly sensitive to the ideological makeup of the lower federal courts even while basically still following a patronage approach.[75] They would use patronage when they could, but they would refuse to nominate certain individuals who deviated too much from their preferred ideological agenda.

After several decades of presidents who followed more of an ideological approach in their federal court nominations (see discussion below), President Bill Clinton returned to a patronage model. Clinton allowed Democratic senators and even some Democratic congressmen to suggest judicial nominees to him, though in a break from the old patronage models of the 1950s and 1960s Clinton's appointments were far more diverse than those of his predecessors. This was due to the fact that Democratic senators needed the support of women and minority voters in their own reelection campaigns, so they were quick to suggest nontraditional judicial nominees to the president. As Figure 3.1 indicates, almost half of the Clinton appointees were women and minorities, which fulfilled a promise he had made in his 1992 campaign to make the courts "look like America."[76] President Clinton promoted diversity on the bench as an important idea, and those politicians who suggested potential nominees also saw diversity among judges as a strong political issue for them. However, when Republicans took control of the Senate following the 1994 elections, they moved to delay the confirmation of almost all of President Clinton's judicial nominees.[77] Three lower court

FIGURE 3.1 Female and Minority Appointments to the Federal Courts by President

PRESIDENT	WOMEN		AFRICAN AMERICAN		HISPANIC		ASIAN		TOTAL	
	#	%	#	%	#	%	#	%	#	%
Roosevelt	1	0.5	0	0	0	0	0	0	1	0.5
Truman	1	0.8	1	0.8	0	0	0	0	2	1.6
Eisenhower	0	0	0	0	0	0	0	0	0	0
Kennedy	1	0.8	3	2.4	1	0.8	1	0.8	6	3.9
Johnson	3	1.8	10	5.9	3	1.8	0	0	15	8.9
Nixon	1	0.4	6	2.6	2	0.9	1	0.4	10	4.4
Ford	1	1.5	3	4.6	1	1.5	2	3.1	7	10.8
Carter	40	15.5	37	14.3	16	6.2	2	0.8	87	33.7
Reagan	29	7.8	7	1.9	15	4.0	2	0.5	51	13.7
G. H. W. Bush	36	19.3	13	7.0	8	4.3	0	0	52	27.8
Clinton	108	29.3	61	16.6	25	6.8	5	1.4	177	48.1
G. W. Bush	69	21.4	24	7.5	29	9.0	3	0.9	106	32.9
Obama (First two years only)	31	50.8	16	26.2	5	8.2	6	9.8	43	70.5

Note: The chart shows appointments to the U.S. District Courts, U.S. Courts of Appeals, and U.S. Supreme Court combined. It does not double-count individuals who fit into more than one category.

Source: Compiled by author using data from Sheldon Goldman, Elliot Slotnick, and Sara Schiavoni, "Obama's Judiciary at Midterm: The Confirmation Drama Continues," Judicature 96 (2011): 301.

nominees were filibustered; one was even blocked by members of his own party, in part because Clinton resorted to nominating some Republican judicial candidates in order to get the rest of his nominations confirmed.[78]

The Ideological Approach

Starting with President Nixon in the late 1960s, the model for making lower court appointments seems clearly to have shifted to an ideological approach.

Many presidents began using the courts as campaign issues in their presidential elections (see Chapter 11), and they also came to realize that the federal courts could support or block the president's policy agenda for decades to come. The ideological makeup of the lower federal courts became very important to presidents and the interest groups who supported them. Many presidents came to see their judicial nominations as a way of protecting their historical legacies, and so they started choosing their lower court nominees primarily for ideological reasons. For a variety of reasons, the ideological approach seems to be more prevalent with Republican presidents than it has been with Democrats.[79] Nixon actively campaigned against liberal activist federal judges in 1968,[80] and his judicial appointments reflected his support for law and order issues and his opposition to expanding civil rights.[81]

Presidents Ronald Reagan, George H. W. Bush, and George W. Bush also used an ideological approach to selecting lower court nominees. When Reagan came to power, he centralized the judicial selection process. Staff from the White House and the Justice Department served on his judicial nomination committee. All potential judicial nominees had to fill out a long questionnaire that was forwarded to the attorney general, and President Reagan would refuse to nominate potential appointees who showed any indication that they might be pro-choice on the abortion issue.[82] Reagan ensured that all of his judicial nominees were conservatives, even if it meant disregarding the preferences of the home state senators for those nominees and further eroding the tradition of senatorial courtesy.[83] Some moderate Republican senators were quite unhappy with the Reagan judicial nominees for their states.

When Reagan's vice president, George H. W. Bush, became president, he tended to follow the same general ideological pattern as his predecessor in his judicial appointments. His son George W. Bush also vowed to appoint judicial conservatives to the federal bench, in part to appease the conservative wing of the Republican Party, which did not fully trust him at that time. Almost all of President George W. Bush's potential judicial appointees had to prove themselves to be acceptable to the most conservative wing of the Republican Party before he would nominate them to the federal bench.[84] These presidents wanted their conservative visions to last long after their presidencies ended, and having a conservative federal court system was one clear way to achieve that goal.

In fact, all of the federal judicial appointees nominated by both President George H. W. Bush and President George W. Bush either were members of the Federalist Society or were approved by that group. The **Federalist Society**, established in the early 1980s, is a group of conservative lawyers, law students, law professors, and judges who advocate for conservative rulings from the federal courts. Chief Justice Roberts and Justices Samuel Alito, Antonin Scalia, and Clarence Thomas are all current or former members of the Federalist Society.[85] The contemporary liberal alternative to the Federalist Society is the **American Constitution Society for Law and Policy**, created at Georgetown Law School in 2001.[86] During President George W. Bush's administration, Federalist Society lawyers dominated not only the federal courts but also the legal offices at the U.S. Department of Justice and many other federal agencies.[87]

The Merit Selection Approach

After Jimmy Carter won the presidency in the 1976 election, he used a new and very different model for selecting lower federal judges. Carter had run as an anti-Washington candidate and, ignoring the tradition of senatorial courtesy, decided that federal judges should be appointed through a merit selection system similar to the Missouri Plan for selecting state judges (this will be discussed in more detail later in this chapter). Carter established Merit Commissions for all nominations for the U.S. circuit courts of appeals and encouraged senators to create merit commissions for the U.S. district courts in their states as well. Senators from thirty-one states complied with President Carter's request.[88] These merit commissions would screen potential judicial candidates and suggest appropriate potential nominees based purely on their qualifications. Carter's merit selection scheme did bring much greater diversity to the federal bench, as illustrated in Figure 3.1. Almost a third of President Carter's judicial appointments were nontraditional, meaning that the appointees were not white males.

The Diversity Approach

President Obama also seems to be following a new path in his approach to nominees for the lower federal bench. Obama seems to be specifically looking for nominees with nontraditional backgrounds who will bring to the bench empathy with the lives of ordinary Americans.[89] One might call this the diversity model. In his first two years in office, only about 30 percent of his judicial nominees were white males, as Figure 3.1 indicates. As of May 2012, 46 percent of President Obama's appointees were women and more than 36 percent were people of color, a far higher percentage than any of his predecessors.[90] However, Obama also looked for safe nominees who were not ideologically extreme. As Charlie Savage, a *New York Times* reporter, commented, "Mr. Obama has also largely shied away from nominating assertive liberals who might stand as ideological counterpoints to some of the assertive conservatives Mr. Bush named. Instead of prominent liberal academics whose scholarly writings and videotaped panel discussions would provide ammunition to conservatives, Mr. Obama gravitated toward litigators, prosecutors and sitting district and state judges, especially those who would diversify the bench."[91]

Figure 3.1 shows how many female and minority judges various presidents appointed to the federal bench during their presidencies. Note that the number of women and people of color on the federal bench has generally been growing over the years, but different presidents certainly vary in the percentage of nontraditional judges they have appointed. Democratic presidents have generally appointed more female and minority federal judges than have Republicans.

Perhaps the Obama approach to judicial nominees can best be understood by looking at his Supreme Court appointments. For his highest-profile nominees, President Obama seemed to prefer not only women and minorities but also those with nontraditional legal backgrounds. Justice Elena Kagan had no prior judicial experience before being appointed to the U.S. Supreme Court, although she did serve as the dean of Harvard Law School and as the U.S. solicitor general. Justice Sonia Sotomayor was once a civil rights attorney before becoming a judge on the U.S. Court of Appeals and then an Obama nominee to the Supreme Court.

The Obama Administration seems intent on bringing not only demographic diversity to the federal judiciary but also a diversity of backgrounds and experiences. For example, President Obama has appointed the first Latina to the U.S. Supreme Court, the first openly gay man to a U.S. district court, and the first female judicial nominees who were of Chinese, Korean, or Vietnamese background.[92] He has also appointed the first openly gay black man to the trial court, the first Asian American lesbian to a trial court, and the first South Asian to sit on the U.S. Court of Appeals for the District of Columbia.[93] In fact, by the end of his first term, almost two-thirds of his judicial nominees were nontraditional.[94] President Obama, the first president from a mixed racial background, seems to enjoy breaking other barriers with his judicial nominations.

SUPREME COURT NOMINATIONS

Not surprisingly, voters and the media pay much more attention to U.S. Supreme Court appointments than they do to nominations for the lower federal courts. Presidents use a variety of criteria in order to decide whom to nominate to the U.S. Supreme Court. One set of criteria includes the qualifications of the potential nominee, including competence, experience, judicial temperament, and ethical standards. A second set of concerns are mostly ideological. Will the nominee advance the president's political and ideological agenda? Almost all Supreme Court nominees belong to the political party of the president. A third consideration is rewarding those who have been active in the president's party. While it is rare, some are direct rewards to close personal friends of the president, as with President Obama's nomination of Elena Kagan or President Johnson's nomination of Abe Fortas. A fourth category involves the pursuit of political support. President George W. Bush wanted the support of the right wing of his party, and he rewarded that support by nominating Samuel Alito to the Supreme Court. Likewise, President Obama nominated Sonia Sotomayor in 2009 in part because he needed the support of Latino voters in the 2012 presidential election. Another criterion might be symbolic representation on the Court. Some might say that President George H. W. Bush nominated Clarence Thomas in large part because he was African American.

Although most appointees for the Supreme Court are easily confirmed, some face great difficulties in the Senate. The next section will look at some of the most famous recent fights over confirmation of nominees to the U.S. Supreme Court.

Abe Fortas and the Filibuster

In 1968, the country was in a time of turmoil. There were massive protests against the Vietnam War and race riots in some of our major cities. The presidential election was a hard-fought contest. Just before the beginning of the contentious Democratic National Convention in Chicago, Chief Justice Earl Warren announced his impending retirement. Although he was not running for reelection, President Johnson nominated Associate Justice Abe Fortas to become the new chief justice. The Democrats controlled the Senate, but the party was deeply divided over issues of the Vietnam War and civil rights. During Fortas's confirmation hearings, conservatives from both political parties tried to make it seem that Justice Fortas was responsible for all of the liberal activism on the Warren Court. This was ironic, because Justice Fortas had only served on the Supreme Court for a few years before his nomination to become chief justice. Conservatives also accused Fortas of financial improprieties. Conservatives from both parties then filibustered the Fortas nomination. Eventually Justice Fortas withdrew his name from consideration and then resigned from the Supreme Court altogether. After Richard Nixon was elected to the presidency in 1968, he named Warren Burger to be chief justice.[95] Burger was easily confirmed by the Senate.

Nixon's Failed Nominations

Following the confirmation of Chief Justice Warren Burger, President Nixon faced several more vacancies on the Supreme Court. He first nominated a southerner, Clement F. Haynsworth, but the Senate rejected him in part because of strong opposition from labor unions and civil rights groups and also because of accusations of conflict of interest in some of his lower court cases.[96] Nixon then nominated the southerner G. Harrold Carswell. He was rejected because of his racist past and his perceived lack of qualifications for the highest court.[97] As presidential scholar Kevin McMahon has so colorfully described these two failed nominations, "It must have seemed as though the president made the worst selections possible, that he had picked two clones of Frankenstein's monster to serve on the nation's highest tribunal."[98] Liberals in both parties found no reason to support the Nixon nominees and probably voted against them as much for ideological reasons as because of the nominees' other problems.[99] Interest group opposition was key to both defeats.[100] Nixon was furious that the Senate had rejected both of his southern nominees, but he eventually nominated Harry Blackmun, a friend of Chief Justice Burger's, and Blackmun was easily confirmed.[101]

Interest Group Involvement

In the late 1980s, interest groups showed their muscle in a couple of Supreme Court confirmation fights. In 1987, President Ronald Reagan nominated Judge Robert Bork to replace Justice Lewis Powell, who was considered a swing vote on the Court. As a member of the Nixon Administration, Bork had fired the Watergate special prosecutor Archibald Cox, and he was well known in Washington political circles.[102] Bork had a long list of academic publications advocating an extreme version of judicial restraint. More than three hundred liberal groups came together to oppose the Bork nomination, and they used a wide variety of tactics, including advertising, grassroots events, polling, and focus groups.[103] Some of the major liberal groups opposing Bork included the American Civil Liberties Union (ACLU), the AFL-CIO labor unions, and the National Organization for Women (NOW).[104] The Senate eventually rejected Bork by a vote of 58–42. Conservatives were shocked that the liberal groups had been able to defeat Bork almost exclusively because of the nominee's ideological views. Eventually President Reagan nominated Justice Anthony Kennedy to the seat, and he was easily confirmed.

Reagan had also nominated Antonin Scalia to fill another vacancy on the Court in 1986. Although Scalia's views were quite similar to Bork's, he was confirmed by a vote of 98–0. This happened because interest groups decided to spend all of their time and resources fighting Reagan's nomination of Justice William Rehnquist to become chief justice instead of opposing the Scalia nomination.[105] Rehnquist was nevertheless confirmed by a vote of 65–33. Once Associate Justice Rehnquist was confirmed as chief justice, Scalia was immediately confirmed as an associate justice by a unanimous vote.

Clarence Thomas

In 1991, another nasty fight broke out over confirmation of a Supreme Court nominee. With the retirement of Justice Marshall, the first African American to serve on the nation's highest court, President George H. W. Bush decided to nominate Clarence Thomas to fill the seat. Although an African American, Thomas was very conservative. Justice Thomas was only forty-three years old when he was confirmed, and he had had only five years of law practice and eighteen months as a federal judge when nominated, making him one of the youngest and least experienced judicial nominees in over a century.[106] None of the members of the ABA Standing Committee on the Federal Judiciary found him to be well qualified for the position. Immediately after the nomination was announced to the public, leaders of the National Organization for Women held a press conference at which they announced, "We're going to Bork him. We need to kill him politically."[107] This was only a prelude to the opposition from many liberal groups to the Thomas nomination, which increased after Anita Hill testified at Thomas's nationally televised confirmation hearings that he had sexually harassed her during his term as chairman of the federal Equal Employment Opportunity Commission (EEOC). The then all-male Senate Judiciary Committee nevertheless sent the nomination to the floor of the Senate, and the Senate confirmed Justice Thomas by a vote of 52–48.

The Recent Past

There were no vacancies on the U.S. Supreme Court from 1994 until 2005. This was the second-longest period of stability in Court membership in history.[108] Justice Sandra Day O'Connor was the key swing vote on the Supreme Court for most of this period. When she announced her retirement, interest groups and others suspected that there might be a fight coming over her successor. President George W. Bush first nominated Judge John Roberts to fill the O'Connor seat. Then, when Chief Justice Rehnquist died in office, President Bush realigned the

Roberts nomination in order to fill the chief justice's seat. Chief Justice Roberts was confirmed by a vote of 78–22 in 2005. Notably, Democratic senators Hillary Clinton (D-N.Y.) and Barack Obama (D-Ill.) voted against the nomination.[109] President Bush next nominated his own White House counsel, Harriet Miers, to fill O'Connor's seat, but the nomination was soon withdrawn due to strong opposition from the religious right wing of the Republican Party. Finally Bush nominated Samuel Alito to the Court. Interest groups on both sides spent huge sums on the Alito nomination, making it one of the most expensive confirmation fights in history.[110] Eventually Justice Alito was confirmed by a vote of 58–42,[111] in the most partisan judicial confirmation vote in history.[112] Only Justice Thomas received more negative votes on his confirmation.

Partisanship continued to be the major theme in the nomination and confirmation process of President Obama's two appointees to the Supreme Court. Justice Sonia Sotomayor was confirmed by a vote of 68–31 in 2009, and Justice Elena Kagan was confirmed by a vote of 63–37 in 2010. Most Senate Republicans voted against both nominees, while almost all Democrats supported them. In addition, interest groups have become very influential in convincing senators that they should vote against nominees on purely ideological as well as partisan grounds.[113]

Sometimes the justices themselves get involved in federal judicial selection issues. For example, Chief Justice Burger was quite active in sending names to the president when vacancies occurred on the Court. He was instrumental in Nixon's nominations of G. Harrold Carswell and Harry Blackmun. He also lobbied President Reagan for Sandra Day O'Connor's appointment to the Court.[114] When President Obama was facing a vacancy on the U.S. Supreme Court, Justice Ruth Bader Ginsburg publicly stated that the Court needed more gender diversity in its membership.[115] In 2010, Justice Anthony Kennedy agreed with President Obama that the Court needed justices who were more empathetic.[116]

STATE JUDICIAL SELECTION METHODS

Unlike the relative simplicity of the federal judicial selection process, the states use a wide variety of methods to select their state judges. The selection method used by a specific state is generally spelled out in the state constitution,[117] but these procedures can be supplemented by state statutes and by executive orders. The choice of method can have significant consequences, as judicial selection and retention mechanisms can help determine who will control political power in the state.[118]

There is some controversy about how best to categorize the various state judicial selection systems. Some scholars focus only on how state judges are selected, not on how they retain their seats on the bench. One of the key debates has been over the importance of merit selection panels in the initial appointment of state judges. These merit selection commissions or panels can be used in conjunction with a variety of state judicial selection methods. Some scholars have used a typology of state judicial selection methods that has focused almost exclusively on whether the state employs these so-called merit selection panels.[119]

I believe, however, that the selection methods should be categorized according to how much the system promotes the value of judicial accountability, defined earlier in this chapter. Thus, I group the state selection systems depending both on how the judges are initially selected and on how they retain their judicial offices. Figure 3.2 shows which states primarily use which judicial selection method. The six categories of state selection methods used in this book are (1) governor appointment for life term, (2) governor appointment with legislative confirmation and retention, (3) legislative appointment, (4) partisan elections, (5) nonpartisan elections, and (6) the Missouri Plan. Each will be explained in more detail below.

FIGURE 3.2 State Judicial Selection Methods for State Supreme Courts

TYPE	STATES
Governor appointment for life	Massachusetts, New Hampshire, Rhode Island
Governor appointment with legislative confirmation and retention	Connecticut, Delaware, Hawaii,** Maine, Maryland, New Jersey, New York,* Vermont
Legislative appointment	South Carolina, Virginia
Partisan elections	Alabama, Illinois, Louisiana, New Mexico, Pennsylvania, Texas, West Virginia
Nonpartisan elections	Arkansas, Georgia, Idaho, Kentucky, Michigan, Minnesota, Mississippi, Montana, Nevada, North Carolina, North Dakota, Ohio, Oregon, Washington, Wisconsin
Missouri Plan	Alaska, Arizona, California*, Colorado, Florida*, Indiana, Iowa, Kansas, Missouri, Nebraska, Oklahoma, South Dakota, Tennessee, Utah,*** Wyoming

Notes: * State uses different selection processes for at least some lower courts
** Legislature is not involved with retention
*** State legislature must approve Governor's appointments to the state supreme court.
Source: Compiled by author using data from the American Judicature Society.

Governor and Legislative Appointments

Only three New England states allow the governor to appoint state judges for what amounts to a life term, or at least until the state's mandatory retirement age, which is usually seventy. The three states using this system are Massachusetts, New Hampshire, and Rhode Island. The judicial selection processes in these states promote the value of judicial independence, much as the federal judicial selection system does.

Appointment by the governor with confirmation by the legislature is used in another eight states, mostly eastern ones, although in these states the state judges serve limited terms. The governor may use a variety of means to determine whom to nominate. Unlike in the first three states, in this group the state legislatures must confirm judicial nominees. When their terms are up, these states generally require that the legislature vote to retain these judges. In this category, judges must be accountable to the other branches of government. Judges for the local courts of the District of Columbia are appointed by the president of the United States and confirmed by the U.S. Senate for fifteen-year terms.

Only two states, Virginia and South Carolina, use the third judicial selection method, legislative appointment. In these states, judges are voted into office by the state legislature. The legislature must then vote to retain the judges when their terms expire. Not surprisingly, many of the judges from these states served in the state legislature prior to their appointment to the bench.[120] Here the judges are accountable to the legislative branch, but not to the governor or to the people directly.

Judicial Elections

The following two systems are very similar, and both involve having the voters directly elect the state judges. Elections of judges first became popular during the era of Jacksonian democracy.[121] In **partisan elections**, candidates from political parties run against each other for election to the bench for fairly short terms of office. The party membership of each candidate appears directly on the ballot. In **nonpartisan elections**, the party label for the candidates does not appear on the general election ballot. However, many of these states choose their candidates for the general election through partisan conventions or primaries. While the voters do not have the party cue on the ballot to help them determine which candidates belong to which party, the parties in these states usually go to great lengths to alert voters to which candidates are supported by which party.[122] Thus, there are in reality very few differences in these two electoral judicial selection systems. In both of these methods, the judges are accountable directly to the voters. In most states with elected judges, governors can appoint judges to fill vacancies for unexpired terms. The appointed judge then runs for election in the next election cycle.

A Compromise: The Missouri Plan

The last judicial selection method, the **Missouri Plan**, is an attempt to balance the values of judicial independence and judicial accountability. In this compromise system, first used in Missouri in 1940,[123] the governor appoints a so-called merit selection commission. These merit panels are usually composed of five members: two Democrats, two Republicans, and one representative of the state bar association. The merit commission screens all applicants for vacant judgeships, determining their qualifications for the bench. The commission then forwards three names to the governor for each judicial opening, and the governor chooses one of the three candidates to appoint as judge. After a set number of years, usually seven to ten, the judge must face the voters in a retention election. In a judicial retention election, the simple question to the voters is whether to retain this judge on the bench or not. If the voters vote to remove the judge from the bench, then the whole process starts all over again for the new judicial vacancy. This somewhat complex judicial selection method is a compromise between those systems that solely promote judicial independence and those that promote judicial accountability.

Several states use a modified Missouri Plan approach, as indicated in Figure 3.2. For example, although Utah generally uses a Missouri Plan system of judicial selection for all of its state judges, the Utah legislature must confirm the governor's appointments to the state supreme court.

RECENT CONTROVERSIES IN STATE JUDICIAL SELECTION

In many states, there is still a great deal of controversy over the processes used to select and retain judges. In a study of the relationships between state supreme courts and state legislatures, 68 percent of legislators interviewed voiced unprompted concerns over judicial selection and retention methods when asked how they perceived overall relations with the state supreme court.[124]

Historically, different judicial selection methods have been most popular in different eras, and some states have changed their judicial selection process over time. These attempted changes usually prove to be quite controversial. Fierce fights often erupt whenever the state government considers changing the judicial selection process. For example, in 1987 voters in Ohio were asked whether they wanted to end their nonpartisan election of judges and instead use the Missouri Plan. More than two-thirds voted against this proposal.[125] In 2000, Florida voters overwhelmingly rejected a proposal to change the way they elected their local trial judges.[126] In 2010, a proposal to replace Nevada's nonpartisan elections with the Missouri Plan received only 42 percent of the vote, despite the best efforts of retired U.S. Supreme Court Justice Sandra Day O'Connor, among others, to promote the change.[127] Voters in Oregon (1978) and South Dakota (2004) have also rejected proposals to adopt the Missouri Plan for state judicial selection.[128] Some even argue that the choice of judicial selection method has become a partisan issue in many states, with Democrats preferring appointment systems while Republicans support elected systems, though that analysis is probably too simplistic.[129] Nevertheless, some states have made recent modifications to their judicial selection processes. For example, both Arkansas and North Carolina have recently moved from partisan elections to nonpartisan judicial elections.[130]

Should Judges Be Elected?

There is a fair amount of controversy over recent judicial elections. Recall that today more than 85 percent of all state judges must win voter approval in order to keep their seats on the bench, either through direct elections or through retention elections.[131] Both Justices Ruth Bader Ginsburg and Sandra Day O'Connor have made a variety of public statements condemning the practice of judicial elections. Both justices have argued that "raising campaign money and promising outcomes on the bench is antithetical to a fair judicial system."[132] These justices are not alone in their opposition to judicial election mechanisms. The ABA has long opposed judicial elections,[133] as does the American Judicature Society, and many other scholars and judges agree. As two judicial politics experts, James Gibson and Gregory Caldeira, have written, "A conversation with virtually any judge in the United States (and, in our experiences, all judges in Europe) about whether judges ought to be elected inevitably elicits the view that the American people know much too little about judges, law, and courts to be able to exercise their democratic duty as electors."[134]

Some scholars fear that judicial elections produce unexpected consequences. For example, judges' need to find campaign contributors may appear to compromise their impartiality.[135] And fears of losing elections may also deter judges from making decisions that might be unpopular with voters.[136] Those who argue that judicial activism is needed to protect minority political interests in our society fear that elected judges lack the job security, the moral stature, and the professionalism to defy deeply entrenched norms or majoritarian views.[137] Finally, some argue that judicial elections create conflicts between the institutional norms of judging and the need of judges to be good politicians. As Keith Bybee, a judicial studies scholar notes, "Many state judges thus appear to be suspended between conventional expectations of impartial judicial conduct and the growing electoral necessity of shrewd political calculation and frankly partisan behavior."[138]

Historically, judicial elections were a fairly routine and boring affair. In retention elections, most judges easily retained their seats. Between 1964 and 2006 only about 1 percent of judges lost their seats in all judicial retention elections.[139] And between 1990 and 2000, only 3 of 177 state supreme court justices (1.7 percent) were defeated in retention elections.[140] Likewise, incumbent judges generally are reelected in direct election systems, even if they have an opposing candidate.

Today, judicial elections of all types are much more competitive and much more contested than before.[141] State supreme court elections increasingly involve attack ads and mudslinging common to other contested political races.[142] Studies show that, while only 33 percent of nonpartisan elections were contested in 1988, 75 percent of nonpartisan elections were contested in 2000. Similarly, 74 percent of partisan elections were contested in 1988, but by 2000 that figure had risen to 95 percent.[143] In 2000, incumbents in partisan judicial elections were defeated in 45.5 percent of the races.[144] However, in 2006 and 2008 incumbent reelection rates were at their highest point since 1984.[145] Today, judicial elections are slightly more competitive than elections for the U.S. House of Representatives.[146]

Judges clearly do not feel safe in retention elections today. For example, California Supreme Court Justice Rose Bird lost her seat in a retention election in 1986 because the public perceived her as opposed to the use of the death penalty in the state. This was the first time in California history that a judge on the state supreme court was removed from office in a retention election.[147] And after the Iowa Supreme Court unanimously approved same-sex marriage in the state, three judges on the state supreme court were removed from the bench in 2010 when they lost their retention elections.[148] Retired U.S. Supreme Court Justice Sandra Day O'Connor actively campaigned in favor of retaining the three judges, to no avail.[149] In 2012, major national Republican figures such as Governor Bobby Jindal of Louisiana and former presidential candidate Senator Rick Santorum of Pennsylvania both campaigned in Iowa to defeat Supreme Court Justice David Wiggins, who had also voted in favor of same-sex marriage under the Iowa constitution, in his retention election.[150] However, despite these efforts by conservatives, Justice Wiggins retained his seat on the Iowa Supreme Court in the 2012 elections when 54 percent of the voters voted to keep him on the bench.[151] Three judges in Florida faced serious opposition in their 2012 retention elections because they helped block a ballot measure in 2010 that was an attempt to allow the state to opt out of the national health care reform legislation. Governor Rick Scott led the efforts to remove the judges.[152] All three justices won their retention elections, with more than two-thirds of the voters opting to keep these judges on the bench.

Money in Elections

Money is certainly a crucial factor in judicial elections today.[153] See Figure 3.3 for more details on total spending in state supreme court elections over the years. As one can see, the general trend is that more and more money is being spent on these judicial elections. Between 1990 and 2004, the costs of judicial campaigns almost doubled.[154] Total spending in state supreme court contests went from less than $6 million at the start of the 1990s to more than $45 million during the 2008 election cycle. Much of the activity occurred in a handful of states with open elections for their high courts, including Alabama, Pennsylvania, Ohio, Illinois, and Texas.[155] One study found that in Texas more than 99 percent of lawyers surveyed and more than 86 percent of the judges surveyed believed that campaign contributions had some influence on judicial rulings.[156] As Justice Kennedy has stated, "We weren't talking about this [thirty] years ago because we didn't have money in [judicial] elections. Money in elections presents us with a tremendous challenge, a tremendous problem, and we are remiss if we don't at once address it and correct it."[157] Regarding money in judicial elections, Justice O'Connor has commented, "Left unaddressed, the perception that justice is for sale will undermine the rule of law that the courts are supposed to uphold."[158]

Attorneys have been the traditional source of campaign contributions in judicial elections, and recent studies show that this professional group still accounts for about a quarter of all campaign fund-raising. There is considerable variation among the states, however.[159] For example, in Texas most of the campaign contributions for judicial elections come from lawyers and law firms with cases before the judges to whom they contribute campaign money.[160] There is some evidence that these costly and highly partisan judicial election campaigns erode the legitimacy of state courts in the public's mind.[161] Bert Brandenburg, the executive director of Justice at Stake, an interest group devoted to limiting campaign spending on state judicial elections, has argued, "There's an instinct among the public that courts are supposed to be different than the rest of the government, at least somewhat. The question is whether the courts can stay impartial if they become overwhelmed with cash."[162]

FIGURE 3.3 Total State High Court Election Spending, 1990–2008

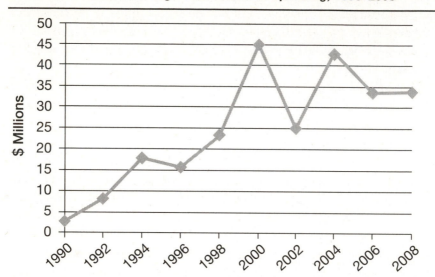

Source: Neal Devins and Nicole Mansker, "Public Opinion and State Supreme Courts," *University of Pennsylvania Journal of Constitutional Law* 13 (2010): 455–509, at 468.

Public Support for Elected Judges

The type of selection system may affect public support for state courts. Some studies have found that there is a lower level of support for the courts in states with elected judges than in those with appointed state judges.[163] There is also a general perception that judges are most vulnerable to defeat in partisan elections and least vulnerable in retention elections. According to one study that covered the period 1980 to 1995, 19 percent of incumbents in states with partisan elections were defeated, compared with 9 percent in nonpartisan elections and 2 percent in retention elections.[164] In states with elected judges who serve short terms, judges are much more likely to vote for criminal defendants to receive the death penalty.

Judicial elections are low-information elections, meaning that the voters often know very little about the candidates. Judicial campaigns were traditionally so uninteresting that voters rarely took advantage of the available sources of information about the races.[165] The media have a difficult time covering these elections, in part because judges remain hesitant to comment on legal issues that might come before them in a case.[166] In all judicial elections, there can be significant **voter roll-off**, the phenomenon where people vote in some races, usually high-information ones such as for president, U.S. senator, or governor, but make no choice in other, low-information races on the same ballot. One study found that from 1980 through 1995, an average of about one-quarter of all people who went to the polls skipped a contest for a state supreme court seat. For all judicial retention elections studied in ten states between 1964 and 1994, roll-off averaged 34.5 percent.[167]

Judicial elections do have their supporters. As Chris Bonneau and Melinda Gann, two pro-election scholars, have written, "Judicial elections are democracy-enhancing institutions that operate efficaciously and serve to create a valuable nexus between citizens and the bench."[168] Elected judges are much more likely than appointed ones to rule in accordance with public preferences on such issues as the death penalty, abortion, and tort litigation.[169] In fact, elected judges are more likely to follow public opinion on all matters of criminal law.[170] An elected judiciary is also somewhat more likely to declare a state law unconstitutional than are appointed judges.[171] And clearly most judges want to be reelected to their seats on the bench.[172] Thus, judicial elections promote the goals of judicial accountability.

An important recent work, *Electing Judges: The Surprising Effects of Campaigning on Judicial Legitimacy* by James Gibson, provides evidence to refute the claim that judicial elections reduce public support for the courts. Specifically, Gibson's research finds that judicial elections actually increase the public's perception that the courts are legitimate. This research also finds that the public holds both elected judges and appointed judges in the same high regard.[173] Thus, judicial elections not only increase judicial accountability but also increase public support for the courts in general.

THE U.S. SUPREME COURT ON JUDICIAL ELECTIONS

There are three important recent U.S. Supreme Court decisions regarding judicial elections. *Republican Party of Minnesota v. White* (2002) declared unconstitutional a state law that prohibited judicial candidates from taking positions on issues that might come before them. In other words, judicial election candidates are now free to announce their views on controversial political or legal issues, though codes of judicial ethics may still prevent judges from commenting on specific legal cases.[174] Judicial candidates can also reveal their broad ideological positions and their party affiliations, even in nonpartisan elections, as long as they do not comment on any potential or pending cases.[175] This decision came down when judicial elections were becoming nastier and much more costly.[176] Justice Scalia's majority opinion seemed to argue that judicial accountability should be an important value for the states.[177] The effects of this ruling are not entirely clear. Some scholars have argued that this ruling has had little if any impact on state supreme court elections.[178] However, as one scholar noted after the Supreme Court's decision, "As judicial campaigns begin to look more like campaigns for legislative and executive offices, states may begin to rethink whether judicial elections continue to make sense."[179]

Caperton v. Massey (2009) concerned the refusal of a new state supreme court justice to recuse himself from a case in which one of the parties had contributed more than $3 million to support his election campaign. Justice Kennedy's majority opinion stressed the potential for the appearance of bias in cases where judges hear cases involving large donors to their campaigns.[180] Newspaper editorials have routinely highlighted the ethical and due process concerns raised by judges' hearing cases that involve contributors.[181] In November 2009, the Michigan Supreme Court became the first state supreme court to adopt new rules that allow the entire court to review recusal motions and disqualify individual justices from cases that pose possible ethics violations.[182]

Citizens United v. Federal Election Commission (2010) declared unconstitutional limits on campaign spending by corporations and unions. Opponents of this ruling fear that interest groups and corporations will spend unlimited funds on judicial elections just as they are currently doing in presidential, senatorial, and gubernatorial races. How does this ruling interact with the two discussed above? As lawyer and scholar Alexander Polikoff argues, the Court's decision in *Caperton v. Massey* (2009) "acknowledges that independent expenditures in candidate elections can lead to an appearance of bias,"[183] and so with unlimited campaign spending on judicial elections could come increased bias. However, it is still to be seen how these three U.S. Supreme Court decisions taken collectively might change the way judicial elections are carried out in the states.

CHAPTER SUMMARY

This chapter examined judicial selection at both the state and federal levels. It began with a discussion of the competing values of judicial independence and judicial accountability, and how the federal judicial selection process promotes judicial independence while most state selection procedures promote judicial accountability. The chapter then detailed the nomination and confirmation processes for federal judges, exploring issues of senatorial courtesy and filibusters in the U.S. Senate. It also looked at the differences in approaches to lower court nominees used by various presidents before moving on to an examination of some of the key fights in the Senate over appointments to the U.S. Supreme Court. The discussion then turned to the six categories of state judicial selection methods, as well as some of the major controversies surrounding the election of state judges. The chapter concluded with a discussion of some recent U.S. Supreme Court decisions regarding judicial elections.

For Further Reading

Bell, Lauren Cohen. 2002. *Warring Factions: Interest Groups, Money and the New Politics of Senate Confirmation.* Columbus: Ohio State University Press.

Binder, Sarah A., and Forrest Maltzman. 2009. *Advice and Dissent: The Struggle to Shape the Federal Judiciary.* Washington, DC: Brookings Institution.

Bonneau, Chris W., and Melinda Gann Hall. 2009. *In Defense of Judicial Elections.* New York: Routledge.

Comiskey, Michael. 2004. *Seeking Justices: The Judging of Supreme Court Nominees.* Lawrence: University Press of Kansas.

Epstein, Lee, and Jeffrey A. Segal. 2005. *Advice and Consent: The Politics of Judicial Appointments.* New York: Oxford University Press.

Gibson, James L. 2012. *Electing Judges: The Surprising Effects of Campaigning on Judicial Legitimacy.* Chicago: University of Chicago Press.

Goldman, Sheldon. 1997. *Picking Federal Judges.* New Haven: Yale University Press.

Scherer, Nancy. 2005. *Scoring Points: Politicians, Activists and the Lower Court Appointment Process.* Stanford, CA: Stanford University Press.

Steigerwalt, Amy. 2010. *Battle over the Bench: Senators, Interest Groups, and Lower Court Confirmations.* Charlottesville: University of Virginia Press.

Tarr, G. Alan. 2012. *Without Fear or Favor: Judicial Independence and Judicial Accountability in the States.* Stanford, CA: Stanford University Press.

4

The Legal Profession

This chapter will explore the American legal profession, which includes both lawyers and judges. Unlike in many other countries around the world, in the United States the legal profession is very broadly defined, and American lawyers do a lot of different things in their work. The American legal profession is the largest in the world, both in terms of absolute numbers and in terms of the proportion of the population who are attorneys. It is also probably the wealthiest.[1] Recall that Alexis de Tocqueville thought of lawyers as the American aristocracy.[2] Lawyers are clearly key players in both criminal law and civil law processes in the United States (see Chapters 5 and 6 for more details). In the United States, anyone with a law degree who has passed a state bar examination may be considered a lawyer, regardless of how that person earns income or what type of work he or she actually does. Lawyers thus play leading roles in our society's governmental, business, political, and civic affairs.[3]

Recently scholars have begun to study the political and professional roles of lawyers in our legal system, and the literature on this area is quickly growing.[4] As Frances Kahn Zemans and Victor Rosenblum, two judicial politics scholars, have noted, "The enormous influence that lawyers wield in both the public and the private sectors makes their professional development of particular concern in a democratic society."[5] Because the United States is part of the Anglo-American common law tradition, our judges are lawyers first. Thus, both lawyers and judges are considered part of the legal profession in this country. The United States does not have specialized judge training schools, as found in many of the civil law countries of Continental Europe. This chapter will examine the working lives of both attorneys and judges in the United States, beginning with a look at the common experience of all American lawyers—law school.

LAW SCHOOL

The entry point for the American legal profession is law school. A **profession** is an occupation with (1) specific requirements for formal training and learning, (2) admission to practice by licensing, and (3) a unique code of ethics and a system to discipline its members for violation of the ethical codes.[6] Law school is where new lawyers are socialized into the profession, including learning the "professional ideology and rhetoric" and the perspectives on problem solving that shape the way members of the profession perceive the world around them.[7] As I have stated in a previous work, "[P]rofessional socialization involves acquiring specialized knowledge and skills, but it also involves learning the norms and jargon of the profession."[8] In other words, professional socialization involves learning how to act and think like a professional in that specific field.

Understanding more about law school will help put the broader legal profession into perspective. Both lawyers and judges must start by gaining a law degree, known in the United States as a Juris Doctor (J.D.). Law schools are accredited by the American Bar Association (ABA).[9] The ABA has also convinced states to regulate the types of legal services that individuals and law firms can offer.[10] In other words, lawyers have a monopoly on providing legal services, as defined by state laws. All lawyers must pass a state bar exam and then be admitted to the state bar before they can become practicing attorneys in that state.[11] The only exception to this rule is Wisconsin, which allows graduates of the University of Wisconsin (Madison) law school to practice law in the state without passing the bar exam first.[12] Today, almost all states require that individuals who take the state bar exam have a degree from an ABA-accredited law school.[13] Only seven states allow apprenticeship to substitute for all or part of a formal legal education for those who take the state bar examination.[14] Some scholars argue that the ABA has imposed unreasonable barriers to entry for the legal profession because its law school accreditation standards are too rigid and because, due to pressure from the ABA, states have allowed members of state bars to have a monopoly on the provision of legal services.[15]

Law schools accept applicants with any undergraduate major, although a technical undergraduate degree is required to take the special patent law exam. Unlike most of the rest of the world, where legal education follows the B.A., M.A., and Ph.D. model, American and Canadian law schools are graduate schools only. Students at American law schools must first complete a four-year undergraduate degree, and then they can study for the J.D. degree. The J.D. generally takes three years of full-time study, although some law schools allow the degree to be completed part-time, usually with evening classes over four years.

Some students will continue on to the LL.M. degree, which for American students is a highly specialized master of laws degree. For international students who already have a law degree from another country, the LL.M. degree is their first American law degree and indicates that they are familiar with American law and legal practices.[16]

Getting into Law School

Entry to law school is highly competitive, and most applicants are not accepted. In 2011, there were about 147,000 students enrolled in J.D. programs in this country. Law schools generally stress two very important numbers in their admissions decisions: the applicant's college grade point average and the applicant's LSAT score. Based largely on these two numbers, law schools then sort the applicants into three groups: automatically accept, automatically reject, and "let's take a closer look." For applicants in this third group, the applicant's personal statement, letters of recommendation, extracurricular activities, work experience, and general sense of maturity can make the difference between being admitted and being rejected.

Recently, the number of applications to law school has fallen dramatically. In early 2013, it was feared that applications would hit a thirty-year low. By May of that year only 55,700 applications had been received for ABA-accredited law schools for the class that was to enter in August 2013, down about 13 percent from the previous year. This was the third year in a row that applications decreased. Law school enrollment hit its peak in 2010, making it more difficult for all those new lawyers to find legal jobs after they graduated.[17] Because of the falling number of applications, many law schools have reduced the size of their entering class, and some have even laid off administrators and professors. Most attribute the decline in applications to concerns over student debt and the difficulty of finding high-paying jobs after law school.[18]

The American legal profession is highly prestige driven, and there is a clear hierarchy of law schools. Many law schools are very sensitive to the rankings prepared by *U.S. News and World Report*.[19] Law schools will often change their policies in order to maintain their *U.S. News* rankings.[20] For example, because a school's average LSAT scores play such a large role in the rankings, most law schools now give that score much more weight than other admissions factors. The prestige of the law school attended can certainly affect an individual's employment choices after law school. Most of the largest law firms in the country, which pay by far the highest salaries, will only interview candidates from a small list of select schools. And most law clerks at the U.S. Supreme Court come from only a handful of law schools, including Harvard and Yale. After Justice Kagan joined the Court in 2010, every justice on the U.S. Supreme Court had attended Harvard Law School or Yale Law School (Justice Ginsburg attended Harvard Law, although she eventually graduated from Columbia Law School).[21]

Teaching Students to Think like a Lawyer

Law schools see their purpose as teaching students to "think like lawyers." Learning how to think like a lawyer requires enormous and sometimes wrenching changes in how students see and understand the world. **Thinking like a lawyer** means learning legal reasoning and analysis, but it also means developing a distinct professional identity.[22] As mentioned earlier in this chapter, sociologists often talk about how professionals adopt a professional ideology and rhetoric that shape the way they experience the world around them.[23] Professionals acquire specialized knowledge, but they also develop a particular shared way of looking at the world, including a common professional approach to problem solving. In many ways, the uniformity of legal education is what produces this common professional culture and set of values among lawyers. Such a professional identity stays with the individual regardless of whether he or she actually practices law in daily working life.[24] As scholar Magali Sarfatti Larson argues, "You cannot really unfrock a priest, unmake a doctor, or disbar a lawyer."[25]

Historically, American lawyers received very little formal training, instead following an apprenticeship model where they worked with experienced lawyers.[26] In the 1870s, Harvard Law School became the first modern law school, stressing both legal research and formal legal education for future lawyers.[27] The dean of Harvard Law School was Christopher Columbus Langdell, and he is credited with creating modern legal education. Langdell and the Harvard Law School stressed formal knowledge that was devoid of context—essentially, law was taught rather like a science.[28] Today, the apprenticeship model has been entirely jettisoned in favor of a formal legal education at one of over two hundred ABA-accredited law schools in the nation. However, much of the current criticism of law schools today is that they provide precious little practical training, focusing instead on the theoretical aspects of "thinking like a lawyer."[29]

Teaching Methods

The teaching techniques in American law schools are amazingly uniform.[30] As several legal commentators have written, "If you could ask first-year students at a hundred law schools to describe their experiences, you'd hear the same things over and over."[31] Students almost exclusively read and study appellate court decisions. This is known as the **case method.** In addition to the case method, most law professors use a form of the **Socratic method** in their classes. What this means is professors call on students, without prior warning, and ask them about the facts of a particular case, the reasoning behind the court's ruling, and hypothetical questions regarding the application of the court's reasoning, often taking students to logical extremes. Through this form of interrogation, students learn how to think like lawyers.[32] In law school, law is presented as a coherent, comprehensive system of rules without political content or context.[33]

Almost all students take the same core of first-year classes, and many take the same elective courses because those classes cover topics on the state bar examinations. Not only is legal education quite uniform throughout the country, but law professors are very likely to come from similar backgrounds and have similar experiences. Law schools are beginning to diversify their faculties by hiring more individuals with an interdisciplinary background—many have a Ph.D. in another field in addition to a law degree. But the teaching approach that law professors favor has changed little. Many still teach similar courses, have similar educational backgrounds themselves, and use the same set of teaching techniques.[34]

While the classes taken and the teaching styles are very similar throughout the country, there are some differences among law schools. At some schools the student body is more communitarian, while at others the students are more cutthroat. The best law schools in the country focus on the law as a total concept regardless of state differences, while more regional law schools may primarily teach the law of the state in which they are located. Some schools such as Yale are known to emphasize theory and policy. Two law schools, Northeastern and Drexel, take a very alternative approach to legal education. Their students take classes for a quarter, and then work at a co-op job or internship for a quarter. Some schools, such as Northeastern, also may not give formal grades. Almost all law schools choose their top students to serve as editors on the school's law reviews or law journals. Since students select which articles will be published and do all the editing themselves, some judges and even some scholars question the usefulness of these legal journals.[35]

In part because of the cost involved in attending law school and in part because of the lack of practical training at most U.S. law schools, some have questioned whether the third year of law school is necessary. For example, President Barack Obama, a former law professor himself, has suggested that law school should be only two years instead of three. Supreme Court Justice Anthony Kennedy, among others, opposes this idea.[36] In September 2013, an ABA task force on legal education released a draft report calling for major changes in law school education and allowing some nonlawyers to provide limited legal services to low-income clients. The task force hopes that its recommendations will allow law schools to be more innovative and get away from a one-size-fits-all model.[37]

Others are taking action to reduce the time that students spend in law school. New York State has considered allowing law students to take the bar exam after only two years of law school.[38] Northwestern Law School already offers an accelerated program in which students can complete the normal three years of study in just two years.[39] Some law schools are allowing students to double-count some of their law courses, thus making it possible for students to complete a B.A. and J.D. in only six years instead of the traditional seven. New York University Law School has recently revamped its traditional third-year course offerings, placing more emphasis on studying abroad, internships, and highly focused concentrations in certain specialized areas of the law.[40] Stanford University Law School and Washington and Lee Law School, among others, have recently announced significant changes in their third-year curriculums. Stanford is making it easier for students to obtain joint graduate degrees, while Washington and Lee provides more clinical and internship experiences.[41] Many law schools are searching for ways to make the third year more meaningful to their students. They are fighting the old law school adage that "in the first year they scare you to death, in the second year they work you to death, and in the third year they bore you to death."

Jobs After Law School

The legal profession was especially hard hit by the nationwide economic downturn that started in 2008. It became harder and harder for recent law school graduates to find jobs in the profession, at least in urban areas. There remains a shortage of lawyers in many rural areas and even in some rural states, and some states have begun to give salary incentives to lawyers willing to work in rural areas, similar to programs that currently offer such incentives to doctors, dentists, and nurses.[42]

This is, unfortunately, the "new normal" in legal employment. Figure 4.1 indicates employment rates over time for recent law school graduates. Notice that employment rates for new lawyers were generally lower after the recession that started in 2008 than they were before that date. Also note that this chart does not indicate what percentage of law school graduates are working in jobs that require a law degree. One report indicates that nine months after graduation, only 55 percent of the members of the class of 2011 were working in full-time jobs that required a law degree. At the twenty law schools with the highest employment rates, 83 percent of graduates were working as lawyers. At the twenty schools

FIGURE 4.1 Legal Employment Market: Employment Rate Nine Months After Graduation (1999–2011)

Class of 2011	85.6%
Class of 2010	87.6%
Class of 2009	88.3%
Class of 2008	89.9%
Class of 2007	91.9%
Class of 2006	90.7%
Class of 2005	89.6%
Class of 2004	88.9%
Class of 2003	88.9%
Class of 2002	89.0%
Class of 2001	90.0%
Class of 2000	91.5%
Class of 1999	90.3%

Source: National Association for Law Placement, *Jobs & JD's: Employment and Earnings of New Graduates, Classes of 2007, 2008, 2009, 2010 & 2011,* used with permission

with the lowest employment rates, that figure was a dismal 31 percent.[43] Some commentators have questioned the employment data released by individual law schools, implying that the law schools are not being honest with their applicants.[44] Law school graduates are also carrying a lot of debt to pay for their education. In 2010, 85 percent of graduates from ABA-accredited law schools had debts to repay, and the average debt load was almost $100,000 per person.[45] Given the large amount of debt that many law students accumulate, some observers are questioning whether law school still makes economic sense for many college graduates.[46]

Law schools counter that society will always need well-prepared and well-educated lawyers. As Lawrence E. Mitchell, dean of the law school at Case Western Reserve University, has written, "The career for which we educate students, done through the medium of the law, is a career in leadership and creative problem solving. Many graduates will find that their legal educations give them the skills to find rich and rewarding lives in business, politics, government, finance, the nonprofit sector, the arts, education, and more."[47] Mitchell continues,

"Investment in [law school] tuition is for a lifelong career, not a first job. . . . Creative, innovative and entrepreneurial lawyers will find ways to capitalize on this."[48]

Employment rates are generally measured nine months after graduation because many legal jobs require new lawyers to pass the state bar examination before they can begin work. Most students take the bar exam in July right after their graduation from law school, and it sometimes takes a few months after that before they learn whether or not they have passed. Almost all state bars use the Multistate Bar Examination, given on a Wednesday. This multiple-choice exam is uniform throughout the country. Specific states supplement the multistate exam with their own essay examinations, usually given on a Tuesday or a Thursday immediately before or after the multistate exam. Some states use both days, meaning that their bar exam takes three days to complete. Most state bars require one to have a law degree from a U.S.-accredited law school before being eligible to take the bar exam, but California and New York are among the exceptions. Bar exam passage rates vary greatly across the country, with a high in Wisconsin of 89 percent in 2009 and a low in California of 49 percent that year. For all first-time takers of the bar exam with degrees from accredited U.S. law schools, 83 percent passed in 2009.[49]

THE CHANGING DEMOGRAPHICS OF THE LEGAL PROFESSION

The legal profession has been growing quite quickly in the United States. Between 1880 and 1980, the number of lawyers multiplied ninefold, while the general population grew at less than half that rate.[50] Since 1970, the legal profession as a whole has grown three times faster than other professions, and now there are more lawyers per capita than medical doctors.[51] There are approximately one million lawyers practicing law today,[52] and more working in other fields. More than forty-four thousand law degrees were awarded in 2010 in the United States, over four times the number awarded in 1965.[53]

Nineteenth-century lawyers were almost exclusively native-born white Anglo-Saxon Protestant men.[54] In 1963, fewer than 3 percent of American lawyers were female, and in 1970 only about 1 percent were African American.[55] Until at least the 1960s, most law firms were unwilling to hire female or minority lawyers. Some firms also refused to hire Jewish attorneys. Today, new lawyers are much more diverse in terms of sex, race, and ethnic background than they were even a generation ago.[56] For example, in a nationwide study of new lawyers first admitted to the bar in 2000, women were 44 percent of the respondents. Members of racial and ethnic minorities made up around 20 percent of the sample, with Asians being 7 percent, African Americans around 6.6 percent, Hispanic/Latino individuals 4.5 percent, Native Americans 1.5 percent, and all others just under 1 percent.[57] However, even today, lawyers still tend to come from families with higher-than-average incomes.

Today, just under half of all law students are women. At one time, women were quite rare in the legal profession; in fact, Harvard Law School did not even begin admitting women until 1950.[58] In 1971, women made up only about 3 percent of the bar, but after great progress women today make up about 29 percent of the total legal profession in the United States.[59] However, according to 2006 statistics, women accounted for only about 18 percent of the partners at large law firms.[60] In a recent study of lawyers first admitted to the bar in 2000, women lawyers were far more likely than men to be unemployed or to be working part-time.[61] This probably reflects the fact that American society continues to be quite gendered when it comes to child rearing, with women still overwhelmingly responsible for that duty. A certain proportion of both men and women may not use their law degrees to practice law, but women tend to interrupt their careers for family responsibilities at much greater rates than do men. Some estimate that as many as 42 percent of women leave the profession mid-career, and more than 76 percent of women whose first jobs are in large law firms leave those firms before making partner.[62]

WHERE LAWYERS WORK

Lawyers work in a variety of employment settings. Figure 4.2 shows the percentages of recent law school graduates who found jobs in various sectors. Notice that where new lawyers are finding jobs is somewhat different today than it was in the recent past. This next section will discuss these various work settings in some detail.

FIGURE 4.2 Legal Employment Market: Where Law School Graduates Got First Jobs

EMPLOYER TYPE	2007	2008	2009	2010	2011
Private Practice	55.5%	56.2%	55.9%	50.9%	49.5%
Business	14.1%	13.4%	13.5%	15.1%	18.1%
Government (including military)	11.7%	11.8%	11.4%	12.8%	11.9%
Judicial clerkships	9.8%	9.6%	8.7%	9.3%	9.3%
Public interest	5.8%	5.4%	5.7%	6.7%	7.5%
Academic	1.8%	2.3%	3.5%	3.7%	3.0%

Source: National Association for Law Placement, *Jobs & JD's: Employment and Earnings of New Graduates, Classes of 2007, 2008, 2009, 2010 & 2011,* used with permission.

Large Law Firms

The most wealthy and powerful lawyers work in **large law firms**. How to define "large" can be somewhat difficult, but many studies define a large law firm as employing at least fifty lawyers. Some boutique law firms, such as many that specialize in patent law or appellate litigation before the U.S. Supreme Court, may be quite small but function in ways very similar to large law firms.[63]

The number of large law firms in the United States has grown exponentially over the years. For example, in 1980 only 5 percent of lawyers worked in firms of fifty or more lawyers.[64] In 2000, at least 735 American law firms employed more than fifty lawyers, and these firms accounted for around 18 percent of all lawyers who practiced law in the United States.[65] Today, large law firms may have thousands of lawyers spread around the globe. These firms may have their main office in New York City, Washington, D.C., Chicago, Houston, Cleveland, Boston, or Silicon Valley, but they usually have other offices in major cities throughout the United States and all over the world. Their primary clients are large corporate interests, often the largest corporations in the country. In 2010, the average hourly fee charged by these firms for work by their partners was $470 per hour, and the average fee for work by associates was almost $300 per hour.[66]

In recent decades, these large law firms have developed a strict hierarchy of employees. At the top are the senior **equity partners**, whose salary is a share of the firm's annual profits. Some of these partners can earn well over $1 million per year.[67] Next in the hierarchy at some firms will be junior partners or non-equity partners. Their salaries are considerably lower than those of equity partners. **Associates** are new lawyers, usually right out of the best law schools in the country. These associates will work six or seven years before they can be promoted to partner. Law firms hire many more associates than they expect to promote.[68] The partnership decision is largely based on the associate's **billable hours**, which is the measure that large firms use to determine how to bill their clients for their lawyers' time. Many of these associates can work seventy to seventy-five hours per week or more in order to amass enough billable hours for the year. Most lawyers at large law firms bill in six- or twelve-minute increments, meaning that partners and associates must account for every minute of their time at work. Partnership decisions are also based on **rainmaking**, which means bringing new business into the firm. Partnership decisions can take into account more subjective factors as well, such as which associates are the "best fit" for the firm's culture and level of prestige. Like a tenure decision for college professors, associates who do not make partner are asked to leave the firm. According to data from 2006, women made up 18 percent of the partners at large law firms in the United States, and minorities constituted only 5 percent.[69] The highly competitive and stressful nature of this competition to become a law firm partner has been called the "tournament of lawyers" by one group of scholars, who chose that phrase as the title for their book on the subject of large law firms.[70]

Figure 4.3 shows starting salaries for recent law school graduates. Beginning salaries for new associates at large law firms are usually around $165,000 per year, as seen in the cluster of salaries at the right of the chart in Figure 4.3. Many other lawyers, especially those who work in smaller firms or who are employed by the government, make much less. And numerous studies have shown that many lawyers working in large law firms are highly dissatisfied with their professional lives, despite their high salaries.[71]

Large law firms hire other types of workers as well. **Summer associates** are law students who work for the firm over the summer months; these stints are often considered tryouts for an associate position after graduation. These summer associates are often quite well paid. Below the associates are **paralegals**, who are individuals without law degrees who do legal research and other work for the lawyers. Traditionally, many of these paralegals were women, while most of the large firm lawyers were men.[72] Today, paralegals might be middle-aged women

FIGURE 4.3 Distribution of Reported Full-Time Salaries, Class of 2011

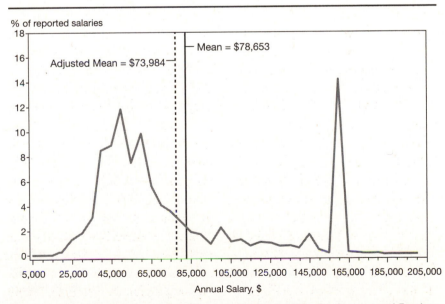

Source: National Association of Law Placement, *Jobs and JD's: Employment and Earnings of New Graduates, Class of 2011,* used with permission.

reentering the workforce after raising their families, or they might be recent college graduates who are working for a few years before applying to law school. Finally, there are a variety of clerical and technical staff.

The Two Hemispheres of the Law

At the opposite end of the scale from large law firms, many more lawyers work in small private law firms or in solo practice. These smaller firms might handle divorce cases, personal injury cases, criminal defense work, wills, real estate, or other types of less prestigious legal problems for individuals and small corporations.[73] Lawyers at these smaller firms often went to less well-known local and regional law schools, or they graduated lower in their classes at law schools higher up in the legal hierarchy. Their salaries are much lower than those in large firms, as one can see in Figure 4.3.

The very different work lives of large firm lawyers and other lawyers at smaller firms have come to be known as the **two hemispheres of the law**. The two hemispheres are divided by the wealth of the clients, the income of the lawyers, and the intellectual difficulty of the lawyers' work. This term was coined by a team of scholars who interviewed lawyers in Chicago to find out what types of legal work were more prestigious and rewarding.[74] In the nation's largest law firms (and many highly specialized boutique firms), or the first hemisphere, the clients tend to be either extremely wealthy corporations or wealthy individuals, the lawyers make an enormous amount of money, and the legal work is intellectually stimulating and challenging. In smaller firms, or the second hemisphere, the clients are generally less wealthy individuals without prior relationships to a lawyer, the attorneys make far smaller salaries, and the legal work is often repetitive and routine. Lawyers in the first hemisphere tend to be specialists with a great deal of expertise in a very lucrative and highly challenging area of the law, such as tax law or securities law; lawyers in the second hemisphere tend to be generalists or to do the majority of their work in less stimulating areas of the law, such as landlord-tenant disputes or family law. Lawyers in the first hemisphere have a great deal of power, prestige, and wealth; lawyers in the second hemisphere do not. Figure 4.3 clearly indicates the salary differences for recent law school graduates who enter the different hemispheres. Starting salaries in the first hemisphere are now around $165,000 per year, while lawyers in the second hemisphere often start out at salaries of around $40,000 to $65,000 depending on the job. The adjusted mean salary for all new starting lawyers is about $74,000 per year, meaning that about half are above that number and half are below. (The adjusted figure takes into account non-respondents to the survey, who tend to have lower salaries.)

Recall that Figure 4.2 shows the numbers of lawyers who are getting jobs in private practice (in both hemispheres). Today, less than half of all new lawyers are working in private law firms. This is a huge shift from previous times, when the vast majority of lawyers worked in law firms. Before World War II, 80–90 percent of the legal profession was engaged in private practice.[75] As recently as 2000, more than 75 percent of all lawyers were in private practice.[76] But the employment patterns for new lawyers have shifted enormously since the economic downturn of 2008. Today only about half of the jobs found by new law school graduates are in private practice.

Beyond Private Firms

So if fewer new law school graduates are going into private practice, then where are they going? More and more businesses are hiring in-house lawyers, instead of paying law firms for their legal work, as shown in Figure 4.2. **In-house lawyers** are employees of a corporation, not of an independent private law firm. Eighteen percent of new lawyers are now employed by business. Around 12 percent are full-time government employees, while an additional 9 percent are working as law clerks for judges, usually for only a year or two before they must find other jobs. Traditionally, government lawyers have earned less than their big-firm colleagues, although their working hours are usually shorter and more predictable.[77] About one-third of governmental attorneys are employed by the federal government in a wide variety of federal agencies, and about two-thirds work in state and local government.[78] About 3 percent of new lawyers become academics, although that figure may be somewhat inflated, as law schools are increasingly hiring their alumni to work in their admissions offices, career services offices, and so on. Some of these jobs are temporary in nature, until the graduates can find a full-time legal job. Although traditionally almost all law professors only had the J.D. degree, or perhaps a LL.M. degree, today more and more law schools are hiring professors with Ph.D.'s and joint Ph.D./J.D. degrees.[79] Chief Justice John Roberts has complained bitterly that many law professors earn higher salaries than federal judges.[80]

WHAT LAWYERS DO

In their professional lives, lawyers perform a variety of tasks. Some scholars have argued that the nature of legal work is changing rapidly, in large part due to the shifting nature of information technology and the changing nature of consumer preferences for legal services.[81] Nevertheless, there are certain basic tasks that lawyers will continue to perform in our society.

From television, movies, novels, and other media, one might assume that the vast majority of lawyers are litigators. **Litigation** means appearing in court during a trial, and **litigators** are those few lawyers who actually appear in court. Lawyers do go to court in both criminal and civil cases, but the most successful lawyers spend most of their time keeping their clients out of court.

Almost all practicing attorneys advise and counsel clients on legal issues. They also represent clients before a variety of nonjudicial governmental bodies, such as federal or state and local bureaucratic agencies. Lawyers certainly spend a fair amount of time and effort drafting legal documents such as contracts, wills, and trusts. Lawyers also spend a substantial amount of time negotiating with others on behalf of their clients. Attorneys might write appellate briefs and appear before appellate courts in oral arguments. They also must educate clients about what the law is. This involves a great deal of research and writing. Probably one of the most important tasks of lawyers is translating client narratives into legally actionable measures.[82]

Note that all of these activities are client-focused. In the United States, the duty of lawyers is to represent the best interests of their clients. The tasks they perform are technical and depend on skill, training, and specialized legal knowledge. However, while lawyers should be putting the interests of their clients ahead of all else, the choices lawyers make (and do not make) have critical political ramifications for our society. Lawyers are professionals, but they are also political actors whose collective decisions have important legal and political consequences.[83] Lawyers often work in a **community of practice**, which means that their professional norms and choices are greatly influenced by the other practitioners with whom they interact on a daily basis. Divorce lawyers in a particular location may form a community of practice,[84] as can criminal prosecutors, judges, and defense attorneys, who often work together for long periods of time in the criminal justice system.[85] What this means is that at times lawyers may face ethical dilemmas, such as whether their clients' needs must come before the needs of the other attorneys and judges with whom they will be working in the future. Nonlawyers often ask how a criminal defense attorney, for example, can represent someone whom he or she knows to be guilty. The response is usually that everyone deserves proper representation in order to maintain the fairness of the overall criminal justice system, even if that means that guilty individuals are not always convicted. Leslie Levin and Lynn Mather edited a very interesting volume called *Lawyers in Practice: Ethical Decision Making in Context,* which examines the ethical issues lawyers face in a variety of practice contexts.[86]

One ethical problem facing many lawyers is how to charge fees. In *Goldfarb v. Virginia State Bar* (1975), the U.S. Supreme Court declared a state bar's minimum fee schedule to be unconstitutional. Thus, all lawyers and/or law firms must set their own fees without interference from the state bar. Lawyers in large law firms usually charge by the hour, often with clients in addition paying an annual retainer to keep the firm available to provide legal services whenever the client needs them. Some criminal defense attorneys, real estate attorneys, divorce attorneys, and other general practice lawyers often charge a flat fee based on the case. They may also charge an hourly fee on top of the per-case fee if they run into unexpected appearances in court, unexpected expenses, and so forth. Personal injury lawyers tend to charge a **contingency fee**, meaning that they do not charge up front for their legal services, but instead take a percentage of any monetary award they earn for their clients. Many contingency fees give the attorneys one-third of the client's monetary award, either from a settlement of a civil dispute or from a court judgment in the case.

A major U.S. Supreme Court decision regarding the legal profession, *Bates v. State Bar of Arizona* (1977), involved lawyer advertising. In this decision, the Court struck down a rule by the Arizona bar that prohibited advertising by lawyers. The Court ruled that advertising is commercial speech, which is protected by the First Amendment. Commercial speech receives less protection than political speech because the government can require that advertising not be false or misleading. The state bar had argued that advertising by lawyers would reduce the professionalism of the practice of law, but the Supreme Court refused to accept that argument. Most of the state bar prohibitions on lawyer advertising had been in place for more than seventy years.[87] In fact, one of the first ethics rules promulgated by the American Bar Association in 1908 prohibited lawyer advertising.[88] Today, the lawyers who do advertise are generally in solo or small firm practices, and their clients rarely have an ongoing relationship with attorneys. Lawyers in large law firms or specialty firms with wealthier clients almost never advertise.

Not all lawyers are client-centered in every case they handle. In some instances, lawyers are using the courts for political purposes. Lawyers who work for interest groups are clearly in this category. Others may work for public interest law firms, on either the political left or the political right. Lawyers can be part of social movements, either intentionally or unintentionally. Generally these **cause lawyers** are using the courts to bring about social change, and they may or may not be concerned about the needs of their specific clients in a case. While a growing number of academics are now studying and publishing on cause lawyers, there is little agreement so far on how to define who is a cause lawyer and who is not.[89] But there is a general agreement that for cause lawyers, the political agenda is far more important then traditional client-centered lawyering.

ACCESS TO JUSTICE

A key question for most industrialized democracies is how or if to provide legal services to those who cannot afford to pay for them themselves.[90] When the U.S. Supreme Court in *Gideon v. Wainwright* (1963) declared that criminal defendants in all serious cases have the right to an attorney, the concept of access to justice at least in criminal cases was constitutionalized. There is also a constitutional right to a speedy trial in criminal cases. Almost all of the states responded to the *Gideon* ruling by establishing a system of government-paid criminal defense attorneys for the poor, known as **public defenders**. Likewise, the federal government established federal defender organizations, which provide federally paid defenders for defendants accused of federal crimes who cannot afford an attorney on their own. To supplement these government-paid public defenders, state and local governments may also pay private attorneys to handle certain criminal cases for the poor. The pay for these **court-appointed attorneys** varies greatly from state to state. However, the fees are generally so low that many commentators worry about the quality of legal services these lawyers provide.[91] The problem is especially troubling in capital punishment cases.[92]

Representing the Poor in Civil Cases

There is no constitutional right at all, however, to an attorney in civil cases in the United States. There is also no constitutional right to a speedy trial in civil cases. In contrast, the indigent have had a right to a lawyer in civil cases in England since 1495 and in Austria since 1781.[93] More than sixty million low-income Americans now qualify for free legal services in civil cases,[94] but many estimate that as much as 80 percent of the civil legal needs of low-income people go unmet in the United States today.[95] One solution would be government-sponsored lawyers for the poor. As part of the Great Society and War on Poverty programs enacted during Lyndon Baines Johnson's presidency in the 1960s, the federal government established the **Legal Services Corporation**, which hires government-sponsored lawyers to help serve the poor in civil proceedings.[96] Beginning in the Reagan Administration, Congress has severely cut the budget for the Legal Services Corporation, as well as imposing stringent limits on the types of cases these lawyers can handle.[97] Most of the funding for local Legal Services offices comes from the interest on the trust accounts in which lawyers deposit their clients' escrow funds. As the economy has faltered and overall interest rates have fallen dramatically, the interest earnings from these trust accounts have also diminished greatly. Thus, around the country many local Legal Services offices are severely underfunded today. The

Legal Services Corporation reports that it can only handle the cases of about half of those who apply for legal assistance, but the number of people who cannot afford a lawyer in a civil case is much higher than that because many low-income people do not even know where to go to get the legal assistance they need.[98]

In the United States, government-sponsored legal aid is only available to the very poor. Roughly fifty million Americans are eligible to receive civil legal aid services. In other countries, government-subsidized legal assistance is often available even to middle-class individuals.[99] Scholars remain pessimistic that government funding in the United States for access to justice will increase anytime soon. Voters seem less interested in funding legal services than they are in health care, education, transportation, or prisons.[100]

Alternative Ways to Provide Legal Services to the Poor

Another option is to have the government pay private attorneys to take civil cases for those who cannot afford to hire a lawyer. In Canada, the government pays private attorneys to handle civil cases for the poor, much the way the Medicare program pays private doctors to provide health care for the elderly in the United States. In Australia, the federal government used to provide similar support to private lawyers who took civil cases for the poor, but in the 1990s the costs for the program were shifted to the Australian states.[101] Some labor unions in the United States have negotiated to have legal services for their members paid for by the employer, but this is still quite rare.

Another option to provide legal aid to the poor is to have private charities provide such services. This was the primary method of access to justice for the poor before the 1960s. A variant of this model is to have lawyers provide their services **pro bono** (for free or at a reduced rate) to certain low-income clients. The American Bar Association recommends that all lawyers provide at least fifty hours of pro bono representation per year.[102] The number of hours that lawyers give in pro bono work nationwide now exceeds the number of hours worked by Legal Services lawyers in the United States.[103] Nevertheless, many feel that lawyers should be willing to devote far more hours to pro bono work than they are currently doing. Some states have even considered making pro bono work mandatory before lawyers can renew their annual licenses. In common law countries around the world, lawyers are providing more and more pro bono services, although this phenomenon is still quite rare in civil law nations.[104]

Many law schools now provide free legal services to the poor through their law school **clinical programs**, where law students supervised by a faculty member provide legal services to those who cannot afford them.[105] The clinics assist low-income clients by providing them with needed legal services, but they also help law students gain practical legal experience. Today the nation's law schools collectively have more than fourteen hundred full-time clinical faculty members.[106] Some law schools are also considering making pro bono work, in clinics or otherwise, mandatory before law students can graduate. As of August 2007, thirty-five law schools in the United States had a mandatory graduation requirement of a certain number of hours of pro bono work as a law student.[107] Providing access to legal services remains a difficult problem in the United States. The demand for legal services always outstrips their availability.[108]

Most of these law school clinics appeal to left-leaning students who want to help out the poor and downtrodden, but options more attractive to conservative students are also being attempted. For example, Stanford Law School has just started a clinic devoted to protecting religious liberties. This clinic is being funded by several religious-right groups who worry that the traditional legal clinic experience in law school promotes the ideological values of liberals.[109]

LAWYERS AS JUDGES

We will now turn to examining lawyers who work as judges. Since the United States has a common law judicial system, our judges work as lawyers before they are selected for the bench. Thus, lawyers and judges are considered parts of the same broad legal profession in the United States. About 3 percent of American lawyers working in the legal profession are employed as judges.[110] Most American judges receive very little training before taking their seats on the bench. This is a far different approach than that used in civil law countries, where judges are specifically trained and remain judges for their entire careers. In the civil law world, judges obtain jobs and eventually are elevated to higher courts because of their substantive knowledge and expertise. There the judiciary is a distinct branch of the national civil service. Thus, in the civil law world, judges and lawyers form two very separate professions.[111] In England, a common law county, judges are drawn from the best and brightest of the barristers (roughly equivalent to American litigators), who have already achieved high social standing. Nowhere in Europe do judges get their jobs because of their political connections or for being active in political parties, as they often do in the United States.

Since the judicial selection processes at both the state and federal levels in the United States are quite political in nature, it is little surprise that most judges were politically active before being named to the bench. Almost all federal judges are members of their nominating president's political party. State judges in both state elected and appointed systems were usually party activists before running

FIGURE 4.4 Number of Active Judges on the Federal Bench, by Appointing President*

PRESIDENT	U.S. DISTRICT COURTS		U.S. COURTS OF APPEALS	
	#	%	#	%
Obama	44	6.6	15	9.0
G. W. Bush	250	37.7	53	31.7
Clinton	197	29.7	46	27.5
G. H. W. Bush	60	9.0	13	7.8
Reagan	37	5.6	19	11.4
Carter	6	1.0	6	3.6
Ford	1	0.2	1	0.6
Nixon	1	0.2	0	0
Johnson	1	0.2	0	0
Vacancies	67	10.1	14	7.8
Total	664	100	167	100

* As of January 1, 2011

Source: Compiled by author using data from Sheldon Goldman, Elliot Slotnick, and Sara Schiavoni, "Obama's Judiciary at Midterm: The Confirmation Drama Continues," *Judicature* 96 (2011): 299.

for office or getting appointed to the bench. Traditionally, a majority of state trial judges come directly from private practice, often from medium-sized or large firms.[112] However, another common career path to become a judge is to be a prosecutor first.[113] Since state district attorneys are almost always elected officials, prosecutors must be active in politics. A fairly large proportion of federal judges have prior experience as state judges.[114] Very few state judges serve life terms, so many of them return to being lawyers after they end their service on the state court bench.

When analyzing the decisions of federal judges, scholars often look at the party of their appointing president.[115] For example, one recent study has found that federal judges appointed by Republican presidents tend to vote more conservatively than judges appointed by Democratic presidents, and the differences are especially pronounced in the area of civil rights.[116] A previous study found that Republican-appointed judges issued rulings that were more conservative on affirmative action questions than did judges appointed by Democrats.[117] As of May 2012, 53 percent of the judges on the U.S. courts of appeals were appointed by Republican presidents. On the U.S. district courts, 54 percent of the judges were appointed by Republican presidents. On the U.S. Supreme Court, five of the justices were appointed by Republican presidents and four were appointed by Democrats.[118] Figure 4.4 breaks down these numbers by providing more detail on how many federal judges serving in January 2011 were appointed by which presidents. This figure clearly illustrates the effects of the life terms of the federal judiciary.

Judicial Socialization

Lawyers who are named to the bench must learn a variety of things before they are fully socialized into being judges. New judges must learn legal procedures, case management techniques, the norms and attitudes accepted by members of the bench, and other aspects of the day-to-day workings of the court.[119] Since American judges receive very little formal training, they must turn for advice to those with more experience. New judges often look to other judges, court staff, and experienced lawyers for advice on how to work and act as a judge.[120]

Let's look at each element of this socialization process. There is no requirement that trial judges must have litigation experience before they come to the bench. Thus, new judges must learn or relearn the rules of civil procedure and criminal procedure in their jurisdictions. Second, new judges must learn how to manage the huge number of cases before them. They must pick up the rhythms of case flow and judicial decision making. Third, judges must learn the norms and expectations of the role of being a judge. They have a new responsibility for making critical decisions that can have enormous effects on the lives of the people before them.

One of the most difficult things for new judges is to learn how to deal with the social and other restrictions imposed by their new status. Lawyers are strong advocates for their clients and their causes, but in our adversary system judges must be neutral and unbiased decision makers. This is a major adjustment. Being a judge is also an extremely solitary and often lonely enterprise. For example, judges must never discuss current cases with lawyers or others who have an interest in the case. When they were lawyers, they could usually seek advice from other lawyers about the specifics of any given case. But once they become judges, they can no longer discuss their work at social gatherings and other events. They can usually ask other judges for advice, but even then they must be careful not to divulge any confidential material. And state judges, who have a short term of office, must also adapt to the procedures for retaining their job. Therefore, there are three types of socialization issues for new judges: legal, administrative, and psychological.[121] As one scholar notes, "[N]ewly selected judges are thrust into a rather alien environment."[122]

As was mentioned earlier, most American judges receive very little training before they assume the bench. The Federal Judicial Center (FJC) is a federal agency in Washington, D.C., that does provide some training for federal judges. The FJC had its own closed-circuit television network for federal judges to help them learn about the job and keep up with changes in judicial administration and other aspects of the work. There are also a variety of state programs for judge training, including the National Judicial College in Reno, Nevada.[123] But many judges find themselves on the bench without much preparation or formal training.

Backgrounds of Judges

The backgrounds of federal judges reveal several things about who becomes a judge. Almost all judges are middle-aged, with lengthy legal careers before they achieve a seat on the federal bench. From 1993 to 2010, 57 percent of the judges appointed to the U.S. district courts were white males, while 53 percent of the appointees to the U.S. courts of appeals were white males. Fifty-five percent of U.S. district court appointees received their undergraduate degrees from private colleges and universities, while 63 percent of the circuit court appointees did so. This figure includes the 11 percent of district court appointees who had Ivy League educations, while 23 percent of the U.S. courts of appeals appointees received their undergraduate degrees from one of the eight Ivy League universities. Forty-four percent of district court and 40 percent of circuit court appointees had previous experience as a prosecutor. Perhaps most significant, 47 percent had a net worth of over $1 million at the time of appointment to the federal trial courts, as did 53 percent of the appellate court appointees. All of the federal appointees were lawyers.[124] Obviously, those named to the federal bench were not representative of the American population at large. Those who become federal judges come from backgrounds of greater wealth and higher social standing than the average American.

Lower state court judges are much more heterogeneous than federal judges and state appellate court judges. As late as 1977, about 96 percent of state supreme court judges were white and 98 percent were male. Women and minorities had a hard time breaking into the legal profession as a whole and thus into the ranks of judges. By 2010, 26 percent of all judges (both state and federal) were women, and all but two of the state supreme courts had at least one female member. This is a far cry from the experience of Sandra Day O'Connor in the early

1950s. When the future Justice O'Connor graduated near the top of her class at Stanford Law School, she could only find a job as a legal secretary after graduation because no law firms to which she applied would hire a female attorney.[125]

How diverse are state judges today? In 2008, the American Judicature Society did a study of diversity among state court judges. Overall, around 29 percent of all state judges in 2008 were women and 12.6 percent were racial and ethnic minorities. The highest percentage of minority judges was found in Hawaii (65.1 percent). The states with the next highest percentages were Louisiana, New York, and Texas, respectively, where minority judges accounted for approximately 20 percent of the bench. At that time, there were no minority judges serving on appellate or general-jurisdiction trial courts in six states: Maine, Montana, New Hampshire, South Dakota, Vermont, and Wyoming. The states with the highest percentages of women judges at that time were Florida, Hawaii, Maryland, Massachusetts, Nevada, and Vermont, where approximately one-third of judges were women.[126] Democratic-dominated states were more likely to have more women and minorities on the bench, while Republican-dominated states were less likely to do so.[127]

Scholars have long wondered whether female and/or minority judges make different decisions than their white male colleagues. The research findings are inconclusive. In most areas of the law, there appear to be few differences in the rulings of white versus nonwhite judges or between male and female judges.[128] However, some studies have found that female judges are more sensitive to sex discrimination and sexual harassment cases than are their male colleagues.[129] Other studies have found that minority judges are more supportive of some civil rights claims than are their white counterparts.[130] Some studies have found that minority judges and female judges are more likely to issue liberal decisions than are white male judges, especially in criminal cases.[131] Other studies have reported that the mere presence of a woman or a minority judge on an appellate court panel changes the decision-making process for the entire panel.[132] However, the most powerful background variable for predicting the rulings of a judge remains the political party of which the judge is a member.[133] Thus, party and ideology seem to have a greater effect on judicial decision making than does the race or sex of the judge.

Although most studies do not show that female judges vote differently than male judges on appellate courts, nevertheless several female justices on the U.S. Supreme Court feel that the presence of women on the Court is very important. For example, Justice O'Connor has expressed concern that her replacement on the Court was a man. Discussing the fact that she was the first woman to serve on the nation's highest court, Justice O'Connor has said, "I've often said that it's wonderful to be the first to do something, but I didn't want to be the last. . . . When I retired, I was not replaced then by a woman, which gives one pause to think, 'Oh, what did I do wrong that led to this?'"[134] Maureen Mahoney is an attorney who has argued well over twenty cases before the Supreme Court and has won the vast majority of them. She is one of the few female litigants who regularly appear before the Supreme Court. When asked about the effects of having women on the Court, she replied, "I think having Sandra Day O'Connor join the Court was very significant for the public and for generations of women. I don't think anyone should say otherwise because role models are important in our country. I'm not saying how that translates into how you interpret the Constitution. But I think it filled young girls, young women with pride to have Sandra Day O'Connor on the Supreme Court."[135] Justice Ginsburg has also discussed the importance of having women on the Supreme Court. After the Court held oral arguments in *Safford Unified School District #1 v. Redding* (2009), which involved a strip search of a thirteen-year-old girl at school, Justice Ginsburg said of her eight male colleagues who were hearing the case, "They have never been a 13-year-old girl. . . . It's a very sensitive age for a girl. . . . I didn't think that my colleagues, some of them, quite understood."[136] Recall that when President Obama was facing a vacancy on the U.S. Supreme Court, Justice Ruth Bader Ginsburg publicly stated that the Court needed more gender diversity in its membership.[137]

As important as ideology and party are to judges' decision making, ideological differences do not prevent judges from forming close friendships. For example, Justices Ginsburg and Scalia are very good friends, despite the fact that they rarely vote together when the Supreme Court is divided along ideological lines. Justice Ginsburg was also good friends with the late Judge Robert Bork.[138] On the other hand, Justice Blackmun and Chief Justice Burger started out as good friends on the Supreme Court, but their friendship disintegrated as they moved farther and farther apart ideologically.[139] In an unusual event across ideological lines, liberal Justice Elena Kagan has even gone antelope and bird hunting with conservative Justice Scalia.[140]

CHAPTER SUMMARY

This chapter examined the American legal profession, which includes both lawyers and judges. It began with a look at the law school experience, which is the one common socialization experience for all American lawyers. This chapter also looked at where lawyers work and what kinds of things they do in their professional lives. The chapter looked at recent employment trends for new lawyers, as well as examining starting salaries. Because the legal profession is so prestige oriented, the chapter discussed the concept of the two hemispheres of the law. It also considered issues regarding access to justice for those who cannot afford to hire an attorney. Finally, the chapter examined the professional socialization of judges when they first come to the bench. It also looked at the demographic backgrounds of both lawyers and judges.

For Further Reading

Baum, Lawrence. 2006. *Judges and Their Audiences: A Perspective on Judicial Behavior.* Princeton, NJ: Princeton University Press.

Greenburg, Jan Crawford. 2007. *Supreme Conflict: The Inside Story of the Struggle for Control of the United States Supreme Court.* New York: Penguin.

Greenhouse, Linda. 2005. *Becoming Justice Blackmun: Harry Blackmun's Supreme Court Journey.* New York: Times Books.

Heinz, John P., Robert L. Nelson, Rebecca L. Sandefur, and Edward O. Laumann. 2005. *Urban Lawyers: The New Social Structure of the Bar.* Chicago: University of Chicago Press.

Levin, Leslie C., and Lynn Mather, eds. 2012. *Lawyers in Practice: Ethical Decision Making in Context.* Chicago: University of Chicago Press.

Mather, Lynn, Craig A. McEwen, and Richard J. Maiman. 2001. *Divorce Lawyers at Work: Variety of Professionalism in Practice.* New York: Oxford University Press.

McGuire, Kevin. 1993. *The Supreme Court Bar: Legal Elites in the Washington Community.* Charlottesville: University of Virginia Press.

Scheingold, Stuart A., and Austin Sarat. 2004. *Something to Believe In: Politics, Professionalism, and Cause Lawyering.* Stanford, CA: Stanford University Press.

Southworth, Ann. 2008. *Lawyers of the Right: Professionalizing the Conservative Coalition.* Chicago: University of Chicago Press.

Toobin, Jeffrey. 2007. *The Nine: Inside the Secret World of the Supreme Court.* New York: Doubleday.

5

Trial Courts: Criminal Cases

When many people think about trials in the United States, they automatically assume that the matter involves the criminal justice system. This chapter will examine the process used for criminal trials by first defining *crime* and then looking at the role of the major actors in the criminal justice process. We will focus on the decision-making procedures and assessments of the police, the prosecutor, the defense attorney, the defendant, and the judge at various points in the process. This chapter will also look at the phenomenon of plea bargaining, since around 90 to 95 percent of state criminal cases and over 97 percent of federal cases end in plea bargains.[1]

A **crime** is a wrong against society. In our country, the courts are the only institution with the power to punish criminals. In a criminal case, the **prosecutor** is the lawyer who represents the interests of the society and argues against the **defendant**, who is the person accused of committing the crime. Recall that the way criminal cases are named—for example, *People vs. Defendant, State vs. Defendant, Commonwealth vs. Defendant, United States vs. Defendant*—indicate that the defendant is accused of breaking society's legal rules.

Almost all prosecutors' offices follow the same geographical boundaries as the courts in which they serve. Most local prosecutors are elected officials, often known as the district attorney or the state attorney; thus, all local prosecutors have political priorities or reasons for the types of cases they might pursue.[2] Federal prosecutors, known as U.S. Attorneys, are technically appointed by the president and confirmed by the U.S. Senate as political appointees in the U.S. Department of Justice. However, U.S. Attorneys are expected to perform their jobs without displaying too much evidence that they have any overt political motivations in specific prosecutions.[3] The burden of proof in a criminal case is "guilt beyond a reasonable doubt," meaning that the prosecutor has the responsibility to prove to a jury or to a judge that all the elements of the crime prove the defendant's guilt beyond dispute. Under most circumstances, the prosecutor cannot appeal a trial court's finding that the defendant is not guilty.

CRIMINAL STATUTES AND THE CONSTITUTION

Since the criminal justice system involves the government using its power against its citizens, the Framers of the Constitution were very concerned about possible abuses in the system. The Fourth, Fifth, Sixth, Seventh, Eighth, and Fourteenth Amendments to the U.S. Constitution all deal with the rights of accused criminals. Both the Fifth and Fourteenth Amendments have a Due Process Clause, stating that no person can "be deprived of life, liberty, or property, without due process of law." The Fifth Amendment applies to the federal government, while the Fourteenth Amendment applies to the states. Other constitutional requirements include a right to a speedy and public trial in a criminal case, the right to a jury in most major cases if the defendant chooses to have one, a prohibition against double jeopardy, the right against self-incrimination, the right to a lawyer in a criminal case, and the right of a criminal defendant to confront and cross-examine the witnesses against him or her. The Eighth Amendment prohibits cruel and unusual punishments, while the Fourth Amendment prohibits unlawful searches and seizures.

There can be no common law crimes in the United States. In other words, judges cannot create crimes on their own; all crimes must be clearly defined by a specific statute, which spells out in detail the prohibited behavior and the potential sentence for that criminal action. If a criminal statute is too vague or unclear, the courts will almost certainly declare that statute to be unconstitutional. The Constitution also prohibits criminal laws that go into force retroactively or apply only to specific individuals.

The vast majority of crimes in the United States are state crimes, but there are also a smaller number of federal crimes. Many of the federal crimes today are drug related. Both state and federal statutes spell out the specifics of a crime in our society and provide a range of possible punishments, but in almost all cases only judges can actually impose a criminal sentence on any given defendant. Criminal sentences are considered a question of law and thus are almost always imposed by judges, not juries. Convicted criminal defendants may face a variety of punishments for their offenses, including prison sentences, fines paid to the government, or even the death penalty.

By worldwide standards, punishments in the United States are considered quite harsh. The United States has the highest incarceration rate in the world, about ten times higher than the average rate in Western Europe.[4] In fact, the percentage of Americans in prison is over four times as high as in Luxembourg, the United Kingdom, or Spain, and those countries have the highest incarceration rates in the European Union.[5] Over four decades, the number of Americans in jail increased by a factor of ten. If we count people who are on probation or parole, more than seven million individuals are currently under legal supervision in the United States.[6] While the United States has a very large percentage of its residents in prison, we do not have a tradition of imprisoning political prisoners or debtors, like much of the rest of the world.[7]

TYPES OF CRIMES AND ELEMENTS OF A CRIME

There are various types of crimes. Some crimes are called sins of commission, while others are called sins of omission. **Sins of commission** mean that the defendant has committed a prohibited criminal act. **Sins of omission** mean that the defendant has not done something that is required by law. A sin of commission would be robbery, while failing to file a federal tax return each year is a sin of omission. A **felony** is a serious crime, one that is usually tried in major state trial courts and is usually punishable by at least one year in prison. A **misdemeanor** is a less serious criminal offense that carries a sentence of less than a year in jail and is usually tried in a minor state trial court. A **juvenile offense** is a criminal action committed by a minor that leads to a finding of juvenile delinquency in a juvenile court. Some juvenile offenses would also be crimes if done by an adult, but other actions are considered juvenile offenses merely because of the age of the perpetrator. For example, school truancy is a juvenile offense but would not be a crime for adults.

The prosecutor must prove all the elements of the crime beyond a reasonable doubt at trial. All of these elements should be clearly spelled out in the criminal statutes. The first element of a crime is the **actus reus**, or the actual criminal act. For example, for murder, the actus reus would be killing another person. The second element is the **mens rea**, which refers to criminal intent. Both murder and manslaughter involve the act of killing another person, but, under most criminal statutes, in order to prove first-degree murder the prosecutor must prove that the killing was premeditated, while manslaughter requires a much lower level of intent. The next element of a crime is the criminal injury or result. For example, the difference between murder and attempted murder is the fact that the prosecutor must prove in a murder case that the victim actually died. The final element is causation. Thus, the prosecutor must prove that the defendant's actions, performed with the required criminal intent, actually *caused* the injury or result. The burden of proof falls on the prosecutor in criminal cases, and guilt beyond a reasonable doubt is a much tougher standard than the standards of preponderance of evidence or clear and convincing evidence, the two burdens of proof in civil cases that will be discussed in more detail in Chapter 6.

STEPS IN THE CRIMINAL TRIAL PROCESS

This next section will examine the steps that lead up to the sentencing of a criminal defendant found guilty of a crime. This section will pay special attention to which actors in the criminal justice process have discretion in their decision making and when they can exercise this discretion. Figure 5.1 provides an overview of the steps in the process and will be discussed in more detail below.

The Role of the Police

Generally the first step in the criminal justice process is the arrest of the suspected criminal. The police have almost total discretion at this step. The police

FIGURE 5.1 Steps in the Criminal Trial Process

Warrant for search and/or arrest
↓
Arrest
↓
Preliminary hearing
↓
Arraignment
↓
Grand jury indictment (may also occur before arrest)
↓
Pretrial conferences and discovery
↓
Jury selection
↓
Trial
↓
Verdict
↓
Sentencing

can make an arrest under two main circumstances: if a judge has issued an arrest warrant or if the police actually see a crime being committed. The police may also make an arrest after a complaint is filed by a third party and that complaint is investigated thoroughly by the police. A 2007 study found that only about 40 percent of all victims report crimes to the police.[8] A judge will issue an **arrest warrant** when he or she feels that there is probable cause that the suspect has committed a crime. This may happen after a grand jury hearing on the case or after the police investigate a crime reported by a victim. For the vast majority of crimes committed in our society, arrests are never made because the police cannot find the alleged criminal, or because the police choose not to arrest the suspect.[9] In fact, one study estimated that arrests occurred in only about one in four incidents of aggravated assault, while only about one in a thousand drug deals ended in arrest in our country.[10]

The police have a great deal of discretion over whether or not to arrest a suspect.[11] In fact, there are many times when the police do not make an arrest even when they are legally allowed to do so. Police departments are often referred to as among the most political of institutions in American cities.[12] At times the police will give an offender a mere warning.[13] At other times the police may decide that the alleged criminal incident is not important enough for them to use their time and resources making an arrest.[14] Police officers might not make an arrest when they feel that the application of the law in this specific case would not be appropriate or would be unfair. At other times, the police just disagree with the underlying purpose of the criminal statute they must implement. For example, some police officers may not fully support hate crime legislation[15] or domestic violence laws, and thus may choose not to make an arrest in such instances.[16] At times, the police officer may have personal, family, or other ties to the suspected criminal that would make arresting the person personally difficult.[17] Some have alleged that decisions to arrest can be influenced by racial or ethnic profiling, meaning that police are more willing to arrest members of various minority groups than whites.[18] This discretion gives the police a great deal of power in the criminal justice process. As Jeannine Bell, a criminal justice scholar, has written, "Because police encounter incidents first, they serve as gatekeepers with the discretion to discard incidents that prosecutors and judges will never see."[19]

There are many important U.S. Supreme Court decisions that constrain the police in their arrests and investigations of crime. This section will just touch on a few of them. An important constraint on police investigations of crime is the **exclusionary rule**, which means that any evidence seized illegally cannot be used at trial. The exclusionary rule for federal crimes originated in *Weeks v. United States* (1914), and the U.S. Supreme Court applied this rule to the states in *Mapp v. Ohio*

(1961). Another important Supreme Court ruling affecting the actions of the police is *Miranda v. Arizona* (1966). In this case, the Supreme Court held that the
police must inform all criminal suspects of their rights at the time of their arrest
and before any formal interrogation. Known as the Miranda warning, it identifies
the right to remain silent, the right to know that anything said to the police may be
used in court against the suspect, the right to consult with an attorney and to have
the lawyer present during interrogation, and the right to have a court-appointed
lawyer if the accused cannot afford to hire a private attorney. The U.S. Supreme
Court constitutionalized the Miranda warning in *Dickerson v. United States*
(2000). If the police do not read the accused his or her rights, any evidence collected resulting from statements to the police cannot be used against the defendant
in court. In some ways, the *Miranda* decision expands and clarifies the Court's
ruling in *Gideon v. Wainwright* (1963), in which the Court declared that all criminal defendants must have a lawyer provided for them in all serious criminal trials.

The Preliminary Hearing and Arraignment

After the arrest, the defendant must appear almost immediately before a judge in
a **preliminary hearing**. The purpose of this hearing is to make sure that the police
have not arrested the wrong person. In other words, at the preliminary hearing
the judge must ensure that there has been no misidentification of the accused by
the police. This step is usually quite routine and occurs very soon after the arrest.

The next step in the process is the **arraignment**, when the arrested individual
appears before a judge to learn the formal criminal charges against him or her.
The defendant must also enter a plea of guilty or not guilty at this step. The prosecutor has all the discretion in the charging decisions. One option is to charge
the defendant with a very serious crime, knowing that later the charges may be
reduced through the plea bargaining process (discussed later in this chapter).
The prosecutor might also present a variety of charges for a single event. Or the
prosecutor might drop the charges completely because of a lack of evidence in
the case. As mentioned previously, it is also at this point that the defendant must
be provided with a lawyer if she or he cannot afford to hire one, as determined
by the *Gideon v. Wainwright* (1963) case. Most states have created a system of
public defenders to provide government-paid criminal defense lawyers for the
poor and indigent.[20] At other times, the court will appoint a private attorney if
the accused cannot afford to hire a lawyer.

At the arraignment, the defendant almost always seeks bail. **Bail** is money a
defendant has to provide to the court to guarantee his or her attendance at trial.
The judge determines appropriate bail based on the formal charges facing the

accused. The judge also takes into consideration the defendant's past criminal history, the probability that the defendant will appear at trial, the gravity of the crime, the strength of the evidence against the defendant, the defendant's ties to the community, the defendant's job status, and other factors when deciding how much bail is appropriate. Some states have very strict guidelines based on these criteria that judges must use when setting the bail amount, and the Eighth Amendment prohibits excessive bail. Bail is available for most crimes except for murder, but the amount of bail may cause hardships for low-income defendants. Defendants who cannot afford the cash bail may hire a bail bondsman, who will usually require a non-refundable fee of 10 percent of the cash bail for state crimes and 15 percent for federal crimes plus other collateral in order to issue a bail bond to the court. Defendants who cannot afford bail must remain in custody unless they raise the bail money or until the court dismisses the charges against them.[21]

Grand Juries

After arraignment, it is possible that the prosecutor will have to convene a **grand jury** to determine whether there is enough evidence for the case to proceed to trial. This step can occur at various points in the criminal justice process before trial. The U.S. Constitution requires a grand jury to bring an indictment of a defendant before a federal criminal trial can proceed. Most states also use the grand jury process, although it is not constitutionally required. The federal grand jury usually consists of twenty-three lay jurors, and twelve or more must agree before an indictment is issued. State grand juries vary in size. The **indictment** lists the formal charges against the defendant, and the trial is limited to the charges listed in the indictment. Grand juries sit for much longer periods than trial juries, and they often consider large numbers of cases. A grand jury investigation may occur prior to, and therefore lead to, arrest warrants, or the grand jury may consider the case after a defendant's arraignment but before trial.

The procedures of the grand jury are very different from those of a regular trial. The grand jury is under the total control of the prosecutor. There is no judge present during a grand jury proceeding, and witnesses may not bring a lawyer with them even though they must answer the prosecutor's questions under oath. The rules of evidence also do not apply. The First Amendment does not protect journalists called before a federal grand jury, nor does it allow them to maintain the confidentiality of their sources. Thus, grand juries are often seen as biased in favor of the prosecution. An old joke says that a grand jury will indict a ham sandwich if the prosecutor asks them to do so.

The Discovery Process in a Criminal Case

The next step in the criminal process involves the discovery period and a variety of pretrial conferences with the prosecutor, the defense attorney, and the judge. **Discovery** means that the two lawyers exchange information about the case, although in a criminal proceeding the defense lawyer has very few obligations to share information with the prosecutor. On the other hand, the prosecution must share with the defense most information it has at its disposal. Part of the discovery process involves both sides sharing their witness lists for trial. The judge may also rule on a variety of evidentiary issues during this phase. It is also a prime opportunity for plea bargaining to occur. The plea bargaining process will be discussed in more detail later in this chapter.

The Trial in a Criminal Case

After all the preliminary business is disposed of, the case then moves to the trial phase. The criminal defendant has the right to a jury in all cases where he or she could receive a jail or prison sentence of more than six months. The defendant also, of course, has the right to waive the jury and have a judge alone decide the case. If there is no jury, it is called a **bench trial**. A jury is mandatory in a capital punishment case, however, and the prosecutor must decide before trial whether or not to seek the death penalty.

A **jury** usually consists of twelve lay individuals, and it must make a unanimous decision in most criminal cases. One of the purposes of the jury in a criminal case is to serve as a popular check on the actions of the governmental actors in the criminal justice system, such as the judge, the prosecutor, and the police. The jury serves as the "conscience of the community" and may substitute the views of the people for the rule of law.[22] Jury reform efforts for both criminal and civil trials will be discussed in more detail in Chapter 6.

Occasionally, juries refuse to convict a criminal defendant, instead rendering a verdict of not guilty, because they feel that the law in question is unjust or because it would be unjust to enforce the law in the specific circumstances of the case. This is often known as **jury nullification**. Some equate jury nullification with a form of civil disobedience,[23] while others feel that jury nullification is always improper and courts should do everything possible to discourage the practice.[24] Nevertheless, juries can and do substitute their own collective sense of justice for that of the prosecutor and/or the judge.

Although most criminal cases never go to trial because they end in plea bargains, the mere threat of a jury trial heavily influences the decisions of all the players at almost every step in the criminal justice system. As scholar Jeffrey Abramson concludes in his study of the jury, "The whole point [of a jury] is to subject law to a democratic interpretation, to achieve a justice that resonates with the values and common sense of the people in whose name the law was written."[25]

Before the jury is seated, the court must select a **jury pool**, and the potential jurors from the jury pool will be summoned to the courthouse. Many states use voter registration rolls to create their potential jury pools, while other states supplement these lists with lists of people who pay utilities in the state, lists of those with driver licenses in the state, hunting and fishing license lists, gun registration lists, et cetera.[26] In the past, many courts used so-called blue ribbon juries, where the jurors were considered to be the most prominent men in the community. These blue ribbon juries were often considered to be exclusionary, elitist, and even racist, and civil rights laws enacted in the late 1960s changed that practice.[27] Today almost all scholars and court officials agree that the jury pool should be broad enough to provide as representative a jury as possible, and one that reflects the actual demographics of the court's geographical jurisdiction.

The prosecutor and the defense lawyer both get to question the potential jurors individually, as does the judge. This process is known as **voir dire**. Jurors who cannot be impartial (perhaps because of their political views), who have connections to the case, or who have some bias (perhaps due to their past experiences) are released through **challenges for cause**. The judge decides which members of the jury pool will be excused for cause, sometimes at the request of one of the lawyers in the case. Each side also gets a certain number of **peremptory challenges**, in which they can excuse a potential juror without giving a reason.[28] The U.S. Supreme Court has said that no potential juror can be excused due solely to race or sex,[29] but this principle is very hard to enforce when lawyers use their peremptory challenges. After this selection process, the trial actually begins. As discussed earlier in the book, the role of the jury is to decide questions of fact, while the judge's role is to decide any questions of law that may arise at trial. If there is no jury, then the judge performs both functions.

At trial, the lawyers examine witnesses and present evidence in order to assist the court in determining the facts of the crime. The lawyers present the facts in the most favorable light for their clients, and the jury (if there is one) determines whose presentation of the facts is most correct. After each side presents its case, the jury then delivers the **verdict**, that is, the decision that determines the guilt or innocence of a criminal defendant. In a criminal case, if the verdict is guilty, then the jury or the judge must have determined beyond a reasonable doubt that the defendant committed all elements of the crime. When a jury decides a verdict of guilty in a criminal case, it reassures the rest of the community that the government has acted fairly and that the punishment prescribed for the convicted defendant will be just.[30] If the verdict is not guilty on all charges, then the process ends. Only under extraordinary circumstances can the prosecutor appeal a not-guilty trial verdict.

Criminal Sentencing

After a guilty verdict, the trial enters the sentencing phase. A criminal sentence is a question of law, and in almost all states the judge imposes the sentence in all cases except for the death penalty. The judge may take several weeks or months after the trial verdict in order to decide on the proper sentence in a major criminal case. In a misdemeanor case, the judge may issue the sentence immediately after the trial ends. In major criminal cases, the judge relies on probation officers to prepare a report on sentencing, which includes information that was not admissible at trial, including the past criminal record of the convicted defendant. The probation officers examine the severity of the crime, the defendant's past behavior, and any mitigating factors that the judge should consider. Prosecutors will also make sentencing recommendations to the judge—they always do so in a plea bargain situation, and often do so after a full trial. Both the federal government and the states have taken a variety of measures to restrict the judge's sentencing discretion, as we will discuss in more detail below.

The goals of criminal sentencing include retribution, incapacitation, deterrence, and rehabilitation. **Retribution** is a form of societal revenge, where the convicted criminal defendant gets the punishment the members of the society feels he or she deserves. **Incapacitation** means that dangerous individuals will be confined to prison as a way of protecting society. There are two forms of deterrence: **general deterrence**, or the hope that strong criminal sentences will deter potential criminals before they commit a crime, and **individual deterrence**, or preventing an individual from committing another crime since he or she is in prison. **Rehabilitation** means changing the individual so that she or he can become a useful member of society when punishment ends.

Today, rehabilitation seems to be much lower on the list than the other goals, except in the juvenile courts. This was not always true. From the late 1940s to the 1970s, rehabilitation seemed to be the ideal and was the dominant force in the sentencing decisions for adult criminals in the United States. It was assumed at the time that one of the key goals of imprisonment was to change the character, attitude, and behavior of offenders, both to benefit them and to make them less threatening to society.[31] Starting in the 1980s, most state legislatures and Congress believed that they needed to toughen sentences in order to promote the other goals of sentencing (retribution, incapacitation, and deterrence), thus downplaying the goal of rehabilitation. Legislators wanted to appear to be tougher on crime, and so criminal statutes prescribed ever harsher sentences in the United States. However, judges did not always choose the harshest sentences for convicted criminals. Judges felt that their sentencing decisions should reflect many different considerations.

RESTRICTING THE SENTENCING DISCRETION OF JUDGES

Beginning in the 1980s, the U.S. Congress and many state legislatures began to enact new schemes that were designed to restrict the discretion of judges in criminal sentencing. The sense was that the courts were too soft on crime, too inconsistent, or both, and that citizens were demanding ever tougher criminal sentences. One such mechanism is sentencing guidelines, and another is mandatory sentences, both of which we will explore in greater detail in the following sections.

Sentencing Guidelines

In 1984, Congress passed the federal Sentencing Reform Act. This act required that a newly created U.S. Sentencing Commission recommend sentencing guidelines to Congress, and the first set of federal sentencing guidelines was enacted by Congress in 1987. Most states soon followed suit with their own sentencing guideline schemes.[32] The **Federal Sentencing Guidelines** are a grid, where one axis is the severity of the crime committed and the other axis is the past behavior of the defendant. Information about mitigating and aggravating factors in the defendant's past may come from probation officers' reports on the defendant or other sources. Placing the crime on the grid, the judge is given a specific sentencing range for the individual defendant.

Although the Supreme Court had found the federal sentencing guidelines to be constitutional in *Mistretta v. United States* (1989), later in *United States v. Booker* (2005) the Court ruled that these guidelines were merely advisory and could not be treated as mandatory restrictions on the discretion of federal judges.[33] Nevertheless, judges today must give reasons for deviating from the sentencing guidelines. The new guideline system seemed to have made criminal sentences more uniform, although various aspects of the system remain controversial.

One of the major controversies involving the federal sentencing guidelines, for example, involved sentencing disparities between powder cocaine and crack cocaine. Powder cocaine is more often used by upper-middle-class whites, while lower-income people and racial minorities tended to prefer the cheaper crack cocaine. Chemically, the two drugs are almost identical. Under the sentencing guidelines, the sentence for the use or sale of crack cocaine was a hundred times greater than the sentence for using or selling powder cocaine. These disparities raised all types of questions regarding race and class in our justice system. After many years of trying to find a politically acceptable solution to the problem, in 2010 Congress passed the Fair Sentencing Act, which reduced the disparity in federal sentencing for crack cocaine versus powder cocaine from over 100 to 1 to a mere 18 to 1.[34]

Mandatory Sentences

Another approach to limiting the discretion of judges is **mandatory sentences**. Here legislatures mandate a specific sentence or a minimum sentence for someone convicted of a particular crime. Almost every state and the U.S. Congress have enacted some form of mandatory minimum sentencing laws.[35] These laws have shifted most or all of the discretion away from judges and given prosecutors the power during the sentencing phase of the criminal justice process by providing them with more weapons to force defendants to accept plea bargains. After these laws were enacted, only one in forty felony cases went to trial, while in the 1970s before these laws were passed around one in twelve felony cases went to trial.[36] Judges have generally opposed these mandatory sentencing schemes. Judges want the freedom to make their own choices, and they also feel that their decisions promote justice and good results.[37]

Some of these mandatory sentencing laws include so-called sentence add-ons. These restrictions on sentencing come in a variety of forms. For example, using a gun while committing a crime might include a mandatory five-year sentence add-on, or a hate-motivated crime might carry a seven-year add-on. The U.S. Supreme Court seems to have approved of this sentencing add-on approach. Although the Supreme Court in R.A.V. v. St. Paul (1992) ruled that hate speech is protected under the First Amendment, it also approved sentence add-ons for hate crimes in Wisconsin v. Mitchell (1993). While hate speech is protected speech, prosecutors can use a defendant's hate speech to prove that the crime committed was motivated by hate and therefore is subject to sentence add-ons.

A variation on the mandatory sentencing laws are "**three strikes and you're out**" laws. These laws generally call for life sentences without parole for individuals convicted of three violent felonies or perhaps just three felonies of any type. One study found that after the three-strikes laws went into effect, prosecutors were more likely to reduce felony charges to misdemeanors as part of the plea bargaining process.[38] California has one of the strictest three-strikes laws in the country. A constitutional challenge to the law went all the way to the U.S. Supreme Court, which upheld the law by a 5–4 vote in *Ewing v. California* (2003). In this case, the defendant was convicted of shoplifting three golf clubs as his third strike, though his previous felonies were more violent. The defendant appealed, stating that a life sentence for the crime of stealing golf clubs was cruel and unusual. The U.S. Supreme Court refused to declare these three-strikes laws to be in violation of the Eighth Amendment's prohibition on cruel and unusual punishment. In her majority opinion, Justice O'Connor made the following statement:

> We do not sit as a "superlegislature" to second-guess these policy choices. It is enough that the State of California has a reasonable basis for believing that dramatically enhanced sentences for habitual felons advances the goals of its criminal justice system in any substantial way . . . To be sure, Ewing's sentence is a long one. But it reflects a rational legislative judgment, entitled to deference, that offenders who have committed serious or violent felonies and who continue to commit felonies must be incapacitated.[39]

In his dissent in this case, Justice Stevens declared the application of the California law to be in violation of the Eighth Amendment's prohibition on cruel and unusual punishments. Justice Stevens also called for judges to have greater sentencing discretion in these situations. As Justice Stevens argued, "By broadly prohibiting excessive sanctions, the *Eighth Amendment* directs judges to exercise their wise judgment in assessing the proportionality of all forms of punishment."[40] In 2012, Massachusetts became the twenty-seventh state to enact three-strikes legislation, although Governor Deval Patrick was highly skeptical that this was the right approach to sentencing reform.[41]

PLEA BARGAINING

A **plea bargain** means that the criminal defendant pleads guilty in exchange for a lesser sentence for the crime, moving the case immediately to the sentencing phase. The expectation is that a defendant who refuses to plea-bargain and is found guilty at trial will face a much harsher sentence. Plea bargains are generally a uniquely American phenomenon, because they are quite rare in most other countries. Plea bargaining has been going on in the United States since the 1830s and 1840s, and it appears to have originated in the Boston courts.[42] The practice quickly spread across the country, and it became quite common by the 1920s.[43] About 90 to 95 percent of all state criminal cases today end up in some type of plea bargain, and the percentage is even higher for federal crimes.

Types of Plea Bargains

There are several types of plea bargains. An **implicit plea bargain** means that the defendant pleads guilty without any direct communication with the prosecutor or the judge in the case. Implicit plea bargains are especially common in misdemeanor cases, but they can happen in felony cases as well.[44] The opposite of an implicit bargain is an **explicit plea bargain**, where the parties to the bargain actually communicate with each other about the deal. There are several types of explicit plea bargains. A **charge bargain** occurs when the prosecutor and the defense attorney reach an agreement where the prosecutor agrees to reduce the charges against the defendant in exchange for the defendant's guilty plea. A charge bargain usually also involves the prosecutor making a recommendation to the judge about the sentence for the new charges. A charge bargain greatly reduces the discretion of the judge in the criminal justice process because the prosecutor has all the discretion during the charging phase. A **prosecutor sentence bargain** occurs when the prosecutor agrees to recommend a reduced sentence to the judge in exchange for a guilty plea. A **judge's sentence bargain** means that the judge suggests a possible sentence if the defendant pleads guilty, but this type of plea bargain is fairly rare because most judges do not get involved directly in negotiations over the details of plea bargains.

Why Are Plea Bargains So Prevalent?

Generally, plea bargains meet the needs of all the members of the **courthouse community**, that is, the prosecutors, criminal defense lawyers, and judges who work together over long periods of time. Their interactions with any specific criminal defendant are quite brief, and so maintaining these long-term professional relationships may become more important than the outcome in any particular case. These courthouse communities,[45] or communities of practice, as they are sometimes called,[46] develop their own norms and expectations. Routines develop about how bargains are reached and who negotiates with whom; the terms of the bargain also tend to follow local norms.[47] Many local courthouse communities develop "going rates" for sentencing of specific crimes in their locales.[48] Let's look at how plea bargains can or perhaps cannot meet the needs of various players in the criminal justice system.

Prosecutors generally favor plea bargains. Most prosecuting attorneys have very heavy workloads, and they are responsible for many more cases than they can possibly take to trial. A plea bargain saves time, money, and resources for the government in general and for the prosecutor in particular.[49] It also guarantees that a defendant will be punished and probably go to jail in serious cases. Plea bargains also avoid the problem of a single juror deadlocking the case and causing a mistrial, since the jury must be unanimous in its guilty verdict.[50] Since head prosecutors are normally elected officials at the state level, plea bargains give them an automatic win on their record. No elected official likes to lose, and local prosecutors are especially sensitive to losing cases at trial. Federal prosecutors generally have strong cases to begin with and are usually able to get everything they want in a plea bargain. A recent study found that more than 97 percent of federal cases are plea-bargained. Local prosecutors may be in a far weaker position in their plea negotiations, which is why plea bargains happen less frequently in state courts.[51] Thus, under most circumstances, prosecutors are eager to make a deal and offer a plea bargain to end a criminal case.

Judges also generally favor plea bargains. They see plea bargains as saving the taxpayers' money and resources. Judges are also very busy people. When they are not sitting on the bench at trial, they are involved in legal research, legal writing, and other administrative tasks. A lengthy trial can be quite draining for a judge and prevent him or her from finishing this other work. Judges also understand the difficulties that courts face in finding jurors for criminal cases. Some judges even actively encourage plea bargains and are involved in the negotiations from the outset.[52] Although judges have the ultimate authority to sentence those criminal defendants found guilty, they routinely follow the sentencing recommendations of a plea bargain even when they did not take part in the negotiations. Even elected state judges will often favor plea bargains because the voters tend not to hold judges responsible for the plea bargains negotiated by defense attorneys and prosecutors.[53] Also, guilty pleas cannot be appealed, so judges have no fear of their decision being reversed by a higher court when they accept a plea bargain.[54]

Defense attorneys have their own incentives to plea-bargain. Public defenders, those government-paid lawyers for the poor in criminal cases, also have very heavy workloads. They may be responsible for an extremely large number of cases at one time. Plea bargains save them time and resources.[55] They also want to be good citizens of the courthouse community. While their clients come and go, public defenders must work with the same prosecutors and judges again and again. Since plea bargains meet the needs of the other members of the courthouse community, public defenders are hesitant to rock the boat and oppose a proposed plea bargain. Public defenders also seek plea bargains in cases where there is very little they can do to win at trial. Thus, they often encourage their clients to accept a plea bargain for the "going rate" in that community of practice. Public defenders feel that most of their cases fall into this category.[56]

Private defense attorneys may have similar incentives to plea-bargain. They too may be part of the courthouse community, and they are aware of the "going rate" for sentencing in their locales. Many private defense lawyers are paid on a per-case basis, so they might make the same amount of money whether the case goes to trial or not. Even when private defense lawyers charge an hourly fee for appearing in court, they are often able to make more money by handling several cases through plea bargaining than if they work on only one trial that occupies all of their professional time.

What about the needs of the defendant? Repeat offenders are often well aware of the plea bargaining system in their communities, and they may even also know the "going rate" for sentencing for specific crimes. Defendants who actually committed the crime will most likely receive a lighter sentence if they plea-bargain than if they demand that the case go to trial. Most defense lawyers will advise their clients to accept a fair plea bargain instead of taking their chances at trial. Trials can be very long and very expensive.[57] Defendants who cannot afford bail have special incentives to plea-bargain because months can elapse between arraignment and trial.[58] Unless they are released on bail, accused defendants must wait in jail during this lengthy period. A plea bargain may mean the sentence is for time served or a shorter additional period of incarceration.

Innocent defendants present a special case. Their lawyers may encourage them to take a plea bargain instead of running the risk of losing at trial. Many defendants may prefer the certainty of a plea bargain over the uncertainly of going to trial. Since defendants may not be familiar with the criminal justice system, they may feel that they should follow the advice of their professional expert, who handles criminal cases on a regular basis.[59] They also worry that judges might impose a much harsher sentence if they have to sit through a lengthy and tiresome trial. Some defendants will plead guilty just to avoid the publicity of a trial.[60] There are, of course, innocent defendants who refuse to plea-bargain, preferring instead to fight for justice at trial.

So When Do Cases Go to Trial?

Perhaps the better question to ask is when criminal cases actually go to trial. Death penalty cases almost always go to a full trial because virtually no criminal defendant will voluntarily accept a death sentence in a plea bargain. Cases that receive a great deal of sensationalized media coverage will probably go to a full trial because the prosecutor will not want the bad publicity that a plea bargain in such a case might bring. For example, James E. Holmes was arrested for killing twelve people and injuring around seventy more in a shooting at a movie theater in Aurora, Colorado, in July 2012. The case received national attention and led in part to the state of Colorado passing stricter gun control laws. When the defendant proposed a plea bargain in order to avoid the death penalty, the prosecutors in the case refused the offer. They wanted to take the case to trial and attempt to convince a jury that the death penalty was the proper conclusion to the tragedy.[61] After the plea bargain proposal was rejected by the prosecutor, the defendant decided to use an insanity defense during the trial.

Defendants who hire private defense attorneys from outside the community of practice or the courthouse community are much more likely to go to trial because their lawyers don't have to work with the other players on a long-term basis. They are free to upset the norms of the community of practice. Truly innocent defendants may demand that their attorneys take the case to trial even when the odds are stacked against them. Attorneys with political agendas might also take a case to trial in order to get the case to an appellate court that can set precedent on the issue. However, trials in criminal cases remain quite rare because the vast majority of criminal defendants actively seek plea bargains.

Debates About Plea Bargaining

Some players in the criminal justice system do not like plea bargains. The police generally oppose plea bargains, especially when they feel that the defendant is getting off too easily for the crime. The victims of crime often oppose plea bargains, because they may feel that plea bargains have not brought them the justice they deserve. The media are often highly skeptical of plea bargains, in part because they can lose a juicy story when the case does not go to trial.[62] Politicians are often opposed to plea bargains, because the public may perceive the plea bargaining system as being soft on crime.[63] In the late 1970s the attorney general of Alaska and the state's supreme court attempted to ban plea bargaining, but the number of defendants who pled guilty dropped very little in the state. While the state officials could try to stop plea bargaining, in reality they could never stop implicit bargains or even charge bargains. By attempting to limit plea bargains, the state just increased the power of the prosecutor to push through charge bargains.[64]

A variety of scholars have criticized plea bargaining, often because they feel that it hurts the poor and powerless in our society. As one scholar has succinctly stated, "There is no glory in plea bargaining."[65] Plea bargains are often seen as coercive, especially when the defendant receives a deal in exchange for testifying on behalf of the prosecutor.[66] However, the views of critics of plea bargaining rarely matter much in our criminal justice system because plea bargaining is so crucial to the functioning of the courthouse community. The U.S. Supreme Court has heard a variety of cases regarding plea bargains. In order to reduce the coercive nature of plea bargains, the U.S. Supreme Court in *Boykin v. Alabama* (1969) required that the defendant state in open court that he or she was accepting the plea bargain voluntarily and that he or she understood the ramifications of the guilty plea, including the waiving of his or her constitutional rights in the process. In *Padilla v. Commonwealth of Kentucky* (2010), the Supreme Court ruled that criminal defense attorneys must advise noncitizen clients about the deportation risks of a guilty plea as part of a plea bargain. In *Missouri v. Frye* (2012), the Court decided that the Sixth Amendment right to effective assistance of counsel extends to all critical stages of the criminal proceedings, including the consideration of plea bargain offers that lapse or are rejected. With this decision, the justices specifically reinforced the idea that plea bargain negotiations are a critical part of the criminal justice process.

CAPITAL PUNISHMENT CASES

So far, this chapter has examined the criminal process for regular trials and plea bargains; however, capital punishment cases follow a very different path. The death penalty remains highly controversial in the United States, in part because almost all other industrialized democracies around the world have abolished its use. For example, it is a requirement for entry into the European Union that member states abolish the death penalty. Most of the death penalties carried out around the world are in the United States, China, Saudi Arabia, Iran, and Iraq.

The popularity of the death penalty in the United States is lower than it used to be. In March 2013, Maryland became the eighteenth state to abolish the death penalty under state law.[67] The District of Columbia abolished its death penalty in 1981. Since 2007, six states (Connecticut, Illinois, Maryland, New Jersey, New Mexico, and New York) have abolished the death penalty. In March 2014 the New Hampshire House voted overwhelmingly to repeal the death penalty statute, and the governor agreed to sign the repeal legislation if it passed.[68] The repeal died, however, in a tie vote in the Senate. However, the federal government retains a death penalty that can be used throughout the nation, even in states that do not have their own death penalty statutes.

The Supreme Court and the Death Penalty

As of this writing, the federal government and thirty-two states allow the use of the death penalty. The death penalty is strongly supported by voters in states such as Texas, Oklahoma, Florida, and Georgia. We will start this section with an examination of a pair of Supreme Court decisions that have set the parameters for modern death penalty procedures, *Furman v. Georgia* (1972) and *Gregg v. Georgia* (1976).

In *Furman v. Georgia* (1972), William Henry Furman was convicted of murder and sentenced to death. The question before the Court was whether the death penalty was cruel and unusual punishment and thus violated the Eighth Amendment. In a 5–4 decision, the Court declared that the death penalty statutes then in force were unconstitutional because of the erratic nature of their application. We now know that the justices were split into three groups on this question. The two liberal justices, Justices Thurgood Marshall and William Brennan, felt that because of evolving standards of decency the death penalty was always cruel and unusual. The four conservative justices voted to uphold the death penalty statutes as they were at the time. The three justices in the middle felt that the death penalty was applied in an arbitrary and racially discriminatory manner, and voted to strike down the laws as they were then written. Georgia, like many other states, rewrote its death penalty statute, and by a vote of 7–2 the Court upheld the new procedures in *Gregg v. Georgia* (1976).

After *Gregg* and some other decisions further clarified the ruling, the federal government and the states changed to a so-called **bifurcated jury** system in death penalty cases. The first jury would decide guilt or innocence, and the second jury would decide whether the sentence should be death or life imprisonment. These two juries were usually made up of the same individuals, but they would hear different evidence in each stage of the proceedings. The prosecutors must indicate before the trial starts whether or not they will be seeking the death penalty. All jurors must be "death qualified," meaning that anyone who opposes the death penalty as a matter of principle must be automatically excused from the pool of potential jurors.[69] In the first stage of the trial, the jury would hear evidence about the facts of the case. In the penalty phase, the jury would hear evidence about aggravating factors such as the defendant's prior criminal behavior and mitigating factors such as elements of the defendant's past. In a regular trial, sentencing decisions are in the hands of the judge, so it matters less when the judge learns about these aggravating and mitigating factors. However, because the jury makes the sentencing decision in death penalty cases, there is much more attention paid to issues such as admission of evidence. In *Gregg*, the Court approved this bifurcated jury process because the group of justices who had been in the middle on the *Furman* decision apparently felt that these new procedures would eliminate the arbitrariness and racial disparities in the capital punishment process.

Over the years, the U.S. Supreme Court has issued a variety of decisions that have expanded or restricted the application of the death penalty. In *McCleskey v. Kemp* (1987), the Court ruled that individual defendants must prove racial discrimination in their own specific cases, but not through aggregate social science data indicating racial discrimination in sentencing patterns, since legislatures are better suited to evaluate such data than courts are. In 1996, a unanimous Court upheld the military's death penalty process in *Loving v. United States*. In *Apprendi v. New Jersey* (2000), the Court ruled that in all criminal cases, including capital punishment cases, a jury had to decide beyond a reasonable doubt if a fact increasing the penalty in a criminal case was true; a judge alone could not make this decision. In *Baze v. Rees* (2008), the Court upheld Kentucky's lethal injection method of execution by a vote of 7–2.

The Court has also narrowed the application of the death penalty. Execution of the insane is unconstitutional, according to *Ford v. Wainwright* (1986). In *Atkins v. Virginia* (2002), the Supreme Court prohibited the execution of the mentally disabled, although it left it to the states to define who is mentally disabled.[70] In *Roper v. Simmons* (2005), the Court prohibited execution of defendants who were juveniles when they committed the crime. In *Kennedy v. Louisiana* (2008), the Court ruled unconstitutional a state statute permitting the death penalty for the rape of a child when the child survived the attack. Thus, the death penalty is a viable sentencing option only for the crime of murder.

The Appeals Process

The appeals process for death penalty cases is also quite complicated. Since the vast majority of death penalty cases are prosecuted under state statutes and by local prosecutors, most cases are heard in state courts. The states have a wide variety of rules governing when new evidence may be introduced on appeal and the time limits for such appeals. The case then usually goes to the intermediate courts of appeals if the state has them, and then on to the state supreme court. If the conviction and the death sentence are upheld by the state supreme court, then the defendant has the right to file a **writ of certiorari** to the U.S. Supreme Court just like any other regular case, asking it to review the lower court's decision. It takes four votes of the justices to accept a writ of certiorari. If the Court refuses to take the case, then the decision of the state supreme court stands. A more detailed discussion of the writ of certiorari process is in Chapter 7.

However, at this point the death penalty defendant has a second road to have the U.S. Supreme Court hear the case. The process starts with the defendant's lawyer filing a writ of **habeas corpus** with the federal district court, which allows the federal courts to review the detention of any prisoner. (*Habeas corpus* means "produce the body.") A writ of habeas corpus generally is a judicial order forcing law enforcement authorities to produce a prisoner they are holding and to justify the prisoner's continued confinement. It has been used by military prisoners, by state prison inmates objecting to their living conditions, by detainees at Guantanamo Bay, and in death penalty cases, among others. The Anti-Terrorism and Effective Death Penalty Act of 1996 established a one-year limit on when habeas corpus petitions could be filed by those convicted in state courts, and it limited defendants to only one chance for the federal courts to review the constitutional issues in their death penalty cases.[71] Under habeas corpus procedures, convicted defendants who face the death penalty under state law can have their cases reviewed by the federal district court. If unsuccessful, defendants can then appeal to the U.S. circuit court of appeals. If unsuccessful at that level, they can then appeal to the U.S. Supreme Court. Thus, capital punishment defendants generally get two chances for the U.S. Supreme Court to review their case: through a normal appeal of a state supreme court decision and through the federal habeas corpus proceedings.

In addition, governors have the right to pardon those convicted under state law or to commute their sentences from death to life in prison. Presidents have the right to pardon or commute the sentences of defendants convicted under federal law.[72] Lawyers for those facing the death penalty often ask these executives to delay execution or to commute their client's death penalty sentence, though governors and presidents rarely grant these requests.

The Debate over Capital Punishment

The use of the death penalty remains highly controversial. The main concern of opponents of the death penalty is the potential for execution of innocent individuals.[73] In 1997, the American Bar Association called for a moratorium on all executions because of the organization's concerns with the death penalty process. The ABA's concerns generally fell into three categories: concerns about ineffective counsel at trial, the difficulties of presenting new evidence and raising new issues before appellate courts in death penalty cases, and continuing unease that the death penalty was racially discriminatory in its application.[74]

Opponents of the death penalty argue that too many defendants facing capital punishment do not receive effective assistance of counsel at trial. The Sixth Amendment has been interpreted to require that all criminal defendants receive the assistance of effective counsel. This concern is especially problematic in capital punishment cases. Death penalty trials are extremely complicated and require the lawyer to have access to a fair amount of resources to defend the client. The lawyer must understand what evidence can be admitted in the initial trial phase and what information should be presented to the jury in the sentencing phase. The lawyer must also investigate potential mitigating factors in the defendant's prior experiences. Public defender offices around the country may employ death penalty specialists, but many defendants facing the death penalty receive a court-appointed attorney who may have no experience at all in this type of case. The appointed lawyer might not even specialize in criminal law, much less in death penalty cases. There have been stories about court-appointed attorneys being drunk and sleeping during trial, being in the parking lot of the courthouse during the testimony of a key prosecution witness, and failing to investigate any mitigating evidence that could be presented to the jury in the sentencing phase. The states in which the death penalty is used most often are also the ones that regularly fail to provide adequate investigatory resources to court-appointed lawyers in these cases.[75]

The second legalistic criticism of the death penalty argues that procedural rules and practices prevent defendants from raising key issues in the appellate courts. Criminal procedures are complicated. If the defendant's counsel at trial is not top-notch, then the job becomes even harder for the lawyer who represents the defendant on appeal. States have a variety of rules about when new evidence can presented and the time limitations for such actions. Because the Anti-Terrorism and Effective Death Penalty Act of 1996 limited the number of appeals that death penalty defendants can pursue, it has become even more critical that a good lawyer handle the client's appeals. As one critic of the death penalty has noted, "New abolitionists argue against the death penalty by claiming that it has not been, and cannot be, administered in a manner that is compatible with our legal system's fundamental commitments to fair and equal treatment."[76]

Racial discrimination in the application of the death penalty has long been a concern among death penalty opponents. Some argue that all sides involved in the criminal justice process may act in ways that promote racial disparities. The statistics appear to be clear. For example, between 1930 and 1997 more than half of those executed in the United States were African American, although blacks only made up around 13 percent of the total population during that period. In

2000, 43 percent of the inmates on death row were African American.[77] Racial disparities are especially striking when the victim is white and the accused is not. Several studies have shown that prosecutors are five times more likely to seek the death penalty when the victim is white than when the victim is African American.[78] Although whites are about 50 percent of all murder victims, since the 1970s about 80 percent of all executions have been for crimes involving white victims.[79] The arbitrariness of the death penalty also promotes claims of racial disparities in its application. As one critic has noted, "Being sentenced to death is the result of a process that may be no more rational than being struck by lightning."[80]

RACE DISCRIMINATION IN THE CRIMINAL JUSTICE PROCESS

Some argue that there are clear racial and class biases in our criminal justice system. These biases are especially clear in death penalty cases, according to their critics, but the biases can present themselves at all stages of the criminal justice process. While the Supreme Court has done a great deal to eradicate overt biases in the criminal justice process, implicit biases including systemic institutional discrimination may still exist in the implementation of the criminal laws.

The evidence is stark. In 2002, 13 percent of black men and an amazing 43 percent of Hispanic/Latino men between the ages of twenty-five and twenty-nine were in jail, compared to fewer than 2 percent of whites.[81] On any given day, one in eight black males between the ages of twenty and twenty-nine is incarcerated, while this is true of only one in fifty-nine white males of the same age. At the beginning of the twenty-first century, black men had a one-in-three (33 percent) chance of serving time in prison over their lifetimes, while white males had a 6 percent chance.[82] Racial and class biases seem to exist at all steps in the criminal justice process, from arrest to sentencing. African American and Hispanic/Latino men are arrested and convicted at much higher rates than whites and serve much longer prison sentences than whites for similar crimes.[83] The Leadership Conference on Civil Rights, a major civil rights organization, has declared that current criminal justice practices "threaten to render irrelevant fifty years of hard-fought civil rights progress."[84]

Racial bias in arrests and incarceration may begin with racial profiling. **Racial or ethnic profiling** means that the police are likely to target or stop an individual based primarily on his or her race or ethnicity rather than because of any individualized suspicion.[85] Various studies have shown that members of minority groups are more likely than whites to perceive that they are being singled out and unfairly targeted by police.[86] In fact, one nationwide study found that 40 percent of blacks, compared to only 5 percent of whites, felt that they had been stopped by the police solely because of their race.[87]

The data are clear that blacks and other minorities are arrested in greater numbers than whites. Why these disparities exist is less clear. Some argue that the general public, and thus law enforcement personnel, believe that African Americans are inherently more inclined to criminal behavior and are more violent than whites. Those who make such arguments find implicit racism in the behavior of the police at the arrest stage of the criminal justice process.[88] Other studies argue that people of color and especially African American youths face multiple layers of disadvantage that ultimately make it more likely that they will be arrested. These studies point to things such as unstable family structures and deleterious neighborhood conditions as contributing to the higher arrest rates for blacks and other minorities.[89]

Many scholars argue that, after the arrest, prosecutors are more likely to bring more severe charges against African Americans than they are against whites for similar crimes.[90] Juries are more likely to convict[91] and judges are more likely to give harsher sentences to minority defendants than to whites.[92] Many of the claims of institutional racism are due to differences in rates of drug convictions. According to a 2000 report by Human Rights Watch, black male drug users in the United States were thirteen times more likely than white male drug users to be sentenced to jail, even though estimated drug usage rates were equivalent for the two groups.[93]

CHAPTER SUMMARY

This chapter examined the criminal justice process, focusing on the discretion that the players in the process have at each step. It examined the definition of crime, the elements of a crime, and the burden of proof that the prosecutor must prove in criminal trials. The chapter then looked at the decision making of the police, the prosecutor, the defense attorney, the defendant, and the judge at various points in the process. It next turned to plea bargaining, which is important since around 90 to 95 percent of state criminal cases and more than 97 percent of federal cases end in plea bargains. The chapter also looked at efforts to reduce the discretion of judges in criminal sentencing at both the state and federal levels. After examining the different procedures used in capital punishment cases, the chapter concluded with a look at the issues of race and social class in the criminal justice system.

For Further Reading

Bach, Amy. 2009. *Ordinary Injustice: How America Holds Court*. New York: Holt.

Bogira, Steve. 2005. *Courtroom 302: A Year Behind the Scenes in an American Criminal Courthouse*. New York: Vintage Books.

Fisher, George. 2003. *Plea Bargaining's Triumph: A History of Plea Bargaining in America*. Stanford, CA: Stanford University Press.

Flemming, Roy B., Peter F. Nardulli, and James Eisenstein. 1992. *The Craft of Justice: Politics and Work in Criminal Court Communities*. Philadelphia: University of Pennsylvania Press.

Lewis, Anthony. 1964. *Gideon's Trumpet: How One Man, a Poor Prisoner, Took His Case to the Supreme Court and Changed the Law of the United States*. New York: Vintage Books.

McIntyre, Lisa J. 1987. *The Public Defender: The Practice of Law in the Shadows of Repute*. Chicago: University of Chicago Press.

Scott, Elizabeth S., and Laurence Steinberg. 2008. *Rethinking Juvenile Justice:* Cambridge, MA: Harvard University Press.

Tyler, Tom R., and Yuen J. Huo. 2002. *Trust in the Law: Encouraging Public Cooperation with the Police and Courts*. New York: Russell Sage Foundation.

Walker, Thomas G. 2009. *Eligible for Execution: The Story of the Daryl Atkins Case*. Washington, DC: CQ Press.

Wert, Justin J. 2011. *Habeas Corpus in America: The Politics of Individual Rights*. Lawrence: University Press of Kansas.

6

Trial Courts: Civil Cases

This chapter will examine civil cases in the United States. Broadly defined, civil cases involve wrongs between private parties. Civil law thus helps to define the duties that private citizens owe to each other. The parties to a civil case might be individuals, corporations, government agencies, or perhaps interest groups. Some civil cases such as a divorce require a court order, while other civil cases can be settled without going before a judge, and in fact most civil cases filed in court settle without going to trial. This chapter will examine the steps in the civil case process, including (1) the goals of civil cases, (2) civil legal remedies, (3) the burdens of proof in a civil case, (4) the role of juries in civil cases, and (5) alternative dispute resolution mechanisms.

The **plaintiff** is the party who files the civil lawsuit, while the **defendant** must defend it. Recall that the case names clearly indicate which cases are civil and which ones are criminal. Thus, a civil case could be *Brown vs. Brown* (perhaps a divorce case), *Brown vs. Jones* (perhaps a real property dispute), *Brown vs. the U.S. Postal Service* (perhaps for a car accident with a postal truck), or *Brown vs. Multinational Corporation* (perhaps a contract dispute or an employment lawsuit). The case could also be *Apple vs. Samsung* (perhaps an antitrust case, a trademark dispute, or a patent case).

Civil cases can be very important in helping to determine how people treat each other in our society. But they often receive less attention than do criminal cases. As Lawrence Baum has noted, "Unlike criminal cases, civil cases seldom garner newspaper headlines or coverage on television news programs before the first commercial. Yet individual cases often have fundamental effects on people's lives, and the work of the courts in civil cases shapes government policy on significant issues."[1]

TYPES OF CIVIL CASES

Almost any court case that is not a criminal case is classified as a civil case, and these cases obviously involve a wide variety of types of lawsuits. Some of these lawsuits are handled in general jurisdiction courts, while others are heard in specialized state courts. Figure 6.1 provides an overview of the proportion of civil cases in state courts by subject matter for the year 2010. The data come from an average of the caseload statistics for seventeen selected states. Note that contract disputes are by far the largest category of civil cases heard by the state courts. Even though they get a lot of attention from the tort reform movement (discussed in more detail later in this chapter), tort lawsuits make up only about 6 percent of all civil cases today, and this proportion has changed very little over the last several decades.[2] The broad categories of civil cases discussed in more detail below correspond to the subjects of classes taken by first-year law students.

A **contract** is a legally enforceable agreement between two or more people or corporations that creates an obligation to do or not do a particular thing.

FIGURE 6.1 Civil Cases in State Courts by Type, 2010*

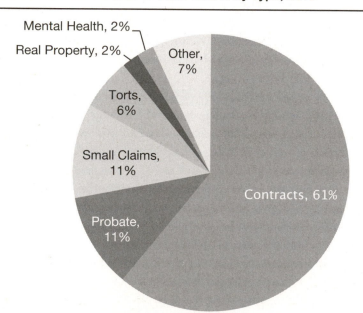

* Averages of caseloads in seventeen selected states, 2010
Source: Compiled by author from data from Robert LaFountain, Richard Schauffler, Shauna Strickland, and Kathryn Holt, *Examining the Work of State Courts: An Analysis of 2010 State Court Caseloads* (Williamsburg, VA: National Center for State Courts, 2012).

Consistent and predictable rules for enforcing contracts are essential in a capitalist society. Civil cases involving contracts thus help clarify these rules because courts determine when a contract is enforceable and what remedies should be afforded to the injured party for breach of the contract. As law scholar Lawrence Cunningham has noted, "Government regulation aims to protect people from the unscrupulous who would take advantage of contract law's freedom."[3]

Torts are civil wrongs where a person's behavior has unfairly caused someone else to suffer loss or harm. In torts, the plaintiff usually claims that the defendant acted negligently or recklessly. Medical malpractice cases, libel or slander cases, a variety of accidental harms, and personal injury cases are all examples of torts. Tort law thus helps to clarify the duties that individuals and corporations owe to each other in our society. Tort lawsuits both make the victim whole again and help to prevent the behavior that caused the harm in the first place. Recent changes in tort laws have become highly controversial, and the issue of tort reform will be discussed later in this chapter.

Commercial law usually involves alleged violations of the Uniform Commercial Code and other laws regulating banking, sales, and other commercial practices. Insurance laws and bankruptcy laws can also produce civil court cases. Consistent rules help keep our capitalist society functioning. **Property law** cases involve real property or personal property issues. This category can include water rights and mineral rights for real property, as well as questions involving access to the property of others.

Family law cases can involve issues of divorce, child custody, adoption, and child support. **Probate law** consists of the rules regarding how property passes to another after a person's death. This type of case includes the probate of wills as well as situations in which an individual dies without leaving a will. This category also encompasses trust and estate mechanisms designed to help mostly wealthy individuals avoid any estate taxes or to address other financial issues. Some states treat both family law issues and probate issues in the same specialized court, but in other states these cases are brought in different types of courts.

GOALS AND REMEDIES IN CIVIL LAWSUITS

Civil cases generally have three goals in the United States: clarification of legal status, dispute resolution, and behavior modification. For most civil disputes in our society, the courts provide an unbiased forum for resolution of the dispute. The case is decided using legal rules and norms, and the judge makes decisions based on the requirements of the law. Civil lawsuits can also be used by private individuals to enforce their constitutional rights and protect them from discrimination.[4] In addition, civil lawsuits may help individuals and groups achieve political goals that they may or may not be able to win through the decisions of other governmental institutions.[5] Many civil disputes can be and are settled without going to trial; about 85 percent of civil cases are settled before a trial concludes.

Recall that some of these civil cases, such as divorces or probating a will, require a judge's signature in order to finalize the resolution of the conflict. All changes in legal status must have a judge's order for the change to be implemented. For example, one cannot get a divorce without a judge's decree, nor can one change the status of a child's legal custody or change one's legal name without a court order. Changes in property ownership after a person's death or changes in real property boundaries also require a judge's signature. Most other civil disputes do not require a judge in order to settle the dispute, although the courts are available when alternative dispute resolution mechanisms such as mediation or arbitration do not resolve the conflict. These alternatives to going to court will be discussed in more detail later in the chapter.

Remedies in Civil Cases

Plaintiffs look to the court to provide them with legal **remedies** in civil lawsuits, which can include money damages, restitution, coercion, injunctions, and a declaration by the court of legal rights. Questions about available remedies in any given case are determined by legislatures and appellate courts. Money damages are further divided into compensatory damages and punitive damages. In a civil case, **compensatory damages** are those things that can be counted or at least given a monetary value, such as lost wages and medical bills. Although much more difficult to calculate, "pain and suffering" is also considered a compensatory damage. Thus, courts may be forced to put a dollar figure on what compensatory damages are appropriate for an injured arm, a lost eye, or even a wrongful death. **Punitive damages**, however, are meant to modify the behavior of the defendant and all potential future defendants. Punitive damages are intended to get the attention of other corporations or individuals so that they do not cause the same harm to another in the future. Punitive damages are often calculated according to the liable defendant's ability to pay. Thus, a wealthy corporation will usually be asked to pay much more in punitive damages than an individual without many resources. In the U.S. system, both compensatory and punitive damages are paid directly to the plaintiff in a civil case, while in a criminal case fines are paid by the convicted defendant to the government.

Restitution means that whatever losses plaintiffs suffer are returned to them, and they are made whole. Under the terms of a restitution order, a defendant might have to return money or property improperly taken from the plaintiff. For example, in a wrongful termination case, the improperly dismissed employee might get his or her job back. **Coercion** means that the defendant is ordered to do something, such as pay back child support payments or rehire an employee who was wrongfully terminated. A liable defendant in a libel case might be forced to publish a public apology to the person whose reputation was harmed. An **injunction** prevents someone from taking an improper action, such as preventing a lumber company from cutting down trees that are essential to the habitat of the spotted owl. An injunction might also prevent a labor union from participating in an illegal strike against an employer. A declaration of legal status includes a divorce decree or a court order determining a real property boundary line when that boundary has been in dispute.[6] Child custody orders are also a declaration of legal status, as is a change in a person's name.

Behavior Modification

Courts may serve as institutions that encourage behavior modification for the parties involved and/or for the broader American public. For example, in a famous 1994 case, an older woman sued McDonald's in a civil lawsuit when the coffee she bought at a drive-through spilled on her and caused her bodily damage. In the lawsuit, the court awarded her $160,000 in monetary damages as compensation for her medical bills and suffering. The jury also awarded her $2.7 million in punitive damages, although an appeals court later reduced that amount. At trial, the jury had heard testimony that McDonald's kept its coffee at a very high temperature in order to maximize its profits even though it was aware that such high temperatures might injure customers. In other words, McDonald's intentionally chose to keep its profits higher even if it meant that some customers would suffer physical harm. In order to modify this behavior and the behavior of other companies that provide goods and services directly to consumers, the jury awarded the plaintiff these sizable punitive damages. Even after the appeals court later reduced the punitive damages award, the media continued to characterize the case as an example of out-of-control jury awards to defendants in civil cases.[7] (Other instances of courts being used for behavior modification are described in the books *The Buffalo Creek Disaster*, about a civil lawsuit that followed an environmental mining disaster in West Virginia;[8] *A Civil Action*, about an environmental suit in Woburn, Massachusetts;[9] and *Lawyers, Lawsuits, and Legal Rights*, in part about lawsuits regarding the Americans with Disabilities Act.[10])

The jury awarded the plaintiff punitive damages in the McDonald's hot coffee case in order to send a clear message that companies could not put their desire for increased profits ahead of the need to protect consumers from foresee-able injuries when their products were used for their intended purposes. In other words, the jury wanted to modify the behavior of all future potential defendants in order to protect individuals from bodily harm in similar circumstances. Awards of punitive damages are actually quite rare in civil litigation, and large monetary awards are even rarer. Statistical studies by law professors and the Department of Justice have found that punitive damages are only awarded in about 2 percent of civil cases that go to trial, and that the median punitive damage award is between $38,000 and $50,000.[11]

BURDENS OF PROOF IN A CIVIL CASE

There are two burdens of proof in a civil case, depending on the nature of the dispute. **Burden of proof** means the level of evidence that the plaintiff in a civil case (or the prosecutor in a criminal case) must prove in order to win the case. Generally the plaintiff must prove a civil case by a preponderance of the evidence or perhaps by a higher standard known as clear and convincing evidence. **Preponderance of the evidence** means that the plaintiff proves the case by tipping the scales of justice just a little in one direction. This is by far the most common burden of proof in civil cases. At times, the law may require the plaintiff to prove the case by a higher standard, known as **clear and convincing evidence**. For example, in *Cruzan v. Director, Missouri Department of Health* (1990), the Supreme Court upheld a Missouri statute requiring that medical patients who could not communicate their own wishes would not have their life support removed unless there was clear and convincing evidence of the patient's preferences. In these circumstances, clear and convincing evidence generally meant written proof or other absolutely clear statements of the patient's intent. Recall that the burden of proof in a criminal case is guilt beyond a reasonable doubt.

Perhaps an American football field analogy will help explain the differences among the three burdens of proof. For guilt beyond a reasonable doubt, the team's offense (the prosecutor) must move the ball across the opponent's goal line. For clear and convincing evidence, the plaintiff must move the ball across the twenty-five-yard line. For preponderance of evidence, the plaintiff must merely move the football beyond the fifty-yard line.

STEPS IN THE CIVIL CASE PROCESS

The civil lawsuit process is part of our adversary system of justice. Each party to the case is represented by his or her own lawyer. The lawyer's job is to represent the best interests of the client. However, there is no constitutional right to a lawyer in a civil case in the United States. There is also no right to a speedy trial in civil litigation. Figure 6.2 provides an overview of the steps in the civil case process. Each step will be discussed in more detail in the following sections.

Many civil disputes are never taken to court because the harmed party cannot afford a lawyer or the expense of a trial. Estimates are that as much as 80 percent of the civil legal needs of low-income people go unmet in the United States today.[12] See Chapter 4 for more details about legal services for the poor.

The Initial Stages of a Civil Lawsuit

The first step in the civil trial process is the filing of a complaint in court by the plaintiff. In the **complaint**, the plaintiff must explain the nature of the dispute and note the remedies being sought. Normally, the complaint will also discuss the threshold requirements for the case to go forward, including the issues of jurisdiction, standing, proper venue, mootness, and ripeness.

FIGURE 6.2 Steps in a Civil Trial

Plaintiff files a complaint
↓
Service of process on the defendant
↓
Defendant files an answer to the complaint
↓
Pretrial conferences among the plaintiff's lawyer, the defense lawyer, and the judge
↓
Discovery of evidence, including depositions, interrogatories, medical examinations, and document delivery
↓
Additional pretrial conferences as necessary among the plaintiff's lawyer, the defense lawyer, and the judge
↓
Voir dire to choose a jury in many cases
↓
Trial
↓
Verdict
↓
Post-trial motions such as a judgment notwithstanding the verdict
↓
Compliance with or enforcement of the court's judgment

After the complaint is filed, the plaintiff must follow the local rules for **service of process**. This means that the defendant must be notified of the lawsuit and given a copy of the complaint. Television shows love to show process servers surprising unknowing civil defendants when they "serve the papers" on them. Usually, service of process is not that dramatic. At times and in certain places it is done by law enforcement personnel. Sometimes the service of process means that notice of the lawsuit is published in the section of a newspaper devoted to such legal notices. Nevertheless, it is the plaintiff's responsibility to make sure that the defendant is properly notified of the lawsuit.

The defendant then files an **answer** with the court explaining his or her view of the issues in the dispute. The defendant may also countersue in the answer, making the case more complicated because technically both sides are acting as a plaintiff in the dispute. Together, the complaint and the answer form the **pleadings** in the case. If the defendant neglects to file an answer in the case after proper service of process, then the judge can immediately issue a **default judgment** against the defendant, meaning that the plaintiff receives the requested remedies without further deliberation by the court.

If further deliberation is needed, the next step is usually a series of pretrial conferences with the judge, the plaintiff's lawyer, and the defendant's lawyer. If both sides can stipulate to (that is, come to an agreement on) any of the facts or issues in the case, they can narrow down the range of issues in the dispute. The judge will then usually hear any preliminary motions, such as on the threshold requirements (jurisdiction, venue, and standing). If the judge sees the case as frivolous or otherwise without merit, he or she can dismiss the lawsuit immediately.[13] The judge will also set the parameters for the discovery phase of the trial, as discussed in more detail below. In rare cases, the judge may also issue a judgment based solely on the pleadings if he or she feels that the law compels a decision in favor of one of the parties at that point in the process.

The Discovery Process in a Civil Case

In the discovery stage of a civil case, both sides can learn more information about the lawsuit and the issues it presents. The two sides must share information with each other. Depositions can be part of the discovery phase. In a **deposition**, the lawyers question potential witnesses in the case under oath with everyone present in the same room. Although a judge is not present for a deposition, the questions are asked under oath and a court reporter or stenographer is present to record the witnesses' answers for the record. Attorneys for both sides are present at a deposition. Any disagreements that arise during a deposition will be settled by the judge at a later time. Another form of discovery is the **interrogatory**, meaning that each party may present the other side with written questions, which must be answered in writing. **Production of documents** may also be required during discovery, where each side's lawyers have the right to review relevant documents in the case. The process may also include **medical examinations**, depending on the nature of the case and the details of the lawsuit. Discovery is crucial to the success or failure of the lawsuit, and each side tries to get as much information as it can without unnecessarily disclosing critical information to the other side. As journalist Reynolds Holding has noted, "The real action, the stuff that wins or loses a case, is far more likely to happen in a conference room than in a courtroom."[14]

Critics of the civil lawsuit process often argue that the side with the most resources can use the discovery process to delay the trial or even to discourage the plaintiff from continuing the lawsuit. Discovery can be time-consuming and expensive—lawyers can demand answers to a large number of interrogatories, one side may give truckloads of unsorted documents to the other side, and parties may have to hire expensive experts to help the lawyers make sense of what they are learning during discovery.[15]

After the discovery process ends, there is usually a pretrial conference attended by the judge and the lawyers for both sides. In some places, this pretrial conference is mandatory. Here the judge further clarifies the issues in the case and decides any pending evidentiary questions. It is a perfect opportunity for the parties to settle the case before proceeding to trial. Some judges will even strongly suggest that the parties settle the case before it goes any further. Judges are certainly more willing to participate in negotiations over settlements in civil cases than in plea bargains for criminal cases.[16] Most judges will almost automatically approve a settlement reached through negotiations by the parties in a civil lawsuit.

The Trial in a Civil Case

If the parties cannot reach an agreement, then the case proceeds to the trial phase. In some complex civil cases such as patent cases and antitrust cases, there is no right to a jury at trial. In what is known as a **bench trial**, the judge will hear the case without a jury. Juries are not permitted in certain types of civil cases, such as bankruptcy proceedings, family law cases, probates of wills, and divorce cases. A higher proportion of civil cases are heard in bench trials than are criminal cases. In 2010, 32 percent of civil cases heard in federal courts were bench trials, while only 14 percent of criminal cases in federal courts that year did not have juries.[17] If the type of case permits a jury, it is usually up to the defendant to decide whether to opt for one, although sometimes either party may request a jury trial in a civil case.

The process for seating a civil jury is very similar to the process for seating a jury in a criminal case. The court will select a **jury pool**, which is the group from which the potential jury is drawn. The potential jurors in the jury pool will be summoned to the courthouse. The same jury pool is usually used to summon potential jurors for both criminal and civil cases. In civil cases, there is the same **voir dire** process as found in criminal trials. The plaintiff's lawyer and the defense's lawyer both get to question the potential jurors individually, as does the judge. The judge decides which members of the jury pool will be excused through **challenges for cause**, sometimes at the request of one of the lawyers in the case. Jurors are excused for cause if the judge feels that they cannot be impartial in the case, perhaps because they have a relationship with one of the parties or because they have filed similar lawsuits in the past. Judges may also exclude individuals for cause if they would suffer physical or economic burdens by serving on the jury. And like in criminal trials, each side gets a limited number of **peremptory challenges**, in which lawyers can excuse a potential juror without giving a reason.[18] Recall that the U.S. Supreme Court has said that no potential juror can be excused solely because of race or sex, but this principle is very hard to enforce when lawyers use peremptory challenges. The voir dire process is a uniquely American phenomenon—it is quite rare in Canada and the United Kingdom, which also have jury trials fairly often.[19]

The main role of juries in civil cases is to decide specific facts in specific cases, while leaving broader legal questions to the judge. Civil juries may also recommend appropriate remedies, including the amounts of compensatory and punitive damages, if they find the defendant liable. The United States is the only major democracy that allows jurors both to determine liability and to set the level of monetary damages to be paid to the successful plaintiff in a civil lawsuit.[20] Journalist and author Stephen Adler describes the role of juries in civil cases thus: "Only in a jury trial can each person's case be treated as unique, as worthy of a fresh look and an independent calculation of its value, based on the best judgment of people unburdened by either expertise or direct self-interest."[21] Although, as noted, very few civil cases actually end in a jury trial—more than 85 percent of lawsuits filed are eventually settled out of court—and some cases can never be heard in front of a jury at all, in many lawsuits the decisions of all of the actors at the various stages of the civil process are clearly affected by the potential of a jury trial.

Civil juries also permit average individuals to participate in the judicial process, allowing them to feel more a part of the democratic system of government, as well as to serve as a check on governmental actors such as judges. As Alexis de Tocqueville wrote, "Juries, especially civil juries, instill some of the habits of the judicial mind into every citizen, and just those habits are the very best way of preparing people to be free. [. . .] Juries invest each citizen with a sort of magisterial office; they make all men feel that they have duties toward society and that they take a share in its government. By making men pay attention to things other than their own affairs, they combat that individual selfishness which is like rust in society."[22]

Jury service also has great educational value to the jurors. As Tocqueville again wrote, "I do not know whether a jury is useful to the litigants, but I am sure it is very good for those who have to decide the case. I regard it as one of the most effective means of popular education at society's disposal."[23]

Once the jury is seated, if there is one, the trial can begin. This phase begins with each side making opening statements. Then the plaintiff's side presents its case by introducing evidence obtained during the discovery phase and by questioning witnesses. Since the role of trial courts is to answer questions of fact, the plaintiff's lawyer will present the facts in such a way as to prove that case, usually by the standard of a preponderance of evidence. At the end of the plaintiff's presentation, the defense lawyer will almost always move for a **directed verdict**. A directed verdict can occur when the plaintiff has not presented enough evidence to meet the burden of proof. If the plaintiff's case is insufficient according to law, then the judge will grant the defendant's motion and end the trial at that point with a verdict favoring the defendant. In most trials, however, the plaintiff would never have gotten this far without having sufficient evidence, and the judge almost always denies the motion for a directed verdict. Then the defendant's lawyer presents the rebuttal evidence. The trial ends with closing arguments from each side's lawyer. The judge may then give instructions to the jury to help them in their deliberations. These **jury instructions** are often suggested by the lawyers on each side, or there may be boilerplate instructions used over and over in a specific jurisdiction.

After the jury deliberates, it hands down the verdict in the case. Recall that the verdict in a civil case determines not only who wins and who loses but also what legal remedies a successful plaintiff should be given. Although the jury can decide on the amount of compensatory and punitive damages a winning plaintiff will receive, as well as other remedies such as restitution, only judges can order injunctive or coercive relief. After the jury's verdict, the defendant may move for a **judgment notwithstanding the verdict** if he or she can convince the judge that the jury verdict violates the law. For example, many states limit the amount of punitive damages to a certain percentage or ratio of the compensatory damages.

The majority of states that have set a limit on punitive damages have decided that punitive damages cannot be more than three times the compensatory damage figure.[24] If the jury awards more in punitive damages than the law allows or the judge feels is just, the judge can then grant the defendant's motion for a judgment notwithstanding the verdict. In other words, the judge can ignore the jury's verdict in a civil case or reduce the damages awarded if he or she believes that the law compels such a result.

Civil Judgments

At the end of the civil case process, the judge grants a judgment to the successful plaintiff. The **judgment** states the legal remedies that are now available to the winning party. Many losing parties voluntarily comply with the judgment of the court, but at times the winning party may have great difficulty collecting on the judgment. This problem seems to be especially acute in the area of child support payments. The judgment is also usually not immediately enforced if the losing party files an appeal in the case. The appellate court may then decide whether the trial court's judgment was proper or not.

This process can be quite lengthy. For example, in 2010 the average time for a civil suit in federal court to go from filing the complaint to trial was more than two years. In 2009, the average time between filing and trial in the Illinois state court system was over three years.[25] Some complicated cases such as antitrust suits can take years or perhaps even decades to conclude.[26]

JURIES AND JURY REFORM

Jury reform has become an important political issue in many areas. Jury reform efforts are generally of two types. One family of jury reform proposals are designed to make the jury pool more inclusive and to improve the quality of jury deliberations. A second family of jury reforms includes so-called tort reform proposals, which are generally designed to reduce the discretion of juries in civil litigation, especially around the issues of monetary damages.

The U.S. Constitution protects the right to a trial by jury in both civil and criminal cases, and juries are deeply ingrained in American legal culture. Juries are far less common elsewhere in the world; some estimate that 80 percent of jury trials worldwide take place in the United States.[27] In our adversary system, juries must decide how to determine the truth from each side's presentation of the facts at trial. Juries thus add a sense of democracy to the legal system. As one scholar notes, "No other institution of government rivals the jury in placing power so directly in the hands of citizens."[28] According to some estimates, over a third of Americans are likely to have served on a jury at some point in their lifetimes.[29] Public opinion polls consistently show that those who have the most favorable view of juries are those who have had prior jury service themselves.[30] Some studies have even shown that Americans who serve on juries are more likely to participate in political activities and vote in elections after their jury service.[31] But many Americans try very hard to avoid jury service if they can.[32] As one scholar has colorfully proclaimed, "Trial by jury is about the best of democracy and about the worst of democracy."[33]

The Jury Pool

The jury in both civil and criminal cases must be drawn from a representative cross section of the community.[34] Court administrators must start by creating a jury pool. Traditionally, juries were chosen from among the most prominent men in a community. In 1968, Congress passed legislation requiring that juries in the federal courts be drawn instead from a fair cross section of the community. In 1975, the U.S. Supreme Court declared that state courts had to make their jury pools representative of the broader population of their areas.[35] How, then, can we make the jury pool more representative of the community at large so that the trial jury is actually a jury of one's peers?

Today, almost all citizens except minors and convicted criminals are eligible to be jurors. In creating the jury pool, the courts tend to draw from a variety of lists: those registered to vote, people with driver licenses, people receiving utility services, those receiving government benefits such as welfare, students from local universities, those with gun licenses or hunting licenses, or even the phone book. The most accurate list of potential jurors, the list of taxpayers, is almost always unavailable to the courts because privacy laws prevent tax departments from sharing this information with other governmental entities. Some courts will automatically exclude certain individuals from their jury pool, such as lawyers, medical doctors, judges, or those who cannot physically show up for jury duty because they live in nursing homes or other institutions. Courts try very hard to make their jury pools as representative as possible, but there are limits on how far they can go to make the jury pool truly a cross section of the community.[36]

From this large group of people in the jury pool, almost every jurisdiction chooses those to be summoned for jury duty by random selection methods, and sends out summonses requiring people to appear at the courthouse for potential jury service. However, in many cities across the United States fewer than half of those summoned for jury duty actually show up at the courthouse. This no-show problem can create a bias in who actually serves on a jury.[37] To combat this, some states have tried to make jury service more attractive by increasing the amount of money they pay jurors for their work. Jury compensation now ranges from about $5 per day to $50 per day, depending on the location. Other states require employers to give employees time off from their regular job for jury service. Some states have greatly increased their jury summons enforcement efforts, giving law enforcement personnel the authority to arrest those who try to avoid jury duty. Others have proposed a "Juror Appreciation Week" in order to educate the public about the benefits of jury duty.

Reforms in Jury Deliberations

Some proposed jury reforms deal with the quality of the jury's deliberations in a case. Some of the frequently mentioned reforms in this area include allowing the jurors to take notes during the trial, giving them notebooks with lists of witness names and key points of their testimony, and allowing them to ask questions of the judge. The Arizona courts were the leaders in using the so-called educational model of jury reforms.[38] According to a 2002 study, forty-eight states now allow jurors to take notes during trials.[39] Whether jurors can ask questions of the judge during the trial is generally at the discretion of the judge. One study found that about 39 percent of state trial judges allow jurors to ask them questions during the trial. The same study found that 21 percent of state judges now use so-called plain English jury instructions in order to make it easier for jurors to understand the issues in a case.[40] Many judges also provide guidebooks to jurors that define common legal terms and provide suggestions for deliberation that draw upon social science research in this area.[41]

Tort Reform

A very different approach to jury reform involves various tort reform proposals. Generally, **tort reform** features efforts to make it more difficult for plaintiffs to win money damage awards in civil lawsuits or perhaps even to prevent them from filing suit in the first place. Starting around the end of World War II, many state supreme courts took on the task of liberalizing their state tort laws, thus making it easier for plaintiffs in tort cases to prove their claims. Then, starting in the 1980s, many state legislatures attempted to rein in these court-initiated changes in tort law in order to protect the defendants in tort cases, especially wealthy and corporate defendants.[42] For many conservatives, state tort laws are today seen as a form of business regulation that distorts free market principles and harms the economy.[43]

Tort reform proposals generally limit the types of cases that can be heard in court or greatly reduce jury discretion in those tort cases that do go to trial. For example, some tort reform proposals would substantially increase the penalties for lawyers who file frivolous lawsuits. Others would require that a plaintiff who loses in civil litigation would have to pay the attorney fees for the defendant. This "loser pays" system is what is used in the United Kingdom and various other countries that have far fewer civil lawsuits than we do in the United States. Between 1986 and 2002, forty-five states and the District of Columbia enacted some form of limits on tort lawsuits.[44]

There is also a feeling among various business groups, medical doctors, and others that civil juries are out of control in our society. They cite very large monetary awards from juries in cases such as the McDonald's hot coffee case, discussed earlier in this chapter. Many Americans also feel that large jury awards in tort cases reward unworthy and greedy plaintiffs who do not deserve this newfound wealth.[45] Critics of jury awards in civil cases fear that the jury makes decisions more on the basis of emotion, sympathy, and prejudice rather than according to the law. As Jeffrey Abramson, a scholar of American juries, has stated, "Jury verdicts are notoriously unpredictable, ad hoc, arbitrary, idiosyncratic, and whimsical. Like cases are not treated alike."[46]

Some advocates of tort reform want to eliminate punitive damages in certain types of cases, for example medical malpractice suits. Other proposals would severely limit the dollar amounts for punitive damages that juries can award to victorious plaintiffs. Some suggestions would limit the amount of money plaintiffs could receive for pain and suffering, even though such money is considered a compensatory remedy. Other tort reform ideas address the **contingency fee** system, in which attorneys are paid a percentage of any monetary award they win for their client. Usually this contingency fee is about one-third of the monetary judgment (including both compensatory and punitive damages) that the successful plaintiff receives. Many argue that the contingency fee system allows plaintiffs without many resources to file civil lawsuits that would not be filed if the party had to pay the lawyers up front. Other tort reform proposals would greatly restrict class action suits.[47] Some of these ideas have already been enacted into law by various state legislatures and by the U.S. Congress.

There is a great deal of controversy about whether our civil litigation system is out of control. Most of the lawsuits brought up as examples are tort cases. In 2005, for example, a spokesperson for the U.S. Chamber of Commerce declared,

"In the last decade, we've had a litigation explosion in this country that is unmatched in the industrialized world."[48] Many argue that this litigation explosion is fueled by Americans who think they can quickly get rich if they win the right lawsuit. This can make Americans seem to be a litigious people who "will sue each other at the slightest provocation."[49] Politicians have certainly sounded this theme many times. Pete Wilson, the former Republican governor of California, has been quoted as saying, "The lawyer's briefcase has become a weapon of terror."[50] Former president George H. W. Bush has been quoted as saying, "Americans are suing each other too much and caring for each other too little."[51] His son, George W. Bush, said during his presidency, "We're a litigious society; everybody is suing, it seems like." The result is to "terrorize small business owners" and drive medical doctors out of their practices. President Bush concluded, "No one has ever been healed by a frivolous lawsuit."[52]

While most tort reform efforts have taken place in state legislatures, the U.S. Congress has also long considered tort reform proposals. These would in essence nationalize tort law and override many state trial court decisions. The technical legal term for this concept is federal **preemption** of state laws, meaning that under the U.S. Constitution's Supremacy Clause federal law preempts enforcement of any contrary state laws.[53] The U.S. House Judiciary Committee, at the time under the control of Republicans, held six hearings between May 2011 and April 2013 on tort reform issues. In a March 5, 2013, hearing on the effects of excessive litigation on U.S. global competitiveness, Judiciary Committee chair Rep. Bob Goodlatte (R-Va.) stated that his committee was

> doing what we can to remove the crushing burden that excessive litigation costs impose on our global competitiveness, economic growth, and our ability to create and retain jobs. . . . Unfortunately, the United States has become the world's most litigious country. This litigiousness has created what amounts to a "tort tax," which imposes an added cost on every product Americans purchase and every service we consume. We need a civil justice system that deters wrongdoers and fully compensates victims. But a prosperous free enterprise economy also depends on a tort system that is efficient and free of meritless litigation and excessive damage awards.[54]

The U.S. House Judiciary Committee has approved various federal tort reform bills over the years, including a bill in February 2011 that would have required that states adopt a three-year statute of limitations on medical lawsuits, cap noneconomic damages at $250,000 in these cases, and limit punitive damages to $250,000 or twice the economic damages, whichever was greater. The bill would have applied to lawsuits in both federal and state courts, but its primary focus was states that did not already have their own tort reform laws.[55] Although medical malpractice cases only constitute about 2 percent of all civil cases, they receive a lot of attention in tort reform efforts because the medical community wants protection from what they perceive to be out-of-control medical malpractice decisions. The full House of Representatives has passed various tort reform bills recently, including various forms of medical malpractice reforms, but these bills have always died in the U.S. Senate.

Trial lawyers oppose tort reform because they argue that civil litigation not only compensates victims for their injuries but also provides a mechanism for behavior modification. Without the courts and the plaintiff bar to protect them, innocent Americans would be overrun by negligent doctors, swindlers, polluters, and manufacturers of unsafe products. They also claim that the contingency fee system used in many personal injury cases actually allows plaintiffs without huge resources at their disposal to file necessary lawsuits. Trial lawyers in this context are generally personal injury lawyers who represent plaintiffs in tort cases filed against corporations and wealthy individuals. Trial lawyers generally support the Democratic Party, while the business and medical interests advocating tort reform generally support the Republican Party. Thus, in many states, and at the federal level, tort reform has become a partisan issue.

In an attempt to provide empirical analysis and perhaps avoid getting involved in the partisan disputes over this issue, a variety of academic studies have attempted to refute the agenda of the tort reform movement. For example, one study found that plaintiffs rarely win large judgments against corporations for selling defective products.[56] Another study found that juries generally produce reasonable outcomes in civil cases.[57] Jurors in cases where businesses are the defendants tend to be more sympathetic to the business concerns than to the plaintiff, according to one influential study.[58] One research work blamed the media for sensationalizing and distorting the work of civil juries.[59] Other studies attempted to provide academic "antidotes" to largely misleading anecdotes about tort reform.[60] Many academics saw the tort reform movement as an effort to increase the advantages of those with extensive experience in litigation and to further disadvantage those who have limited contact with the legal system.[61]

ALTERNATIVES TO GOING TO COURT

As we've seen, the civil lawsuit process can be so time-consuming and costly that most civil cases filed in court in the United States are settled before trial. Sometimes plaintiffs do not wish to go to trial at all but file suit merely to demonstrate to the other party in the dispute that they are serious about resolving the issue. This next section will focus on alternatives to civil cases (known collectively as **alternative dispute resolution**) that do not require a court order to end the dispute.[62]

One of the first things that a party to a dispute has to calculate is whether it is worth pursuing a resolution to the problem. Many people may decide just to ignore the potential conflict, possibly because of the time and money involved in filing a lawsuit.

Parties to a dispute may try to solve the problem privately by contacting the other party informally to see if a solution to the conflict can be found quickly and easily. For example, many retailers have return policies that allow the consumer to return an item with few questions asked, especially if the consumer still has the sales receipt. Another example is when both parties agree not to report a minor car accident to their respective insurance companies, but instead work out some plan for fixing the cars without filing a formal insurance claim. A more formal variation on this approach is to have a lawyer draft a letter to the other party suggesting a solution to the conflict. In many circumstances this is enough to encourage the parties to find a compromise to end the dispute.

Third-Party Dispute Resolution Approaches

One clear alternative to filing a lawsuit is **mediation**. This means that the parties to the dispute agree to have a neutral third party help them find a negotiated solution to the problem. The mediator hears both sides of the conflict and then suggests a compromise solution. The parties must agree to all aspects of the mediator's recommendation before it goes into force. The mediator can also meet with each party individually in what are known as **ex parte communications**, meaning that the other party is not privy to those conversations. The parties are under no obligation to accept the mediator's recommendations. The mediator may be a professional trained in the subject matter of the dispute or may just be a helpful third party. Religious officials can sometimes function as informal mediators, for example, as can marriage counselors. Resident assistants in college dormitories can also serve this function when they help college roommates work out conflicts between them.

Mediation has the advantage that it is usually far less costly than litigation. The proceedings are private, which makes them attractive to many parties. Mediation may be advantageous when the parties wish to preserve their future relationship with each other. Mediation is a less contentious form of dispute resolution than some of the other alternatives. The aggrieved party can still file a lawsuit if the mediation process is unsuccessful.[63]

Another alternative to going to court is **arbitration**. This involves a neutral third party listening to both sides of the conflict. Unlike mediation, however, both parties must agree in advance that they will abide by the arbitrator's decisions. The arbitrator should not meet with or communicate with the parties individually (i.e., no ex parte communications). The arbitrator is almost always a trained professional with experience in the subject matter of the dispute who understands the industry norms. For example, many salary disputes between professional athletes and their teams are handled through arbitration. These arbitrators are quite familiar with the salary practices of similarly situated teams and athletes with similar records and skills. Most credit card companies are now requiring arbitration to resolve any disputes between the consumer and the credit card companies. When consumers apply for a new credit card, they must sign an agreement acknowledging that any conflict between the cardholder and the issuing bank company must be resolved through arbitration. In this situation, the arbitrator is someone who is quite familiar with banking practices. This is how the major banks avoid lawsuits. There is some question, however, about whether this arbitration process is fair to consumers.

If the parties will have no future relationship, arbitration is often preferred over mediation, even though mediation is considered a less intrusive form of dispute resolution. Arbitration is also the norm in certain industries and professions. Arbitration and mediation have been used in the United States for many years,[64] although their popularity has increased since the 1970s.[65]

There is also the so-called **rent-a-judge** option. In these situations, the parties choose a lawyer or former judge who agrees to hear both sides and then suggest a decision based on the law. Most of these instances are similar to arbitration, in that the parties agree in advance to abide by the decision of the rent-a-judge. Famous examples of this approach are television shows such as *Judge Judy* or *The People's Court*. While these programs can be entertaining, they can also serve as legitimate conflict resolution devices. What actually happens in these cases is that the parties agree in advance to follow the judge's ruling in the dispute.

The main difference between arbitration and the rent-a-judge option is that in the former case, arbitrators usually make decisions based on industry standards and other norms, but, in the latter, judges or lawyers make decisions based on legal reasoning using legal rules and sources of law. The parties will agree in advance which state's laws apply in the case. Apart from the television shows, rent-a-judge proceedings are private, thus appealing to parties who want to avoid the publicity of a trial in a regular court. This process is often much quicker and less expensive than formal litigation.

So When Don't Cases Settle?

Given all these alternatives to formal litigation, under what circumstances do cases actually go to trial if it is not required by law? Civil cases that go to trial almost always involve parties that want no future relationship. If the relationship between the parties can be salvaged, then they usually settle the dispute before it goes all the way through a costly trial. A case may go to trial because each side may feel it has truth and justice on its side. A case may also go to trial as a delaying tactic, given the cost and complexities associated with the discovery phase; some parties may refuse to settle in order to wear the other side down to the point that they drop the suit. This has been the tactic of some drug manufacturers and tobacco companies, who felt that they were better off fighting each individual case instead of settling any of them.

Cases may also go to trial when the parties see clear benefits from the publicity that a trial can bring. This is often true when the party is more interested in the long-term benefit than the short-term win. When parties are using the courts to advance a political agenda, then the cases almost always go to trial. In fact, cause lawyers may not only want a trial verdict but also may be seeking an appellate court decision in order to create a precedent in a certain area of the law.

DO THE "HAVES" COME OUT AHEAD?

One question for those who study judicial politics is whether there are any patterns in who wins and who loses in civil litigation. In 1974, Marc Galanter published an extremely influential article entitled "Why the 'Haves' Come Out Ahead."[66] This article has spurred an enormous number of research projects in the law-and-society tradition. All of these research studies consider the question of whether the prior experience of litigants affects their probability of winning in civil lawsuits.

Galanter divided litigants in civil lawsuits into two groups: repeat players and one-shotters. A **repeat player** has already had a great deal of litigation experience and anticipates having further repeated contact with the courts. Repeat players may be corporations, governmental organizations, or interest groups. For example, the ultimate repeat player at the U.S. Supreme Court is the U.S. solicitor general, who is the lawyer for the executive branch at the Supreme

Court of the United States. These repeat players either employ lawyers in-house or have long-standing relationships with lawyers in private law firms. Repeat players may be far less concerned about the specific lawsuit in which they are currently involved than they are with their long-term litigation strategy. They want judges to create legal rules that will help them in their future cases. They often have sustained informal contacts with judges and other decision makers. According to Galanter, repeat players approach potential civil disputes in the following manner:

> Repeat players usually have low stakes in the outcome of any particular case and have the resources to pursue long-term interests. They can anticipate legal problems and can often structure transactions and compile a record to justify their actions. They develop expertise and have access to specialists who are skilled in dealing with particular types of cases or issues. They enjoy economies of scale and encounter low start-up costs for any particular case. [. . .] The credibility and legitimacy that flow from repeated contacts [with the courts] may help to sustain a repeat player's claims.[67]

On the other hand, **one-shotters** deal with the legal system quite infrequently. They might be a business or an organization, but they are most likely to be individuals. They usually do not have regular relationships with a lawyer, and they pursue a short-term litigation strategy. By definition, they have had little prior contact or experience with the courts. They want to resolve the specific dispute before them in the most favorable way possible. Thus, they are keenly interested in winning the lawsuit in which they are involved.[68]

Repeat players usually have far greater power than their one-shot opponents. They certainly have more experience with the courts and are better known there. Repeat players also know how to use the civil litigation process to their advantage, and they often have superior resources, which allow them to hire the best available attorneys and to incur legal expenses, such as those associated with extensive discovery and expert witnesses, that may increase the chances of winning at trial.[69]

Repeat players and one-shotters therefore have very different approaches to civil litigation. One-shotters will often settle a lawsuit that a repeat player would not—especially if the case in question would harm the long-term interests of the repeat player. Repeat players might settle low-visibility cases in which they expect an unfavorable verdict or in which going to trial might set a bad precedent for them. Rarely is one lawsuit that important to repeat players. However, repeat players are also likely to fight hard in other suits that could cause long-term problems for them. They are not overly concerned about the outcome in any particular case, focusing instead on the results of all of their cases taken collectively.[70] One-shotters may find the litigation strategies of repeat players to be confusing and strange if they cannot see the big picture themselves and anticipate the long-term needs of these actors.

Galanter argued that when one-shotters sue repeat players, the repeat players usually have enormous advantages and therefore rarely lose such lawsuits. The American adversary system assumes that the lawyers on each side have equal skills and resources available to them. This is likely to be true when a repeat player sues another repeat player, or when a one-shotter sues another one-shotter. However, Galanter argued that scholars needed to pay more attention to the lawsuits where the two sides are not equal in litigation experience or in resources available to them. The fact that there is no constitutional right to a lawyer or a right to a speedy trial in civil cases means that repeat players can often use delaying tactics to their advantage. Crowded dockets can spur judges and legislators to impose restrictive rules in order to discourage litigation.

Galanter does not say that the "haves" always win; rather, they have incredible advantages in our civil litigation system.[71] However, a variety of studies have shown that governmental actors (the ultimate repeat players) are more successful in civil litigation than are businesses or other organizations, and that organizational interests are far more successful than are individuals.[72] One study found that between 1925 and 1988, governments won about 68 percent of the time in the U.S. courts of appeals, business interests won just under 50 percent of the time, and individuals won less than 40 percent of their cases.[73] The findings are similar for civil cases in both trial courts and appellate courts.

One mechanism that might level the playing field a bit for one-shotters is the **contingency fee**. The plaintiff usually does not need to pay his or her lawyer up front; only if the lawsuit is successful will the lawyer get a certain percentage of the judgment, usually one-third of the money damages awarded. Almost all tort cases filed by individuals are handled on a contingency fee basis. After the trial, the winnings are paid directly to the lawyer in the case, and the lawyer then pays the plaintiff his or her share of the money damages awarded. Lawyers like contingency fees because they have no difficulties collecting their fees when due, and clients like them because they have no out-of-pocket expenses for the case.[74] It is these contingency fee arrangements that are usually being described in television commercials that state clients can get free consultations and pay no money up front. Lawyers who work on a contingency fee basis may try to settle cases as soon as possible because they don't want the financial risks of a long and drawn-out trial where the outcome is uncertain. But contingency fees do allow plaintiffs without many resources to sue wealthier and more powerful repeat players.[75]

Another mechanism for increasing the odds that one-shotters will win against repeat players is the award of punitive damages to successful civil plaintiffs, in the hopes of discouraging the same kind of behavior in the repeat player or in others.

CHAPTER SUMMARY

This chapter examined the process in civil trials. Civil law in this country helps to define the duties that private citizens owe to each other. Some civil cases such as a divorce require a court order, while other civil cases can be settled without going to court in a process similar to plea bargaining in criminal cases. About 85 percent of all civil cases settle without going to trial.

This chapter looked at the broad categories of civil cases, the goals of civil litigation, and the remedies that plaintiffs seek in these lawsuits. The chapter then compared the standards of proof in civil cases with the prosecutor's burden of proof in criminal cases. It also explored the role of juries in civil litigation and various proposals for jury reform, before moving on to a discussion of the alternatives to going to court. Finally, the chapter concluded with a look at the question of whether the "haves" come out ahead in civil trials.

For Further Reading

Abramson, Jeffrey. 1994. *We, the Jury: The Jury System and the Ideal of Democracy*. New York: Basic Books.

Burke, Thomas F. 2002. *Lawyers, Lawsuits, and Legal Rights*. Berkeley: University of California Press.

Burns, Robert P. 2009. *The Death of the American Trial*. Chicago: University of Chicago Press.

Gastil, John, E. Pierre Deess, Philip J. Weiser, and Cindy Simmons. 2010. *The Jury and Democracy: How Jury Deliberation Promotes Civic Engagement and Political Participation*. New York: Oxford University Press.

Haltom, William, and Michael McCann. 2004. *Distorting the Law: Politics, the Media, and the Litigation Crisis*. Chicago: University of Chicago Press.

Hans, Valerie P. 2000. *Business on Trial: The Civil Jury and Corporate Responsibility*. New Haven: Yale University Press.

Kritzer, Herbert M. 1990. *The Justice Broker: Lawyers and Ordinary Litigation*. New York: Oxford University Press.

————. 1998. *Legal Advocacy: Lawyers and Nonlawyers at Work*. Ann Arbor: University of Michigan Press.

Kritzer, Herbert M., and Susan S. Silbey, eds. 2003. *In Litigation: Do the "Haves" Still Come Out Ahead?* Stanford: Stanford University Press.

Sunstein, Cass, Reid Hastie, John W. Payne, David A. Schkade, and W. Kip Viscusi, eds. 2002. *Punitive Damages: How Juries Decide*. Chicago: University of Chicago Press.

The Appellate Court Process

Appellate courts serve two basic functions in the United States: they correct errors that occurred in the trial courts, and they create precedent for all the courts below them in the judicial hierarchy. While error correction is relatively routine and the appellate courts can handle many cases without extensive deliberation, the creation of precedent requires the judges on appellate courts to make important public policy decisions. This public policy function is often of great interest to political scientists and other sociolegal scholars. This chapter will explore the processes that appellate courts use in their decision making.

While appellate courts may have **original jurisdiction** over limited types of cases, meaning that the cases originate in the appellate courts, the vast majority of cases in appellate courts come to them on appeal from lower courts through their **appellate jurisdiction**. Since all litigants have an absolute right to one appeal, many appellate courts have a mandatory docket, meaning that these courts must hear all appeals in order to make sure that there were no errors at trial. Appellate courts in the United States accept the facts as determined by the trial court, but they will correct any errors of law that occurred in the court below. The U.S. circuit courts of appeals have a mandatory docket, and they collectively resolve more than fifty-six thousand cases per year.[1] The state supreme courts have a mixture of mandatory and discretionary dockets, and these appellate courts collectively hear around a hundred thousand cases per year. In contrast, the U.S. Supreme Court with its discretionary docket hears an average of only seventy-five to eighty-five cases per year. Because the U.S. Supreme Court takes so few cases, the U.S. courts of appeals are usually the last word on federal legal precedents, while the state supreme courts are the last word on state law precedents.

In the United States, appellate courts are structured differently than trial courts. First, in American appellate courts panels of multiple judges hear each case, rather than the single judge who normally presides over a trial. In the U.S. circuit courts of appeals, cases are mostly heard by panels of three randomly selected judges, while state appellate courts have between three and nine judges hearing a single case. The U.S. Supreme Court, of course, has all nine of its justices hear a case unless there is a vacancy on the Court or a justice recuses himself or herself. **Recusal** means that judges may disqualify themselves from a case if there might be a perception that they could not be impartial. For example, Justice Clarence Thomas recused himself from *United States v. Virginia* (1996), the case in which the Supreme Court ruled that women had to be admitted to the Virginia Military Institute, because his son was a student there. In her first year on the Supreme Court, Justice Elena Kagan recused herself from about a third of the cases because she had previously worked on them in her position as solicitor general of the United States. In *Caperton v. Massey* (2009), the U.S. Supreme Court laid out criteria for when state judges should recuse themselves if one of the parties to a case is a major financial contributor to their judicial election campaigns.

Appellate courts also differ from trial courts because most of the work on the appeals courts is done in writing—the appeal is filed through written briefs, and appellate courts issue their opinions in writing. Appellate decisions have two components: the outcome of the case (who wins and who loses) and the reasoning of the opinion. It is the reasoning of the majority of judges on the appellate court that becomes precedent for all future cases brought to the courts below them in the judicial hierarchy. While the outcome of a case before an appellate court is quite important to the parties involved, it is the reasoning of the written opinions that answers the questions of law and thus becomes precedent.

If **oral arguments** occur before appellate judges, their purpose is to clarify the arguments in the written briefs to the court. Oral arguments are one of the few public aspects of decision making on appellate courts, and so the media often focus on these, even though most of the work of appellate courts occurs out of public view.

THE U.S. SUPREME COURT: STRUCTURE AND PROCESS

Perhaps at this point it would be helpful to examine the process that the U.S. Supreme Court follows. Because the U.S. Supreme Court has a discretionary docket, meaning that it decides which cases it will hear and which ones it will refuse to hear, the process is somewhat different from the process in appellate courts with a mandatory docket. While in some ways the steps discussed below are unique to the U.S. Supreme Court, in other ways they are illustrative of the functioning of all appellate courts with discretionary dockets.

A very small number of cases do originate in the U.S. Supreme Court—generally only about one case per year. Article III, Section 2 of the Constitution spells out the original jurisdiction of the Supreme Court. Generally, today this is interpreted to mean cases between the states, cases where a state is a party, and cases involving ambassadors, ministers, and consuls. However, recall that in *Marbury v. Madison* (1803), the Supreme Court held that it is unconstitutional for Congress to add to the original jurisdiction of the Supreme Court. And in *Cohens v. Virginia* (1821), the Supreme Court ruled that under its original jurisdiction it did not have to hear all cases in which a state is a party. Thus, while Congress cannot add to the Supreme Court's original jurisdiction, it can direct those original jurisdiction cases to other courts.[2] So while federal statutes require that the U.S. Supreme Court have both original and exclusive jurisdiction over disputes between the states, meaning that no other court can handle them, those statutes also say that in cases where a state is a party, other courts can hear the case in addition to the Supreme Court. And while the U.S. Supreme Court does have original jurisdiction in cases affecting foreign diplomatic officials, today most such questions are handled by the U.S. Department of State. As a practical matter, today the cases heard by the Supreme Court under its original jurisdiction are generally limited to boundary disputes between the states, such as the question of whether New York or New Jersey should control the gift shop on Ellis Island. The steps that a case follows at the Supreme Court of the United States are summarized in Figure 7.1.

The Writ of Certiorari

Because the U.S. Supreme Court hears so few cases under its original jurisdiction, almost always there must be a final decision from one of the U.S. courts of appeals or from a state supreme court before the U.S. Supreme Court will hear a case. In addition, the U.S. Supreme Court will not take a case from a state supreme court unless there is a federal issue involved.[3] Thus, the state supreme court is the final word on matters of purely state law. For example, when the Supreme Judicial Court of Massachusetts decided that the state constitution required that marriage licenses had to be issued to same-sex couples, the U.S. Supreme Court at the time did not see a federal issue in the case. Thus, the Massachusetts Supreme Court had the last word on interpreting the Massachusetts constitution.

FIGURE 7.1 The Steps in the Process Used by the U.S. Supreme Court

Lower court decision
↓
Writ of certiorari from losing party in court below
↓
Reply brief on certiorari from winning party below
↓
Amicus curiae briefs on certiorari
↓
Law clerk memos for the justices on certiorari
↓
Conference on certiorari
↓
Four votes required to grant writ of certiorari
↓
Briefs on merits from parties
↓
Amicus curiae briefs on merits
↓
Oral arguments
↓
Conference on merits
↓
Preliminary vote on the outcome of the case
↓
Opinion assignment (both majority and dissent)
↓
Opinion drafting
↓
Opinion negotiations
↓
Justices may write concurrences and additional dissents
↓
Final vote occurs when justices sign written opinion
↓
Final opinions released to the public

The losing party in the lower court files a petition for a **writ of certiorari**, which is the formal written request for the U.S. Supreme Court to hear the case. The winning party at the lower court files a reply brief, explaining why the U.S. Supreme Court should refuse to take the case. The Court also accepts **amicus curiae briefs** in support of or opposition to the writ of certiorari. These formal "friend of the court" briefs are often used by interest groups and others to try to lobby the Supreme Court. A very special type of amicus curiae brief can come from the **solicitor general,** who is the lawyer for the federal executive branch in cases before the Supreme Court of the United States (for more details on the role of the solicitor general, see Chapter 11). The U.S. Supreme Court receives more than ten thousand petitions for writs of certiorari each year.

In order to assist the justices with the task of sorting through all these petitions to find the few cases that the Court will actually hear, the law clerks for the justices read all these submissions. Since 1972, instead of having all the law clerks read all the petitions and the accompanying materials, almost all of the justices have pooled their clerks. This means that only one clerk from the entire Court prepares a memo for all the justices spelling out the importance of a particular case and the legal issues it raises.[4] Some justices prefer to keep their clerks out of the pool, and they divide all of the petitions for writs of certiorari among their own four clerks.[5] At the moment, Justice Samuel Alito's clerks are not part of the pool; previously, Justices Thurgood Marshall and John Paul Stevens did not have their clerks participate in the certiorari pool either.[6]

Conference on Certiorari

Having read the memos about the petitions, the justices then gather for the Court's **conference on certiorari.** This is the meeting at which the justices vote on whether to accept or reject a petition for a writ of certiorari. At this meeting of the nine justices, no law clerks or secretaries are present, and the most junior associate justice on the Court must answer the door to the conference room if anyone dares to knock. The most junior justice also keeps the formal record of the votes on certiorari.[7]

For the conference on certiorari, the chief justice prepares a **discuss list** of the cases the justices will discuss. Any other justice can add a case to the discuss list if he or she so chooses. If a case does not make the discuss list, then the petition for the writ of certiorari is automatically rejected by the Court. While the justices seem to depend on the memos written by the law clerks, certainly they will read all the materials for the cases in which they have a special interest. It is reported that Justice William J. Brennan read all of the certiorari materials himself except during the summer months,[8] but most justices seem to read only those petitions that the law clerks' memos describe as worthy of review.

It takes four votes to accept the petition for the writ of certiorari; that is, four justices must agree to have the Court hear the case in full. The Supreme Court hears fewer than a hundred cases per year, meaning that about 98 percent of the time the petition for the writ of certiorari does not receive the necessary four votes at the conference. If certiorari is denied, then the outcome and reasoning of the lower court stand in the case. A denial of certiorari in a specific case does not prevent the Court from hearing a different case on a similar issue if that later case receives the necessary four votes. Thus, while a denial of certiorari is extremely important to the parties to the case, it does not mean that the legal issues in the case won't come to the Court again in the future. Perhaps the justices would prefer a different set of facts, or they may wait for more lower court judges to weigh in on the issues in the case. The justices on the Supreme Court are quite emphatic that a denial of certiorari has no precedent value, even though the media often neglect to mention that key fact when reporting on the Supreme Court's actions.

Each justice seems to have different criteria for deciding when to vote in favor of a writ of certiorari and when to refrain from supporting a specific writ—it's almost as if the Court operates as nine separate law firms.[9] Although it takes four votes to accept a writ of certiorari, the justices do not seem to lobby each other on which cases to accept. Their decisions on certiorari appear to be made individually, without consulting other justices first. However, the justices and their own clerks often communicate about certiorari issues, and law clerks may attempt to influence their justice's decisions on certiorari.[10]

Political scientists are always trying to predict which petitions for writs of certiorari the Court will accept and which ones it will deny. The Court's Rule 10 explicitly states that conflict among the lower courts is an important criterion for accepting a petition for certiorari, but the Court does not automatically take all cases in which there is a conflict. Lawyers will always assert in their petitions for writs of certiorari that a conflict exists among lower judges, but in their memos the law clerks must distinguish between a mere assertion of a conflict among the lower courts and true splits in the lower court rulings. Rule 10 also states that the Court is interested in hearing cases regarding important issues of federal law on which the Court has not yet ruled, cases that reveal conflicts between a lower court decision and a Supreme Court precedent, and cases in which a lower court has dramatically departed "from the accepted and usual course of judicial proceedings."[11] Although Rule 10 on its face may appear to be rather straightforward, the actual process of choosing which cases to hear in full is anything but. W. H. Perry Jr. is one of the few academics who have been able to interview justices and law clerks about the decision-making process at the certiorari stage, and, despite his insights, much of this process remains a mystery. As Perry concludes, "The processing of cert. petitions is complex, involving several decision makers and several points of decision."[12]

Cue Theory

One attempt to make sense of all the confusion surrounding the Court's decisions on certiorari is known as **cue theory**. Cue theory, according to political scientists, states that since the justices are so busy with the other aspects of their duties, they must find some method for quickly processing the huge volume of petitions for writs of certiorari. Thus, the justices look for specific cues in the petitions to help make the process easier. If no cue is present, then that specific petition deserves no further attention.[13] So the processing of petitions for certiorari is a two-step process: separating out the cases worthy of further discussion, and then deciding which of the cases deemed worthy of further discussion will receive full consideration by the Court.[14] Some of the earlier work in this area suggested that viable positive cues include when the solicitor general seeks review of the case by the Court, when there is disagreement among judges on the lower courts, and when there is a civil liberties issue present in the case.[15] Later works debated which specific cues might be more or less useful in predicting which cases the Court would take,[16] but, in general, cue theory seems to be a valid method of attempting to explain how the justices approach their certiorari decisions. Cues regarding specific issue areas seem to be the least predictive of the behavior of the justices. Clearly, the Court has shifted from accepting mostly economics-based cases before World War II to accepting many more civil liberties cases today.[17] But within those broad categories, it is very difficult to predict which specific issues the Court will choose to hear at any given time.

Nevertheless, judicial politics scholars want to know more about how the justices make their certiorari decisions. Recall that the justices seem to make their decisions on whether to grant or deny certiorari individualistically rather than collectively.[18] One piece of information that all justices appear interested in is what judge authored the lower court decision and who, if anyone, dissented from that opinion.[19]

Some justices may also be sensitive to which interest groups are bringing the case to the Court or even supporting the case through amicus briefs.[20] Repeat players may have some significant advantages at the certiorari stage. Lawyers and interest groups known to the justices may have an easier time having their cases accepted for full consideration by the Court. Justice Anthony Kennedy has explained that when reviewing the petitions for certiorari, "[w]e look at the names of counsel for lawyers we trust."[21]

Some political scientists argue that justices are more likely to vote for a petition for a writ of certiorari when they disagree with the ideological direction of the lower court decision. Cue theory suggests that the justices would want to hear cases in which they believe the lower court came to the incorrect ideological re-sult. As one study concluded on this point, "[T]he justices grant cert because they believe that the legal rule adopted by the lower court represents a serious devia-tion from the legal rule that a majority of justices prefer."[22] In fact, more than two-thirds of the time the Supreme Court overturns the lower court ruling when it issues its final opinion in the case.[23] As Chief Justice William Rehnquist once explained, "[T]he most common reason members of our Court vote to grant cer-tiorari is that they doubt the correctness of the decision of the lower court."[24]

However, individual justices also may be strategic in their votes for certiorari because they may not want to accept a case and then end up with a Supreme Court precedent that goes against their own preferred policy outcomes. Consid-ering this in terms of cue theory, this means that the justices consider both their own preferred ideological outcome from the case and the likelihood that a ma-jority of their colleagues have the same preferred ideological outcome. In her confirmation hearings to become solicitor general of the United States, Elena Kagan admitted as much. She stated that when she clerked for Justice Marshall the law clerks would always inform the justice when they thought a full Supreme Court decision would go against his preferred ideological stance in order to help him decide whether to vote in favor of the petition for certiorari.[25] The implica-tion is that Justice Marshall would not vote to grant certiorari if he thought the majority of his colleagues would create a precedent with which he disagreed. This is a clear indication of strategic behavior by justices at the certiorari stage.

Settling disagreements among lower court judges on any given issue is clearly important to many of the justices. Cue theory places a lot of importance on ac-tual conflicts among the lower courts. From his interviews, Perry argues that this variable is the most crucial to those sitting on the high court.[26] Chief Justice John Roberts has noted that conflict between the circuits is an important variable when selecting cases to hear: "Our main job is to make sure federal law is uni-form across the country."[27] While conflict among the circuits is an important criterion for accepting a writ of certiorari and perhaps even a crucial cue, it is neither necessary nor sufficient. The justices will not grant a petition for certio-rari just because there is a conflict among the circuits, but they are far less likely to take the case if there is no real conflict below.[28] The justices may want to wait until more lower courts rule on an issue before they decide to grant certiorari in any given instance. As Justice Stephen Breyer has described the certiorari pro-cess, "The primary job is to take the case where there is a need for a nationally uniform decision on the meaning of the particular law."[29]

Perry does offer an important caveat to cue theory. Because the Court ap-proves such a small percentage of the petitions for writs of certiorari today, the overwhelming majority of petitions are denied. Therefore, Perry cautions about putting too much faith in cue theory: "The mere presence of an issue that disposes a justice favorably toward a grant is easily overwhelmed if there exists any reason to deny."[30]

Political science research has generally found two key predictors of when the Supreme Court will be most likely to accept a writ of certiorari: (1) a large number of amicus briefs supporting or even opposing the granting of certiorari, because this is a good indicator of the importance of the case to the larger society,[31] and (2) a request by the solicitor general to have the Court take a case. When the solicitor general makes such a request, the Court accepts the petition about 70 percent of the time[32] (in some years that acceptance rate has been 90 percent or even higher).[33] But conflict among the circuits remains an important factor: another study found that in the 2004–2006 terms, about 70 percent of cases decided by the Supreme Court involved resolving real conflicts among the lower courts.[34]

Although it is extremely rare, at times the justices will issue written dissents from a denial of certiorari. Because of their firm opposition to the death penalty, Justices Brennan and Marshall always issued a written dissent to the denial of certiorari in every capital punishment case that came before the Court. Outside of these circumstances, a written dissent from a denial of certiorari remains quite rare. Perhaps this is because the mere threat of a published dissent from the denial of certiorari may lead the other justices to vote to accept the case for full consideration.[35] Justices may file a dissent from a denial of certiorari because they want to signal litigants to find another case on the same issue, perhaps with better facts. But the justices strongly prefer that there be no published dissents on denials of certiorari. As Perry concludes, "[T]he justices do not really want the bar to know precisely why cases are granted or denied."[36]

The Rare Case Heard:
Briefs on the Merits and Oral Arguments

Once the petition for a writ of certiorari is accepted, then the parties prepare new briefs on the merits for the case. While the briefs at the certiorari stage argued why the Court should or should not take the case, the **briefs on the merits** argue how the Court should decide the case. The Court also accepts additional amicus curiae briefs at the merits stage, including amicus briefs from the solicitor general if the U.S. government is not already a party to the case. The Supreme Court then schedules oral arguments.

In general, the purpose of the oral arguments is to have the lawyers clarify the arguments in the written briefs, although at times it seems as if the justices are really talking to each other through their probing questions and just using the lawyers as intermediaries. Normally, each side in the case has thirty minutes to answer the justices' many questions during oral argument, although if the solicitor general requests it, someone from that office may take as much as fifteen minutes away from the allotted time for the party they support. The solicitor general's office may present its views at oral argument on almost any case if it chooses to do so and sometimes when the Court requests that it do so.

Oral arguments are open to the public and receive a great deal of coverage, but television cameras are not allowed in the Supreme Court courtroom. Oral arguments at the Supreme Court of Canada have been televised since the mid-1990s, and the newly created Supreme Court of the United Kingdom now allows cameras at its proceedings.[37] The justices of the U.S. Supreme Court, however, have refused to televise their oral arguments. At the U.S. Supreme Court members of the press may only take notes during oral arguments, although the Court does allow sketch artists to make drawings of the justices during these proceedings. In February 2012, the U.S. Senate Judiciary Committee again approved legislation to require the Supreme Court to televise their oral arguments, but many justices remain strongly opposed to that practice and such bills have never passed both houses of Congress at the same time.[38] In fact, even though some of the more recent appointees to the Court, including Justices Sonia Sotomayor and Elena Kagan, said in their confirmation hearings that they might support having cameras at the Supreme Court, all of them now seem to have changed their minds on the issue. Chief Justice Roberts has also opposed the use of cameras.[39] Fearing that cameras in the courtroom at the highest court would change the dynamic of oral arguments, one commentator has argued, "Let's not let them ruin the nation's last bastion for serious discussion of serious issues by serious people."[40]

Scholars are split on the question of how important oral arguments are in the decision-making process at the U.S. Supreme Court. Some argue that justices tend to make up their minds based solely on the written briefs and that oral arguments do little to change their positions.[41] Others maintain that the questions that justices ask during oral arguments are not a good indication of how a particular justice will vote on the case in question.[42] Yet other scholars hold that oral arguments are a key part of the decision-making process at the nation's highest court, helping the justices determine how to frame the majority opinion in order to incorporate the views of enough justices to get the necessary five votes in the case.[43] Because oral arguments are the first point in the decision-making process where justices express their views on a specific case, the justices themselves seem to take oral arguments very seriously.[44] As Chief Justice Rehnquist once noted,

"In a significant number of cases in which I have heard oral argument, I have left the bench feeling different about the case than I did when I came on the bench."[45]

Opinion Drafting and Negotiation

Following oral arguments, the justices meet again in a private **conference on the merits**. At this meeting of the justices, which takes place without any clerks or secretaries present, the case is discussed and a preliminary vote is taken on the outcome. The preliminary vote is not released to the public. If the chief justice is in the majority on that preliminary vote, he then assigns the opinion-writing task for the majority opinion. If the chief justice is in the minority, then the most senior associate justice in the majority assigns the opinion-writing task for the presumed majority opinion, and the chief justice assigns the dissenting opinion to a colleague in the minority. On today's Court, the most senior justice in opposition to the position of the usually conservative Chief Justice Roberts is typically Justice Ruth Bader Ginsburg, as she is almost always part of the liberal bloc on the Court.

The chief justice may consider a variety of factors when assigning the opinion-writing task. First, there are workload issues. The chief justice has to make sure that all justices have about the same number of opinions to draft. As Chief Justice Roberts has so colorfully stated, "You want to make sure everyone has their fair share of interesting cases and has their fair share of what we call the dogs, the uninteresting cases."[46] Second, some justices are more expert in certain areas of the law than others. For example, one reason Chief Justice Warren Burger assigned the majority opinion in the abortion case of *Roe v. Wade* (1973) to his good friend Justice Harry Blackmun was because Blackmun had been the lawyer for the Mayo Clinic. Being familiar with the needs of the medical community, Justice Blackmun wrote about the abortion issues in *Roe* from the perspective of the doctor.

Another factor that the chief justice must consider is whether the assigned justice can keep the five votes necessary to make the final opinion the majority opinion and thus the opinion of the Court. Since the final vote comes when justices sign on to a written opinion, the preliminary vote can change over the course of opinion drafting and negotiations, as discussed below. Therefore, the chief justice may assign the majority opinion to a moderate member of the majority in order to keep the necessary fifth vote.[47] In highly important cases, the chief justice may feel the need to take on the task of writing the majority opinion personally. This occurred in *Brown v. Board of Education* (1954), when Chief

Justice Earl Warren wrote the opinion for the Court himself. This also occurred more recently, when Chief Justice Roberts wrote the majority opinion on the constitutionality of President Obama's health care reform legislation in *National Federation of Independent Business v. Sebelius* (2012). Extremely unusual leaks from the Supreme Court indicate that originally Chief Justice Roberts was going to write a majority opinion that was more in line with the views of the Court's conservatives. Instead, during the opinion drafting stage the chief justice changed his views and wrote an opinion upholding the mandate that individuals must buy health insurance.[48] Since he had assigned the opinion to himself, Chief Justice Roberts's change of heart led to the Court upholding the constitutionality of the individual mandate to buy health insurance instead of striking it down, as the preliminary vote on the issue might have indicated.

Each justice carefully drafts his or her preliminary written opinions and circulates them to the eight other justices for their comments. A period of negotiation then follows, during which a justice may agree to sign on to an opinion but only if certain changes are made. This negotiation is not like logrolling in the U.S. Congress, where a politician may say something like, "I'll vote for your bill if you vote for mine." The justices are well aware that the reasoning in their written majority opinions becomes binding precedent on all lower courts for all future cases, and so the negotiations at the Court are much more intellectual and based on legal analysis and legal reasoning. In other words, a justice may agree to sign on to an opinion if its reasoning is changed in a way that he or she finds acceptable. That may mean adding or subtracting specific wording from the draft opinion. A justice may say that he or she will sign on to a preliminary opinion if a new paragraph is added or if certain paragraphs are dropped.

These negotiations are quite common on the Supreme Court. For example, one study found that during the seventeen years Chief Justice Burger held the position, requests for changes in the draft opinion occurred in about a third of all cases, and more often in the more important cases. About 70 percent of the time the draft opinion was changed to incorporate the requested modifications.[49] Not surprisingly, justices are less likely to make suggested revisions when they already have the necessary five votes for a draft opinion. Most of these negotiations are done in written form through formal memoranda. According to Justice Breyer, "Things take place in writing because that is a mode through which appellate judges are most comfortable communicating."[50] When the papers of a justice are made public after the justice's death or retirement, scholars and others use them to learn as much as they can about the negotiations over opinion drafting on the Supreme Court.[51]

A very famous example of negotiations at the Supreme Court occurred during the writing of *Brown v. Board of Education* (1954). We now know from the release of the papers of the justices that the preliminary vote in *Brown* was probably 6–3 in favor of ending racial discrimination in public schools. Chief Justice Warren assigned the majority opinion-writing task to himself, in large part because he felt the opinion should be unanimous in such a landmark case, which could signal the end of de jure racial discrimination in the United States. The chief justice then asked the conservative justices who were in dissent on the preliminary vote in *Brown* what they would need to sign his majority opinion. The response from the conservatives was that they did not want the Court to order desegregation in the public schools to begin immediately. Instead, they wanted integration to proceed "with all deliberate speed." The chief justice inserted this phrase into his majority opinion, and eventually all the justices signed on to the unanimous opinion.[52] Instead of forcing school desegregation to begin in 1954, in reality the "with all deliberate speed" phrase meant that in many parts of the country school desegregation would not begin until the federal bureaucracy cut off federal funding to segregated public schools starting in 1966. The cost of a unanimous Court was a delay of more than a decade in desegregation efforts.

Given that the reasoning of the majority opinion becomes precedent for all future cases, the justices do try to coalesce around as few opinions as possible. But at any point in the negotiation process, any justice may write his or her own concurring or dissenting opinion. Eventually the chief justice decides that the negotiation period has come to a conclusion, and then the opinions are released to the public in open court and quickly made available by the Court's Office of Public Information to the public in both written and electronic form. On rare occasion, dissenting judges may give an oral summary from the bench of their dissent if they feel especially strongly that the majority opinion in a case is incorrect.

Supreme Court Law Clerks

As mentioned above, many appellate judges, including the justices on the Supreme Court, hire law clerks to help them with their work. **Law clerks** at the U.S. Supreme Court are recent law school graduates who finished at or near the top of their law school classes at some of the most prestigious law schools in the country.[53] For example, some estimate that roughly 40 percent of all recent law clerks at the Court have graduated from Harvard or Yale Law Schools.[54] They normally spend a year clerking for a judge on the U.S. courts of appeals before they are selected by the justices of the Supreme Court to assist them for a one-year term. Most of the justices hire four law clerks per year, and retired justices can hire one clerk each. When they served on the Court, Chief Justice William Rehnquist and Justice John Paul Stevens would generally only hire three clerks per year instead of their allotted four.

Some justices seem to hire clerks who agree with them ideologically, while others seem to want ideological diversity among their clerks. One study found that the partisan makeup of a justice's clerks can and does influence that justice's decisions,[55] but one must wonder whether that is because justices tend to hire clerks with similar ideologies in the first place. In particular, the most conservative justices on the Court seem to prefer to hire clerks who share their political views.[56] Many of the justices on the Supreme Court tend repeatedly to hire clerks who have worked for one of a small number of ideologically like-minded judges on the U.S. courts of appeals, who have become known as "feeder judges."[57]

After clerking on the U.S. Supreme Court, the former law clerks often go into private practice, where they can sometimes earn signing bonuses of well over $200,000 and salaries higher than those of the judges for whom they worked.[58] On the U.S. Supreme Court, Justices Stephen Breyer, Byron White, Elena Kagan, and John Paul Stevens as well as Chief Justices William Rehnquist and John Roberts were all former law clerks on the high court.[59] Judges on state supreme courts also hire law clerks, but many of them are now relying more and more on full-time staff attorneys instead. Most of the academic study of law clerks has focused on those who work at the Supreme Court of the United States.

The clerks at the Supreme Court perform a variety of functions. As discussed earlier in this chapter, they write memos to the justices regarding the certiorari petitions. They also help the justices understand all the materials in the cases that get a full hearing at the Court. They do whatever legal or other research their justice requests. They write bench memos to the justices on the cases heard in full, which outline the basic facts and issues of the case, suggest questions for oral arguments, and perhaps recommend how the justice should vote on the merits of the case. As Justice Alito has described some of the duties of law clerks on the Supreme Court, "They help me decide how I'm going to vote, and they help me prepare to make the decision on how to vote. [. . .] They give me the opportunity to discuss the case and the strengths and weaknesses of the arguments that are made before going into the oral argument and before voting at conference."[60] Many of the clerks prepare the initial draft of the written opinions, which the justices then carefully edit and usually totally rewrite. They also serve as informal ambassadors to the clerks in other justices' chambers.[61] So that they may talk among themselves about cases without having anyone overhear their conversations, the law clerks have their own private dining room in the cafeteria at the U.S. Supreme Court building.

The clerks sign a confidentiality agreement when they begin their work at the Supreme Court each July.[62] Nevertheless, at least two famous books on the U.S. Supreme Court were written with the direct or indirect assistance of former clerks. *The Brethren* was published in 1979 by two *Washington Post* reporters who seemed to have a great deal of access to former law clerks at the Court.[63] *Closed Chambers*, published in 1998, was actually written by a former law clerk.[64] Both sought to provide a look behind the scenes at the Court, and neither book was well received by the justices at the time. As scholar Barbara Perry, who was quite critical of these books, has commented, "The Court was portrayed as a petty, back-stabbing gathering of nine prima donnas."[65] Perry goes on to note that both books were highly problematic because they "relied too heavily on anecdotal evidence from the law clerks, whose notorious egos may not have made them the most dependable sources."[66] It is unclear whether the leaks from the Supreme Court about Chief Justice Roberts's decision in the health care reform case in 2012 (discussed above) came from law clerks, but many suspect that they did.[67]

There are perennial questions about why the justices hire so few female and minority law clerks. These questions seem to arise every year when the justices go across the street to ask the House Appropriations Committee for funding for the federal courts.[68] In 1944 Justice William O. Douglas hired the first female law clerk, and in 1948 Justice Felix Frankfurter hired the first African American clerk. The second female and African American clerks would not make it to the Court until nearly two decades later. By the 1990s women made up about a third of the law clerks, and in 2002 nine of the thirty-five clerks on the Court at that time were minorities.[69] This was clear progress over the past. In a study of law clerks on the Supreme Court from 1882 to 2004, only 15 percent during that long historical period were female and only 6 percent were from racial and ethnic minorities.[70] On the Rehnquist Court, Justices Sandra Day O'Connor, Ruth Bader Ginsburg, John Paul Stevens, and Stephen Breyer tended to hire the most female law clerks. Chief Justice William Rehnquist and Justice Antonin Scalia were the least likely to hire minority law clerks, while Justices Stevens and Breyer were the most likely to hire nonwhite law clerks.[71]

The normal response from the justices to questions about the continued lack of female and minority law clerks is that they hire their clerks from a very small pool of people clerking for judges on the U.S. courts of appeals. Until that pool becomes more diverse, the clerks at the Supreme Court are unlikely to become less homogeneous.[72] For all law clerks in all the federal courts in 2010, African Americans were only 2.4 percent of the total, and Hispanic/Latinos were only 2 percent. These figures were much lower than the figures for 2006, when African Americans were 3.5 percent and Hispanic/Latinos were 3.1 percent, respectively, of the total number of clerks in the federal courts.[73]

The lack of female and minority law clerks on the Supreme Court has led to protests. Several newspaper articles from 1998 pointed out the tiny number of minority law clerks at the high court at that time.[74] In response, that year the NAACP held a rally outside the Supreme Court attended by more than a thousand people demanding more minority law clerks at the high court. Several high-profile professors and politicians were arrested in the protest.[75] Academics began to publish articles in law reviews and other venues complaining about the lack of diversity among Supreme Court law clerks.[76] Members of Congress also expressed their unhappiness about the situation.[77] In 2006, women's groups complained that of the thirty-seven law clerks hired at the Supreme Court that year, only seven were female, the lowest number since 1994.[78]

APPELLATE COURT PRECEDENTS

The U.S. Supreme Court and other courts interpret multiple sources of law in their work. These sources include constitutions, statutes, executive orders, and agency decisions. Recall that the courts have the power of judicial review, which is the power to declare the actions of other actors unconstitutional. When appellate courts base their decisions on the Constitution, it is much harder for other governmental institutions to overturn them. Appellate courts also interpret statutes, and these **statutory interpretation** cases are far easier for legislatures to overturn. The legislative branch just needs to pass a new statute in order to overturn a statutory interpretation decision that it does not like. Appellate courts can also interpret executive orders and administrative agency decisions. Later chapters will discuss the interactions between the courts and the other branches of government.

Appellate courts can and do overturn their own precedents. The principle of *stare decisis* states that the courts should decide the current case before them based on past court rulings, but since top appellate courts are the creators of precedent for the courts below them, when those top appellate courts overturn past rulings, the precedent for all the courts below them change as well. For example, since many state supreme court justices are elected, some states will change their precedents when party control of the state supreme court changes. Likewise, the U.S. Supreme Court can and does modify its precedents when the makeup of the Court changes. Although some justices are hesitant to overturn past rulings, the fact of the matter is that Supreme Court precedent will change whenever five justices vote to do so. For example, on the question of whether state anti-sodomy laws violated the constitutional right of individual privacy, the Supreme Court said no in *Bowers v. Hardwick* (1986). The Court later overruled this decision in *Lawrence v. Texas* (2003), when it declared the Texas anti-sodomy law to be unconstitutional on both privacy and equal protection grounds. The facts in the two cases were almost identical, but the change in justices over time led the Court to overrule its previous precedent. In *Minersville School District v. Gobitis* (1940), the U.S. Supreme Court said that Jehovah's Witness children could not be excused from laws requiring mandatory flag salutes at the beginning of the school day in public school even though such activities violated their religious beliefs. Just a few years later, the Court reversed itself in *West Virginia State Board of Education v. Barnette* (1943); in fact, several justices switched their votes in this case.

Sometimes even a single new justice can rapidly effect a dramatic change in precedent. In *Stenberg v. Carhart* (2000), the Supreme Court by a 5–4 vote had struck down a Nebraska statute outlawing a specific type of late-term abortion, called "partial-birth abortion" by abortion opponents. The Court stated that the statute was unconstitutional because it did not include an exception from the abortion ban if the health or life of the mother was at risk. However, after Justice O'Connor retired from the Court in 2006 and was replaced by Justice Alito, the Supreme Court majority shifted and the Court voted 5–4 to uphold an almost identical federal statute in *Gonzales v. Carhart* (2007). Although the new majority on the Supreme Court claimed that they were not overruling the first decision, the two rulings are logically and legally inconsistent.

DECISION MAKING ON OTHER APPELLATE COURTS

Decision making on the U.S. courts of appeals is complicated by the fact that in these courts, cases are generally heard by panels of three randomly selected judges. That is, a new panel is created for each specific case, but, when a panel makes a decision, it speaks for the entire circuit court. Thus, the decision from the three-judge panel usually serves as precedent for the entire court. However, there are times when the majority of judges on the entire circuit court disagree with the decision of the panel. So there is a mechanism to have the entire court review certain decisions of the three-judge panels in order to have uniform precedents from the circuit.

When they think the decision of a three-judge panel may not reflect the view of the entire circuit, litigants can ask for an **en banc** review, meaning that the case will be reheard by the entire membership of the circuit (or in the largest courts, such as the U.S. Court of Appeals for the Ninth Circuit, by a significant portion of the membership).[79] The *en banc* mechanism allows the entire court to make sure that all the precedents established by the three-judge panels reflect the views of most of the judges on the circuit. A majority of the judges on the circuit must vote for the *en banc* rehearing of the case. *En banc* reviews are quite rare, occurring in less than 1 percent of all the cases heard by the circuit courts.[80] Although *en banc* reviews are infrequent, judges on the panels must always keep the possibility of such a review in mind when they write their initial opinions.[81]

The three judges on each panel may write their opinions with the possibility of Supreme Court review in mind as well.[82] Some research suggests that circuit court judges often write decisions that they perceive to be consistent with the current views of the Supreme Court rather than with its actual precedents.[83] Other research suggests that judges on the U.S. courts of appeals follow the legal model, and thus their decision making reflects current precedent and not the presumed ideological preferences of the current Supreme Court justices.[84]

Because many of the U.S. courts of appeals have huge caseloads and are greatly overworked, a number of the circuit courts have resorted to using senior judges and designated U.S. district court judges to help them get their work done. The situation is not helped by the fact that it is getting increasingly difficult to get presidential nominations for the U.S. courts of appeals confirmed by the U.S. Senate. A **senior judge** is someone who is technically retired from the bench but continues to hear cases, although with a reduced caseload. A senior judge's seat on the court is officially considered vacant, and the president can nominate a replacement at any time.[85] Even retired U.S. Supreme Court justices may sit as senior judges; David Souter often sits as a senior judge, hearing cases on the U.S. Court of Appeals for the First Circuit in Boston.[86] Senior judges are now considered essential for the proper operation of the U.S. courts of appeals.[87] The circuit courts also use U.S. district court judges, who are designated to hear a specific case or set of cases. Designation of a district court judge is at the discretion of the chief judge of the circuit.[88] Designated district court judges are less likely to file separate opinions in a case, while senior judges are more likely to do so.[89]

Different circuits have different norms.[90] One of the clear norms on most circuits is that dissenting opinions remain somewhat rare.[91] When dissents do occur, they are often a result of ideological differences among the judges. Dissents are most frequent in First Amendment and privacy cases and least frequent in criminal cases and economics-based cases.[92] Judges may dissent in order to signal their allies on higher courts that they should review and probably reverse the rulings of these intermediate courts.

IMPLEMENTATION ISSUES

How are U.S. Supreme Court precedents actually put into practice? In other words, how does **implementation** of court policies occur? The conventional wisdom is that the U.S. Supreme Court is best able to enforce its own decisions when it reviews and overturns the rulings of lower courts that have deviated from Supreme Court precedent.[93] However, the Supreme Court can only enforce the decision of each case with the parties to that specific case, and, since the Supreme Court hears so few cases each year, implementation issues are often left to state supreme courts or to the U.S. courts of appeals. Generally speaking, the Court must depend on the goodwill of the executive, the legislature, and the people to enforce most of its rulings. Thus, the question arises of how the Court's policies are actually put into practice by these other actors.

Sometimes other political actors will ignore a Supreme Court decision with which they disagree. For example, after the Court ruled in *Worcester v. Georgia* (1832) that the state could not remove the Cherokee Nation from its lands in Georgia, President Jackson ordered U.S. federal personnel to ignore the Court's order. And in *Immigration and Naturalization Service v. Chadha* (1983), Congress simply refused to accept the Supreme Court's declaration that a one-house legislative veto is unconstitutional. In this case, the Immigration and Naturalization Service ordered Jagdish Chadha to be deported, but the U.S. House of Representatives voted to overturn the agency's decision using a one-house legislative veto, which was allowed by the statutes dealing with illegal immigration. The Supreme Court ruled that Congress could overturn a decision of an executive-branch federal agency only by having both houses pass a bill that the president could either sign or veto—the regular method. Congress, however, simply ignored the *Chadha* judicial ruling, and it continues to pass a variety of statutes that include one-house legislative vetoes even though the Supreme Court has declared this practice to be unconstitutional.[94] Although the Supreme Court, in a variety of decisions including *Engel v. Vitale* (1962), *Lee v. Weisman* (1992), and *Santa Fe Independent School District v. Doe* (2000), has declared that organized prayer at public school events is unconstitutional, many local governments in some parts of the country continue to ignore the Court's decisions on this issue.

Bradley Canon and Charles Johnson came up with a model for analyzing the implementation and impact of U.S. Supreme Court policies and precedents.[95] These scholars note that different populations have different experiences with the implementation of a Supreme Court ruling. The "interpreting population" includes lawyers and lower court judges who must initially interpret the Supreme Court's policy. The Supreme Court seems to have the most control over this population.

The "implementing population" must put the Court's policy into practice. For example, the police must give the *Miranda* warnings, while the state legislatures had to change their abortion laws after *Roe v. Wade* (1973). The "consumer population" is the group the Court is trying to help with their policies. After *Roe v. Wade*, women who might want to have abortions were the consumer population. Accused criminals were the consumer population for the large number of Supreme Court decisions dealing with the rights of criminal defendants. Finally, the "secondary population" includes everyone else who reacts to the Court's policy. For example, *Roe v. Wade* resulted in the emergence of many interest groups on both sides of the abortion issue. State legislatures have also enacted a variety of restrictions on abortions, some of which the Court later declared to be constitutional or unconstitutional. Members of Congress can also be part of the secondary population. Regarding the rights of criminal defendants, in 1968 Congress passed legislation to overturn the Court's policy pronouncement in *Miranda v. Arizona* (1966). Eventually the Court declared the federal statute to be unconstitutional in *Dickerson v. United States* (2000), meaning that the *Miranda* warnings were constitutionalized.

The Court does have some control over lower courts and over repeat players such as the police. For example, the Supreme Court's exclusionary rule decisions, stating that any evidence improperly collected by the police is not admissible at trial, has had a direct effect on police activities. Many observers believe that police have become more professionalized because they have a great deal to lose if the evidence they collect cannot be used in a specific criminal trial. Thus, the Court can indirectly control the behavior of the police.

The Court can also control the behavior of lower court judges by overturning decisions that the Court feels violate its policy decisions. Most judges strongly prefer that their decisions not be overturned on appeal, and so most judges do follow the precedent of higher courts such as the U.S. Supreme Court when they make their decisions.[96] Some even argue that it is the threat of reversal instead of the actual number of reversals that motivates judges.[97] As Judge Richard Posner explains, "The judge wants to be a good judge and thus decide cases in accordance with the law. He also does not want to be reversed."[98] Because of judicial norms and the threat of reversing a decision below, the Supreme Court can and does exert control over how lower court judges interpret its rulings.

However, implementation of Supreme Court policies remains complicated. Lower court judges have a variety of ways to prevent full implementation of Supreme Court policies if they are determined to do so. First, lower court judges might say that the facts of the case before them do not fit with the high court's precedential cases.[99] The lower courts might also interpret the Supreme Court's precedent quite narrowly, not giving it full application.[100] They could dispose of the case on procedural grounds, or they might criticize the Supreme Court precedent while following it.[101] They might also cite their own precedents instead of those from the U.S. Supreme Court.[102] Or they could just ignore precedents they do not like.[103] This happened in *Hopwood v. Texas* (1996), when the Fifth Circuit ruled that the Supreme Court's precedents allowing affirmative action were no longer valid, and in *Dickerson v. United States,* 166 F.3d 667 (Fourth Circuit, 1999), when the Fourth Circuit ruled that the Supreme Court's policy in the *Miranda* case had been overturned by Congress. The U.S. Supreme Court then later overturned both of these appellate court decisions.

Implementation problems can occur because of communications issues, compliance issues, or both. The Supreme Court's policy must be clearly communicated. If the Supreme Court policy in its majority opinion is unclear or ambiguous, then putting that policy into practice will be much more difficult. Most litigants will bring U.S. Supreme Court precedents to the attention of lower court judges, so knowledge of a policy's existence is rarely a problem, but the precedent still must be understood by the lower court judges.[104] To prevent communication issues, the Court needs to make sure that its policies are not too vague or too tentative. The Supreme Court can create all sorts of implementation problems when it is fractured on any given issue. If the Court issues too many individual opinions in any given case, it is very difficult for lawyers and judges to interpret the policy the Court is actually articulating. Sometimes the U.S. Supreme Court will take a case just to make the precedent on the issue clearer. As Justice Louis Brandeis argued, "Stare decisis is usually the wise policy, because in most matters it is more important that the applicable rule of law be settled rather than that it be settled right."[105]

There are also compliance issues if lower courts willfully refuse to follow Supreme Court precedents. **Compliance** in this context means that lower court judges follow the law and precedent as determined by the courts above them. (*Compliance* can also be used to mean the general willingness of citizens to follow the law or the willingness of various actors to follow the ruling of the Supreme Court in general.) The lower courts may have ideological views different from those held by the majority on the Supreme Court. Lower court judges may also be subject to various political forces that may affect their willingness to comply with Supreme Court precedent. This problem is especially crucial for state supreme court judges, who often must face some sort of election to retain their seats on the bench. Thus, state supreme court implementation of U.S. Supreme Court precedents is highly influenced by the political context facing the state judges. The state's governors and legislatures also have various means to overturn or avoid the policy decisions of state supreme courts.[106] However, many recent studies have found that in general lower courts do follow Supreme Court precedents.[107]

CHAPTER SUMMARY

This chapter examined the primary goals of appellate courts in the United States: correcting errors from the trial and setting precedent for all future courts. It detailed the steps that the U.S. Supreme Court uses to decide cases, including how the Court decides which cases to accept for full consideration, the conference on certiorari, the procedures involved in opinion writing and negotiating, and the role of law clerks. Political scientists use cue theory as one way to try to understand why the Supreme Court accepts the few cases that it does. The chapter also examined when the U.S. Supreme Court will change its precedents. It then explored some of the differences in the process used by the U.S. circuit courts of appeals, which generally decides cases using panels of three randomly selected judges. Finally, the chapter discussed issues regarding the implementation and impact of U.S. Supreme Court policy decisions.

For Further Reading

Baird, Vanessa. 2006. *Answering the Call: How Litigants and Justices Set the Supreme Court's Agenda.* Charlottesville: University of Virginia Press.

Banks, Christopher P. 1999. *Judicial Politics in the D.C. Circuit Court.* Baltimore: Johns Hopkins University Press.

Black, Ryan C., Timothy R. Johnson, and Justin Wedeking. 2012. *Oral Arguments and Coalition Formation on the U.S. Supreme Court: A Deliberate Dialogue.* Ann Arbor: University of Michigan Press.

Canon, Bradley C., and Charles A. Johnson. 1999. *Judicial Policies: Implementation and Impact.* 2nd ed. Washington, DC: CQ Press.

Cross, Frank B. 2007. *Decision Making in the U.S. Courts of Appeals.* Stanford, CA: Stanford University Press.

Hettinger, Virginia A., Stefanie A. Lindquist, and Wendy L. Martinek. 2006. *Judging on a Collegial Court: Influences on Federal Appellate Decision Making.* Charlottesville: University of Virginia Press.

Klein, David E. 2002. *Making Law in the United States Courts of Appeals.* New York: Cambridge University Press.

Perry, H. W., Jr. 1991. *Deciding to Decide: Agenda Setting in the United States Supreme Court.* Cambridge, MA: Harvard University Press.

Tarr, G. Alan, and Mary Cornelia Porter. 1988. *State Supreme Courts in State and Nation.* New Haven, CT: Yale University Press.

Ward, Artemus, and David L. Weiden. 2006. *Sorcerers' Apprentices: Law Clerks at the U.S. Supreme Court.* New York: New York University Press.

8

Studying Decision Making
on Appellate Courts

This chapter will focus on how political scientists and other sociolegal scholars study decision making on U.S. appellate courts, and specifically on the U.S. Supreme Court. It will look at the historical development of theories of and approaches to judicial decision making. Most of the scholarly work in this area has focused on the U.S. Supreme Court, but these approaches can apply to other appellate courts as well.

In the early part of the twentieth century, the dominant view of judicial decision making among scholars and judges alike in the United States was the **legal model**, or what some have called the "slot machine" view of justice. Law was a science, and judges just had to find the one right legal answer to all legal issues. Judges did this only through legal analysis and reasoning.

Then thinkers such as Oliver Wendell Holmes in the early 1900s challenged this conventional wisdom, instead using the approach of **legal realism.** The legal realists claimed that judges had a great deal of discretion in their decision making, and that political factors did influence how a judge ruled in a case. In other words, the law is not set in stone but instead is indeterminate.[1] Legal realism is sometimes called *political jurisprudence.* The legal realists thus rejected natural law, positivist approaches, and a purely legalistic approach to judicial decision making. They saw these approaches as too mechanical and unrealistic.[2] They came much closer to today's sociological and political science understandings of the law because they emphasized dynamic factors in judicial decision making. There are a variety of famous legal realists from that era. For example, Roscoe Pound argued in favor of sociological jurisprudence, where the social sciences would help shape the development of law. Benjamin Cardozo argued that while many legal principles could be found through the proper analysis of legal texts and precedents, at times judges must create new rules or refashion old ones as society changes. In this approach, ultimately the law was whatever the judge said it was. As Holmes wrote, "The life of the law has not been logic; it has been experience. The felt necessities of the time, the prevalent moral and political theories, intuitions of public policy, avowed or unconscious, even the prejudices which judges share with their fellow-men" produce the judges' understanding of the law and legal decision making.[3] Chief Justice Evan Hughes put it much more simply when he said, "We live under a Constitution, but the Constitution is what judges say it is."[4]

MODELS OF JUDICIAL DECISION MAKING

This next section gives a historical overview of several models used by political scientists and other scholars to understand and examine judicial decision making, including the legal model, the behavioral revolution and the attitudinal model, post-behavioralist models, and strategic models. It is important to remember that all scientific models simplify the world in order to help us understand what is important and what isn't.

Legal Model

As mentioned above, the traditional legal model assumes that judges make their decisions purely on the basis of legal analysis and legal reasoning. Other factors, such as ideological and political considerations, do not come into play. Some have labeled this approach as "law as a science," where the duty of the judge is merely to find the one right legal answer to any legal questions. The law, in this context, means "a body of preexisting rules found in canonical legal materials, such as constitutional and statutory texts," as well as the precedents from previous courts that have interpreted those texts.[5] Judges use logical analysis to find the right legal answer based solely on the use of these legal texts. Thus, the legal model assumes that law has its own internal logic and order. The legal model includes rules of interpretation, or canons of construction, so that judges always know how to apply the legal rules to the facts before them.

The legal approach treats law as an autonomous discipline with its own internal logic and decision-making style. Thus, the judge does not look to other academic disciplines, such as the social sciences, for guidance. The legal approach remains the judiciary's "official" theory of judicial behavior, because most if not all judges maintain even today that their decisions are derived entirely from proper legal analysis and reasoning.[6] Evidence of the fact that judges use the legal model comes from the fact that between 1950 and 2004 about 38 percent of all Supreme Court decisions were unanimous, suggesting that political considerations played no role.[7] Most political scientists are highly skeptical that judges consider the law and nothing else. One set of scholars argued: "The naive legal model states that justices will 'find' the law and that there is a determinative answer to every legal question in statutes, constitutional provisions, or extant precedents."[8]

The legal model of judicial decision making complemented the **traditionalist** approach that was dominant in political science until the 1960s. Traditionalist scholars in political science were most interested in examining the formal structures and rules that were the foundation of political and governmental institutions. These studies were often descriptive in nature, using mostly qualitative methods, and traditionalist scholars usually did not use broad theories in order to ground their observations in a larger theoretical perspective.[9] Therefore, traditionalist scholars were often highly normative in their work. **Normative** in this context is the opposite of **empirical**. Empirical studies look at what is, while normative studies propose what ought to be.

The Behavioral Revolution and the Attitudinal Model

Gaining steam in the 1960s was a **behavioral revolution** in political science. Instead of looking at institutional rules and structures, behavioralist political scientists began to examine political behavior at the individual level of analysis. These scholars also wanted to do more work that was empirical in nature, rather than normative. The idea was to make the study of politics more scientific. The stress was on empiricism, theory building, observation, measurement, and the testing of hypotheses. Although the behavioral revolution in American politics really took hold in the 1960s, its roots can be traced back twenty years earlier to the works of C. Herman Pritchett.[10] After the behavioral revolution, political scientists were urged to "look at what justices do rather than what they say."[11]

Since good quantitative studies demanded large sample sizes, the more qualitative studies of institutions and institutional rules waned. For example, instead of studying the structures and rules of the courts, behavioralist political scientists studied specific case votes of individual judges. The behavioralists stressed rigorous empirical analysis of the behavior of individual political actors. They wanted to be able to predict the decisions of judges and other political decision makers.[12] Almost none of this work was normative in character.

One of the outgrowths of this new behavioral empirical focus was the **attitudinal model** of judicial decision making. The attitudinal model assumed that the judge is acting in a purely ideological fashion, unconstrained by any other forces.[13] The judge's only motivating factor is to make good public policy,[14] but a judge's definition of good public policy is driven by his or her own political and ideological preferences. As Lawrence Baum has argued about this model, "Devoted to good policy as a goal, attitudinal judges act directly on their policy preferences without calculating the consequences of their choices."[15] In other words, judges can rule based only on their ideological views because the law is ambiguous enough to allow multiple interpretations.[16] A variety of 5–4 decisions by the Supreme Court, with liberal justices on one side and conservative justices on the other, would be examples of the attitudinal model at work. Most cases dealing with abortion or other privacy issues seem to be highly ideological in nature. Many would argue that ideology was also driving the Supreme Court's decision in *Bush v. Gore* (2000), where the Court decided the 2000 presidential election.[17]

However, many political scientists, law professors, and others remain skeptical that judges' decision making is based only on ideology. Other factors such as legal reasoning seem also to be at work. For some scholars, the attitudinal model is seen as tautological or circular—for example, it seems to be saying that some judges are liberals because they vote in a liberal fashion. Other scholars critical of the attitudinal model have explained, "This naive political model sees justices as unconstrained political actors furthering their deeply held policy goals through the cases that sit on their docket."[18]

A great deal of empirical research has found that ideology is a statistically significant variable in judicial decision making.[19] Thus, almost all quantitative studies of judicial decision making include a variable that measures the ideology of individual judges. Chief Justice John Roberts has called the attitudinal model "the political science approach" to studying judicial decision making.[20] He claimed that the Supreme Court uses a more legal approach instead of the policy approach inherent in the attitudinal model. In fact, most judges would describe their approach to judging as anything but ideologically driven.[21] However, in a June 2012 poll, more than 75 percent of the public felt that the rulings of Supreme Court justices were sometimes driven in part by their personal political views.[22] In a similar poll taken in June 2013, 68 percent of respondents agreed that judicial decisions in part reflect the personal political views of the justices.[23] Of course, many political scientists today question whether the attitudinal model captures everything that goes into judicial decisions.[24] Critics are especially concerned that most quantitative studies of judicial decision making ignore unanimous decisions because their statistical models have trouble with a lack of variation in judicial votes.

Post-Behavioralist Models: New Institutionalism

Starting in the late 1980s, an alternative approach to behavioralism began to take root among political scientists. The **new institutionalist model** explores how institutional cultures, structures, rules, and norms constrain the choices and actions of individuals when they serve in a political institution. New institutionalism thus combines the interests of traditionalist scholars in studying formal institutional rules and structures with the focus of behavioralist scholars on examining the actions of individual political actors. As one scholar has summarized the main approach of this model, "In a nutshell, judges' decisions are a function of what they prefer to do, tempered by what they think they ought to do, but constrained by what they perceive is feasible to do."[25] Since traditionalist political science had its roots in the approaches of law and philosophy, perhaps it is not surprising that many scholars in the field of judicial politics have strongly embraced the new institutionalist model.[26]

While behavioralists often studied the decision-making processes of individual judges using mostly quantitative methods, some political scientists argued that legal rules, structures, and doctrines were also quite important. Political institutions establish guidelines for deliberation, help aggregate individual preferences into collective decisions, and provide for the implementation of those decisions.[27] As Douglas North, an expert on judicial politics, has written, "Institutions are the rules of the game in society or, more formally, are the humanly devised constraints that shape human interaction."[28] Role theory, discussed in more depth later in the chapter, may also be thought of as a new institutional approach to judicial decision making.

The new institutionalism allowed scholars to move between different levels of analysis. For example, one could study the voting behavior of individual members of Congress, of congressional committees, or of the parties. In terms of judicial politics, one could study the voting behavior of individual judges, but one could also look at the effects of the makeup of three-judge panels on the U.S. courts of appeals, or examine the hierarchical relationships between different levels of courts. New institutionalism also allowed scholars to explore the interactions between and among institutions of government. Thus, scholars began to explore how courts interact with the legislative and executive branches, as well as how they interact with interest groups, the media, and public opinion.

New institutionalism is an umbrella term for several more specific approaches. There are at least three branches of new institutionalism: rational choice institutionalism, sociological institutionalism, and historical institutionalism. **Rational choice institutionalism** has its roots in economics and formal modeling analysis.

In rational choice models, the political actors are assumed to be acting rationally and institutions are assumed to be seeking the most efficient decision-making processes. A popular approach within this stream is the use of game theory in order to explain political decision making.[29] That is, rational choice institutionalists look at organizations as though they are systems of rules and incentives.[30] These rules are often contested so that one set of political actors can gain an advantage over a different group. This stream of institutionalism is often highly quantitative, with formal mathematical modeling frequently part of this line of scholarship.

Sociological institutionalism has its roots in sociology, anthropology, and cultural studies. This stream stresses the idea of institutional cultures and norms. These scholars see institutional rules, norms, and structures not as inherently rational or dictated by efficiency concerns, but instead as culturally constructed. Sociological institutionalists argue that "even the most seemingly bureaucratic of practices have to be explained in cultural terms."[31] These scholars tend to define institutions more broadly than do scholars in the other two streams.

The third branch of new institutionalist analysis, **historical institutionalism**, has received a great deal of attention among political scientists, especially those who use more qualitative methodologies. Historical institutionalism has its roots in the disciplines of history and law.[32] This branch includes an eclectic group of scholars with a wide variety of research agendas. Generally, historical institutionalists define political institutions broadly and are interested in changes in institutions over time. Historical institutionalists tend to define institutions as "the formal or informal procedures, routines, norms, and conventions embedded in the organizational structure of the polity or political economy."[33] They see political institutions as constitutional, procedural, or programmatic in nature. Other scholars note that historical institutionalists see institutions as continuities, meaning that they usually do not examine only one institution or process at a set point in time but rather tend to look at politics as very complex and complicated sets of processes and institutions that vary over time and interact in interesting and unexpected ways.[34]

Strategic Models

An outgrowth of the new institutional approaches is the strategic models, which can be sorted into two main categories: internal and external. All of these **strategic models** assume that judges are both legal actors and ideological actors, acting within the institutional constraints of the judiciary. But judges also strategically anticipate the reactions of others in their decision-making processes, meaning that judicial decisions are interdependent with the needs and wants of others.

One definition of the strategic model states, "To say that a justice acts strategically is to say that she realizes that her success or failure depends on the preferences of other actors and the actions she expects them to take, not just on her own preferences and actions."[35] One of the first works to promote a strategic model of judicial making was Walter Murphy's *Elements of Judicial Strategy,* first published in 1964.[36] All of the contemporary scholars who use the strategic model trace their intellectual roots to this book.

The internal type of strategic model posits that justices anticipate the reactions of their colleagues in their decision making.[37] A good example of this is the way in which the Court treats sex discrimination cases. All discrimination cases are based on the Fourteenth Amendment's Equal Protection Clause. In analyzing the Equal Protection Clause, the Court uses three tests to determine if a law is unconstitutional: strict scrutiny (for race discrimination cases and cases that impede a fundamental right), intermediate review (mostly for sex discrimination cases), and the rational basis test (most other cases). In strict scrutiny, the law is almost always declared unconstitutional; the rational basis test almost always means that the statute is upheld. When using the intermediate review test, the law may or may not be upheld.

Reed v. Reed (1971) was the first case in which the Court recognized that sex discrimination could violate the Equal Protection Clause, but the justices used the rational basis test in this case. This case declared unconstitutional a state law that preferred fathers over mothers as the administrators of their deceased children's estates. In *Frontiero v. Richardson* (1973), the Court struck down a military rule that allowed male soldiers to receive spousal benefits for their wives automatically, but forced female soldiers to prove that their husbands were financially dependent before their husbands could receive spousal benefits. Most of the justices agreed that this was unconstitutional sex discrimination, but the Court could not agree on what level of scrutiny to use for future sex discrimination cases. Justice William Brennan, among several other justices, felt that sex discrimination cases should receive strict scrutiny just like race discrimination cases. The next sex discrimination case was *Craig v. Boren* (1976), where Oklahoma had a lower drinking age for women than it did for men. Anticipating the reactions of his colleagues and thus using the internal type of strategic model, Justice Brennan wrote the majority opinion in *Craig.* Instead of pushing for strict scrutiny for all sex discrimination cases, as he had in *Frontiero,* Brennan created the intermediate review test. Thus, the Court gave sex discrimination less protection than race discrimination, but Justice Brennan was able to get at least five votes for the new higher level of scrutiny. In this case, Brennan gave up his true ideological preferences in order to get the five votes needed to create a majority on the Court.[38]

The external type of strategic model says that the justices anticipate the reactions of other institutions of government before making their decisions.[39] For example, the Court may back off from a fight with Congress or the president in order to protect the Court from external attack. A pair of cases from the McCarthy era illustrates this type of strategic action on the part of the justices. In *Watkins v. United States* (1957), the Court directly challenged the practices of the House Un-American Activities Committee. The committee would call witnesses to its hearings and demand to know whether they were Communists. The committee members would also demand that witnesses reveal the names of any others in government, academia, or the arts who were members of the Communist Party. In *Watkins,* the Court said that the congressional committee had gone too far and violated the due process rights of the witnesses. In *Barenblatt v. United States* (1959), just a few years later, the Court reversed itself and allowed the congressional committee to ask whatever questions it felt necessary, without judicial interference. Thus, *Barenblatt* is often thought of as the Court's great surrender to McCarthyism. The justices had acted strategically in order to prevent possible retaliation against the Court by an extremely angry U.S. Congress.

The justices are well aware of how the other branches may react to their rulings. According to one study, more than three-quarters of the briefs submitted to the Court contain information about how other governmental institutions might react to the Court's decision.[40] The solicitor general also provides valuable information to the Supreme Court about the preferences of the other branches.[41] Recall that the solicitor general is the lawyer for the executive branch who argues cases at the U.S. Supreme Court.

Sometimes the chief justice in particular feels that he or she must exert leadership and act strategically to save the Supreme Court from potential institutional attacks. For example, Chief Justice William Rehnquist wrote the majority decision in *Dickerson v. U.S.* (2000), which declared the Miranda warnings to be constitutionally required. Rehnquist had been a strong opponent of the decision in *Miranda v. Arizona* (1966) during all of his previous time on the Court. But in his role as chief justice, he felt the need to protect the Court from outside attack. Thus, he authored the majority opinion upholding the Miranda warnings as constitutionally required. Linda Greenhouse, a journalist and commentator on the Supreme Court, has described Rehnquist's strategic approach thusly:

> Chief Justice William H. Rehnquist was a master of the long game, willing to tack left if necessary. In 2000, for example, he wrote a majority opinion, over the furious dissents of Justices Antonin Scalia and Clarence Thomas, upholding the *Miranda* decision against a Congressional effort to declare it inoperative.

William Rehnquist didn't like *Miranda v. Arizona* when the Warren Court decided it in 1966, and he didn't like it any better in 2000, but what he liked even less was an attempted Congressional incursion on the Supreme Court's authority to interpret the Constitution.[42]

Many commentators are wondering if Chief Justice Roberts voted to uphold President Obama's Affordable Care Act in the presidential election year of 2012 because he feared partisan attacks on the Court. The Roberts Court included five conservatives, appointed by Republican presidents, and four liberals, appointed by Democratic presidents. It was the first time in many years that the partisan makeup of the Court mirrored the ideological makeup of the Court. In other words, did Roberts fear public reaction if the Court struck down the Affordable Care Act in an opinion signed by five conservative Republican justices and opposed by four liberal Democratic justices?

As you might recall from the previous chapter, there was also speculation that Chief Justice Roberts changed his vote late in the negotiation process in this case.[43] The conventional wisdom is that Roberts could not bear to face the problems that might have arisen had there been a 5–4 vote striking down the health care reform law, especially if the five activist justices were all Republican appointees and the four restraintists were all Democratic appointees. A clear Republican-Democratic split among the justices on such an important issue could have left the Court vulnerable, and certainly so if President Obama was reelected. Linda Greenhouse colorfully noted:

> [Roberts's] decision to call the mandate a tax and to provide a clearly reluctant fifth vote for upholding it as within the Congressional taxing power was a deeply pragmatic call that saved the Affordable Care Act. Certainly by no coincidence, it also saved the Supreme Court from the stench of extreme partisanship that has hung over the health care litigation from the moment more than two years ago that Republican state officials raced one another to the federal courts to try to erase what they had been unable to block.[44]

Other Approaches

Some political scientists worry that all of these models of judicial decision making are incomplete, and they have developed other approaches. One study suggests that judges care deeply about the reactions of various "audiences." Like most human beings, judges are concerned with maintaining their professional reputations and their friendships with other professionals. Their decision making will reflect this need to please those who matter to them.[45] Other studies have focused more on adding social and cognitive psychological elements to these models. In attempting to combine the legal model and the attitudinal model, one study promoting the use of cognitive psychology variables concluded that judges are "predisposed to find authority consistent with their attitudes more convincing than cited authority that goes against desired outcomes."[46] And some scholars have attempted to create "integrative" models that combine elements of the legal, attitudinal, and strategic models.[47] For these models, precedent, ideology, and the views of other governmental institutions all matter, but none alone can explain judicial decision making. The effects of these factors change over time and across multiple dimensions.[48]

Another integrative approach is the concept of **jurisprudential regimes**. This idea focuses on cases or groups of cases that change the way the Supreme Court deals with future cases; some might call it a paradigm shift. A jurisprudential regime is "a key precedent, or a set of related precedents, that structures the way in which the Supreme Court justices evaluate key elements of cases in arriving at decisions in a particular legal area."[49] Thus, the Court creates an analytical framework for a certain kind of case, and that framework shapes the way that the justices approach the next set of facts and constrains their choices in the future. These new legal rules change the weight that the justices give to different considerations in the future. Therefore, this jurisprudential regime concept includes both legal factors and policy concerns. This concept provides another way to combine the legal, attitudinal, and strategic models.[50]

Judges often seem to be surprised by how political scientists study judicial decision making. Most judges claim that they solely use the legal model. After sitting through a conference about the interconnectedness of law and politics, one judge remarked, "The critique of some in the political science academy that judicial decision-making is not based on law but on politics is disheartening. And I think that critique is wrong."[51] Another judge noted, "There has been an underestimation of the role of precedent in our discussions here. It's very important this thing called precedent. What we have been trained to do is to follow precedent."[52] A third judge complained, "I have come to the end of this conversation feeling a little like a lab rat being analyzed."[53] Judges will claim that they decide all cases based on the law and the facts only. Political scientists usually disagree.

THEORIES OF JUDICIAL DECISION MAKING

Judicial scholars and political scientists have also developed theories to explain how things such as the role of a judge, the structure of the appellate court, and the court's position in the larger political landscape can have an effect on judicial decision making. The following section looks at those theories, including role theory, small group theory, principal agent theory, and regime politics theory.

Role Theory

Role theory is the idea that individuals may make very different decisions in their role as judge than they would in other roles, such as legislator or president.[54] While the courts are clearly political institutions that make public policy, judges must nevertheless explain their decisions using the law and legal reasoning.[55] Any differences between the sort of decisions individuals would make in the role of judge and the decisions they would make in other roles can be attributed in part to differences in institutional roles and decision-making styles. Different institutional constraints and institutional norms also play a part. Stressing the similarities among judges, one scholar has argued, "Most of the time, as far as we can tell, judges of all political stripes, outlooks, backgrounds, and philosophies tend to come to the same *legal* conclusions in ordinary cases."[56] As Judge Richard Posner of the Seventh Circuit has written, "To regard oneself and be regarded by others, especially one's peers, as a good judge requires conformity to the accepted norms of judging."[57] Thus, serving in the role of judge can lead individuals to make different decisions than they would in a different role.

Justices on the Supreme Court have often said that they are constrained in making their decisions by the role of being a judge. For example, Justice Sandra Day O'Connor said exactly that in her dissent in *Roper v. Simmons* (2005), in which the majority ruled that the death penalty was unconstitutional for defendants who were juveniles when they committed the crime. She could not agree with the ruling of the majority, in large part because of her perception of her role as a judge. Justice O'Connor wrote in that case, "Were my office that of a legislator, rather than a judge, then I, too, would be inclined to support legislation setting a minimum age of 18 in this context."[58] Justice O'Connor made a similar argument in her dissent in *Gonzales v. Raich* (2005), in which the majority said that the California law allowing the use of marijuana for medical purposes had to yield to federal drug laws: "If I were a California citizen, I would not have voted for the medical marijuana initiative; if I were a California legislator I would not have supported the Compassionate Use Act. But whatever the wisdom of California's experiment with medical marijuana, the federalism principles that have driven our Commerce Clause cases require that room for experiment [by the states] be protected in this case."[59]

Other justices have also indicated that they wish they could act like legislators but that their role as judge requires them to make a different decision. Take Justice Potter Stewart's dissent in *Griswold v. Connecticut* (1965), where the Court declared unconstitutional a state law banning the use or sale of contraceptives. He stated, "I think this is an uncommonly silly law. . . . But we are not asked in this case to say whether we think this law is unwise, or even asinine. We are asked to hold that it violates the United States Constitution. And that I cannot do."[60] Justice Thomas made a similar claim in *Lawrence v. Texas* (2003), where the Court ruled the state anti-sodomy law to be unconstitutional. After echoing Justice Stewart's claim in *Griswold* that the statute was "uncommonly silly," Justice Thomas wrote, "If I were a member of the Texas legislature, I would vote to repeal it. [. . .] Notwithstanding this, I recognize that as a member of this Court I am not empowered to help petitioners and others similarly situated. My duty, rather, is to decide cases agreeably to the Constitution and laws of the United States."[61] Justice John Paul Stevens on several occasions said that he would have decided a variety of cases differently if he had been a politician rather than a judge. He noted, "In each [decision] I was convinced that the law compelled a result that I would have opposed if I were a legislator."[62] While politicians have the luxury of making decisions based on purely political considerations, judges (and especially appellate judges) must explain how legal reasoning and analysis compel their rulings. With their life terms and judicial independence, Supreme Court justices do not feel obligated to follow public opinion in their decisions. Justice Stevens has commented, "It's part of the job to write unpopular decisions. No doubt about it."[63]

Let us now turn from theories about individual judicial decision making to collective decision making.

Small Group Theory and the U.S. Supreme Court

Since appellate courts are collective bodies, sociolegal scholars often use **small group theory** to help us understand how appellate courts function, shifting the focus away from the individual judge as a lone decision maker. As defined by judicial scholar Sidney Ulmer, small group theory "holds that group variables influence the individual participant to behave differently from the way he would act alone toward the same task."[64]

Remember that justices on the U.S. Supreme Court work together as a group for years at a time, as do many judges on other appellate courts. Thus, the Supreme Court has numerous attributes of a harmonious small group. But the collegial nature of the U.S. Supreme Court should not be overemphasized; in some ways the Court is a collection of extremely independent individuals. As Chief Justice Rehnquist once said, the Court is primarily dominated "by centrifugal forces, pushing toward individuality and independence."[65] At times the Supreme Court has been referred to as "nine separate little law firms" or even as "nine scorpions in a bottle."[66]

The Role of the Chief Justice and Other Leadership Roles

One of the first aspects to consider in small group theory is the role and leadership of the chief justice on the U.S. Supreme Court. The chief justice is often considered first among equals on the Supreme Court and has many duties beyond just voting with his or her colleagues on the Court. Chief Justice Rehnquist received quite a bit of attention when he added four metallic gold stripes to his judicial robe in January 1995, apparently to signal that he was first among equals, since the robes of the other justices did not have such adornments. Rehnquist evidently took the idea for the gold stripes from a costume in a Gilbert and Sullivan light operetta.[67] Chief Justice Roberts has abandoned this practice.

Among the chief justice's unique duties is presiding over the Court in oral arguments and in conference. The chief justice prepares the discuss list for the conference on certiorari and speaks first at the conference meeting if he or she so chooses. If the chief justice is in the majority on the preliminary conference vote on the merits, he or she assigns the task of writing the majority opinion. The chief justice also hires the officers of the Supreme Court and technically hires all the staff for the Supreme Court building. The chief justice is assisted by the Counselor to the Chief Justice, who serves as a kind of chief of staff for the Supreme Court employees. The chief justice also names the head of the Administrative Office of the U.S. Courts, and chairs the Judicial Conference, which is the policy-making body for all federal judges. The chief justice prepares the annual state of the judiciary report for the Court and assigns justices to travel across the street to lobby Congress annually for adequate funding for the federal judiciary. He or she presides over presidential impeachment trials in the U.S. Senate, as Chief Justice Rehnquist did during the removal trial of President Clinton. The chief justice also sits on the oversight board for the Smithsonian Institution, which manages all of the federal museums and zoos in Washington, D.C.

In many ways the chief justice is the public face, and the leader, of the Supreme Court of the United States and of all the federal courts. However, leadership has many aspects, and not all of these are found in the person with the official title of "leader." Clearly the chief justice is the **administrative leader** of the Court. As stated earlier, he or she hires the other officers of the Court and indirectly all Supreme Court employees. He or she also manages the certiorari conference and the conference on the merits at the Court. The chief justice chairs the Judicial Conference of all the district and circuit courts in the country. These jobs come with the title, and all chief justices serve as administrative leader of the Court.

There are other aspects of leadership, however, that do not automatically come with the title. These leadership qualities may or may not be found in the chief justice. Some chief justices have also been the **intellectual leader** of the Court, with the power to persuade the other justices to follow a preferred approach to specific legal questions. For example, it appears that Chief Justice Earl Warren was clearly the intellectual leader of the Supreme Court when he served. He was able to persuade other justices to follow his legal vision. Chief Justice Rehnquist was also the intellectual leader when he served on the Court, though probably only for those in the conservative bloc. But other justices have filled this leadership role on the Court without sitting in the chief justice's seat. For example, Justice Brennan was clearly the intellectual leader of the liberals on the Court during the period when Warren Burger was chief justice. Today, Justice Scalia is probably the intellectual leader of the conservatives on the current Court.

Small groups also need task leaders and social leaders.[68] These roles may or may not be filled by the chief justice. The **task leader** is the person who makes sure the group gets its work done, unofficially chiding the others as needed, and the **social leader** makes sure that the others remain happy in their jobs and maintain good relationships with other members of the group. The chief justice may or may not have the characteristics of these specific types of leaders. Chief Justice Warren may have been both the task and social leader of his Court,[69] but certainly Chief Justice Rehnquist was neither. One might guess that Justice Harry Blackmun was the task leader when he was on the Court[70] because his papers reveal that he was constantly demanding that his colleagues complete their work on time. Justice O'Connor certainly seemed to be the social leader during her years on the highest court.[71] She went out of her way to try to prevent philosophical disagreements among the justices from becoming too personal. For example, she demanded that all the justices eat lunch together instead of isolating themselves in their offices after discussions or hearing oral arguments.[72]

The Freshman Effect

Another aspect of small group theory about the workings of the Supreme Court is the so-called **freshman effect**. This term refers to a phenomenon that might occur when a new justice joins the Supreme Court. Usually, this means that the new justice experiences a period of uncertainty at the beginning of his or her service on the highest court. The new justice may be unwilling to join one of the strongly ideological blocs on the Court, and the new arrival's early decisions may not reflect his or her later views. Sometimes the new justice joins a moderate bloc; other times the new justice finds a more senior justice (perhaps the chief justice) and votes with him or her in most cases.[73] Freshmen are usually assigned fewer and less important decisions to write than are the other justices. They also write fewer concurrences and dissents.

The results of academic research on the freshman effect are mixed. Clearly some new justices go through a period of instability in their voting behavior on the Court. Justices Sandra Day O'Connor, Anthony Kennedy, and David Souter all come to mind. But other justices seem to know from their first day on the Court how they will approach the issues before them. Justices Antonin Scalia, Clarence Thomas, and Samuel Alito are good examples of justices who have not changed their ideological positions over time. Some justices seem to move further to the left the longer they serve on the Supreme Court, with Justices Blackmun and Stevens being good examples. Some research has found this same freshman effect for new justices on lower appellate courts as well.[74]

Small Group Theory and Other Appellate Courts

While a great deal of small group theory focuses on the members of the U.S. Supreme Court, this theory can be used to analyze the behavior of judges on lower appellate courts as well. On state supreme courts, especially those where the judges serve short terms and must face some type of election to retain their seats, there can be a fair amount of turnover among the justices. This fairly rapid pace of change creates small group dynamics different from those found on the U.S. Supreme Court, where membership is comparatively stable. In some states, party control of the state supreme court can change quite often, and so the precedents of the court can change rapidly as well. Michigan and Ohio are good examples of state supreme courts that modify their precedents according to which political party has the majority on the court.[75]

Studying small group effects on the U.S. circuit courts of appeals is a more difficult endeavor because these courts sit in panels of three randomly selected judges. However, each federal circuit court has a chief judge. The **chief judge** is the most senior judge on the circuit court who has been on the court for at least one year and who is under the age of sixty-five when the vacancy occurs. The chief judge has unique administrative responsibilities on the circuit court and within the broader judicial hierarchy. For example, the chief judges sit on the

U.S. Judicial Conference, the policy-making body for all federal judges. The term for the chief judge is seven years or until the age of seventy, whichever comes first.

Scholars have found some other differences between chief judges and the rest of their colleagues on the circuit courts. For example, when chief judges are part of a three-judge panel, they write the majority opinion more often than their colleagues. They are also far less likely to file dissenting or concurring opinions.[76] Chief judges do not, however, have all the leadership opportunities available to the chief justice of the United States, as discussed above, and so they have fewer opportunities to influence their colleagues. Nevertheless, these judges seem at times to behave differently than their peers. As one study has observed, "Chief judges have few, if any, tools at their disposal to bend their fellow appeals court judges to their will. Yet qualitative and quantitative evidence demonstrates that chief judges engage in behaviors that are different from their peers and that reflect concern for the institutional functioning of the circuit."[77]

Another aspect of small group theory as applied to the U.S. courts of appeals looks at whether diversity (either ideological or demographic) on the three-judge panels affects the panels' ultimate decisions. The idea is that having a more diverse panel would prevent like-minded individuals from choosing extreme conclusions.[78] Some studies have found that ideological diversity on a panel does affect the decisions of that panel as a whole, with split panels producing less extreme ideological decisions than unified panels.[79] Other studies have examined the effects of gender diversity on these panels, finding that the presence of a female judge may change the way the entire panel approaches most cases.[80] Clearly, having members with different ideological and background characteristics can affect the panel's decisions.[81]

Principal Agent Theory

Another way to understand the work of appellate courts is through **principal agent theory**. This theory states that the lower courts should act as the agents of the higher courts and follow the precedents set out by their superiors. A good analogy would be the relationship between an employer and an employee—the employee is supposed to carry out the wishes or orders of the employer. Thus, the lower courts should act as agents of the higher courts and follow their wishes as expressed through precedent. In the U.S. courts of appeals, the Supreme Court is the principal and the circuit courts are the agents, meaning that circuit court judges should follow the principle of *stare decisis* and faithfully apply Supreme Court precedents. But the U.S. courts of appeals are also the principals for the

U.S. district courts and various executive branch bureaucratic agencies below them—the agents.[82] The goals of the appellate judges may be different from those of the justices on the Supreme Court.[83] However, according to this theory, even if the ideological preferences of the judges on the circuit courts don't align with the majority on the Supreme Court, the lower court judges still will put aside their ideological differences and follow the precedents of their principal.[84]

Do judges on the U.S. courts of appeals faithfully apply the precedents of their principal, the U.S. Supreme Court? One study examined circuit court rulings on First Amendment and substantive due process cases and found that the lower court judges did generally follow those precedents.[85] Another study examined search-and-seizure law and found that usually judges on the U.S. courts of appeals followed Supreme Court precedent in this area as well.[86] Some broader studies have also found circuit court compliance with U.S. Supreme Court precedents.[87] As one set of scholars has argued, "Judges, at least at the lower court levels, seem to treat precedent seriously."[88]

Some scholars are quite skeptical of principal agent theory because it seems to assume that the principals will be able to sanction agents if they deviate from the principal's preferred outcomes. Since the U.S. Supreme Court reviews so few cases from the U.S. courts of appeals each year, such sanctions are unlikely.[89] One study of anti-trust decisions plus search-and-seizure cases found that the judges on the U.S. courts of appeals did not seem at all concerned about the possibility that the U.S. Supreme Court might reverse their decisions.[90] This study concluded, "Circuit judges are given numerous chances to make law unimpeded by the Supreme Court, and they seem to take advantage of these opportunities."[91] On the other hand, the number of reversals by the U.S. Supreme Court may not be the right measure of usefulness of the principal agent theory, because "[i]t is the threat, not the actuality, of review that can control agents."[92] Despite these disagreements, principal agent theory may be a useful way to approach the role of the U.S. courts of appeals in the judicial hierarchy.

The Anti-Majoritarian Dilemma and Regime Politics Theory

When the courts are activist, they seem to be protecting minority political views against the will of the political majority. Thus, are judicial activism and judicial policy making inherently anti-democratic? In a very famous article published in 1957, political scientist Robert Dahl disagreed with this assertion.[93] Dahl argued that we should not worry about an overly activist Supreme Court because the justices have almost always acted "in alliance with the governing coalition of which they themselves are generally members."[94] Treating the Court matter-of-factly as a policy-making institution, Dahl insisted that the judicial appointment process ensured that "the policy views dominant on the Court are never for long out of line with the policy views dominant among the lawmaking majorities of the United States."[95] In other words, the Supreme Court follows the election returns and supports the current governmental regime in power.

In his article, Dahl only examined cases in which the Court declared acts of Congress to be unconstitutional. He did not consider statutory interpretation cases or cases where the Court struck down the actions of the states. Dahl found that the Supreme Court declared acts of Congress unconstitutional only "after the lawmaking majority was already dead" or when the cases involved "trivial pieces of legislation." Otherwise, the Court often found its decisions "reversed, overridden, or overturned."[96] Both Dahl and his successors believe that the Supreme Court makes public policy in our society, but as part of, and in line with, the broader governing coalition, which includes the president and the Congress.

This idea that the Supreme Court is a willing partner in the coalition that controls politics and policy has become known as **regime politics theory**. Scholars who study this theory "trace the connections between the Court's decisions and the demands of governing elites."[97] According to one advocate of this approach, "'Regime politics' refers to the various ways in which governing coalitions organize their power and advance their political agenda within a system of interrelated institutions," including the Supreme Court.[98] Therefore, political parties, interest groups, and other political actors will attempt to influence the decisions of the judiciary just as they do the decisions of legislatures or executive branch agencies. There is a large and growing body of literature that ties judicial decision making to specific patterns of party politics, group coalition building, critical elections, the policy agenda of the governing elites, and other features of the political regime.[99] Some scholars have argued that the Supreme Court is unable to check the will of the majority even if the justices want to because the political elites in the governing coalition would block such change. Therefore, relying on the courts for broad social change is a "hollow hope."[100]

Also disputing the notion that unelected judges impose their personal views and values on an unwilling American public, scholar Terri Jennings Peretti has argued instead that the justices on the Supreme Court overwhelmingly reflect the views of the current president and Congress. The key is the highly political selection process used to nominate and confirm federal judges. Because federal judges are appointed by the president and confirmed by the Senate, the values of the justices reflect the range of those views currently held by the other branches of government.[101] Or as Robert McCloskey, a famous political scientist writing just three years after Dahl, stated, "[T]he Supreme Court has seldom, if ever, flatly and for very long resisted a really unmistakable wave of public sentiment."[102]

Another indication of the validity of the regime politics theory approach is the fact that the Supreme Court varies over time in how much respect it gives to precedent and other legal factors. Precedent seemed to matter very little for the Court in the 1950s and 1960s, then became more important in the 1970s, and had its greatest impact on the justices in the 1990s.[103] According to this research, the justices choose when to use precedent and when to ignore it based on the needs of the governing coalition at the time.

Almost twenty years after Dahl, political scientist Jonathan Casper wrote a strong rebuttal to Dahl's claims, raising both methodological and substantive criticisms of Dahl's research. Casper noted that Dahl only focused on times when the Supreme Court declared acts of Congress invalid. Thus, Dahl ignored the Court's policy-making roles in statutory interpretation decisions and in declaring state actions to be unconstitutional. Casper also argued that by focusing only on "winners and losers," Dahl missed the important role that the Court plays in creating the nation's policy agenda.

> The notion of a "winning" and a "losing" policy when institutions clash imposes an artificial distinction that obscures a dynamic process in which even the "losers" contribute importantly to outcomes that eventually emerge. [. . .] Many of the issues in which national political institutions become involved are not "settled" but continue to recur. Conflicts among political institutions produce not "winning" and "losing" policies, but rather tentative solutions that become the basis for future policy making.[104]

Writing some fifty years after Dahl, other political scientists also criticized the assumptions of the regime politics theory. Dahl seemed to think that the elements of the governing regime were always in agreement regarding policy choices. However, the justices may have a range of possible choices available to them because the governing coalition is so often divided on important matters. As one study concluded, "The Court's decision in a given case may be supported by some members of the governing coalition, but if the opposite decision would have been supported by other members of the coalition, then the justices may well have significant room for independent action."[105]

Still others have objected to Dahl's approach and the resulting regime politics theory because it ignores the fact that the courts are distinctive in their use of legal reasoning in the decision-making process. Their jurisprudence proves that both ideas and institutions matter.[106] Unlike Dahl, however, some of his contemporaries insisted that the Court blends this policy-making role with the traditional judicial functions of legal reasoning and analysis of multiple sources of law, forming a complex mixture.[107]

GOVERNANCE AS DIALOGUE MOVEMENT

We cannot assess the decision making of U.S. Supreme Court justices without some discussion of the Governance as Dialogue movement. This movement argues that the Supreme Court is not the last word on interpreting the Constitution, but instead is part of a continuing conversation among political actors and institutions that ultimately determines the Constitution's meaning. As one research study concluded, "American political institutions by design are inextricably linked in a continuing dialogue."[108] Recall that Casper argued that public policy making in this country is a "dynamic process" in which "issues recur."[109] Although he did not use the language of the Governance as Dialogue movement, Casper was previewing what was to come. Judges and scholars now acknowledge that there is a continuing conversation among political institutional actors. Justice Ruth Bader Ginsburg has stated that constitutional interpretation often requires courts to enter into "a continuing dialogue with other branches of government, the States, or the private sector."[110] And as Justice Robert H. Jackson argued more than fifty years ago, "No sound assessment of our Supreme Court can treat it as an isolated, self-sustaining, or self-sufficient institution. It is a unit of a complex, interdependent scheme of government from which it cannot be severed."[111] Thus, the Governance as Dialogue movement looks at how all the institutions of government interact with one another and in so doing negotiate the meaning of the Constitution.

Among American academics, Alexander Bickel was among the first to promote the Governance as Dialogue approach. In his famous book *The Least Dangerous Branch* (1962),[112] Bickel stated that the courts must engage in a "continuing colloquy" with the more political branches of government and with other political actors. This was in direct rebuttal to the notion then prevalent in law schools that the courts were supreme in their interpretation of the Constitution. Others have also argued against the notion of judicial supremacy. In his famous book *Constitutional Dialogues* (1988)[113] and in many other works, Louis Fisher has argued that the courts and especially the U.S. Supreme Court are not solely responsible for making constitutional interpretations. Instead, determining constitutionality involves a very complicated conversation among various political and institutional actors. As Fisher notes, "Throughout its history, the

Supreme Court has understood that its 'independence' relies on an astute appreciation of how dependent the judiciary is on the political system for understanding, supporting, and implementing judicial rulings."[114]

CHAPTER SUMMARY

This chapter has explored various theories and approaches political scientists use to help us understand decision making on appellate courts. Most of this research focuses on the U.S. Supreme Court, but the theories can apply to other appellate courts as well. This chapter began with a look at the historical development of the study of judicial decision making in political science, including the traditionalist era and the behavioral revolution. It explored several models of judicial decision making within these schools of thought, including legal, attitudinal, new institutionalist, and strategic models. The chapter then examined role theory, small group theory, principal agent theory, and regime politics theory before concluding with a brief discussion of the Governance as Dialogue movement, which states that policy making and constitutional interpretation consist of a series of continuous inter-institutional conversations or dialogues.

For Further Reading

Bailey, Michael A., and Forrest Maltzman. 2011. *The Constrained Court*. Princeton, NJ: Princeton University Press.

Baum, Lawrence. 1997. *The Puzzle of Judicial Behavior*. Ann Arbor: University of Michigan Press.

Braman, Eileen. 2009. *Law, Politics, and Perception: How Policy Preferences Influence Legal Reasoning*. Charlottesville: University of Virginia Press.

Bybee, Keith J. 2010. *All Judges Are Political: Except When They Are Not*. Stanford, CA: Stanford University Press.

Epstein, Lee, and Jack Knight. 1998. *The Choices Justices Make*. Washington, D.C.: CQ Press.

Gillman, Howard. 2001. *The Votes That Counted: How the Court Decided the 2000 Presidential Election*. Chicago: University of Chicago Press.

Maltzman, Forrest, James Spriggs II, and Paul Wahlbeck. 2000. *Creating Law on the Supreme Court: The Collegial Game*. New York: Cambridge University Press.

Maveety, Nancy, ed. 2003. *The Pioneers of Judicial Behavior*. Ann Arbor: University of Michigan Press.

Murphy, Walter F. 1964. *Elements of Judicial Strategy*. Chicago: University of Chicago Press.

Pacelle, Richard L., Jr., Brett W. Curry, and Bryan W. Marshall. 2011. *Decision Making by the Modern Supreme Court*. New York: Cambridge University Press.

Peretti, Terri Jennings. 1999. *In Defense of a Political Court*. Princeton, NJ: Princeton University Press.

Segal, Jeffrey, and Harold Spaeth. 2002. *The Supreme Court and the Attitudinal Model Revisited*. New York: Cambridge University Press.

9

Public Opinion, Interest Groups, the Media, and the Courts

American courts do not exist in a vacuum. Instead, the courts interact with a variety of other aspects of American society. This chapter will examine how the courts interact with three of those aspects—public opinion, interest groups, and the media.

PUBLIC OPINION AND THE COURTS

Courts depend on the goodwill of the American people and the other institutions of government to enforce their rulings. As Philip Kurland has proclaimed, "The only power that the Court can assert is the power of public opinion."[1] Unless they consider the courts to be legitimate and their decisions well reasoned, the public or political actors have no reason to abide by those decisions. This is especially true of the U.S. Supreme Court. According to Alexis de Tocqueville, "The power of the Supreme Court Justices is immense, but it is power springing from opinion. They are all-powerful so long as the people consent to obey the law; they can do nothing when they scorn it."[2]

The relationship between public opinion and the courts is therefore quite important in a democracy. When examining the interactions between public opinion and the courts, there are three key issues to consider. The first is the level of support the American public gives to the courts in general and also to specific court decisions. The second is whether the Supreme Court and other courts are constrained by public opinion. That is, are the courts free to issue rulings that the public opposes? The third is whether the Supreme Court leads or creates public opinion when it hands down decisions that require change in our society.

Diffuse Public Support for the Supreme Court

Traditionally, public approval ratings for the U.S. Supreme Court have always been higher than those for Congress and the president. Using data from 1972 through 1994, one study found that during this entire time Americans always had more confidence in the Supreme Court than in either of the other federal institutions of government.[3] This broad level of support of the Supreme Court without regard to its rulings in any specific case is known as **diffuse support**. The public support for the U.S. Supreme Court is part of the general diffuse support for the entire justice system in this country. Some scholars even equate diffuse support for the courts with the public's view of the courts' legitimacy.[4] Legitimacy and diffuse support for the courts mean that the public has enduring institutional loyalty to the judiciary.[5] Scholar James Gibson defined diffuse support as "a fundamental commitment to an institution and a willingness to support the institution that extends beyond mere satisfaction with the performance of the institution at the moment."[6] The Supreme Court has enjoyed a relatively long and stable period in which the American public found the Court to be a highly legitimate governmental institution with high levels of diffuse support.[7] As Justice Sonia Sotomayor has noted, "It always thrills me, amazes me, and gives me faith in our country to know how much people trust the courts."[8]

Some have speculated that the American public holds courts and judges in high respect, even reverence. In fairly early academic studies of public opinion toward the U.S. Supreme Court, scholars generally found that the Supreme Court enjoyed a "reservoir of goodwill and commitment among the mass public."[9] James Bryce, a scholar writing in 1891, observed that the courts in general, and particularly the U.S. Supreme Court, were held in high esteem by the American people. And even though many specific court rulings provoked intense public opposition, "the credit and dignity of the Supreme Court stand very high."[10] Drawing on their analysis of how and why the courts had survived strong rhetorical attacks throughout our history, many scholars in the 1950s and 1960s arrived at the conventional wisdom that the courts were protected by a popular reverence for the judiciary. Judicial politics scholar Walter Murphy, writing in 1962, even labeled this phenomenon "the cult of the robe."[11] Other scholars have used the term "judicial mythology" to refer to the reverence, respect, secrecy, and mystery that over the years have protected the American courts from institutional attacks.[12]

In addition to holding the courts in high regard, Americans also seem to revere the U.S. Constitution, almost to the point of treating it as a sacred document. Some scholars have noted that the magic and mystery surrounding the Constitution have spilled over into the popular perception of and support for the courts. As Murphy colorfully noted, "The sacred, mysterious character of the Constitution has been caught by the Justices in the performance of their priestly duty of expounding the meaning of that holy writ."[13] In tune with this theme, one book about the U.S. Supreme Court is even called *The Priestly Tribe: The Supreme Court's Image in the American Mind.*[14] The author of this book, Barbara A. Perry, concludes, "The Court has cultivated positive symbolic impressions through the language of its opinions, the emblems of its power and physical environment, and the honorable behavior of its justices and support personnel."[15]

Other scholars have also noted how important the symbols of the legal system are in maintaining high public support for the courts.[16] These legal symbols help the public see the courts as legitimate and increase diffuse support for them. In other words, the symbols of the judiciary, such as the fact that judges wear robes and many courthouses are majestic public buildings, remind the average person that judges make their decisions based on legal principles instead of on purely political considerations.[17] As James Gibson and Gregory Caldeira noted in their book *Citizens, Courts, and Confirmations,* "Exposure to legitimizing judicial symbols reinforces the message that 'courts are different,' and owing to such difference, courts are worthy of more respect, deference, and obedience—in short, legitimacy."[18]

Is Public Support for the Supreme Court Falling?

But are public reference and respect for the judiciary starting to fade? An April 2012 poll done by the Pew Research Center reports that public approval of the U.S. Supreme Court hit a twenty-five-year low, with only 52 percent of those surveyed stating that they approved of the way the Supreme Court does its job. A March 2013 Pew Research Center report also showed public approval ratings for the Court at the same low figure of 52 percent. Supreme Court approval ratings in Pew Research Center polls peaked in July 1994, when 80 percent of those surveyed expressed approval.

It is always difficult to compare approval ratings in polls from different companies due to methodological differences in how the polls were conducted. Nevertheless, in a June 2012 poll done by the *New York Times* and CBS News, the U.S. Supreme Court's approval rating was an extremely low 44 percent. In the same poll, the approval rating for President Obama was 47 percent, and the approval rating for the U.S. Congress was 15 percent.[19] *New York Times*/CBS News polls from the late 1980s showed that 66 percent of the public approved of the way the Supreme Court did its job.

The two 2012 polls were taken before the Court announced its decision in the health care reform case, *National Federation of Independent Business v. Sebelius* (2012). The media reported that the opinion upheld the constitutionality of the most important parts of President Obama's signature Affordable Care Act, although the opinion itself was actually extremely complex and the president did not win on all issues in the case. After that ruling was released to the public, the Supreme Court's approval rating fell to 41 percent in a *New York Times*/CBS News poll, with most of the drop attributable to Republicans who were very unhappy that the Court upheld the penalty for individuals who do not buy health insurance, known as the individual mandate.[20] The effects of this case on the Supreme Court's approval rating may have lingered. In a June 2013 *New York Times*/CBS News poll, the Supreme Court's overall approval rate remained a fairly low 44 percent. In the same poll, the approval rating for President Obama averaged 47 percent and the approval rating for the U.S. Congress was 13 percent.[21] In recent history, it has been very unusual that the approval rate for the Supreme Court was lower than it was for the president.

The overall approval rating for the Supreme Court may cloak variations among groups in that support. Figure 9.1 shows snapshots of the approval ratings from the Pew polls for the U.S. Supreme Court over time and breaks down the approval ratings by party and by presidential administration. While the overall approval rate for the U.S. Supreme Court has held relatively steady over the years, there has been something of a downward trend, particularly in recent years, with the high of an 80 percent approval rating reached in 1994 and the lowest approval ratings coming very recently.

Figure 9.1 also shows that, generally speaking, members of the president's political party support the Supreme Court more than do members of the opposition party. This is true even when a majority of the justices were appointed by presidents from the other party. Under President Reagan and President George H. W. Bush, Republicans were more supportive of the Supreme Court than were Democrats. This reversed during the Clinton presidency, where Democrats were more supportive of the Supreme Court than were Republicans. The trend reversed again during the presidency of George W. Bush, when Republicans again were strongest in their approval of the Supreme Court. Poll numbers during the Obama Administration have been somewhat mixed, but, since the Court's June 2012 decision upholding the constitutionality of most of the president's health care reform legislation, Democratic support for the Court has increased while Republican approval

FIGURE 9.1 Supreme Court Favorability by Party and Administration

% Favorable	TOTAL	REP.	DEM.	IND	REP.-DEM. DIFF.
	%	%	%	%	
Obama					
2013 (March)	52	47	56	52	−9
2012 (July)	53	38	64	51	−26
2012 (April)	52	56	52	52	+4
2010 (July)	58	52	65	58	−13
2009 (April)	64	70	63	64	+7
G. W. Bush					
2007 (July)	57	73	49	58	+24
2005 (June)	57	64	51	51	+13
2001 (Jan.)	68	80	62	69	+18
Clinton					
1997 (May)	72	69	78	73	−9
1994 (July)	80	79	83	80	−4
G. H. W. Bush					
1991 (Nov.)	72	83	67	69	+16
1990 (May)	65	71	58	67	+13
Reagan					
1987 (May)	76	80	75	75	+5

Source: Compiled by author from data from Pew Research Center.

of the Court has diminished. Thus, the overall approval rating number for the Supreme Court masks the specific variations in support for the Court among various groups, and especially among partisan groupings.

It is unclear how decisions in big cases may affect the public's view of the U.S. Supreme Court, and this is especially true of cases perceived to be decided along political lines. Some have speculated that a significant proportion of the public believes that the Supreme Court acted in a very political fashion in handing down *Bush v. Gore* (2000), which decided the 2000 presidential election, and in *Citizens United v. Federal Election Commission* (2010), where the Court said that it was unconstitutional to limit campaign expenditures from corporations and unions. Did these so-called political rulings result in lower public approval ratings for the Supreme Court? While the answer is unclear, one thing we do know is that in a June 2013 *New York Times*/CBS News poll, more than two-thirds of the respondents (68 percent) reported believing that the justices on the U.S. Supreme Court often base their rulings on their own personal and political views.[22]

Figure 9.2 shows how the general public reacted immediately following a variety of landmark U.S. Supreme Court decisions. Some of these decisions have been quite unpopular among the public, while others show the Court following public opinion on these issues. For example, the Court's ruling in *Clinton v. Jones* (1997) that civil lawsuits filed against sitting presidents could proceed during their presidency was extremely popular among the public at the time. Likewise, the Court's decision in *Parents Involved in Community Schools v. Seattle School District No. 1* (2007), where the Court ruled that race could not be considered in public school assignment decisions, was also very popular among the general population right after the decision was announced. On the other hand, the Supreme Court has not hesitated to hand down less popular decisions, even extremely unpopular ones. The Court's ruling in *Citizens United v. Federal Election Commission* (2010), allowing unlimited corporate and union spending during election campaigns, was supported by a mere 17 percent of the public right after the decision was handed down. Likewise, the Court's ruling that burning the American flag is protected political speech in *Texas v. Johnson* (1989) received very low public support right after it was announced.

Do the Courts Follow Public Opinion?

Moving to our second question, does the Supreme Court follow public opinion in its rulings? Certainly, deciding cases in alignment with popular opinion can bring benefits to the Supreme Court, including increasing the diffuse support for courts in general.[23] Many research studies have found that the decisions of the U.S. Supreme Court generally reflect broad public opinion on the matter.[24] As scholar Michael J. Klarman has argued, Supreme Court justices "rarely hold views that deviate far from dominant public opinion."[25] And as Chief Justice Rehnquist has noted, "Judges, so long as they are relatively normal human beings, can no more escape being influenced by public opinion in the long run than can people working at other jobs."[26] One study from the late 1980s indicated that the Supreme Court followed public opinion in just over 60 percent of the cases examined.[27] As legal scholar Paul Freund has quipped, "Judges [. . .] should not be influenced by the weather of the day, but they are necessarily influenced by the climate of the age."[28]

In refining this view, some scholars have argued that because the U.S. Supreme Court cannot enforce its own rulings, it is dependent on other institutions

FIGURE 9.2 Public Approval of Major Supreme Court Decisions

ISSUE	YEAR	CASE	RULING	% APPROVAL
Abortion	1973	*Roe v. Wade*	Women have right to abortion	52
	2007	*Gonzales v. Carhart*	Upheld federal Partial-Birth Abortion Ban Act	47
Affirmative action	2003	*Grutter v. Bollinger*	Colleges may consider race and sex in admissions	24
Civil procedure	1997	*Clinton v. Jones*	Civil lawsuits can proceed versus president while in office	59
First Amendment	1971	*New York Times v. U.S.*	Protected right of *New York Times* to publish Pentagon Papers about Vietnam War	43
	1989	*Texas v. Johnson*	Destroying or burning American flag as protest is protected freedom of speech	20
	2010	*Citizens United v. Federal Election Commission*	Corporations and unions may spend unlimited money in political elections	17
Gay rights	2000	*Boy Scouts of America v. Dale*	Boy Scouts can prohibit gay Scouts and leaders	56
	2003	*Lawrence v. Texas*	Overturned Texas law prohibiting gay sex	40
Health care reform	2012	*National Federation of Independent Business v. Sebelius*	Upheld most of Obama's health care reform law	46
Race	1954	*Brown v. Board of Education*	Racial segregation in public schools is unconstitutional	55
	2007	*Parents Involved in Community Schools v. Seattle Schools*	Race cannot be a factor when assigning students to public schools	71
Religion	1966	*Engle v. Vitale*	Children cannot be required to utter a spoken prayer in school	30
	2000	*Santa Fe Independent Schools v. Doe*	Bans student-led prayer before football games at public school	29
Terrorism	2008	*Boumediene v. Bush*	Detainees at Guantanamo Bay have a right to challenge detentions in civilian courts	34
Voting rights	2000	*Bush v. Gore*	Rejected 2000 presidential election recounts in Florida	50

Note: These approval ratings were measured soon after the ruling was released to the public.
Source: Compiled by author using data from the *New York Times*.

of government. Since the other branches are sensitive to public opinion, the Court must be too.[29] If the Court is not sensitive to the views of public opinion, it runs the risk of having the other branches overturn or ignore its decisions.[30] Judge Richard Posner of the Seventh Circuit seems to agree with this assessment. When discussing the differences between justices on the U.S. Supreme Court and other American judges, Judge Posner observes, "The Justices operate with even fewer constraints than the lesser federal judges, except for the political constraint imposed by public opinion."[31] Other scholars disagree, stating that since the Supreme Court justices and other federal judges have lifetime appointments, they do not need to care at all about public opinion when making their decisions.[32] To bolster their point, these scholars point to the relatively large number of Supreme Court rulings that did not enjoy broad public support when they were handed down.

The Supreme Court may be freer in some cases to ignore public opinion than it is in others. Does the Supreme Court have greater freedom to ignore public opinion in cases that are less well known to the public? Cases that are widely known by the public and reported on by the media are referred to as **salient** by political scientists. Somewhat counterintuitively, one study concluded that the justices feel the strongest incentives to ignore public opinion in salient cases, while ignoring public views in less well-known cases can bring negative media attention and negative attention from the other branches of government.[33] This is so because salient cases commonly involve issues where justices face the strongest competing desires to follow legal considerations and to follow their personal ideology.[34] Also, the justices' personal policy preferences are likely to be more clearly defined in more salient cases.[35] In addition, a case may become more salient because the Court's decision is expected to deviate from public opinion.[36] Thus, this study of salient versus non-salient judicial rulings concludes that justices must consider public opinion in their non-salient cases in order to increase the diffuse support for the courts in general.[37] Other studies show a decline in public support when the Supreme Court issues salient decisions that the public opposes.[38]

Are the Courts Creating Public Opinion?

There is also a great deal of controversy among political scientists about whether the Supreme Court actually shapes public opinion with its rulings. There is a long line of research that argues that public support for an issue inherently goes up after the Supreme Court rules on that question.[39] However, at least one study found that the theory did not hold at all on the issue of abortion.[40] In fact, several studies have shown that the Supreme Court's abortion opinions polarized the public.[41] One study shows that Supreme Court decisions on abortion can influence future interest group actions.[42] However, another study of the effects of Supreme Court decisions on the abortion issue found that the impact was variable. Additionally, this study, by Timothy R. Johnson and Andrew D. Martin, found that the initial rulings on salient issues can influence public opinion, even if later ones do not have as much effect.[43] The researchers write, "If the public is unsettled on an issue, if the issue is not accessible to most people, the Court can put an issue on the public agenda, generate discussion, and alter public opinion. If the issue is central or salient to voters, the court case should not matter regardless of how many previous rulings the Supreme Court has made."[44]

On some issues, the Court does seem to be leading public opinion. A study of death penalty cases as well as abortion cases found that the Supreme Court rulings can have major impacts on public opinion, depending on the context.[45] The U.S. Supreme Court has also affected public opinion in its decisions regarding the display of the Ten Commandments on public property.[46] Likewise, another study found that the U.S. Supreme Court did have an impact on gay and lesbian rights after ruling on the issue, with decisions in favor of gay rights increasing public support for those rights.[47] A study of state supreme court rulings on same-sex marriage shows that the court decisions in favor of same-sex marriage "have transformed the political culture," creating much more public acceptance of the rights of gays and lesbians to marry.[48] This public acceptance has led to legislative and executive branch institutions also becoming more supportive of same-sex marriage.[49]

But judicial scholars have had a very hard time coming up with broad theories about when the Supreme Court's rulings will change public opinion and when they won't. As Johnson and Martin conclude, "While citizens often accept the Court's choices, their reactions are affected more strongly by the political context within which they live."[50] It is simply not clear whether the U.S. Supreme Court follows public opinion, shapes public opinion, or does neither.

Public Opinion and the State Courts

In state judicial systems where the judges gain and/or retain their seats on the bench through elections, one might assume that the judges are more attentive to public opinion, at least in cases that receive a great deal of media attention. If these judges rule against public opinion, they are likely to lose their jobs. Judges who run in contested judicial elections act like other politicians, and they must value their reputation with the mass public much more than judges who do not need to face the voters to retain their seats on the bench.[51] For example, recall that after the Iowa Supreme Court approved same-sex marriages in the state, three judges on the state supreme court were removed from the bench when they lost their retention elections.[52] Voters can also express their dissatisfaction with state court decisions in other ways. For example, in eighteen states the voters can fairly easily overturn a decision of the state supreme court by amending the state constitution through the initiative and referendum processes.[53]

Clearly, elected judges must be cognizant of the views of the public in their states if they want to retain their seats on the bench. This is certainly true in the so-called big cases, where the issues are salient to the public. One study found that in states with contested elections, judges were much more likely to favor the state in death penalty appeals than were judges in states without election mechanisms, thus signaling that elected state judges can be quite sensitive to public opinion on the issue.[54] Another study showed that state trial judges handed down harsher criminal sentences as their retention elections drew near.[55] In fact, various academic studies have demonstrated that elected judges respond to their constituents by ruling in ways that reflect the preferences of the voters.[56] Thus, elected judges do seem to care about public opinion. As Judge Otto Kaus, a former justice on the California Supreme Court, has stated, "There's no way a judge is going to be able to ignore the political consequences of certain decisions, especially if he or she has to make them near election time. That would be like ignoring a crocodile in your bathtub."[57]

Various studies have found that public support for state courts also depends on personal interactions with those courts.[58] Generally, the more knowledge one has of the courts, the higher one's level of support for the state judiciary. For example, former jurors tend to have a more favorable view of the state courts; unsurprisingly, however, the losers in high-stakes cases tend to have a less favorable view of the state courts in general.[59] Some studies have found that overall support for the state courts is about the same whether the judges are elected or appointed,[60] while other studies have shown that diffuse support for the judiciary is lower in states with elected judges.[61]

Is the level of support for state courts higher or lower than public approval of the federal courts? One study by Christine A. Kelleher and Jennifer Wolak found that public confidence in the state courts is much lower than for the U.S. Supreme Court and other federal courts.[62] When examining variations among the states, this study found that when people perceived their state government to be corrupt, confidence in the state courts also fell. Interestingly, this study also found that gender diversity on state supreme courts promoted confidence in the leadership of state courts, and lack of African American representation on the state supreme courts reduced confidence.[63] Finally, some scholars have concluded that public confidence in state courts is lower than confidence in state executive branches, even though the opposite is true at the federal level.[64] Overall, state judges and state courts seem to have lower approval ratings than their federal colleagues.

INTEREST GROUPS AND THE COURTS

Organized interest groups will, of course, lobby the legislative branch and the executive branch in order to obtain their policy goals, but they are also quite active in using the courts for their public policy purposes. There has been an explosion in the number and breadth of interest groups active in American politics.[65] The numbers and variety of groups who attempt to influence court decisions have also grown enormously.[66] These groups include corporations, unions, governments, public advocacy organizations, public interest law firms, and ad hoc associations of individuals of all ideological views.[67] Judges can also have various links to interest groups. Some judges have developed close relationships with political interest groups before they became judges, and those ties tend to endure.[68] This section will examine how interest groups interact with the courts.

Interest groups can interact with the courts in a variety of ways. Interest groups can file test cases in both state and trial courts. They can also sponsor cases in the appellate courts. Under certain circumstances, interest groups can intervene in existing litigation, meaning that the group can sometimes be added as a party to lawsuits that have already been filed. A fourth and extremely popular method for interest groups to attempt to influence court precedent is through the filing of amicus curiae briefs in appellate courts, especially the U.S. Supreme Court. A fifth way organized interests interact with the courts is by influencing the judicial selection processes. This may include endorsing candidates in state judicial elections or by lobbying the president or U.S. senators regarding the selection of federal judges, including the nominees for the U.S. Supreme Court. Of course, interest groups can also contribute money to judicial campaigns and spend money during judicial elections. All of these interest group activities will be discussed in more detail below.

Test Cases and Case Sponsorship

In test cases, the interest groups take the time to find the right cases with the right set of facts before the lawsuit is filed. Then the groups provide the lawyers and other resources necessary to carry out the litigation in the trial courts. The goal is to have the courts give the interest group the policy statements it wants. Some of these test cases are **class action lawsuits**, which are lawsuits brought on behalf of a named plaintiff and all others in similar situations. For example, a class action could be brought on behalf of all those harmed by a new pharmaceutical drug or all those improperly charged a fee by their credit cards. Interest groups choose to be involved with class action suits because it is much harder for a specific plaintiff to settle the suit. If a single plaintiff can end the lawsuit, this can deprive the interest group of the final court ruling it desires. But whether or not the case is a class action, interest groups must choose their clients carefully.

Sometimes a group can litigate in its own name. For example, in *McCreary County Kentucky v. American Civil Liberties Union of Kentucky* (2005), the ACLU challenged the constitutionality of the display of the Ten Commandments in courthouses and courtrooms in the county. Often, however, the groups must find an individual with actual harm in order to make sure that the courts agree that the party has standing. **Standing** is a technical term meaning that the person bringing the lawsuit is the right party in the case and has actual harm, as the courts have defined the Case and Controversy requirement of Article III of the Constitution. The classic example of a test case is *Brown v. Board of Education* (1954), where the NAACP Legal Defense Fund recruited litigants in Topeka, Kansas, and other cities to challenge the laws and practices that required public schools to be segregated by race. The NAACP could not bring suit on its own in this case because the group would not have had standing. Instead, the NAACP found parents to bring the suits on behalf of their children who attended segregated public schools. Another example of a test case was *District of Columbia v. Heller* (2008), where the conservative think tank lawyer handling the case interviewed a wide variety of gun owners in the District before choosing the right litigant to challenge the constitutionality of the District's then extremely strict gun control laws. The Supreme Court majority agreed with the conservative group's position, ruling that the Second Amendment protected an individual's right to own a gun for protection purposes.

Sponsoring Cases on Appeal

A second interest group tactic is to sponsor the case on appeal. This often happens in death penalty and other criminal cases.[69] It is also done by interest groups without the resources needed to find the proper test cases at trial. A famous example of sponsoring a case on appeal occurred in the early 1900s, when the National Consumers' League asked litigator Louis Brandeis to handle the appeal of a case involving an Oregon law prohibiting women from working more than ten hours per day. In arguing the appeal in *Muller v. Oregon* (1908), Brandeis provided the Court with a great deal of social science evidence about the harms that excessive working hours caused for women. Thus was born the famous Brandeis Brief, the first legal brief to rely more on scientific information and social science than on legal citations. Of course, Brandeis was later appointed to a seat on the U.S. Supreme Court.[70]

A third approach is for interest groups to intervene in a case, thus becoming a party to the dispute. This is more common in federal court than in state court. For an organized group to intervene in a federal case, it often must show that a federal statute authorizes intervenor status.[71] The group must also prove that the original parties to the case will not adequately represent the group's interests in the dispute. The lower federal courts have a myriad of rules about when an organized group can and cannot intervene in a case.[72] Since this approach is highly technical and cannot guarantee that a group will be able to intervene in a specific case, it is rarely used by interest groups.

Filing Amicus Briefs

Interest groups file amicus curiae briefs in great numbers in American appellate courts, and this number has increased over time (see Figure 9.3). Recall that an amicus brief is a "friend of the court" brief that supplements the briefs filed by the parties to the case. Interest groups use amicus briefs to lobby the courts by providing judges with information that is not readily available in the parties' briefs. Because the groups often have expertise in a particular public policy area, judges use the amicus briefs to educate themselves on the ramifications of various issues.[73] In addition to filing amicus briefs on the merits, in which interest groups argue how the court should ultimately rule in the case, interest groups also file amicus briefs that attempt to influence the Supreme Court's decision on whether or not it will even consider the case at the certiorari stage. As we have discussed earlier in the book, several academic studies have found that the number of amicus briefs filed at the certiorari stage is a good indicator of whether the Supreme Court will hear the case or not. The more briefs filed at certiorari, the more likely it is that the Court will hear the case in full.

It is rare for the U.S. Supreme Court to refuse a request to file an amicus brief, either on the merits or at the certiorari stage.[74] In fact, in its 1994 term the Court denied only one request to file an amicus curiae brief.[75] The number of cases at the U.S. Supreme Court that receive amicus briefs on the merits has been steadily rising. From 1946 to 1960, the percentage of cases with at least one amicus brief was relatively stable, averaging 23 percent. However, amicus brief

FIGURE 9.3 Percentage of Supreme Court Cases Accepted for Full Review that Included Amicus Briefs

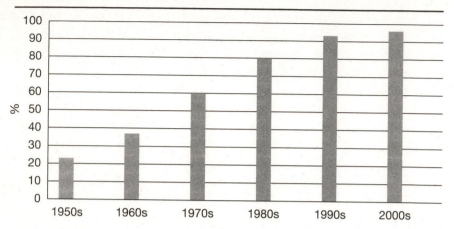

participation went from 31 percent in 1961 to 44 percent in 1969. The percentage of cases with amicus briefs continued to rise over the decades, and by the mid-1990s over 90 percent of all cases heard by the Court included amicus curiae briefs.[76] In 2007, over 98 percent of all cases heard in full by the Supreme Court involved amicus briefs.[77] Figure 9.3 indicates the number of amicus briefs filed in all Supreme Court cases in recent history.

In addition, the number of amicus briefs on the merits per case has greatly increased over time. From 1946 to 1969, the justices likely would receive only a single amicus brief in a case. By the 2000s, the average had risen to eight amicus briefs per case.[78] Some cases have drawn a huge number of amicus briefs on the merits. For example, the Supreme Court received sixty-seven amicus briefs in *District of Columbia v. Heller* (2008), where the Court declared for the first time that the Second Amendment guarantees an individual right to own a gun. Twenty of those briefs supported the gun control law in the District of Columbia, while forty-seven wanted the law declared unconstitutional. More than a hundred amicus briefs were filed in the two University of Michigan affirmative action cases, *Gratz v. Bollinger* (2003) and *Grutter v. Bollinger* (2003). Seventy-eight amicus briefs were filed in the 1989 abortion case *Webster v. Reproductive Health Services* (1989).[79] The Court's decision in *Arizona v. U.S.* (2012) regarding the constitutionality of the Arizona law restricting the rights of illegal immigrants drew over a hundred amicus briefs, many from state and local governments.[80] And there were 136 amicus briefs filed in the Court's 2012 case regarding the constitutionality of the Affordable Care Act, *National Federation of Independent Business v. Sebelius* (2012).[81]

There is a fair amount of academic literature discussing justices' citation of amicus briefs in their opinions. The bottom line is that the amicus briefs seem to have a great deal of importance to the justices. The Court often incorporates into its opinions arguments made by the solicitor general in his or her amicus briefs,[82] as well as from the briefs provided by a variety of interest groups.[83] Looking at Supreme Court decisions from 1946 to 1995, one study found that when an amicus brief was filed, 28 percent of majority opinions in such cases cited it.[84] Former law clerks revealed in interviews that they read almost all the amicus briefs filed in a case and that the briefs from the most experienced litigators were more influential at the Court.[85] Amicus briefs are also now being filed in the U.S. circuit courts of appeals[86] and in the state supreme courts.[87]

One study found that on three state supreme courts, disadvantaged groups were able to overcome their resource disadvantages when their positions were supported by amicus briefs.[88] As Justice Breyer has argued, amicus briefs "play an important role in educating the judges on potentially relevant technical matters, helping make us not experts, but moderately educated lay persons, and that education helps to improve the quality of our decisions."[89] But organized interest groups don't just help to educate judges, they can also play a role in bringing previously little known issues to the public's attention.[90]

Interest Groups and Judicial Selection

Interest groups also attempt to influence the selection of judges at both the state and federal levels. As Chapter 3 indicated, interest groups have long been involved in attempting to influence the federal judicial selection process, usually by lobbying members of the U.S. Senate on specific judicial confirmation votes. Recall that in 1968 conservatives filibustered President Johnson's nomination of Associate Justice Abe Fortas to replace the retiring chief justice, Earl Warren.[91] In 1987, more than eighty liberal interest groups showed their muscle when they joined forces and waged an extraordinarily successful campaign to block the nomination of Robert Bork to the Supreme Court.[92] Both liberal and conservative interest groups have weighed in on Supreme Court nominations ever since. In fact, the 2006 confirmation vote on Justice Samuel Alito was the most partisan vote in history, in part due to heavy interest group involvement.

Filibusters of lower court judicial nominees became much more common in the 1990s and 2000s because interest groups took more interest in these lower court confirmation battles. Recall that when the Republicans took control of the Senate following the 1994 elections, they moved to delay the confirmation of all of President Clinton's judicial nominees.[93] During the presidencies of George W.

Bush and Barack Obama, filibusters of lower court nominees became quite common as interest groups paid more attention to the confirmation process for lower federal court judges. One academic study found that groups will sound a "fire alarm" when they perceive federal lower court nominees to be ideologically extreme, thus bringing public attention to the nomination.[94]

Interest groups have also become much more involved in state judicial elections. Interest groups have come to understand that the decisions of the state courts, and especially the state supreme courts, can have enormous economic, political, and social consequences. For example, the U.S. Chamber of Commerce now routinely spends a great deal of money on state judicial elections, as does the American Association of Trial Lawyers.[95] Tort reform efforts have greatly increased interest group participation in state judicial elections (see Chapter 6). Starting after the end of World War II, state courts began making it easier for plaintiffs to win tort suits. Then in the 1980s, conservative interest groups demanded that the state legislatures protect tort defendants. The state legislatures took action to do so, and many state supreme courts declared these new tort reform laws to be unconstitutional. The interest groups with an interest in tort reform responded by getting much more involved in the judicial selection process. These groups included the medical community, insurance companies, drug manufacturers, car manufacturers, and other corporate interests. For example, judicial elections in Alabama have been described as "a battleground between businesses and those who sue them."[96] Some have even argued that the increasing costs of elections for the state supreme courts are directly correlated with the percentage of tort cases on a particular supreme court's docket.[97] As the president of the Ohio Bar Association has stated, "The people with money to spend who are affected by court decisions have reached the conclusion that it's a lot cheaper to buy a judge than a governor or an entire legislature, and he can probably do a lot more for you."[98]

Interest groups are certainly pouring millions of dollars into state judicial elections.[99] In 2000, interest groups spent an estimated $2.8 million on radio and television ads in just four states: Alabama, Michigan, Mississippi, and Ohio. In the 2000 judicial elections, about 80 percent of all ads run by interest groups attacked a candidate whom the group opposed.[100] In 2010, special interests spent over $1 million in Iowa alone to defeat three state supreme court judges who had voted in favor of legalizing same-sex marriage in that state. A total of $38.4 million was spent on state supreme court elections in 2009–2010, with $16.8 million of that total being spent on television advertising. Almost one-third of this campaign spending was contributed by outside interest groups. A 2011 report critical of money in state judicial elections concluded, "More than ever, a small number of super spenders played a dominant role in influencing who sits on state supreme courts."[101] Interest group activity concerning the courts is increasing at a rapid rate, and many scholars are predicting that this trend will continue to expand in the future.[102] Some scholars worry that increased campaign contributions from interest groups can eventually undermine the legitimacy of the state courts.[103]

THE MEDIA AND THE COURTS

Let us now turn to look at the very complex relationship between the courts and the traditional media. On one hand, most Americans learn about U.S. Supreme Court decisions almost exclusively through the media interpretation of those decisions.[104] On the other hand, the U.S. Supreme Court certainly receives less press coverage than the president or the Congress.[105] And scholars have not spent as much time studying the relationship between the media and the courts as they have other judicial politics issues. As scholars Richard Davis and Vincent J. Strickler noted in a journal article on the relationship between the Supreme Court and the press, that relationship "has been but a footnote in scholarly analysis of political institutions and the press."[106]

Judicial Silence

In the United States, judges and other court officials almost never talk to journalists, and no court employee will comment on specific cases.[107] American appellate courts let their written decisions speak for themselves because any additional comment might endanger the respect and reverence the public has for judges. For their part, many judges seem to enjoy the sense of secrecy and majesty that surrounds the judiciary. As Joe Mathewson has written, "While presidents and governors and legislators hold news conferences [. . .] the justices of the Supreme Court hide behind a red velvet curtain."[108] Especially on the U.S. Supreme Court, the justices promote images of expertise, unanimity, and independence for the Court whenever possible.[109] Barbara Perry concluded that the "image of majesty and mystery has allowed the Court to weather occasional storms of protests from the people, the press, the president, and Congress."[110]

Recently, however, more and more justices are allowing their public speeches to be televised, and some have been interviewed on television programs such as *60 Minutes, Larry King Live,* and the PBS show *Charlie Rose,* though they never discuss upcoming cases.[111] While it seems that many judges in the United States try very hard to ignore the media,[112] some scholars have found that a certain number of justices do engage in an intentional public relations strategy. Justices are students of history and therefore realize that historically the Supreme Court has had to rely on public support in order to achieve general compliance with its policies.[113] Both Justices Clarence Thomas and Sonia Sotomayor have recently authored autobiographies, and they spent a great deal of time promoting their books in the press. Justices Sandra Day O'Connor and John Paul Stevens have also authored several books on the workings of the Supreme Court.

The Supreme Court Beat

It can be a highly prestigious but also frustrating job for the traditional media to cover the U.S. Supreme Court. Davis and Strickler noted, "The Court beat is high in prestige because of its proximity to power but low in satisfaction because of the need to rely on documents and the paucity of interviews with sources."[114] The U.S. Supreme Court has had a Public Information Office since 1935,[115] and a full-time public information officer since 1947. Lower courts also provide press offices, but their main function is to get the courts' decisions to the press, not to help the journalists interpret those decisions.[116] The press must use sources beyond the courts to help them understand judicial rulings. As former *New York Times* reporter Linda Greenhouse described her job covering the U.S. Supreme Court, "I see myself as a kind of translator."[117] To accommodate the needs of the journalists who cover the Supreme Court, the Court has ended its practice of announcing decisions only on Mondays. Now new decisions are spread out through the week. However, as we have seen, the U.S. Supreme Court still refuses to allow cameras in the courtroom.[118]

On the other hand, at the Canadian Supreme Court a court official will routinely explain the court's rulings to the press.[119] The most important oral arguments before the Supreme Court of Canada are also broadcast on the Canadian equivalent of C-SPAN.[120] Another difference between the United States and Canada is the fact that American journalists seem automatically to discuss the U.S. Supreme Court in political terms, while that is still rare in Canada. For example, one academic study comparing media-court relations in the two countries found that American reporters almost always refer to the justices by naming the political party of the president who appointed them, while this is almost never the case in Canada.[121] This study also concludes that in the United States, "judges are skewered with the same sharp knives and in the same merciless fashion as politicians."[122] Some American journalists are beginning to refuse to reveal the political party of the appointing president when they cover judicial rulings,[123] but most still refer to judges as Democrats or Republicans.

Some would argue that there is a certain symbiotic relationship between the judiciary and the press.[124] Both are concerned about truth and justice. Lyle Denniston, a longtime journalist who covered the U.S. Supreme Court for years, has written, "Truth is the common pursuit of the professions of law and journalism. Each, of course, pursues it in its own way. But when either succeeds, the result is the same: a free and self-governing society's most basic interests are served. Indeed, the establishment of truth often is the very achievement of justice."[125] Many journalists admire the judiciary they cover. Another journalist has noted, "If the American people could see the Supreme Court from my vantage point, I believe they would be as impressed—and proud—as I am. [. . .] I believe the best kept secret of the judiciary is how well they work."[126]

The journalists who cover the Supreme Court tend to be highly regarded experts, and some of them may even help shape public opinion about the Court. For example, Linda Greenhouse covered the Supreme Court for the *New York Times* for many years. She was highly regarded in both academic and legal circles. After she retired from the *Times,* she went to work as a distinguished professor at Yale Law School. She was also thought to be very influential in her coverage of the Supreme Court. Some scholars note that the justices were quite sensitive to what she wrote about them, referring to this as the "Greenhouse effect."[127] This term has been used by some conservatives to describe the fact that certain justices have become more liberal the longer they serve on the bench. The idea is that justices respond to the praise and criticism that elite Washington journalists—notably Greenhouse, a liberal—provide them. The usual examples given of justices who change their orientation over time are Justices Harry Blackmun, David Souter, Anthony Kennedy, and Sandra Day O'Connor.[128] All were appointed as conservatives but moved to the left the longer they served on the bench. While there is certainly evidence that elite journalists tend to be liberals,[129] many scholars, such as Lawrence Baum, discount the impact of the so-called Greenhouse effect. Baum wrote, "The idea of a Greenhouse effect has the ring of a search for a scapegoat by unhappy political partisans. More important, it does not fit into the dominant theories of judicial behavior."[130] Nevertheless, scholars have had a great deal of trouble disproving this hypothesis.

Legal Analysis in the Media

Academic studies of the interactions between American courts and the press tend to conclude that the media do not do a good job of communicating complicated legal issues to the public, often putting journalistic concerns above legal ones.[131] The conventional wisdom seems to be that media coverage of the Supreme Court and its decisions tends to ignore important legal principles and important legal details.[132] For example, after the oral arguments on President Obama's health care reform act, many media analysts predicted that the Supreme Court would declare the legislation to be unconstitutional. Instead, the Court upheld the constitutionality of most of the program, although in very narrow terms. Another example is that the media often report that the U.S. Supreme Court upheld a lower court opinion when in fact the Court denied certiorari in a case, acting as if a denial of certiorari is equivalent to a Supreme Court ruling on the issue. However, the Court is quite adamant that the denial of certiorari has no precedent value; it merely means that the Court has chosen not to decide whether the lower court decision is proper or not.

Other scholars disagree with the perspective that the media do not accurately report legal issues, feeling that academic critics of journalists may not understand their extremely demanding job. Scholar William Haltom argued, "If professors at prestigious law schools take months and even years to unravel the reasoning of the justices, it is hardly fair to expect journalists to make sense of the justices in minutes or hours."[133]

Certainly journalists focus on what they consider to be the most newsworthy cases, while often ignoring other, more routine decisions. Evidence suggests that politically controversial cases attract significantly more attention from the media.[134] The U.S. Supreme Court can cause the media to pay more attention to certain issues "by interjecting new or rediscovered social problems or policy alternatives into the national dialogue."[135] But non-routine cases can cause problems for reporters, especially those new to the court beat. In cases that raise novel legal issues, journalists become much more dependent on their expert sources to help them interpret the rulings.[136] That often means ignoring routine cases and simplifying more complex ones. For example, journalists tend to ignore concurring opinions in favor of discussing the dissents. This is likely because there is more drama in the conflicts between the majority opinion and the dissents, while understanding concurring opinions can be a highly technical undertaking.[137] Nevertheless, the concurrences are important to understanding the effects and limits of the majority opinion's reasoning.

Some cases clearly get more media attention than others. For example, the Supreme Court's civil liberties cases seem to get more attention from the media than do other issues.[138] And not all media outlets use the same care in reporting on the judiciary. For example, one study looked at variation in the media coverage of *Lawrence v. Texas* (2003), the case that declared state anti-sodomy laws to be unconstitutional. This research found that newspapers with strong national reputations such as the *New York Times* and the *Washington Post* provided quite detailed stories about the legal issues in the case, but that smaller, local media outlets did not. This study concluded that the media provide more coverage of a legal case when the case has a local angle.[139] Another study found that local media cover court cases differently than the national media do. It also demonstrated that, although there is a perception that tort cases receive a majority of the coverage of civil cases, this is untrue. While national media outlets may focus on the outcomes of civil cases, most news stories at the local level focus on the initial filing of the lawsuit rather than its resolution. National media report only on the most unusual civil cases, often involving large damage awards, while the local media are much more likely to report on less sensational issues that civil lawsuits are attempting to solve.[140]

Most parties to Supreme Court cases understand how important media interpretation of a court ruling can be. Interest groups also see the clear need to lobby the media, because journalists not only interpret court rulings but also help determine what stories are printed or aired and which are not.[141] As Davis and Strickler noted, "Competition to serve as sources for Court stories is intense among interest groups. Their representatives mill about the Supreme Court plaza after decisions, hoping to share their spin with reporters. Elite reporters avoid the plaza and let the groups chase them."[142] When reporters pay special attention to a judicial issue, it is more likely that the court ruling may in fact change public opinion.[143] As political scientists Elliot Slotnick and Jennifer Segal have concluded, "The mass media play an important role in what we think about, how we think about it, and, indeed, they may even influence what we think."[144]

Although the news media may cover all levels of the judicial system, their coverage of local courts concentrates mostly on the fate of criminal defendants rather than on the nature of the courts as an institution.[145] Since many state courts allow television cameras in the courtrooms,[146] media attention to criminal trials has increased. There are now entire cable TV networks dedicated mostly to airing criminal trials. Civil trials rarely receive any attention from journalists.[147] If civil cases do receive press attention, it is usually in the form of broad stories complaining about frivolous lawsuits and the so-called litigation explosion.[148] Journalists also have a very difficult time covering judicial elections, in part because judges remain hesitant to comment on many legal issues that might come before them in a potential case.[149]

State supreme courts, however, tend to attract far less media attention than the U.S. Supreme Court or even trial courts. Even if the media do cover the state appellate courts, journalists will often restrict their reporting to who wins and who loses, leaving out such important factors as the reasoning of the court and contextual aspects.[150] State supreme court decisions often receive little attention from journalists or academics. Complaining about the poor coverage of his court, one Ohio Supreme Court justice has stated, "The media coverage reflects a lack of knowledge about how the court functions and what its purposes are."[151] There are also very little data available on public reaction to state supreme court decisions.[152]

As of June 2009, thirty-four state supreme courts allowed at least limited television coverage of their proceedings.[153] While the presence of cameras in the state supreme courts should in theory lead to more careful media coverage of the rulings of these appellate courts, there is no clear evidence that this is actually occurring. Nevertheless, Ronald M. George, the former chief justice on the California Supreme Court, called the videos of his court "the best P.R. you can imagine."[154]

CHAPTER SUMMARY

This chapter explored the relationship and interactions between the courts and public opinion, interest groups, and the media. In terms of the relationship between the courts and public opinion, it considered three major questions: (1) How does the public view the courts compared to other governmental institutions? (2) Do court rulings generally follow public opinion on the issue? (3) Do court rulings change the public's views on the issues? The chapter then examined the interactions between interest groups and the courts. Interest groups can sponsor cases both at trial and on appeal, and they can intervene in certain cases. Interest groups are also quite active in writing amicus curiae briefs for appellate courts and have only gotten more so in recent years. They are also fairly involved in the judicial selection processes at both the state and federal levels. Finally, this chapter explored the relationship between the courts and the media, including the issues of judicial silence, the Supreme Court beat, and the influence of well-respected journalists on the courts and on public behavior, as well as the kinds of coverage in the news media for all levels of courts.

For Further Reading

Barclay, Scott, Mary Bernstein, and Anna-Maria Marshall, eds. 2009. *Queer Mobilizations: LGBT Activists Confront the Law.* New York: New York University Press.

Collins, Paul M., Jr. 2008. *Friends of the Court: Interest Groups and Judicial Decision Making.* New York: Oxford University Press.

Davis, Richard. 2011. *Justices and Journalists: The U.S. Supreme Court and the Media.* New York: Cambridge University Press.

Gibson, James L., and Gregory A. Caldeira. 2009. *Citizens, Courts, and Confirmations: Positivity Theory and the Judgments of the American People.* Princeton, NJ: Princeton University Press.

Haltom, William. 1998. *Reporting on the Courts: How the Mass Media Cover Judicial Actions.* Chicago: Nelson-Hall.

Hoekstra, Valerie J. 2003. *Public Reaction to Supreme Court Decisions.* Cambridge: Cambridge University Press.

Mathewson, Joe. 2011. *The Supreme Court and the Press: The Indispensable Conflict.* Evanston, IL: Northwestern University Press.

Schlozman, Kay Lehman, and John T. Tierney. 1986. *Organized Interests and American Democracy.* New York: Harper and Row.

Slotnick, Elliot E., and Jennifer A. Segal. 1998. *Television News and the Supreme Court: All the News That's Fit to Air?* Cambridge: Cambridge University Press.

Teles, Steven M. 2008. *The Rise of the Conservative Legal Movement: The Battle for Control of the Law.* Princeton, NJ: Princeton University Press.

10
CHAPTER

Legislatures and the Courts

This chapter will explore how courts interact with legislative bodies at both the state and federal levels. These interactions may be routine and mundane at times, harmonious and cooperative at others, but sometimes they can be deeply contentious. For a variety of reasons, the legislative branch may even find it in its best interests to defer decisions to the judiciary[1] or even increase the power of the courts.[2] For its part, in its decisions the Supreme Court often invites Congress to enact more legislation.[3] In fact, about 7 percent of all majority decisions suggest this in some way, and an even greater proportion of dissenting opinions make that suggestion.[4]

Most of the time, the relationship between the courts and Congress is quite cooperative.[5] For example, the legislative role in the judicial selection process has traditionally been rather routine—the U.S. Senate must confirm all federal judicial nominees, and until fairly recently the Senate almost always approved the president's choices. As political scientist Mitchell J. Pickerill notes, "Those who expect a constitutional revolution, a constitutional moment, or other form of severe confrontation between the Court and Congress simply do not appreciate the more routine and typical type of interaction between Court and Congress in the political process."[6] At the state level, interactions between the courts and legislative bodies also tend to be routine. In two state legislatures (Virginia and South Carolina), the legislature alone appoints state judges. Eight more state legislatures have the responsibility of confirming the governor's nominees for state judgeships.

Many scholars who study the interactions between courts and legislatures, however, start with the notion that judges and legislators do not understand each other very well. The potential for conflict between the branches and a general mistrust of the courts started early in our history. During the Constitutional Convention there was little discussion of the role of the courts in the new constitutional order. In Federalist No. 78, Alexander Hamilton even referred to the courts as "[t]he least dangerous branch." However, during the ratification debates over the new Constitution, Anti-Federalists proposed a great many amendments regarding the new federal courts. Some of these proposals would have created a legislative review committee to oversee decisions of the Supreme Court.[7] None of the Anti-Federalist amendments was adopted, of course.[8] But the potential tension between the legislative and judicial branches has continued to this day.

CONFLICTS BETWEEN THE TWO BRANCHES

Conflicts between the courts and legislatures are not uncommon, and they get a great deal of attention. For example, one recent book on the relationship between Congress and the U.S. Supreme Court is entitled *Strangers on a Hill: Congress and the Court*.[9] A leading law professor who studies the interactions between courts and Congress entitled one of his book chapters "The Choreography of Courts-Congress Conflicts."[10] In the fall of 2006, I interviewed various members of Congress, their staffs, federal judges, and lobbyists in order to understand better the interactions between Congress and the federal courts. At that time the interviewees described the relationship between the two branches as "venomous," "hostile," "tense," "deteriorating," "contentious," "strained," "adversarial," and filled with "animosity."[11] Even though the conflicts between the two branches rarely result in Congress attacking the institution of the courts, the mere threat of retaliation may alter the way judges approach their rulings.[12]

Institutional Differences and Lack of Understanding Between the Branches

These two independent branches of government also have very different approaches to problem solving. In the United States, both courts and legislatures produce public policy, but they do so in very different ways. One of the largest differences is that, although courts are certainly political in nature, judges base their decisions not only on ideology but also on legal reasoning and the law. For example, the fact that judges must explain their decisions in legal and constitutional terms constrains how courts make public policy in a way that does not affect legislators, who can make decisions based purely on political considerations.[13] Members of Congress must be reelected in order to carry out their public policy goals and are therefore always attuned to the needs of the next election cycle, while the justices of the U.S. Supreme Court have life terms. Harvard law professor Mark Tushnet argues that both justices and legislators make decisions based on political considerations, but their understandings of politics differ: "Usually the justices have a longer time frame for their form of politics than presidents or politicians do: the justices care about what's going to happen over the next few decades, the politicians about what's going to happen before the next election."[14] Logrolling, or "I'll vote for your bill if you vote for my bill," is quite common in the legislative branch, while this practice is unheard of in the courts. This difference in institutional cultures and decision-making styles often leads to conflict between the two branches.

Another reason for conflict between judges and legislators is that they do not always know how to communicate effectively with each other. As a lobbyist told me in an interview, "The courts and Congress don't talk to each other enough."[15] Scholars tend to agree with this analysis. Roger H. Davidson and Walter J. Oleszek, two leading congressional scholars, have noted, "Communications between Congress and the federal courts are less than perfect. Neither branch understands the workings of the other very well."[16] Robert Katzmann, a law professor and political scientist who is now a judge on the U.S. Court of Appeals for the Second Circuit, was one of the first academics to spend a great deal of time studying the interactions between courts and legislatures. He has noted, "Congress is largely oblivious of the well-being of the judiciary as an institution, and the judiciary often seems unaware of the critical nuances of the legislative process. But for occasional exceptions, each branch stands aloof from the other."[17]

Others, too, have observed the tense relationship between Congress and the federal courts. Journalist David J. Savage noted, "Congress is not held in very high regard by most of the justices. In public and private comments, they often speak with disdain of the politicians in the House and Senate."[18] The situation was not improved when President Obama openly criticized the Supreme Court's decision in *Citizens United v. Federal Election Commission* (2010) in his 2012 State of the Union address, at which six of the Court's justices were present. Many of the justices were upset with the president's actions, but Democrats in Congress seemed quite excited.[19] In defense of the president's attacks on the Supreme Court, a leading Democratic senator, Sheldon Whitehouse (D-R.I.), said, "I think that there comes a point when you have to be able to tell the truth about a Supreme Court that is activist and that is threatening to become even more activist." He continued, "The Republicans themselves have spent a generation decrying Supreme Court activism, but suddenly when President Obama points out that this would be activist, there's something wrong with saying that? It doesn't seem very logical."[20]

This lack of understanding between legislators and judges does not occur only at the federal level. The relationship between state supreme courts and their state legislatures can also be quite antagonistic at times. In their study of the interactions between state legislatures and state supreme courts, Laura Langer and Teena Wilhelm have concluded, "At the state level, extraordinary tensions have ensued between state courts of last resort and state legislatures, which can have alarming consequences on the policy-making process."[21] Many of these conflicts have revolved around issues of tort reform, where the courts were making it easier for plaintiffs to win court cases while the state legislatures were trying to make it more difficult for the plaintiffs to succeed.[22]

The Congressional Caucus on the Judicial Branch

Concerned about the lack of communication and understanding between judges and legislators, U.S. Representatives Judy Biggert (R-Ill.) and Adam Schiff (D-Calif.) founded the Congressional Caucus on the Judicial Branch in 2003. The purpose of this informal group in Congress was to improve communication between Congress and the courts. This bipartisan group in the U.S. House of Representatives had about forty-five members in 2010,[23] and it continues to grow in number. Over the years this informal organization has brought a variety of Supreme Court justices and other federal judges to Congress to hold informal meetings and talks in order to have members of these two branches get to know each other and their respective institutional cultures better. The caucus has introduced legislation to raise judicial salaries and the salaries of judicial staff, to increase the number of judgeships authorized by Congress where there are severe workload issues, and to increase federal funding for courthouse construction and other such projects.

In describing the goals of the caucus, Schiff has said, "The issues the Caucus gets involved in are driven by what we're hearing from judges. We start from the premise that it is absolutely vital to ensure a strong and independent federal Judiciary to administer justice quickly and fairly. Some of the key issues I see as related to that are the need for additional judgeships, assisting with judicial compensation, securing funding for courthouse construction, addressing security concerns in the courts, and other necessities."[24] In discussing the importance of the face-to-face meetings between judges and legislators, Biggert noted, "These meetings provide a critical and rare opportunity for Members of Congress to interact with senior judges in a context where no pressing decision, legal dispute, or Constitutional question is at stake. It's a chance to communicate on a personal level about the challenges facing our justice system, discuss priorities for funding, and share experiences and perspectives on matters that might otherwise be neglected."[25] These efforts are supported by various members of the U.S. Supreme Court as well. As Chief Justice John Roberts has written, "The separate Branches may not always agree on matters of mutual interest, but each should strive, through respectful exchange of insights and ideas, to know and appreciate where the other stands."[26]

LEGISLATIVE OVERSIGHT OF JUDICIAL OPERATIONS

Both state and federal courts are dependent on their respective legislatures for a variety of issues related to their operations, including their annual budgets, their salaries, their jurisdictions, and the number of judges per court. We will look at each of these areas in more detail in the following sections.

Judiciary Budgets

Although the judiciary is an independent third branch of government, courts are nevertheless dependent on the other branches for their budgets. While the executive branch usually proposes the details of judicial spending, the legislative branch has the ultimate power of the purse. In the U.S. Congress, funding for the federal courts comes each year from an appropriations bill that originates in the House Appropriations Committee. Typically, two justices of the U.S. Supreme Court travel across the street every year to testify before the House Appropriations Committee about the budgetary needs of the federal courts.[27] The Administrative Office of the U.S. Courts sends spending requests to the executive branch and to the Congress. Congress must then approve the annual appropriations for the courts.

Often the executive and legislative branches fail to protect the judiciary's budget. For example, in the automatic sequester cuts that went into effect in March 2013, the federal courts saw their $6.97 billion annual budget cut by over $322 million, a 5 percent reduction.[28] The cuts required furloughs and layoffs for many employees of the federal judicial branch. Since there is no constitutional right to a civil trial, the most immediate effect of the spending cuts was to slow the federal courts' handling of civil cases. Federal prosecutors' offices nationwide also saw about $100 million in cuts, which meant they could handle around sixteen hundred fewer civil cases and one thousand fewer criminal cases.[29] Some federal courts stopped hearing criminal cases on Fridays because the federal prosecutors and defenders were furloughed (not allowed to work) for certain periods of time.[30] In his January 2014 year-end report on the state of the judiciary, Chief Justice Roberts complained bitterly about the unfairness of the sequester cuts imposed on the federal courts.[31] He noted, "The impact of the sequester was more significant on the courts than elsewhere in the government, because virtually all of their core functions are constitutionally and statutorily required. Unlike most Executive Branch agencies, the courts do not have discretionary programs they can eliminate or postpone in response to budget cuts."[32] Echoing a theme that is common in many of his year-end reports, the chief justice argued that the budgets of the federal courts should be protected from partisan politics, concluding, "The United States courts owe their preeminence in no small measure to statesmen who have looked past the politics of the moment and have supported a strong, independent, and impartial Judiciary as an essential element of just government and the rule of law."[33]

Similarly, state legislatures must approve the budgets for the state courts.[34] The overall appropriations for the judiciary have long been a source of conflict and concern for the courts.[35] Since the economic downturn that started in 2008, many state courts have faced cuts in their budgets of around 10 to 15 percent. Almost half the states stopped filling some judicial vacancies for a time, and more than thirty have frozen salaries of judges and judicial branch staff. Some state courts have reduced their opening hours, and many courthouses around the country are "physically eroding" and "functionally deficient."[36]

Judicial Salaries

More specifically, salaries for judges and other judicial branch staff have long been a point of contention between legislatures and the courts. While the U.S. Constitution provides that the salaries of federal judges cannot be lowered, it says nothing about whether judges should get annual cost-of-living increases in their pay. In 2013, the salary for U.S. district court judges was $174,000, and for judges on the U.S. courts of appeals the salary was $184,500. Justices on the Supreme Court earned $213,900 per year, while the chief justice of the United States earned a salary of $223,500. Note that these salaries are far below those earned by partners in large firms and even below those of many law professors.

For many years, the chief justice of the Supreme Court has used his annual year-end report on the state of the judiciary to call for Congress to grant salary increases for federal judges and their staffs. For example, in his 2007 report, Chief Justice Roberts noted, "I am resolved to continue Chief Justice Rehnquist's twenty-year pursuit of equitable salaries for federal judges."[37] The next year he wrote, "I suspect many are tired of hearing it, and I know I am tired of saying it, but I must make this plea again—Congress must provide judicial compensation that keeps pace with inflation. Judges knew what the pay was when they answered the call of public service. But they did not know that Congress would steadily erode that pay in real terms by repeatedly failing over the years to provide even cost-of-living increases."[38] On congressional appropriations for federal courts, the chief justice concluded, "The Judiciary is resilient and can weather the occasional neglect that is often the fate of those who quietly do their work. But the Judiciary's needs cannot be postponed indefinitely without damaging its fabric. Given the Judiciary's small cost, and its absolutely critical role in protecting the Constitution and rights we enjoy, I must renew the Judiciary's modest petition: Simply provide cost-of-living increases that have been unfairly denied! We have done our part—it is long past time for Congress to do its."[39]

Congress can use its budget decisions to signal its overall approval or disapproval of the decisions of federal judges in general and the Supreme Court in particular.[40] For example, in 1964 Congress approved salary increases for lower federal judges of $7,500 per year but only increased the salaries of Supreme Court justices by $4,500, a clear indication that Congress was upset with several U.S. Supreme Court decisions.[41] More than forty years later, Representative Steve King (R-Iowa) expressed his frustration with the courts, telling a reporter, "When their budget starts to dry up, we'll get their attention."[42] Likewise, former House majority leader Tom DeLay (R-Tex.) has stated that Congress should be more forceful in using its appropriations powers to send a clear message to the courts: "We set up the courts. We can unset the courts. We have the power of the purse!"[43] Although politicians often threaten to reduce the budgets for the judiciary out of frustration with some of the judges' decisions, it is not at all clear that legislatures actually carry out most of these threats.

While funding for the federal courts is sometimes problematic, many state courts are currently facing a severe budget crisis. This crisis is due in part to the economic downturn that the United States faced starting in 2008, but it may also be due in part to concerns over state court actions. In fact, at the February 2012 meeting of the American Bar Association in New Orleans, ABA president William Robinson noted, "State court underfunding is the most pressing issue facing the legal profession."[44] The ABA was so concerned about funding for the state courts that it established a special Task Force on Preservation of the Justice System, which was charged with finding innovative ways to help solve the budgetary crisis facing the state courts.

State judicial salaries have long been an issue. In 2012, the salaries of state supreme court justices ranged from a low of $112,530 to a high of $228,856. What is most telling is that, since the 2008 recession, most states have not given any annual salary increases to their state judges. In 2009, only nine state legislatures gave any pay increases to their state judges, in 2010 only eight states did so, and in 2011 only ten states paid their state judges more than they had in the previous year.[45] Thus, since 2008 state judicial salaries have largely been flat. In New York State, for example, many judges began leaving the bench, citing low salaries as the main reason.[46] Things may be changing, however. For example, the Massachusetts state legislature in May 2013 approved a $30,000 increase for state judges, to be paid over three years. Judges in Massachusetts had not received pay increases for many years, and they remain paid far less than many judges in similar states—this is only the second pay raise in fifteen years for them.[47]

In addition to judicial salaries, courts often ask legislatures to spend money on judicial branch staffing, new technologies for the courts, security, and new courthouses, among other things. While the courts see themselves as an independent third branch of government that deserves legislative respect, the legislators often see the courts as just another governmental agency begging for money. Sometimes the courts get the funding they ask for, but frequently both federal and state legislatures do not approve all of these requests.

Determining Numbers of Judges and Judicial Jurisdiction

In addition to the routine annual budgets, courts and legislatures also interact over other issues. For example, Congress determines how many U.S. district courts will exist and how many judges will serve in each district. Congress also draws the boundaries for the U.S. circuit courts of appeals, as well as determining how many judges will be authorized for each circuit court. Early in U.S. history, the circuit boundaries were determined by transportation realities; recall that the circuit courts were staffed by district court judges and even Supreme Court justices who rode on horseback from court to court. Thus, the circuits on the East Coast were (and remain) relatively compact. Now, however, circuit court boundaries are much more likely to be determined by political concerns as well as by workload issues.

Congress has at times changed the size and geographic location of the circuits to convey its approval or disapproval of the courts' decisions.[48] For example, in 1980 President Jimmy Carter was able to convince Congress to split up the old Court of Appeals for the Fifth Circuit, creating the new Eleventh Circuit and decreasing the size of the Fifth Circuit (see Chapter 2 for a map of the current circuit boundaries). This was done in part due to the heavy caseload in the old Fifth

Circuit, but it was certainly done for political reasons as well.[49] There was great fear that the old Fifth Circuit judges would remain hostile to civil rights issues, and splitting up the circuit was a way to allow President Carter to appoint more circuit court judges who were favorable to civil rights claims. Today, many conservatives would like to split up the large and unwieldy Ninth Circuit Court of Appeals, largely because it is perceived to be the most liberal circuit court in the country. There have been numerous legislative attempts to change the boundaries of the Ninth Circuit,[50] but so far none has been successful.

Once Congress determines how many judges will be authorized for each court, it is the role of the U.S. Senate to confirm presidential appointments to these courts. Likewise, there are similar issues with numbers of judges and court boundaries at the state level, although very few state legislatures have any role in the selection of specific judges to fill these vacancies.

LEGISLATIVE REACTIONS TO COURT DECISIONS

Legislatures can react to the rulings of the judiciary in a variety of ways. Legislators might accept court decisions and even take action to implement them. They could also ignore them. Or the legislature might try to overturn unpopular judicial actions. It is quite common for politicians to criticize individual court decisions with which they disagree, but it is less common for angry legislators to attempt to undermine the legitimacy of the courts as an institution.

Not surprisingly, scholars pay scant attention when Congress accepts a court decision with very little fuss or controversy because this is what usually happens. There is a little more heed paid, however, when Congress simply ignores a court ruling. For example, one leading constitutional scholar, Louis Fisher, has written quite a bit about Congress's refusal to accept the Supreme Court's declaration in *Immigration and Naturalization Service v. Chadha* (1983) that a one-house legislative veto is unconstitutional.[51] As you may recall from earlier in this book, in this case the Immigration and Naturalization Service ordered Jagdish Chadha to be deported, but the U.S. House of Representatives voted to overturn the agency's decision using a one-house legislative veto, which was allowed by statutes dealing with illegal immigration. But the Supreme Court ruled that Congress could only overturn a decision of an executive branch federal agency through the regular method of having both houses pass a bill that the president would either sign or veto. The majority of the justices in the *Chadha* case held that the Presentment Clause of the Constitution meant that a vote of one house was not sufficient to overturn an agency ruling. Congress, however, has simply ignored the *Chadha* ruling, and it continues to pass a variety of statutes that include one-house legislative vetoes.

Some would argue that individual lawmakers in Congress have little incentive to participate in inter-institutional dialogue regarding constitutional interpretation. In his work arguing that Congress as a whole gave very little consideration to constitutional issues when enacting the Affordable Care Act, Neal Devins, a scholar of Congress and the courts, argues, "While all members of Congress have a stake in preserving Congress's institutional authority to independently interpret the Constitution, lawmaker desires to seek reelection, gain status within their party, and serve interest group constituents overwhelm this 'collective good.'"[52] In other words, Congress doesn't waste a lot of time thinking about whether the laws it passes are constitutional. However, collectively the legislative branch often participates in the inter-institutional dialogue by attempting to overturn, change, or blunt a judicial ruling with which a majority of legislators disagree.

Statutory Interpretation Cases

When legislatures are unhappy with a court decision, the nature of the decision provides the context for legislative action. If the case is a **statutory interpretation** case, then the job of the legislative body is theoretically quite easy. If the legislature disagrees with the judicial interpretation of a statute, then the legislature merely needs to enact a new statute with new language that would clarify the ambiguous situation. Several studies have noted, however, that, with the current partisan gridlock in Congress, it has become much harder for the legislative branch to overturn a Supreme Court statutory interpretation decision, thus increasing the power of the Court on many issues.[53] Nevertheless, Congress can and often does enact a new statute under such circumstances. For example, Congress enacted the Civil Rights Restoration Act of 1991 in order to overturn at least a dozen Supreme Court decisions that had made it more difficult to sue for discrimination.[54]

A more recent example of overturning a Supreme Court statutory interpretation occurred when Congress enacted the Lilly Ledbetter Fair Pay Act of 2009, making it much easier for employees to sue employers for sex discrimination based on claims of unequal pay. The new statute was designed to overturn the Supreme Court's ruling in *Ledbetter v. Goodyear Tire & Rubber Co.* (2007), where the Court had interpreted the Civil Rights Act of 1964 to say that the statute of limitations for filing a sex discrimination lawsuit started as soon as the alleged discrimination occurred instead of when the employee found out about the discrimination. The 5–4 Supreme Court decision thus made it much harder to sue employers for sex discrimination, especially when the employees were asserting illegal salary discrimination. Justice Samuel Alito, writing for the conservative majority in the case, argued that the decision was a straightforward reading of the wording of the civil rights statute. Justice Ruth Bader Ginsburg, writing for the liberal dissenters, strongly disagreed. In a rare dissent read from the bench when the Court announced its opinion to the public, Justice Ginsburg attacked the majority opinion and its signers for making a poor public policy choice. She specifically called on Congress to overturn the Court's decision in this case. Said Justice Ginsburg, "In our view, the court does not comprehend, or is indifferent to, the insidious way in which women can be victims of pay discrimination."[55] The majority in Congress agreed with the Court's dissenters when it overruled the Supreme Court ruling and enacted the 2009 act.

Constitutionally Based Decisions

The Supreme Court also issues many constitutional interpretation rulings. An example of such a ruling would be the Supreme Court's recent decision upholding the constitutionality of most of President Obama's Affordable Care Act in *National Federation of Independent Business v. Sebelius* (2012)—clearly an important decision in a presidential election year. The Court upheld the power of Congress to require individuals to purchase health insurance, the key element in the president's health care reform program. Although the Court ruled that Congress could not require individuals to purchase health insurance under its power to regulate interstate commerce, under its taxing powers Congress did have the power to penalize anyone who did not purchase health insurance. Thus, the Supreme Court upheld the so-called individual insurance mandate as a tax or penalty. On the other hand, the Court did rule that Congress had exceeded its constitutional powers when it required the states to expand the Medicaid program, which is health care for the poor. Congress could give financial incentives to the states to expand coverage under the Medicaid program, but it could not require the states to participate in the new, broader version of the program. More details about the many twists and turns in the extremely complicated story of health care reform can be found in Figure 10.1.

A constitutional interpretation decision is generally much harder for the legislature to overturn than a statutory interpretation decision. At the federal level, Congress must in theory pass a constitutional amendment in order to overturn this kind of judicial ruling. This is a very difficult process, although the Eleventh,

FIGURE 10.1 The Affordable Care Act: A Time Line of Executive, Legislative, and Judicial Branch Actions on Health Care Reform

November 4, 2008:	President Obama is elected and promises to reform health care in the United States.
March 5, 2009:	Obama holds first health care forum at White House
August 25, 2009:	A longtime champion of health care reform, Senator Ted Kennedy (D-Mass.), dies.
September 9, 2009:	In a joint session of Congress, Obama urges immediate action on health care reform.
November 7, 2009:	U.S. House of Representatives passes its version of health care reform, with no Republican support.
December 24, 2009:	U.S. Senate passes its version of health care reform, with no Republican support.
January 19, 2010:	Senator Scott Brown (R-Mass) is elected in a special election to fill Ted Kennedy's seat. Brown's election deprives Democrats of sixty votes needed to end filibusters.
March 21, 2010:	House approves Senate health care bill. Obama signs it into law several days later.
October 7, 2010:	U.S. district court judge in Michigan rules law constitutional.
November 30, 2010:	U.S. district court judge in Virginia rules law constitutional.
December 13, 2010:	A different U.S. district court judge in Virginia rules parts of law unconstitutional.
January 31, 2011:	U.S. district court judge in Florida rules parts of law unconstitutional.
February 22, 2011:	U.S. district court judge in the District of Columbia rules the law constitutional.
June 29, 2011:	A divided panel of the Sixth Circuit rules law constitutional.
August 12, 2011:	Eleventh Circuit Court of Appeals rules part of law is unconstitutional.
November 8, 2011:	U.S. Court of Appeals for the District of Columbia rules the law constitutional.
March 26–28, 2012:	U.S. Supreme Court hears six hours of oral arguments on the case.
June 29, 2012:	U.S. Supreme Court upholds most parts of the law in a complex decision.

Thirteenth, Fourteenth, Fifteenth, Sixteenth, and Twenty-Sixth Amendments to the U.S. Constitution were passed by Congress and ratified by the states in order to directly overturn various Supreme Court decisions. In practice, however, Congress often attempts to overturn a decision by merely enacting a statute. The courts usually declare these statutory attempts to be unconstitutional. For example, when the Supreme Court ruled in *Texas v. Johnson* (1989) that flag burning was a form of protected political speech, Congress answered by passing a federal statute to ban flag burning, which was then declared unconstitutional in *United States v. Eichman* (1990). Or when Congress passed the Religious Freedom Restoration Act of 1993 in reaction to the Supreme Court's ruling in *Employment Division, Department of Human Resources of Oregon v. Smith* (1990), the Supreme Court responded by declaring this act to be unconstitutional in *City of Boerne v. Archbishop Flores* (1997).[56] Congress eventually found a way to narrow the impact of the Court's ruling in *Boerne,* at least as it applied to federal government actions and to federal contractors, when it enacted the Religious Land Use and Institutionalized Persons Act of 2000. The Court upheld this act in *Cutter v. Wilkinson* (2005). Various scholars have looked at how Congress can weaken constitutional interpretation decisions with which it disagrees.[57]

Congress was successful, however, when it passed a statute to overturn the Supreme Court's ruling in *Stenberg v. Carhart* (2000), which had struck down a Nebraska statute outlawing a specific type of late-term abortion that the right-to-life movement called "partial-birth abortion." Because Justice Sandra Day O'Connor had retired from the Court, her replacement, Justice Alito, joined with the other four conservatives to vote to uphold the congressional statute in *Gonzales v. Carhart* (2007).

Moving from the federal level to the states, in some states it is quite easy for legislatures or voters to amend state constitutions when they disagree with state courts' interpretations of their state constitutions, though it is much harder in others. For example, in Massachusetts it can be quite difficult to amend the state constitution in reaction to state high court rulings.[58] Thus, it was almost impossible for the state legislature to overturn the Massachusetts Supreme Court's decision declaring a right to same-sex marriage in the state, while it was much easier for the voters of California to overturn a similar decision there.

Types of Constitutional Decisions

The Supreme Court may make a decision about the constitutionality of a statute in a variety of ways. In other words, we should look beyond the simple question of whether the Court declared the statute in question to be constitutional or unconstitutional. Sometimes the Court gives Congress a great deal of latitude to address the issue in another manner, while in other cases the Court seems to issue such a broad opinion that the legislature has very few options available to it. Figure 10.2 provides a typology of outcomes in the Court's constitutional cases.

FIGURE 10.2 Typology of Judicial Review Decisions

UPHOLD BROADLY	UPHOLD NARROWLY	STRIKE DOWN AS APPLIED	STRIKE DOWN ON FACE NARROWLY	STRIKE DOWN ON FACE BROADLY
• Uphold in entirety • No limitations on decision or state action	• Uphold with limitations on decision or state action • Uphold as applied	• Struck down as applied • Struck down based on facts	• Specific provisions severed and struck down • Strike down on face but with direction for alternatives to achieve policy ends	• Strike down on face broadly because policy area is not within the power of state actor

Source: Compiled by author using data from J. Mitchell Pickerill and Artemus Ward, "Keep on Keepin' On? Rethinking the Conceptualization and Operationalization of Judicial Review," paper prepared for the annual meeting of the Law & Society Association, June 2012, Honolulu, Hawaii. Used by permission of the authors.

The Court may uphold a statute on quite broad terms, indicating that it is approaching the issue from a clear judicial restraintist point of view. This type of decision would signal to Congress or the state legislature that it could produce similar laws in the future with little or no judicial interference. For example, in *Gonzales v. Raich* (2005), the Supreme Court used very broad language to uphold the right of Congress to criminalize the use and sale of marijuana even after some states had passed laws legalizing medical marijuana, ruling that the federal drug laws superseded the state laws. This ruling gave Congress enormous latitude in deciding how to address future federalism issues.

The Court may also uphold a statute on quite narrow grounds. This type of decision could restrict the actual effects of the statute while also signaling that the Court is willing to entertain future cases where the outcome might be different. This kind of narrow ruling would thus send a very different message to Congress or to the state legislatures. For example, even though the Court in *R.A.V. v. St. Paul* (1992) had declared hate speech to be constitutionally protected political speech, in *Virginia v. Black* (2003) the Court upheld a Virginia statute outlawing the burning of a cross—but only if the statute was interpreted to outlaw just cross burning intended to intimidate a specific individual. If the statute was interpreted to outlaw cross burning that did not intend to intimidate an identifiable individual, such as during a rally in a public park, then it would be unconstitutional under the *R.A.V.* precedent. This judicial decision gave the legislature less leeway to address hate speech issues in the future, even though it did not declare the statute in question to be unconstitutional in all circumstances.

Just as the Court can uphold a statute in a number of ways, it can do the same when declaring a statute unconstitutional. The narrowest type of ruling in this group would strike down the law only as it applies to the specific set of facts before the Court. For example, in *Wisconsin v. Yoder* (1972), the Supreme Court did not say that all mandatory school attendance laws were unconstitutional. Instead, the Court said that the state law requiring school attendance until the eighth grade violated the defendant's right to free exercise of religion, because for religious reasons the Amish did not want their children to be forced to attend school beyond the age at which they had acquired the skills necessary to the community's agrarian lifestyle. The overall statute was constitutional, but not as applied to the Amish under these specific facts. This type of decision gives the legislative branch a fair amount of leeway in enacting future legislation.

A fourth type of case would be where the Court strikes down a law on its face, but on quite narrow terms. In *Califano v. Goldfarb* (1976) the Supreme Court declared unconstitutional a federal statute that awarded Social Security survivors' benefits to women almost automatically but forced men to prove that their wives had provided over half of their financial support while alive before they could collect survivors' benefits. The Court struck down the statute on its face, meaning that under no circumstances could it be seen as constitutional. However, the language of the Court was quite guarded in this ruling. After this ruling, Congress would have had some wiggle room to craft a new statute in this area if it so desired.

The last category would be when the Court strikes down a law on very broad terms. For example, in *Citizens United v. Federal Election Commission* (2010), the Supreme Court issued a sweeping ruling that declared unconstitutional almost any restrictions on the spending of corporations or unions during elections. Justice Kennedy's majority opinion used wide-ranging language, including the following statement: "If the First Amendment has any force, it prohibits Congress from fining or jailing citizens, or associations of citizens, for simply engaging in political speech."[59] This broad language would make it very difficult for Congress to pass a new law to blunt the effects of the *Citizens United* ruling. Instead, opponents of the ruling are attempting to amend the Constitution in order to overturn the decision.[60]

LEGISLATIVE EFFORTS TO CURB THE COURTS

When legislators get very angry with judges over their judicial decisions, they have a variety of measures other than overturning court decisions that they can use in attacking the courts as institutions. Impeachment of federal judges is one such option. Although federal judges have life terms, there is a growing willingness to call for the U.S. House of Representatives to impeach federal judges over their decisions and for the U.S. Senate to then remove them from office. This is a drastic measure, and, since the failed attempt to impeach Justice Samuel Chase in the early 1800s, Congress has never removed a federal judge solely because politicians disagreed with his or her decisions. But the movement favoring impeachment for political reasons seems to be gaining steam. For example, Justice at Stake found that between 2002 and 2006 there were at least fifty-eight serious impeachment threats against federal judges.[61]

The movement to impeach state judges is also acquiring momentum. According to the National Center for the Study of State Courts, the year 2011 saw the greatest number of threats of impeachment against state judges to date. Of course, because so many state judges are elected in some way (see Chapter 3), unhappy legislators can simply call for judges to be removed from the bench through the election mechanism. Recall that in 2010 three judges on the Iowa Supreme Court lost their retention elections because they had ruled that under the Iowa constitution same-sex couples had the right to marry. As the *Des Moines Register* reported on the outcome of those retention elections, "Their removal marked the first time an Iowa Supreme Court justice has not been retained since 1962, when the merit selection and retention system for judges was adopted. The decision is expected to echo to courts throughout the country, as conservative activists had hoped."[62]

Jurisdiction and Jurisdiction Stripping

Another drastic measure legislatures have for curbing the courts is stripping the courts of jurisdiction over certain cases or types of cases. Recall that jurisdiction is the power of a court to hear a specific case. As Chapter 2 indicated, the state court systems are systems of open jurisdiction, meaning that most types of cases can be heard in some state court. State legislatures often determine the structure of the state courts, including questions regarding which state courts will have jurisdiction over what types of cases. At the federal level, however, Congress determines what types of cases the federal courts can hear when it set up the tests for federal jurisdiction, which means that Congress could theoretically prevent the federal courts from hearing certain cases—a phenomenon that is often referred to as **court stripping**.

The Exceptions Clause in the U.S. Constitution seems to give Congress the ability to restrict the jurisdiction of the federal courts, but this power has rarely been used and it remains an open question whether such court stripping actions would be declared unconstitutional by the courts.[63] In the late 1800s and early 1900s, when the Supreme Court was dominated by conservative judicial activists, many labor leaders and other progressives called for the enactment of various court-stripping proposals.[64] When conservatives were upset with the liberal judicial activism of the federal courts in the 1950s, 1960s, and 1970s, many politicians from the right demanded passage of various court-stripping measures. For instance, there were calls to prevent the federal courts from hearing abortion, desegregation, affirmative action, or prisoner rights cases. Almost none of these proposals were enacted into law, but court stripping remained a potential tool that some would threaten to use against the courts, among them Edwin Meese, who served as attorney general under President Ronald Reagan.[65]

Then the tide began to change, and Congress started to give serious consideration to court stripping. For example, in 2004 the U.S. Senate Republican Policy Committee published a report entitled *Restoring Popular Control of the Constitution: The Case for Jurisdiction-Stripping Legislation*. In this report, these conservatives argued, "The American people must have a remedy when they believe that federal courts have overreached and interpreted the Constitution in ways that are fundamentally at odds with the people's common constitutional understandings and expectations."[66] Lately Congress has passed several court-stripping provisions, including one in the Military Commissions Act of 2006 that would have prevented the federal courts from hearing cases dealing with the detainees at Guantanamo Bay. However, the Supreme Court declared this act to be unconstitutional in *Boumediene v. Bush* (2008).

The Supreme Court and Court Stripping

It remains highly controversial whether such court-stripping actions by Congress are constitutional. Right after the Civil War, the Supreme Court issued two conflicting rulings that help to fuel this debate. Supporters of court-stripping legislation usually cite *Ex Parte McCardle* (1869) for the proposition that there are few if any limits on the power of Congress to take away federal court jurisdiction over a specific case or over a class of cases, or to change federal jurisdiction in any way. Opponents of court-stripping usually cite *United States v. Klein* (1872) for the proposition that there are clear limits on the power of Congress in this area. Opponents also typically cite equal protection, due process, and separation of powers arguments to support their view that Congress cannot strip the federal courts, or at least the U.S. Supreme Court, of jurisdiction in controversial cases.[67]

William McCardle was a southern journalist who was highly critical of Reconstruction. He was arrested for publishing articles that had "incited insurrection, disorder, and violence" and was awaiting trial by a military commission (not a regular federal court) in the militarily occupied South when he filed a writ of habeas corpus, asking the regular federal courts to hear his case. The Radical Republicans who controlled Congress after the Civil War were afraid that the Supreme Court would use this case to declare the Reconstruction Acts unconstitutional, so Congress passed legislation stripping the Supreme Court of jurisdiction to hear the case. A unanimous Court upheld the constitutionality of the congressional court-stripping action. In *Ex Parte McCardle*, the Supreme Court stated that the justices were "not at liberty to inquire into the motives of the legislature. We can only examine into its power under the Constitution; and the power to make exceptions to the appellate jurisdiction of this court is given by express words."[68] Thus, one could cite *McCardle* for the proposition that Congress can take away federal jurisdiction, just as it can grant jurisdiction to the federal courts.

A few years later, however, in the *Klein* case the Supreme Court issued the opposite ruling. In this case, President Andrew Johnson had been issuing pardons to former Confederate soldiers so that they could get back land and property confiscated after the Civil War. The Radical Republicans in Congress opposed this and passed legislation to nullify the president's pardon power and to strip the courts of the ability to hear any cases dealing with the pardons. In a 7–2 decision, the Supreme Court ruled that Congress had acted unconstitutionally in restricting the president's power and in trying to prevent the federal courts from hearing these cases. Coming to the opposite conclusion from *Ex Parte McCardle*, in *U.S. v. Klein* the majority of the Court stated that Congress "has inadvertently passed the limit which separates the legislative from the judicial power."[69] Thus, one could cite *Klein* for the proposition that Congress cannot strip the federal courts of jurisdiction over specific cases.

This complicated pair of precedents has left a great deal of confusion about the constitutionality of court-stripping legislation. Justice Felix Frankfurter followed the *McCardle* precedent when he dissented in *National Mutual Insurance v. Tidewater Transfer Co.* (1949), writing, "Congress need not give this Court any appellate power; it may withdraw appellate jurisdiction once conferred and it may do so even while a case [is pending before the court]."[70] On the other hand, Justice William O. Douglas cited the *Klein* precedent when he wrote in his dissent in *Glidden Co. v. Zdanok* (1962), "There is a serious question whether the *McCardle* case could command a majority view today."[71] The scholarly debate on this issue is equally confused,[72] but many scholars seem uncomfortable today with the *McCardle* precedent. There is general agreement that court-stripping efforts cannot be successful if they would destroy the courts' fundamental role, interfere with the Constitution's Supremacy Clause, or deprive any person of life, liberty, or property without due process of law.[73] Laurence Tribe, a Harvard Law professor, puts it more directly: "Laws *designed* to hinder the exercise of constitutional rights are, to that degree, unconstitutional."[74] William French Smith, the U.S. attorney general under President Ronald Reagan, stated his opposition to court-stripping legislation when he wrote, "Congress may not [. . .] consistent with the Constitution, make 'exceptions' to Supreme Court jurisdiction which would intrude upon the core functions of the Supreme Court as an independent and equal branch in our system of separation of powers."[75] The debate over the constitutionality of court-stripping efforts continues.

STATE LEGISLATURES AND STATE SUPREME COURTS

State legislatures and state supreme courts often interact. State supreme courts both influence and are influenced by other political actors in the state.[76] Some state legislatures and state supreme courts have formal inter-branch communications mechanisms. One such mechanism is the **advisory opinion**. In this process, the state legislature or the governor asks the state supreme court before passing a bill if the bill is constitutional.[77] This process can also be used when the legislature asks the state supreme court to clarify a previous ruling, as the Massachusetts legislature did when it asked the state supreme court if civil unions would satisfy the court's requirement for equal treatment for same-sex couples. The Massachusetts Supreme Judicial Court responded to the advisory opinion request by declaring, "The dissimilitude between the terms 'civil marriage' and 'civil unions' is not innocuous; it is a considered choice of language that reflects a demonstrable assigning of same-sex, largely homosexual, couples to second-class status. [. . .] The history of our nation has demonstrated that separate is seldom, if ever, equal."[78] According to Laura Langer, a judicial politics scholar, formal advisory opinions are used regularly in about eleven states.[79]

On certain issues, conflict between the state legislature and the state supreme court seems inevitable. For example, in states such as Massachusetts where the courts have declared a right to same-sex marriage, many legislators roundly criticized those decisions.[80] School financing is another issue where the courts directed state legislatures to take action. After the Supreme Court's ruling in *San Antonio Independent School District v. Rodriguez* (1973) that there is no federal right to an education and that for federal purposes the unequal funding of school districts within a state was not unconstitutional discrimination on the basis of poverty, proponents of changing state education financing programs filed many lawsuits in state courts based largely on state constitutional claims. As of 2007, at least twenty-five state supreme courts had ordered their state legislatures to change their educational funding systems. As scholar Christopher Berry has concluded, "Taken together, these school finance judgments represent perhaps the most important reform movement in American public education since 1954, when *Brown v. Board of Education* ended racial segregation in schools."[81] The conflicts between the state supreme courts and the state legislatures on this issue were especially notable in New Jersey, Texas, and Montana, but the Kentucky legislature seized on the court decision in that state to make major educational reforms without resisting the court's ruling.[82] Court rulings in Vermont, New Hampshire, and Maine caused those state legislatures to impose new statewide property taxes in order to pay for the education financing reforms ordered by their respective state supreme courts.[83]

Tort reform issues are another area where state courts and state legislatures may clash. Beginning after World War II, many state supreme courts took it upon themselves to liberalize their state tort laws, thus making it easier for plaintiffs to win tort cases. Starting in the 1980s, many state legislatures attempted to rein in or even overturn these court-initiated changes. The legislatures were generally more interested in protecting the defendants in tort cases, especially when these defendants were wealthy individuals or large corporations. Thus, many state courts took the more liberal view that the main purpose of tort law is to modify behavior, while the legislatures took the more conservative view that tort lawsuits distort free market principles. When the legislatures enacted various tort reform measures, many state supreme courts declared them to be unconstitutional. During the 1980s and 1990s, supreme courts in twenty-six states declared more than ninety new tort reform laws to be unconstitutional.[84] The pro-tort-reform interest groups and politicians responded by pouring money into judicial elections and retention elections in order to remove anti-tort-reform judges from the bench. Much of the increase in the costs of judicial campaigns in a given state can be directly correlated with the percentage of tort cases on the state supreme court's docket.[85]

How state legislatures interact with their state courts may depend in part on the judicial selection system used in the state (see Chapter 3). Not surprisingly, where state supreme court membership is determined by the state legislature, such as in Virginia and South Carolina, the courts generally promote the legislative political agenda.[86] In eight states, the state legislature must confirm most gubernatorial appointments to the state's supreme court (Connecticut, Delaware, Hawaii, Maine, Maryland, New Jersey, New York, and Vermont). Although Utah generally uses a Missouri Plan system of judicial selection for all of its state judges, the Utah legislature must confirm the governor's appointments to the state supreme court, making it the ninth state to give the legislature this power. The other thirty-nine state legislatures do not have any role in judicial selection.

In a state such as Massachusetts, where the governor appoints judges to life terms and the legislature plays no role in the selection process, there is often little conflict with the state courts except on highly salient issues such as the right to same-sex marriage or campaign finance reform.[87] As one state legislator observed, "In the history of Massachusetts, the legislature has had little reaction to the courts. The legislature does not view itself in a contentious mode with the courts, maybe with the governor, but never with the courts."[88] As another state representative explained, "The governors in this state have generally been in the mainstream of thinking in Massachusetts, and they have appointed mainstream judges. Thus the Massachusetts courts are very much in step with the legislature."[89]

New Hampshire has a very similar state judicial selection process. However, there have been several direct conflicts between the New Hampshire legislature and the state supreme court. In a series of decisions in the 1990s, the New Hampshire Supreme Court declared the state's school financing system to be unconstitutional. This forced the state legislature to enact a statewide property tax system in order to equalize school funding. Many in the legislature were furious with the court's decisions. Then a question arose whether the chief justice of the New Hampshire Supreme Court, David Brock, should have recused himself in a divorce case before the court. Angered by the court's school finance ruling, the New Hampshire House impeached Chief Justice Brock, although the state senate narrowly refused to remove him from office. This episode shows how state legislators upset with the courts over one issue may attack the courts on other issues.[90]

In states where judges are elected, judicial decisions may be more likely to become campaign issues for state legislators. For example, the Ohio legislature has long been at odds with the state supreme court. Although judicial elections in Ohio are technically nonpartisan, the decisions of the state supreme court often vary according to which political party has the majority on the court. Thus, legislators in Ohio see the courts as playing a highly partisan role in the policy-making process in the state. As one member of the Ohio legislature argued, "Judges in Ohio are subject to the same influences as legislators. All business interests seek to control their future, to press their influence, to maintain control over the courts' decisions, basically to keep us out of their decisions."[91] When asked how he would respond to a decision of the Ohio Supreme Court with which he disagreed, another Ohio legislator proclaimed, "I would issue a press release to scare the courts to their senses. I don't hesitate to overturn court decisions. The courts are just another political group, in my opinion."[92]

One recent study interviewed state supreme court judges and state legislators in a variety of states in order to explore the interactions between the two institutions of government. The researchers chose six representative states with six different methods of judicial selection and retention and found that the relationships were generally tense and strained in almost all of these states.[93] Among legislators, the greatest mistrust of state supreme courts came in states where the judges were popularly elected. In states with both partisan and nonpartisan judicial election systems, a tiny proportion of legislators described the relationship with their state supreme court as very good and a high proportion said the relationship was very poor. A large proportion of these legislators also saw judicial rulings as retaliatory because the legislature had criticized the courts. However, a very high proportion of legislators in states with other types of judicial selection systems described their relationship with their state supreme court as very good, and few said it was very poor.[94] While tensions seem to be growing between most state courts and their legislatures, the worst relationships exist where the state judges are directly elected by the voters.

It is unclear how much state judges weigh legislative views in making their judicial decisions. In a study of state supreme court rulings in cases involving the establishment of religion, one scholar found that state supreme court judges paid almost no attention to the positions of the governor and the state legislature.[95] Some state legislatures have attempted to force the courts to consider their wishes. For example, in 2001 the Oregon legislature enacted a statute that elevated the role of legislative history when the courts engaged in statutory interpretation decisions. The Texas legislature has also enacted similar rules of statutory interpretation.[96] In fact, many states have enacted such rules in an attempt to restrict the discretion of state judges.[97]

THE SUPREME COURT AND THE SEPARATION OF POWERS

While it may appear that legislators are the ones expressing their anger with the courts, we should also keep in mind that the courts and especially the U.S. Supreme Court often issue rulings involving Congress and the separation of powers. Sometimes the Court rules in favor of congressional authority, but at other times the Court seems to be attempting to restrict congressional discretion.

The issue of whether Congress must follow constitutional principles in seating or rejecting its own members arose in the Supreme Court case *Powell v. McCormack* (1969). Adam Clayton Powell had been serving in the U.S. House of Representatives since 1945, but after his 1966 reelection the House passed a resolution refusing to seat him because of charges of ethical violations, including misappropriation of public funds because he allegedly made illegal salary payments to his wife. Powell sued the Speaker of the House in order to get his properly elected seat in Congress. The Supreme Court ruled that the House had to follow exactly the procedures spelled out in the Constitution for seating one of its members, but that a two-thirds majority could also vote to expel Congressman Powell after he took his seat. In other words, Congress could not exclude Representative Powell, since he had been properly elected to the House, but it could expel him later.

The limits on Congress's investigation powers are somewhat unclear due to a pair of cases from the McCarthy era, mentioned in an earlier chapter. In the first case, *Watkins v. United States* (1957), John Thomas Watkins complained that questions members of the House Committee on Un-American Activities posed to him violated his constitutional rights. When he refused to answer, Watkins was convicted of the crime of contempt of Congress. In a 6–1 decision, the Court agreed with Watkins, stating that there were clear constitutional limits to Congress's investigatory powers, and threw out the conviction. The negative reaction from the McCarthy-era Congress was swift and forceful, with many Members of Congress claiming that it was the Supreme Court that had overstepped its authority. Then two years later the Court appeared to reverse itself in a case with very similar facts, *Barenblatt v. United States* (1959). In a 5–4 decision, the Court upheld the criminal conviction of Lloyd Barenblatt for refusing to answer questions from the House Committee on Un-American Activities, allowing Congress great leeway in the limits of its investigatory powers. Many commentators feel that the Court surrendered because it feared intense pressure from the legislative branch over its ruling in this case.

The Court has also made it clear that there are limits on how much of its own legislative power Congress can delegate to others. In *Hampton & Co. v. United States* (1928), the Court ruled that it was constitutional for Congress to delegate certain administrative details to the executive branch. In this case, Congress enacted a general tariff law but allowed the president to adjust the tariffs up or down using some very specific criteria. However, in *Schechter Corp. v. United States* (1935), the Court ruled that Congress had unconstitutionally delegated its legislative powers to a private nongovernmental industry board. In an attempt to stabilize agricultural prices, Congress allowed industrial and trade associations to draw up codes of conduct for their industries in order to minimize competition, raise prices, and restrict production during the Great Depression. The Court declared the congressional action unconstitutional, stating that it could not delegate to nongovernmental actors strictly legislative duties such as writing these codes of conduct. In another case, the Court also ruled that Congress had unconstitutionally delegated its legislative duties, this time to the president as part of a line-item veto law. In *Clinton v. City of New York* (1998), the Court ruled that the Constitution required the president to sign or veto an entire bill presented by Congress, and it prohibited the congressional action that allowed the president to veto only a portion of the bill. Thus, the Supreme Court decided that Congress was giving too much power to the president with line-item veto authority. If Congress wanted to create the line-item veto system, then it would need to pass a constitutional amendment to do so; it could not do so by merely passing a statute delegating that legislative authority to the president.

The Court has certainly reined in Congress when it feels that Congress has violated the separation of powers. For example, in *Buckley v. Valeo* (1976) the Court ruled that parts of the Federal Election Campaign Act amendments of 1974 were unconstitutional. This legislation set up reporting requirements for federal campaign contributions and created a new Federal Election Commission (FEC) to oversee the provisions of the new law. Originally Congress had reserved the right to appoint half of the FEC commissioners itself. The Court ruled that Congress had overstepped its constitutional authority because only the president can appoint these executive branch officials. Likewise, in *Bowsher v. Synar* (1986), the Supreme Court ruled that Congress had violated separation of powers principles when it enacted the Gramm-Rudman-Hollings Act of 1985. This deficit reduction legislation set up a new system for reducing the deficit when Congress could not agree on necessary spending cuts or revenue increases. The comptroller general, the head of the General Accounting Office, would draft the order calling for automatic spending cuts, and the president would have no discretion to modify or veto the comptroller general's order. The constitutional problem for the Supreme Court was the fact that the comptroller general could only be removed from office by a vote of both houses of Congress or by impeachment. The Court ruled that this deficit reduction scheme was unconstitutional because the comptroller general was part of the legislative branch of government, but the act required him to carry out executive branch functions. In a different line of cases, the Court ruled that only Congress could determine proper procedures to follow in impeachment proceedings against a sitting federal judge. This case was *Nixon v. United States* (1993), and the Court ruled that it would not interfere in this internal congressional process.

CHAPTER SUMMARY

This chapter has examined the interactions between the courts and the legislative branch, at both the state and federal levels, that are the focus of the Governance as Dialogue movement. Many of these interactions are routine, including annual budget issues and judicial selection. The chapter then examined the different reactions legislatures have to statutory interpretation decisions and to constitutional interpretation decisions. Court-legislature interactions can become quite contentious. There are a variety of weapons available to Congress when it is extremely unhappy with the federal courts, such as court-stripping proposals, but few of these have ever been put into effect. Nevertheless, the threats of impeaching judges for their political views remain real. This chapter also examined a variety of U.S. Supreme Court decisions that deal with congressional powers and processes.

For Further Reading

Barnes, Jeb. 2004. *Overruled? Legislative Overrides, Pluralism, and Court-Congress Relations in an Age of Statutes.* Stanford, CA: Stanford University Press.

Clark, Tom S. 2011. *The Limits of Judicial Independence.* New York: Cambridge University Press.

Devins, Neal, and Keith E. Whittington, eds. 2005. *Congress and the Constitution.* Durham, NC: Duke University Press.

Fisher, Louis. 1988. *Constitutional Dialogues: Interpretation as Political Process.* Princeton, NJ: Princeton University Press.

Geyh, Charles G. 2006. *When Courts and Congress Collide: The Struggle for Control of America's Judicial System.* Ann Arbor: University of Michigan Press.

Katzmann, Robert A. 1997. *Courts and Congress.* Washington, DC: Brookings Institution Press.

Langer, Laura. 2002. *Judicial Review in State Supreme Courts: A Comparative Study.* Albany: State University of New York Press.

Lovell, George I. 2003. *Legislative Deferrals: Statutory Ambiguity, Judicial Power, and American Democracy.* Cambridge: Cambridge University Press.

Miller, Mark C. 2009. *The View of the Courts from the Hill: Interactions Between Congress and the Federal Judiciary.* Charlottesville: University of Virginia Press.

Pickerill, J. Mitchell. 2004. *Constitutional Deliberation in Congress: The Impact of Judicial Review in a Separated System.* Durham, NC: Duke University Press.

11

Executives and the Courts

Clearly in the United States we have an independent judiciary, in large part due to our system of separation of powers. Federal judges have life terms, and Congress cannot reduce their salaries. Governors and presidents often play a key role in the judicial selection process, and the executives certainly want courts that will help them carry out their political agendas. However, courts are often called upon to referee disagreements between the executive and legislative branches. Should the judiciary side with one branch over the other? This raises an interesting question about how the courts interact with the chief executive. This chapter will examine the interactions between the courts and presidents or state governors.

The relationship between the president of the United States and the U.S. Supreme Court is very important to the separation of powers. Over various periods in our history sometimes the Supreme Court has supported the president's positions, sometimes it has supported the position of Congress, and sometimes it has been in conflict with both at the same time. Clearly, the Supreme Court and the other federal courts are an independent voice in the inter-institutional dialogue about the meaning of the U.S. Constitution.[1]

MAJOR HISTORICAL CONFLICTS BETWEEN THE PRESIDENT AND THE SUPREME COURT

Some scholars have argued that the Framers intended the president and the Supreme Court to work together as partners in order to check the potential power of an overly aggressive legislative branch.[2] This view seems to be contradicted by Alexander Hamilton in Federalist No. 78, where he wrote, "Liberty can have nothing to fear from the judiciary alone, but would have everything to fear from its union with either of the other departments."

Although the president has a strong role in judicial selection, the Supreme Court throughout American history has often ruled against the president's wishes. In response, presidents have long criticized the Supreme Court and its rulings. Very early in our history the relationship between the Supreme Court and the president became quite contentious. Presidents Thomas Jefferson, Andrew Jackson, Abraham Lincoln, and Franklin Roosevelt all had very tense relationships with the Supreme Court because these presidents felt that the Court was blocking their necessary policy initiatives. Let us now look at some of these grand historical executive-judicial conflicts.

The Early Years

Following Thomas Jefferson's victory in the 1800 presidential election, the federal courts quickly became both a partisan and ideological issue in American politics. The Federalist Party supported strong federal courts, while the Jeffersonians feared that the federal courts would become too powerful. The Jeffersonians argued that the federal courts should defer to the decisions of the elected branches and uphold majoritarian principles. The Federalists, on the other hand, believed that the courts should serve as a check on the power of both Congress and the president, hinting that they should play an anti-majoritarian role in the U.S. system of government. Both parties understood that life appointments for the new federal judges would change the nature of law and politics in the United States.

When the Federalist Party lost both Congress and the presidency in the elections of 1800, the Federalists very quickly realized that federal judges would be their last hope of retaining any power and influence in the government. Before the Jeffersonians could take power after the election, the Federalists created many new federal judgeships and packed them with Federalists. These new judgeships became known as the "Midnight Appointments." The Jeffersonians were not happy. One southern senator proclaimed, "I am more afraid of an army of judges [. . .] than an army of soldiers."[3] Another Jeffersonian senator asserted that he was "in favor of an independent judiciary but not of judges who were 'independent of the nation itself.'"[4]

Obviously, the Jeffersonians were furious with the tactics of the Federalists. This was the first period in which sustained national anger was directed at federal judges.[5] At the urging of Thomas Jefferson, the new Democratic-Republican (Jeffersonian) Congress passed a variety of anti-court measures, including one that prevented the Supreme Court from meeting for more than a year.[6] One consequence of these Midnight Appointments was the famous case of *Marbury v. Madison* (1803), which established the courts' power of judicial review.

Thomas Jefferson himself was quite angry at the Federalist judges and their decisions when he took office, but, as president, he mostly refrained from attacking the courts in public. In private, however, he referred to the Supreme Court as "that subtle corps of sappers and miners constantly working underground to undermine the foundations of our confederated fabric."[7] Jefferson fundamentally disagreed with the idea that the president was required to follow the policies articulated by the Supreme Court. In 1804 he said, "Nothing in the Constitution has given them [the Supreme Court] a right to decide for the executive, more than to the executive to decide for them."[8] This was probably in response to the Court's statement in *Marbury v. Madison* (1803) that "[i]t is emphatically the province and duty of the judicial department to say what the law is."[9] Following the Court's ruling in *Marbury,* the Jeffersonians impeached one federal judge and removed him from office because of his alcoholism and probable insanity. The Jeffersonians failed, however, in their efforts to remove Justice Samuel Chase from the Supreme Court. Justice Chase was impeached by the House of Representatives merely because he was a staunch Federalist partisan, but the Federalists did not have enough votes in the U.S. Senate to remove him from the bench. Thus, President Jefferson and the other Jeffersonians were not able to overturn the Court's landmark decision in *Marbury v. Madison.* But they did have enough power that the Supreme Court did not declare another federal statute to be unconstitutional until 1857.

Jacksonian Democracy and the Courts

First elected in 1828, President Andrew Jackson was equally mistrustful of the Supreme Court and the other federal courts. Jackson was elected as a populist who opposed the elitists previously in control of the government. The Jacksonians had inherited the Jeffersonians' mistrust of the federal judiciary, which was augmented by the personal distain that Jackson felt toward Chief Justice John Marshall.[10] Strong supporters of majoritarian democracy, the Jacksonians introduced many bills aimed at weakening the federal courts, but none was ever enacted.[11] The Jacksonians also introduced the idea of electing state judges wherever possible. On this front, they were quite successful, as many states moved to an elected state judiciary.

When Jackson was unhappy with a U.S. Supreme Court decision, he would simply refuse to enforce it. For example, after the Court ruled in *Worcester v.*

Georgia (1832) that the state could not remove the Cherokee Nation from its lands in Georgia, President Jackson refused to allow U.S. federal personnel to enforce the court's order. Journalist Horace Greeley reported that President Jackson allegedly said, "John Marshall has made his decision, *now let him enforce it!*"[12] Although most scholars now believe that Jackson never actually uttered those exact words,[13] they clearly reflect his general views on the power of the judiciary.

While Jackson never opposed judicial independence per se, he did oppose judicial supremacy. In *McCulloch v. Maryland* (1819), the Supreme Court had declared that the newly chartered national bank was constitutional and protected against state efforts to destroy it through extremely heavy state taxes levied on it. The Jacksonians hated the national bank, and, when Congress extended its charter in 1832, Jackson vetoed the bill. In his veto statement, he revealed his belief that the Supreme Court did not have the final word on the meaning of the Constitution: "Mere [judicial] precedent is a dangerous source of authority, and should not be regarded as deciding the questions of constitutional power except where the acquiescence of the people and the States can be considered as well settled. [. . .] The Congress, the Executive, and the Court must each for itself be guided by its own opinion of the Constitution."[14] Thus, President Andrew Jackson and his supporters refused to implement the decisions of the Supreme Court in part because they viewed the Court as an elitist body that could not be reconciled with their concept of majoritarian democracy.[15]

Lincoln and the Courts

In another historical time of conflict between the executive and the courts, Abraham Lincoln became president in large part because of his vocal opposition to the Supreme Court's ruling in *Dred Scott v. Sandford* (1857). In this infamous decision, the Court ruled that blacks could never have any rights that the nation would recognize. The Court also declared the Missouri Compromise of 1820 to be unconstitutional because it limited the spread of slavery. This decision contributed to the rise of the Republican Party, which had been created three years earlier. Lincoln and his party opposed "aggression by the judiciary" and "judicial usurpation,"[16] and *Dred Scott* became the dominant issue in the 1858 Illinois Senate election between Democrat Stephen Douglas and Republican Abe Lincoln. These two men would again face off in the 1860 presidential election. Lincoln often repeated the Jeffersonian and Jacksonian views that the Supreme Court was not the only institution that could interpret the Constitution.[17] In his

First Inaugural Address, Lincoln stated, "If the policy of the government, upon vital questions, affecting the whole people, is to be irrevocably fixed by the decision of the Supreme Court, . . . the people have ceased to be their own rulers."[18] Once in office, Lincoln did not further attack the courts; he merely ignored them and their decisions.[19]

The New Deal and the Courts

Another period of great conflict between the president and the Supreme Court occurred during the early 1930s when the Court declared large parts of Franklin Delano Roosevelt's New Deal to be unconstitutional. FDR responded with his so-called court packing plan, where he vowed to add one new justice to the Court for every member who was then over the age of seventy. In other words, FDR wanted to almost double the size of the Supreme Court in order to ensure that the Court would uphold the constitutionality of his New Deal programs. FDR accused the Supreme Court of "improperly set[ting] itself up as a third house of the Congress—a super-legislature" and of "reading into the Constitution words and implications which are not there, and which were never intended to be there."[20] After the 1936 presidential election, one justice eventually changed his vote, allowing the Court to uphold the New Deal. This 1937 incident is often called the "switch in time that saved nine." Although Congress refused to go along with the president's court packing plan, it did pass a generous early retirement program for the justices.[21] In part because of these financial retirement benefits, Roosevelt was able to appoint eight justices to the Supreme Court over the next six years, thus giving his supporters a huge majority among the justices on the high court and dramatically affecting the Court's future rulings.

Scholars have paid a great deal of attention to this epic struggle between these two branches of the national government.[22] It is worth remembering that the conflicts between the Court and the president that reached their zenith in 1937 had started nearly half a century earlier.[23] As will be explained in more detail below, liberals and progressives had been angry with the conservative activism of the U.S. Supreme Court since the 1890s. Despite FDR's pointed criticisms of the Supreme Court, popular opinion in the United States did not support institutional attacks on the judiciary. As judicial politics scholar Howard Gillman concludes, "In the late 1930s, after nearly a half century of sustained efforts to curtail the powers and responsibilities of state and federal courts, the American judiciary found itself barely bruised and more powerful than ever."[24]

The Supreme Court and Early Presidential Campaigns

Not only have presidents historically attacked specific Supreme Court decisions with which they disagreed, but the Court has also become an issue in many presidential election campaigns. For many decades, it was liberals and progressives who attacked the Court. Starting in the late 1800s the Supreme Court was dominated by conservative judicial activists who focused almost exclusively on economic issues. They saw their job as protecting business interests because they thought that government regulation of the economy would ruin the nation. For example, the Court declared the federal income tax to be unconstitutional in *Pollock v. Farmers' Loan and Trust Co.* (1895), and *United States v. E. C. Knight* (1895) significantly weakened the Sherman Antitrust Act of 1890. In this era, which became known as the *Lochner* era after the justices declared unconstitutional a state law setting a maximum of ten working hours per day or sixty hours per week for bakers in *Lochner v. New York* (1905), the Court struck down a large number of federal and state laws that attempted to improve working conditions. During this period, presidential candidates who represented business interests saw the Supreme Court as the protector of economic freedoms, while those favoring government regulation of the economy attacked the Court for being improperly activist.

The presidential elections of 1896 and 1900 set the tone for future elections in the early part of the twentieth century. In both elections, Republican William McKinley supported the Supreme Court's economic decisions and painted his opponent, Democrat William Jennings Bryan, as a radical because of his party's attacks on the Court. The Republicans were successful in convincing voters in these elections that the Democrats were against law and order and also against constitutional government.[25]

A major fight over judicial power occurred in the presidential election of 1912. Although former president Teddy Roosevelt had recommended William Howard Taft for the Republican presidential nomination in 1908, he tried hard to block Taft's nomination for reelection in 1912. Taft eventually won the 1912 Republican nomination, and he campaigned as a pro-courts conservative. Taft won the Republican nomination in part because many in his party felt that Teddy Roosevelt's views on the courts were too radical for the mainstream of voters. Taft repeated his support for the Supreme Court many times over the course of the fall election campaign.[26]

Despite losing the Republican nomination in 1912, Teddy Roosevelt nevertheless ran for president that year, this time as the nominee of the Progressive Bull Moose Party. After leaving the presidency in 1909, Roosevelt had come to believe that the courts in general and the U.S. Supreme Court in particular were the major impediments to progressive reforms in the country. Starting with his triumphant return to the United States in 1910 after spending time in Africa on safari, Roosevelt began an all-out assault on judicial power and activism. In a speech to the Colorado legislature in August 1910, Roosevelt "accused the courts of blocking effective state and federal action to solve urgent national problems. Roosevelt charged that the courts had imposed artificial limits on the powers of the state legislatures and Congress to exercise control over the activities of large corporations."[27] He then called for the voters to be able to overturn any court decision striking down a statute as unconstitutional. This **decision recall proposal** would have resulted in greatly reduced power for the courts. As Roosevelt stated at the Progressive Party convention, "[P]eople themselves must be the ultimate makers of their own Constitution."[28]

Teddy Roosevelt's attacks on judicial power were far less radical than the ideas promoted by the Socialist Party and its nominee for president in 1912, Eugene Debs. The Socialists called for the elimination of all federal courts below the U.S. Supreme Court, and they advocated the abolition of judicial review. Under the Socialist proposals, federal statutes could be repealed only by an act of Congress or by the voters in a national referendum.[29] The Socialists also wanted all judges (including federal judges on all three levels) to be elected by the voters for very short terms.[30] The eventual winner of the 1912 presidential election was Democrat Woodrow Wilson, who basically ignored the issue of the judiciary in his campaign. Wilson would go to win both the 1912 and 1916 elections.

In the presidential election of 1924, the courts would again appear as a major campaign issue. The Progressive Party nominated Senator Robert M. La Follette as their candidate for president to run against Republican Calvin Coolidge and Democrat John W. Davis. The Progressive Party in 1924 adopted the Socialist Party position of 1912 that judicial review was illegitimate. The Progressive Party platform called for a constitutional amendment to outlaw judicial review and thus severely restrain the power of the courts. In fact, during the campaign La Follette often referred to the justices as "petty tyrants and arrogant despots."[31] Both the Republicans and the Democrats in 1924 warned voters of the dangers of the Progressive plan for the courts. In fact, the Republicans characterized the Progressive proposals concerning the judiciary as revolutionary attacks on judicial independence.[32] Coolidge won the election in a landslide, and anti-court proposals quickly faded away. After the Supreme Court eventually reversed its view that the New Deal was unconstitutional (the "switch in time that saved nine"), liberal and progressive presidential candidates generally stopped attacking the Supreme Court and instead came to see the Court as an ally.

MODERN-DAY CONSERVATIVE
ATTACKS ON THE SUPREME COURT

Starting in the mid-1950s, the Supreme Court switched from being a conservative activist body to being a liberal activist one. Under Chief Justice Earl Warren, the Court seemed uninterested in economic cases, instead focusing almost exclusively on civil rights and civil liberties issues. The Warren Court became the epitome of liberal judicial activism because the justices believed among other things that the Court should protect the rights of unpopular political minorities. Before Chief Justice Warren joined the Supreme Court, in a very famous footnote in *United States v. Carolene Products* (1937), the Court's liberals outlined their preference for hearing civil liberties and civil rights cases over economic ones. These civil rights and liberties issues, especially ones dealing with "discrete and insular minorities," would receive heightened scrutiny from the newly liberal activist Court.[33] When Earl Warren was named chief justice, the liberal activist orientation of the Supreme Court grew even stronger. The Warren Court handed down a long series of liberal activist decisions touching on many different aspects of American life.

Conservatives reacted with alarm. American conservatives had seen the Supreme Court as the great protector of economic freedoms from the late 1800s until 1937. Starting in the 1950s, however, conservatives began to fear that unfettered judicial power was advancing the liberal agenda. Conservatives were furious about a wide variety of Warren Court rulings, including decisions on race discrimination, congressional investigations of Communism, other national security issues, freedom of speech and expression, the rights of accused criminals, and the redrawing of legislative districts to ensure the "one person, one vote" principle. After the Supreme Court's ruling in *Brown v. Board of Education* (1954), which declared an end to racial discrimination in the public schools, there were bumper stickers and billboards all over the South calling for the impeachment of Chief Justice Earl Warren.[34] Congressional opponents of the Court's desegregation decisions even drafted the infamous Southern Manifesto, which stated that the *Brown* decision was a "clear abuse of judicial power."[35] Conservatives remained angry with the Court for decades to come.

The courts became an issue in the 1964 presidential elections. Barry Goldwater, the 1964 Republican presidential candidate who ran against President Lyndon B. Johnson, started talking about the failure of the national government to fight "crime in the streets" and to ensure "law and order." Goldwater did not attack the Supreme Court directly, although it was clear from his rhetoric that he thought the Supreme Court was taking the country down the wrong path.[36]

In 1968, Republican Richard Nixon made the courts a centerpiece of his presidential campaign. He blamed almost all of the country's social problems on the liberal activism and permissiveness of the federal courts in general and of the U.S. Supreme Court in particular. Thus, conservatives did everything they could to end the liberal activism of the Warren Court era. In their eyes, "the Court's recent rulings had aided Communist forces, abetted criminals intent on causing harm, threatened to dislodge schoolchildren from the security of their neighborhoods, unleashed a wave of pornographic smut, released murderers from death row, forced prayer out of the schools, and loosened society's constraints on sexual promiscuity."[37] Southerner George Wallace, the candidate of the American Independent Party in 1968, attacked the Supreme Court whenever possible on the campaign trail. One of his favorite lines was something like this: "If you walk out of this hotel tonight and someone knocks you on the head, *he'll* be out of jail before *you're* out of the hospital, and on Monday morning they'll try the *policeman* instead of the criminal."[38]

After a bruising party convention in Chicago that was marred by riots outside the convention hall, the Democratic Party in 1968 chose LBJ's vice president, Hubert Humphrey, to be its nominee for president. The Democratic convention was complicated even more by the fact that Chief Justice Earl Warren announced just before the gathering convened that he would step down from the Supreme Court, giving the new president the chance to fill the chief justice's seat. Humphrey expressed his strong support for the Supreme Court's rulings and for its chief justice. The Democrats lost the once solidly Democratic South in part because their pro-civil-rights agenda was skillfully exploited by Nixon and Wallace in that region. They also lost many northern ethnic voters who were unhappy with the recent riots and other unrest in the streets and who perceived the Democratic Party as "car[ing] too much about advancing civil rights and not enough about their own concerns."[39]

Thus, for both Richard Nixon and George Wallace in 1968, the Supreme Court became a powerful tool for attracting votes and a mechanism for constructing a new electoral coalition. In Nixon and Wallace's telling, the liberal activist Supreme Court under Chief Justice Earl Warren had done much more wrong than right.[40] Richard Nixon's strategy of attacking the Supreme Court paid off, and he was elected president in 1968. One of Richard M. Nixon's finest moments was the appointment in early 1969 of Warren Burger to be chief justice.

Nixon firmly hoped that the Warren Court period of liberal judicial activism had come to an end.

In the election of 1980, Republican Ronald Reagan again used attacks on the Supreme Court to fire up his conservative base. Reagan needed to attract voters from the growing religious right movement. These social conservatives were angry that the Supreme Court had ruled in favor of abortion rights, and the Republican Party platform that year called for the "appointment of judges who respect traditional family values and the sanctity of innocent human life." To counter concerns that he would use an ideological litmus test for his appointments to the Supreme Court, Reagan pledged to nominate the first woman to the high court. But Reagan made his attacks on the Supreme Court the centerpiece of his appeals to the religious right and other conservative voters.[41] Even though the Supreme Court was quite conservative by this time, right-wing voters were still focused on the liberal activism of the Warren Court era.

Conservative resentment toward the federal courts has continued. When George W. Bush was president, he attacked "activist judges" in both his 2004 and 2005 State of the Union addresses.[42] Various conservatives called for restrictions on the power of the courts, while some even advocated impeaching federal judges because of their rulings. During the 2008 presidential elections, Republican candidate Senator John McCain of Arizona pledged to appoint only federal judges who believed in the philosophy of judicial restraint.

In the 2012 campaign for president, the Supreme Court again became an issue. During the primary season, many of the more conservative Republican candidates for president attacked the federal courts in general and specifically the Supreme Court. As two journalists noted, "Republican presidential candidates are issuing biting and sustained attacks on the federal courts and the role they play in American life, reflecting and stoking skepticism among conservatives about the judiciary."[43] For example, Governor Rick Perry of Texas called for term limits for Supreme Court justices, who of course currently have life appointments to the bench. Representatives Michele Bachmann and Ron Paul said they would forbid the Supreme Court to rule on cases regarding same-sex marriage. Newt Gingrich and Rick Santorum wanted to abolish the U.S. Court of Appeals for the Ninth Circuit because of its perceived liberal activism. Many of the candidates seemed to want to limit the judicial review power of the federal courts. As Gingrich argued, "Judicial supremacy is factually wrong, it is morally wrong, and it is an affront to the American system of self-government."[44] And as Santorum proclaimed, "If you want to send a signal to judges that we are tired of them feeling that these elites in society can dictate to us, then you have to fight back."[45] Notice how many of these Republican attacks on the courts sound very similar to the Socialist Party proposals put forward in the election of 1912.

PRESIDENT OBAMA'S CRITICISM OF THE COURTS

While liberals have for several generations generally supported the federal courts, that period may be coming to a close as the federal courts become more conservative in their rulings. More and more liberals are attacking the U.S. Supreme Court for its conservative activist decisions. President Barack Obama has certainly strongly criticized various Supreme Court decisions with which he disagrees. Obama even took the unusual step of condemning the Court's decision in *Citizens United v. Federal Election Commission* (2010) during his State of the Union address a few days after the decision was handed down, when six of the justices were in attendance. As noted above, President George W. Bush had criticized "activist judges" during his 2004 and 2005 State of the Union addresses. But President Obama went much further in attacking the *Citizens United* decision directly. The ruling declared unconstitutional federal limits on campaign spending by corporations and unions, and liberals were especially upset because the Supreme Court implied that corporations had the same First Amendment rights to free speech as individuals do. In his State of the Union address, President Obama said, "With all due deference to separation of powers, last week the Supreme Court reversed a century of law that, I believe, will open the floodgates for special interests, including foreign corporations, to spend without limit in our elections."[46]

Liberal groups were thrilled with the president's harsh comments on the decision, but conservative groups blasted the president for bringing up the case in that setting, with the justices present. Justice Alito appeared to mouth the words "Not true, not true" as he shook his head during the president's comments about the *Citizens United* case. Some media commentators argued that the president's statements were an "ill-advised attempt to draw the Court, at times viewed as a bastion of independence, into the political fray."[47] As one leading conservative said at the time, "The president's swipe at the Supreme Court was a breach of decorum, and represents the worst of Washington politics—scapegoating 'special interest' boogeymen for all that ails Washington in attempt to silence the diverse range of speakers in our democracy."[48]

A few years later, Justice John Paul Stevens, who by then had retired, praised the president's criticism of the Court's majority opinion in *Citizens United* (Justice Stevens had dissented in the case). At a lecture in Little Rock, Arkansas, in May 2012, Justice Stevens stated that he supported the president's 2010 State of the Union address: "In that succinct comment, the former professor of Constitutional Law at the University of Chicago [Obama] made three important and accurate observations about the Supreme Court's majority opinion. First, it did overturn a century of law; second, it did authorize unlimited election-related expenditures by America's most powerful interests; and third, the logic of the opinion extends to money spent by foreign entities."[49] It is quite unusual for a justice of the Supreme Court to praise the president for criticizing the Court, but after his retirement apparently Justice Stevens felt able to do so.

Soon after the Supreme Court's oral arguments in the health care reform case in the spring of 2012, President Obama again criticized the Court. Many in the media after the oral arguments assumed (incorrectly, as it turned out) that the Court would declare the president's signature health care reform legislation to be unconstitutional. Perhaps in a preemptive strike, the president strongly implied that he would consider such a decision a clear example of conservative judicial activism: "Ultimately, I'm confident that the Supreme Court will not take what would be an unprecedented, extraordinary step of overturning a law that was passed by a strong majority of a democratically elected Congress."[50] Clearly, the president was attempting to make the Supreme Court and its conservative activist decisions a key campaign issue for the 2012 elections. As one commentator noted, President Obama's comments were in line with an "emerging Democratic strategy to paint the court as extreme."[51]

Some Republican-appointed judges and justices did not hesitate to fire back at the president. For example, Justice Scalia took the unusual approach of reading his dissent aloud when the Supreme Court announced its decision in *Arizona v. United States* (2012), which struck down most of the provisions in an Arizona law aimed at preventing illegal immigration. During his oral comments, Justice Scalia attacked President Obama's recent refusal to deport almost 1.4 million illegal immigrants who had entered the country as children. The president's executive order was not part of the case before the Court, and many commentators were shocked that Justice Scalia even mentioned it.[52] In another incident, a Reagan appointee to the U.S. Court of Appeals took offense at President Obama's remarks warning the Supreme Court not to strike down the Affordable Care Act. This judge ordered Attorney General Eric Holder to write a three-page letter explaining that the president respected the courts' power of judicial review.[53] Evidently it was not just Democrats who intended to make the Supreme Court a campaign issue in the 2012 presidential election. The interest in the Supreme Court was heightened even further by the fact that there were four justices over the age of seventy on the Court in 2012.[54] It seems highly likely that President Obama will have the opportunity to make several appointments to the Court in his second term.

In January 2013, the United States Court of Appeals for the District of Columbia Circuit opened yet another battle in the fight between the president and the federal courts. The Court of Appeals declared that President Obama had acted unconstitutionally in making several recess appointments to the National Labor Relations Board after the Senate failed to approve his nominates to this federal agency. A **recess appointment** is when the president makes a temporary appointment to a federal agency or to the federal courts when the Senate is not in formal session. The individual can then serve until the next annual session of Congress begins. The practice started in the 1820s, and presidents have claimed since 1867 that they may determine when the Senate is out of formal session. Obama has made fewer recess appointments than any other recent president,[55] and the D.C. Circuit Court is a prestigious court to which President Obama had none of his appointees confirmed during his first term.[56] The Court of Appeals disagreed with the constitutionality of this recess appointment practice, and, if the ruling is not overturned by the Supreme Court of the United States, then the practice of recess appointments may be dead.

The Court of Appeals might have been reflecting the views of many conservative members of Congress on this issue. In February 2012, the House Judiciary Committee held a hearing on the recess appointments, and several Republican members of the committee argued that the president's actions were unconstitutional.[57] These arguments were similar to those eventually adopted by the federal appeals court in its ruling on the case. A former Justice Department lawyer who handled recess appointments for President George W. Bush disagreed with the committee members, commenting, "If this opinion stands, I think it will fundamentally alter the balance between the Senate and the president by limiting the president's ability to keep offices filled."[58] A spokesperson for the Obama Administration criticized the ruling: "The decision is novel and unprecedented. It contradicts 150 years of practice by Democratic and Republican administrations. So we respectfully but strongly disagree with the ruling."[59] In January 2014, the U.S. Supreme Court heard oral arguments on this issue in *National Labor Relations Board v. Noel Canning* (2014). The Court was expected to issue its ruling in the case by the summer of 2014.

ROUTINE INTERACTIONS BETWEEN EXECUTIVES AND THE COURTS

Of course, the relationship between the executive branch and the judicial branch is not always marked by conflict—many of the interactions are fairly routine. A large number of these regular interactions between the president and the U.S.

Supreme Court occur through the **solicitor general** of the United States, the lawyer for the president and the executive branch at the U.S. Supreme Court. The solicitor general is the only official with an office at the Supreme Court who is not part of the judicial branch.[60] Appointed by the president and confirmed by the U.S. Senate, the solicitor general serves at the will of the president, meaning that the president can fire this individual at any time. Recent research has come to the conclusion that the solicitor general has a great deal of influence over decision making at the U.S. Supreme Court in every stage of the process.[61]

Created in 1870, the Office of the Solicitor General is part of the federal Department of Justice. In addition to the solicitor general, the office includes a small staff of career civil service lawyers who are considered some of the best and brightest in the government. This office was originally designed to relieve the U.S. attorney general of litigation responsibilities in the federal appellate courts.[62] In addition to representing the executive branch before the Supreme Court, the Office of the Solicitor General must also approve all appeals by the federal government in all federal courts. Thus, no one in the federal government can appeal an unfavorable U.S. district court decision or one from a U.S. court of appeals without the express approval of the Office of the Solicitor General.

The solicitor general participates as a party before the Supreme Court when the federal government is directly involved in a case. However, the solicitor general also plays a very large role at the Court as an amicus. The solicitor general often files amicus briefs on certiorari and then again on the merits after the Court has agreed to take a case. When the solicitor general supports a party through an amicus curiae brief, someone from that office is able to participate in oral arguments by taking up to fifteen minutes of the normal thirty-minute argument on that party's side. At times, the Court even requests that the solicitor general file an amicus brief in a particular case and therefore appear at oral arguments.[63] Such frequent appearances make the solicitor general the ultimate "repeat player,"[64] benefiting from this extensive experience and from the professional reputation thereby established in the legal profession.[65]

Even though there is often potential for conflict between the president and the U.S. Supreme Court, the solicitor general nevertheless has a strong success record at the Court.[66] At the certiorari stage, most litigants have a success rate around 1 percent. Petitions supported by the solicitor general, however, generally have a success rate around 70 percent,[67] reaching as high as 90 percent in some years.[68] This is in part due to the fact that solicitors general are very cautious about which cases they recommend that the Supreme Court hear. In many ways, the solicitor general serves as a gatekeeper for the Supreme Court. As one expert has noted, "The Solicitor General's office is far more selective in asking for hearings than are private litigants. This restraint allows the government generally to take only its strongest cases to the Court. One benefit is that the justices expect government petitions to be meritorious."[69]

The solicitor general also has a strong record of winning on the merits. During the Rehnquist Court era the solicitor general won about 62 percent of the time, and during the Burger Court period the solicitor general won more than two-thirds of the cases in which the United States was a party.[70] When the solicitor general filed an amicus brief in a case, in some years the side supported by the solicitor general won an incredible 100 percent of the time, with the average win percentage being between 70 percent and 80 percent.[71] As one recent study concluded, "We know that the Office of the Solicitor General wins an astonishingly high percentage of its Supreme Court cases."[72] The justices also often incorporate into the Court's opinions the arguments the solicitor general's office makes in its briefs on the merits and in oral arguments before the Court.[73] Having argued so much before the Court, "[t]he Solicitor General also knows all the catchwords, and they just know how to write them in a brief."[74] Some notable examples of when the solicitor general has lost at the Supreme Court will be discussed later in this chapter.

The solicitor general must have a good relationship with the president, the attorney general, and the U.S. Supreme Court. These relationships vary from administration to administration, but the solicitor general is respected by the Court, enough to be often referred to as the "tenth justice."[75] This high level of respect and influence afforded to the Office of the Solicitor General is probably due to its objectivity, professionalism, and independence.[76] However, there is a clear tension between having the solicitor general make decisions based purely on legal considerations and having the solicitor general further the president's political agenda.

Presidents certainly use the solicitor general in an attempt to affect the Supreme Court's rulings. One recent study has shown that the Supreme Court defers to the wishes of the solicitor general less often when that office is perceived to be politicized.[77] As political scientist Peter N. Ubertaccio III has stated, the Office of the Solicitor General "exists at the intersection of judicial and executive politics, law and partisanship, public policy, and jurisprudence."[78] Thus the solicitor general must constantly balance legal and political approaches.

Presidents have also used their solicitors general and their attorneys general to advance certain political agendas by refusing to file certain appeals. For example, President Obama signaled his disagreement with the federal Defense of Marriage Act by refusing to appeal a court decision declaring the act to be unconstitutional. Basically, this 1996 federal act prevented the federal government from recognizing same-sex marriages that were legal in various states at the time. It also said that the states had no duty to recognize same-sex marriages performed outside their state borders. The attorney general of Massachusetts, among others, sued to have the courts declare this act unconstitutional because it discriminated against married same-sex couples in that state. A federal district court judge in Massachusetts declared that the Defense of Marriage Act was unconstitutional. Two federal district court judges in California reached similar decisions.[79] A unanimous three-judge panel on the First Circuit Court of Appeals agreed in May 2012.[80] In the appellate litigation before the First Circuit, as we have seen, the Obama Administration refused to defend the constitutionality of the act. Republicans in the U.S. House of Representatives then hired their own lawyer to argue in favor of the Defense of Marriage Act.[81] By refusing to appeal and having the attorney general announce the administration's new position, the Obama Administration clearly advanced its political agenda. The U.S. Supreme Court eventually agreed with the arguments of the Obama Administration, striking down the federal Defense of Marriage Act as unconstitutional in *United States v. Windsor* (2013).

Another way that presidents may attempt to influence judicial interpretation of legislation is through presidential signing statements. When presidents sign legislation, they may add a signing statement that reflects their understanding of the intent of the new law. These signing statements are often issued after extensive consultation with various individuals within the Department of Justice and other executive branch officials.[82] Courts may or may not give weight to these signing statements,[83] although President George W. Bush strongly argued that the courts should look to the signing statements in order to understand the president's position in the inter-institutional dialogue about the constitutionality and intent of the legislation.[84] In this way, presidential signing statements could serve much the same purpose in court as legislative history produced during congressional consideration of the proposed new statute.[85]

There are also routine interactions between the executive branch and the courts at the state level. Traditionally, state and local governments have lacked the centralized control over governmental appeals that the federal government enjoys. In order to begin to emulate the success of their federal colleagues, since the 1970s many states have created their own versions of the Office of the Solicitor General. This trend greatly accelerated in the late 1990s. At least thirty-two states now have a state solicitor general or equivalent, and almost all of these are housed in the office of the state attorney general. The solicitor general is the state's chief appellate attorney and usually has the authority to decide on all state appeals in civil cases, whether in the state supreme court or in federal appellate courts, including the U.S. Supreme Court.[86] (Most state attorneys general have a separate office for appeals in criminal cases.) These lawyers also help coordinate the state's arguments in a wide variety of civil cases, as traditionally the states had no centralized body for making collective decisions in the wide range of non-criminal cases.

Executives and courts clearly interact during the judicial selection process as well. As Chapter 3 indicated, presidents nominate all federal judge candidates, and federal judges are often associated with their nominating president in the media and in the public mind. Governors in eleven states directly nominate judicial candidates for state courts, and in eight states the legislature confirms these appointments for full terms. However, in almost all states except Illinois and Louisiana the governor can appoint judges in order to fill unexpired terms regardless of the selection process. Therefore, the relationship between executives and judges can be quite close because judges often owe their jobs to the governor or to the president.

GOVERNORS AND THE COURTS

There are certainly times when governors are unhappy with the decisions of their state supreme courts. For example, Governor Christine Todd Whitman of New Jersey was certainly upset with the New Jersey Supreme Court in 1997 when it declared the state educational funding system unconstitutional for the third time.[87] In 2010, Governor Rick Scott of Florida became very angry with the state's supreme court when the justices blocked a ballot measure that was an attempt to allow the state to opt out of the national health care reform legislation. In 2012, Governor Scott strongly backed efforts to defeat three of the justices in their retention elections, although these efforts failed.[88] Sometimes governors even get involved in judicial retention elections outside their state's borders. In 2012, Governor Bobby Jindal of Louisiana and former presidential candidate Senator Rick Santorum of Pennsylvania both campaigned in Iowa to defeat a state supreme court justice who had voted in favor of same-sex marriage under the Iowa constitution; again, the effort failed.[89] At times, judicial selection processes become important political tools for state governors. For example, in December 2011 New Jersey's governor, Chris Christie, refused to nominate any candidates to judgeships in the state because of a conflict with the state legislature over his appointments to other positions in the executive branch.[90]

As another example of the importance of judicial selection to governors, when Mitt Romney became governor of Massachusetts in 2003 he vowed to reform the state's judicial selection mechanisms. In Massachusetts, all state judges are appointed by the governor for life terms until the mandatory retirement age of seventy. The governor's appointments must be approved by the Governor's Council, a directly elected statewide body that confirms all judicial appointments and approves parole requests. The state legislature has no role in judicial selection. Although Romney was a Republican, the Governor's Council was dominated by Democrats throughout Romney's term in the statehouse. Claiming that the state's judicial selection procedures were riddled with patronage and backroom deals, Romney issued an executive order in 2003 requiring that all judicial nominees first be vetted by an independent, nonpartisan judicial screening commission similar to the merit selection commissions used by almost all Missouri Plan states (see Chapter 3). Those wishing to be nominated for judgeships would apply directly to the commission, and the commission would first review nominees without knowing their identities, focusing only on their judicial qualifications. Romney thus claimed to have removed politics from the judicial selection process.

This commission rejected almost 80 percent of the applicants for the bench between 2003 and 2006, many of which were supported by Governor Romney. The governor was not happy. In 2006 Romney fired members of the commission who were resisting his judicial nominees, effectively stripping the so-called merit selection commission of any influence over the judicial nominating process. In his last seventeen months in office, Romney nominated mostly political allies and campaign contributors to the courts, thus dropping any pretense that his judicial nominations were based solely on merit. In his first few years in office, Romney had appointed mostly moderate Democrats to the bench in the state. In Romney's final year as governor, his nominees were largely supporters of the right wing of the Republican Party. His reform efforts failed because of the realities of politics in the Bay State and his desire to win the future Republican nomination for president.[91]

Judicial elections can also affect governors. The April 2011 special election for the Supreme Court of Wisconsin became a referendum of sorts on the leadership of Governor Scott Walker, a Republican. Among other hot-button issues, Walker and his narrow Republican majority in the state legislature enacted legislation that greatly reduced collective bargaining rights for public employees in the state. These moves infuriated union members and partisan Democrats, who held numerous protest rallies at the statehouse in Madison. Although judicial elections in Wisconsin are technically nonpartisan and often receive little notice in the media, Republican incumbent Justice David T. Prosser had a very close race against Democrat JoAnne Kloppenburg, an assistant attorney general in the state. The 2011 Supreme Court election clearly became a surrogate for voters' feelings about the governor and his policies. In its coverage of the election, the *New York Times* noted, "[T]he Supreme Court contest—once imagined as a dull race with an all-but-certain outcome—captured the greatest interest."[92] After statewide recounts were completed, Justice Prosser survived and was reelected to the Wisconsin Supreme Court by a little over seven thousand votes.[93] In June 2012, Governor Walker survived an extremely rare recall election, becoming the first governor in the United States to stay in office following a recall vote.[94]

It is unclear how much state judges weigh the views of their governor before making their judicial decisions. In one study of state supreme court rulings in establishment of religion cases, political scientist Kevin T. McGuire found that state supreme court judges paid almost no attention to the positions of the governor and the state legislature in these cases.[95]

THE U.S. SUPREME COURT AND PRESIDENTIAL POWER

The Supreme Court has issued a variety of rulings that have strengthened presidential power, while other decisions have restricted presidential prerogatives. This section will first discuss some of the more notable decisions increasing presidential power. In *Mississippi v. Johnson* (1867), the state sued the president in order to prevent him from enforcing certain parts of the Reconstruction Acts. A unanimous Supreme Court ruled that executive acts require presidential discretion, and the president is immune from lawsuits regarding these executive actions. In the case *Ex Parte Grossman* (1925), the Court heard a case involving President Calvin Coolidge's commutation of the sentence for an individual convicted of violating the alcohol prohibition laws. In a unanimous decision, the Court ruled that the president's pardon power is extremely broad and includes the power to commute sentences as well as issue total pardons for federal offenses.[96]

Perhaps the area in which the president has the greatest power is in foreign affairs and war emergencies. During the Civil War, the Supreme Court decided that President Lincoln did indeed have the power to order the blockade of southern ports and the seizure of neutral ships trying to enter those harbors. In the *Prize Cases* (1863), the Supreme Court approved of the president's wartime actions even though Congress had not in advance authorized Lincoln to act. After the Civil War ended, however, in *Ex Parte Milligan* (1866) a unanimous Court ruled that Lincoln acted unconstitutionally when he suspended the writ of habeas corpus without prior congressional approval.

Probably the greatest judicial grant of power to the president in foreign affairs came from the Court's decision in *U.S. v. Curtiss-Wright Corp.* (1936). Congress had enacted a statute allowing the president to stop arms sales to warring factions in South America, and President Franklin Delano Roosevelt issued an executive order forbidding weapons sales to certain countries. The Curtiss-Wright Corporation sued, claiming that the president's order was unconstitutional. The majority opinion by Justice George Sutherland granted extraordinary power to the president to make foreign policy decisions. The opinion stated that the president has extremely broad inherent and extraconstitutional powers in cases of foreign emergencies and wars, and so this case is often read as the zenith of presidential power in wartime. Presidential wartime powers were also upheld in *Korematsu v. United States* (1944), in which the Supreme Court ruled that the president had broad powers to force all Japanese Americans on the West Coast to enter internment camps, regardless of their citizenship or proven loyalty to this country.

On the other hand, the Court scaled back presidential wartime powers in *Youngstown Co. v. Sawyer* (1952). In this case, a steel mill was having severe labor problems. In order to protect the war effort in Korea, President Harry S. Truman ordered the Secretary of Commerce to seize the steel mill so that it would continue to produce steel needed for the war. Congress did not authorize this action. In a 6–3 decision, the Court ruled that President Truman had acted unconstitutionally. Some commentators see this as a domestic labor dispute rather than a wartime powers case. Nevertheless, in addition to restricting presidential power, this case is also remembered for Justice Robert H. Jackson's famous concurrence, which spells out how the Court approaches presidential power using three categories of circumstances. Jackson noted that the president's power is at its highest when the president's actions are authorized by Congress. On the other hand, presidential authority is at its lowest when the president is acting in clear conflict with the will of Congress. There is a third option, a "twilight zone," when Congress is silent. In such circumstances, congressional inaction may allow the president to take independent action in the matter.

There are several cases that have since clarified that "twilight zone." For example, in *Goldwater v. Carter* (1979), the Supreme Court declared that the president could abrogate our treaty with Taiwan without prior congressional approval. The president also had the right to revoke the passport of a former CIA agent who announced his intension to expose the identity of current CIA agents, according to the Court's ruling in *Haig v. Agee* (1981). Both decisions increased the power of the president in foreign affairs. The president, however, could not solely determine when national security concerns would prevent the publication of certain classified materials. In *New York Times v. United States* (1971), the Court ruled that it, not the president, would decide whether publication of the so-called Pentagon Papers would jeopardize national security. When the Pentagon Papers were published, they revealed that the government had exaggerated various casualty figures in the Vietnam War and had not been truthful with the American people about various aspects of the war effort.

A number of cases have involved the power of the president to appoint and remove various executive branch officials. In *Myers v. United States* (1926), the Supreme Court ruled that the president has the power to remove a regular executive branch official from office without the approval of Congress. However, in *Humphrey's Executor v. United States* (1935), the Court did allow Congress to prevent the president from removing members of the newly created independent regulatory commissions or boards before their terms expired. On the other hand, the Court declared that Congress had unconstitutionally impinged upon the president's removal powers when it created the Public Company Accounting Oversight Board as part of the Sarbanes-Oxley Act of 2002. In *Free Enterprise Fund v. Public Company Accounting Oversight Board* (2010), the Court ruled that the president must have the right to fire members of this board because its unique structure did not make it a regular independent regulatory commission covered by the *Humphrey's Executor* case.

There have also been notable cases where the Supreme Court has greatly restricted presidential power. Some have argued that the trend over the last several decades has been for the Supreme Court to interpret the president's powers relatively narrowly in order to protect the balance of power among the branches.[97] One such case, *United States v. Nixon* (1974), which involved the so-called Watergate tapes, greatly reduced broad claims of executive power and executive privilege. The Watergate scandal involved break-ins at Democratic Party headquarters at the Watergate apartment complex, break-ins that were ordered by President Nixon during his 1972 reelection campaign. The real scandal involved efforts by the president and his staff to cover up the break-ins. When Congress was investigating the incidents, they discovered that President Nixon had illegally made tapes of all of his conversations in the Oval Office without the knowledge of his visitors. Members of Congress demanded that Nixon turn over the tapes to them and to the special prosecutors investigating potential federal crimes arising from the break-ins and the cover-up. Nixon refused to turn over the tapes, citing executive privilege among other reasons. **Executive privilege** means that the president has the right to withhold certain information from the other branches because of the need for confidentiality in the internal workings of the White House or because of national security issues. In a unanimous decision, the Supreme Court ruled that Nixon had to turn over the recordings. The Court stated that the president is not above the law and that there are very strong limits on the president's power to assert executive privilege. Although President Nixon considered ignoring the Court's order that he turn over the recordings,[98] he nevertheless resigned from the presidency within several weeks of the Court's ruling in this case.

While *United States v. Nixon* (1974) dealt with presidents and criminal investigations, *Clinton v. Jones* (1997) dealt with civil cases brought against the president for actions outside of his official duties. In this case, Paula Jones brought a sexual harassment suit against President Bill Clinton for things that happened while Clinton was governor of Arkansas, before he became president. The solicitor general for the Clinton Administration argued that the president should not have to defend civil lawsuits while in office because these civil cases are almost always politically motivated and the president does not have the time to be distracted by them. The solicitor general argued that civil suits against the president should not go forward until the president has left office. Since there is no constitutional requirement for a speedy trial in civil cases, these lawsuits could wait. In a unanimous decision, the Supreme Court ruled that the president is not immune from these civil lawsuits, and there is no presidential immunity for actions outside the president's official responsibilities. Congress could decide to postpone these lawsuits, but the Court would allow them to go forward even while the president was still in office. As a result of this decision, Bill Clinton testified under oath in a deposition for this lawsuit that he had never had sexual relations with an intern named Monica Lewinsky. Many Republicans in Congress felt that President Clinton had lied in this deposition, and the House voted to impeach him. After a trial in the Senate, however, the senators did not vote to remove him from office.

The president, even when acting in concert with the Congress, could not alone determine the constitutional rights of so-called enemy combatants being held by the U.S. military in Guantanamo Bay in Cuba. In a series of cases, the Supreme Court disagreed with the actions of both Congress and the president in this area. Following the 9/11 attacks on the World Trade Center in New York and on the Pentagon near Washington, D.C., President George W. Bush declared that potential terrorists would be treated as "enemy combatants," which was not a term recognized by international law. They would not be entitled to the rights of prisoners of war, however, nor would they be entitled to any rights under the Geneva Conventions. These enemy combatants were held indefinitely in a U.S. military facility at Guantanamo Bay in Cuba, without access to lawyers or even the right to know the charges against them. The Supreme Court in *Hamdi v. Rumsfeld* (2004), *Rasul v. Bush* (2004), and *Hamdan v. Rumsfeld* (2006) basically ruled that President Bush's proposals for trying the accused terrorists were unconstitutional, rejecting the Bush Administration's assertions that the detainees' fate was a question for the executive branch alone.[99] More specifically, in

Hamdan the Court ruled that the military tribunals set up to try accused terrorists were unconstitutional. In *Rasul,* the Supreme Court decided 6–3 that detainees at Guantanamo Bay had habeas corpus rights, and in *Hamdi* the Court ruled that U.S. citizens suspected of being terrorists also have habeas corpus rights.[100]

In response to these decisions and at the urging of the Bush Administration, Congress passed the Military Commissions Act of 2006. Among other things, the act attempted to strip the federal courts of jurisdiction to hear habeas corpus appeals from any noncitizen designated as an enemy combatant. It also prohibited federal judges from consulting foreign or international sources of law in these cases, leaving that power to the president alone. It also banned the invocation of treaty rights by litigants in the federal courts. This act clearly supported President Bush's assertion that the president alone could determine how enemy combatants would be treated in the U.S. justice system. The Supreme Court would declare this act unconstitutional in its decision in *Boumediene v. Bush* (2008).[101]

The Supreme Court also ruled in *Clinton v. City of New York* (1998) that the Congress could not give the president line-item veto authority by passing a mere statute. If Congress wanted to create the line-item veto system and thus increase presidential power, a constitutional amendment would be necessary.

CHAPTER SUMMARY

This chapter examined the interactions between courts and executives, whether they be presidents or governors. It began with a look at some of the famous historical fights between the president and the U.S. Supreme Court, before looking at the Supreme Court as an issue in early presidential campaigns. The chapter then discussed the modern-day attacks on the Supreme Court from conservatives as well as from President Obama. The chapter also looked at some of the more routine interactions between executives and the courts, in particular exploring the role of the solicitor general, who must balance the need for political and legal considerations in the job of representing the views of the presidency at the U.S. Supreme Court. It then examined the relationship between governors and state court judges. The chapter ended with a discussion of some of the most important U.S. Supreme Court decisions regarding presidential power.

For Further Reading

Black, Ryan C., and Ryan J. Owens. 2012. *The Solicitor General and the United States Supreme Court: Executive Branch Influence and Judicial Decisions.* New York: Cambridge University Press.

Caplan, Lincoln. 1987. *The Tenth Justice: The Solicitor General and the Rule of Law.* New York: Alfred A. Knopf.

Crouch, Jeffrey. 2009. *The Presidential Pardon Power.* Lawrence: University Press of Kansas.

Fisher, Louis. 2007. *Constitutional Conflicts Between Congress and the President.* Lawrence: University Press of Kansas.

Kelly, Christopher S., ed. 2006. *Executing the Constitution: Putting the President Back into the Constitution.* Albany: State University of New York Press.

McMahon, Kevin J. 2011. *Nixon's Court: His Challenge to Judicial Liberalism and Its Political Consequences.* Chicago: University of Chicago Press.

Pacelle, Richard L., Jr. 2003. *Between Law and Politics: The Solicitor General and the Structuring of Race, Gender, and Reproductive Rights Policy.* College Station: Texas A&M University Press.

Peabody, Bruce, ed. 2011. *The Politics of Judicial Independence: Courts, Politics, and the Public.* Baltimore: Johns Hopkins University Press.

Scigliano, Robert. 1971. *The Supreme Court and the Presidency.* New York: Free Press.

Whittington, Keith. 1999. *Constitutional Construction: Divided Powers and Constitutional Meaning.* Cambridge, MA: Harvard University Press.

12

Courts and Governmental Bureaucracies

Situated in the executive branch, governmental bureaucratic agencies are responsible for the implementation of policies formulated in the legislative branch and perhaps modified by the courts. Agency decisions have the force of law, and agency rules and adjudication rulings are clearly one of the multiple sources of law in American society. In fact, many refer to the permanent governmental bureaucracy as the fourth branch of government.[1] These federal and state agencies help the president or the governor to enforce the law. This chapter will examine the interactions between courts and administrative agencies at both the federal and state levels.

The term **bureaucracy** means any large, complex organization where employees work in a hierarchy and are charged with the performance of specific tasks.[2] Universities, corporations, and military units are all examples of bureaucracies. In this context, bureaucracy refers to executive branch governmental agencies at both the state and federal levels, and, by that logic, **bureaucrats** are simply executive branch employees. This book uses the terms *bureaucracy* and *bureaucrats* not in a pejorative manner but simply as descriptive terms. These agencies produce regulations and rules that fill in the details of legislation. They also implement public policy decisions; in other words, they put public policy into practice. Thus, governments need bureaucracies in order to carry out their policy objectives.[3] The United States has experienced an enormous growth in administrative agencies resulting from the enactment of Franklin Delano Roosevelt's New Deal and Lyndon Baines Johnson's Great Society programs, as well as other, more recent programs such as the creation of the federal Department of Homeland Security after the 9/11 attacks.

Bureaucratic agencies are a major source of law in the United States at both the federal and state levels. Their decisions affect many aspects of the day-to-day workings of our society. For example, agencies regulate economic activities, environmental practices, workplace safety, immigration policies, agricultural practices, transportation, and education.

Agencies produce generally applicable **rules**, which are often called **regulations.** The federal Administrative Procedures Act of 1946 defines a rule as "the whole or part of an agency statement of general or particular applicability and future effect designed to implement, interpret, or prescribe law or policy."[4] These agency rules and regulations have the force of law and are one of the sources of law used in the United States.

Agencies also have the power to enforce their rules through an **adjudication** process that is presided over by an administrative law judge and resembles a trial for a civil lawsuit.[5] When agencies are involved in rule making, they are acting like little legislatures; when they are involved in adjudication, they are acting like little courts.[6] All of these agency decisions are interpreted by courts to make sure that the agency rules and adjudication decisions are correctly following legal requirements. The agency cannot be acting in ways that are unconstitutional, the agency rules must be consistent with the intent of Congress, and the agency must have followed the proper procedures when creating its rules and adjudication decisions. The courts want to make sure that agencies are not becoming too powerful and that they are abiding by the necessary legal standards in their decision-making processes. In general, the courts are more focused on procedural issues than on substance when they review agency decisions.[7]

AGENCY DECISIONS AS A SOURCE OF LAW

Agencies are a clear source of law in the United States. Courts must routinely interpret agency rules and adjudication decisions. Recall from Chapter 1 the hierarchy of sources of law and where agency decisions fall in that hierarchy. With the huge growth in the size and number of bureaucratic agencies in the United States, interactions between agencies and the courts have also increased. As judicial politics scholar R. Shep Melnick has pointed out, "Today, federal judges spend much of their time regulating the behavior of government bureaucrats, and virtually all government agencies must deal with the courts on a regular basis."[8] Courts have heard cases involving schools, state prisons, housing authorities, social service agencies, environmental agencies, and the police, just to name a few. In many ways, the courts and especially the federal courts have used their power to impose national standards on state and local bureaucratic agencies. The federal courts have reviewed many of the actions of federal agencies as well. As the power of bureaucratic agencies has grown, federal judges have paid more and more attention to the effects of these agency decisions.[9]

Congress creates the federal bureaucratic agencies, and state legislatures create the state agencies. On rare occasions, some bureaucratic agencies can be created by presidential or gubernatorial orders. As scholars Ernest Gellhorn and Ronald M. Levin note, "Administrative agencies usually are created to deal with current crises or to redress serious social problems. Throughout the modern era of administrative regulation, which began approximately a century ago, the government's response to a public demand for action has often been to establish a new agency, or to grant new powers to an existing bureaucracy."[10]

During the early 1900s, the conservative activists on the U.S. Supreme Court were often hostile to governmental agencies, frequently voiding the agencies' decisions on substantive due process grounds.[11] These judicial activists felt that governmental regulation of the economy was unconstitutional under the liberty provisions of the Due Process Clauses of the Fifth and Fourteenth Amendments. In addition to the activist judges, some of the most vocal criticisms of agency rule making in the 1930s and 1940s came from the American Bar Association. Lawyers were concerned that agency rules and regulations would contravene the judge-made common law.[12] After the Supreme Court majority reversed its position in 1937 and began to uphold the constitutionality of the New Deal programs, the courts became more accepting of the legitimacy of agency decision making.

Lawyers, however, remained skeptical of agency rule making practices. The American Bar Association and other lawyers turned to the legislative branch in order to transform the rule making process into something more consistent with traditional lawyerly practices. There was some fear that without legal controls on the bureaucracy, administrative decision making would allow "creeping socialism" to take over our country. According to one academic work, "The specter of unelected and essentially invisible bureaucrats writing, in virtual secrecy, laws that could curtail freedom and confiscate property was a compelling, if somewhat melodramatic, argument for reforming the administrative process."[13]

Agency Rule Making

Congress sought a compromise between the needs of the New Dealers, who wanted a large and quick-acting federal bureaucracy, and the fears of the conservatives, who wanted to make sure that the judiciary had a role in oversight of the growing—and, in their eyes, potentially dangerous—bureaucracy.[14] In 1946 it enacted the **Administrative Procedures Act** (APA) in order to bring some uniformity to federal agency decision making. Today, all federal agencies must follow the rule-making procedures outlined in the APA. When courts review agency decisions, one of the things they consider is whether the agency properly followed the APA requirements. Many states have their own state-level administrative procedure acts.[15]

Among other things, the APA spells out the necessary steps in the agency rule-making process (see Figure 12.1 for the steps generally followed in federal rule making). Agencies cannot begin the rule-making process without authorization from Congress. When a rule is being developed, the public must be informed

FIGURE 12.1 Steps in the Federal Agency Rule-Making Process

1. *Statute authorizes rule making.* Agencies cannot conduct rule making unless authorized by Congress.

2. *Agenda-setting stage.* Information may come from inside or outside the agency.

3. *Political leaders of agency must approve beginning of rule-making process.* Some statutes will have hammer clauses that force agencies to act within a specified time frame.

4. *The Planning Stage.* The agency must identify exactly which employees will be responsible for creating the new rule. Issues to be covered by the new rule must be identified.

5. *Developing the draft rule.* This step will probably involve a great deal of informal consultation not just within the agency but also with groups and individuals from outside the agency. The agency must follow the legal requirement of the Administrative Procedures Act, among others. Notice of the proposed rule making must be posted in the *Federal Register*.

6. *Review.* Office of Management and Budget (OMB), among other agencies, must review draft rule.

7. *Comment period from the public on the draft rule.* Agencies receive written comments on the draft rule. They may also hold public hearings on the draft rule.

8. *Language of rule is finalized.* Notice of the final language must be posted in the *Federal Register*. All rules must be sent to both houses of Congress, and major rules cannot go into effect for at least sixty days to allow for congressional review of the final language. Final language must also be sent to OMB and to the Government Accountability Office (GAO) for their review.

Source: Compiled by author using Cornelius M. Kerwin and Scott R. Fullong, *Rulemaking: How Government Agencies Write Law and Make Policy,* 4th ed. (Washington, DC: CQ Press, 2010).

that the rule making process is under way. This is usually done by placing a notice in the *Federal Register*. Then the agency must have in place a procedure by which interested groups, individuals, and other government agencies can comment on the draft regulation before it goes into effect.[16] Sometimes this step involves public hearings on the proposed rule, but agencies also accept written comments at this point in the process. Courts have generally interpreted the Administrative Procedures Act as requiring agencies to allow interest groups and others the right to participate directly in agency deliberations as well as to bring their complaints to the courts if the agency ignores their concerns.[17] These steps are collectively known as the "notice and comment" process.

The proposed rule must also be approved by the Office of Management and Budget (OMB) and the Government Accountability Office. OMB is a federal agency within the Executive Office of the White House, and its leaders are loyal to the president's agenda; thus, the president must indirectly approve the proposed rule. The agency must also send the final language of the proposed rule to both houses of Congress for their review, as major agency rules cannot go into effect until Congress has had sixty days to review the final language of the rule. Only after the regulations are published in final form in the *Federal Register* can they be challenged in court. Through this lengthy and often time-consuming process, all federal rules receive a great deal of attention and review before they go into force. This is important because the final agency rules and adjudication decisions have the force of law.

The courts have been quite active in reviewing the rule-making process. Judicial oversight of agency decisions actually came before Congress gave careful attention to these agency decisions.[18] The normal standard for courts to review agency rules on both procedural and substantive grounds is that the rules cannot be "an arbitrary or capricious abuse of discretion."[19] This standard gives the courts a great deal of flexibility in how they review agency decisions. Agencies have the technical expertise that allows them to write very complex and targeted rules, but federal judges are generalists and can force agencies to look at the big picture. As scholar Susan Rose-Ackerman concluded, "Agencies' expertise is generally superior to that of courts, but agencies may deviate from technically competent and democratically legitimate procedures in order to favor political insiders. Thus, courts can require officials to listen to a wide range of facts and opinions and to explain their decisions."[20]

The courts can exert a great deal of power when they review and interpret agency rule-making procedures. As Shep Melnick has noted, "Because administrative law decisions immediately affect federal bureaucrats, not private citizens, and because they bring judges directly into conflict with appointed rather than elected officials, they have not incited as much passion or received as much scholarly attention as have constitutional rulings. But their effect has been profound nonetheless."[21]

Agency Adjudication

When agencies enforce their own rules, the process is known as **adjudication**. When someone is accused of violating an agency regulation, he or she appears before an **administrative law judge** (ALJ). The ALJ is an employee of the agency and hears disputes between individuals, groups, or others and the agency's personnel. Depending on the statute that created the agency, appeals of ALJ decisions are usually heard in one of the U.S. courts of appeals. More than a third of the cases heard by the U.S. Court of Appeals for the District of Columbia are appeals from administrative agencies.[22] The U.S. Court of Appeals for the Federal Circuit hears administrative law appeals regarding patents, trademarks, international trade (including cases decided by the Court of International Trade), and some claims for money to be paid by the federal government (including cases from the Court of Federal Claims).[23] Most appeals of immigration law cases are heard in the Ninth and the Second Circuits because most immigrants live on either coast.[24] The standard used by the appellate courts is the "substantial evidence" test, which means that a court will defer to a federal agency's findings of fact and other decisions if those are supported by substantial evidence. In other words, the courts will only strike down agency rules if they are "arbitrary and capricious."[25] In 2010, by one count, 14 percent of all the cases heard by the U.S. circuit courts of appeals were from administrative agencies.[26]

TYPES OF FEDERAL AGENCIES

At the federal level, there are four different types of administrative or bureaucratic agencies, and all types have rule-making and adjudication powers. The first type is **cabinet-level departments**. These agencies are headed by a secretary (or, for the Department of Justice, the attorney general) who serves in the president's cabinet. The top officials in these departments are appointed by the president and confirmed by the U.S. Senate. These political appointees serve at the will of the president, meaning that the president has the power to remove them from the position. Examples of these agencies include the Department of State, the Department of the Treasury, the Department of Defense, and the Department of Homeland Security. Those chosen as cabinet members must have the managerial skills to run these huge agencies, plus political ties to important interest groups or presidential constituencies.[27] For example, the secretary of agriculture almost always has ties to agricultural groups, and the secretary of labor must always be acceptable to organized labor groups. The president's power to remove these political appointees was confirmed by the U.S. Supreme Court in *Myers v. United States* (1926).

The second type of federal agency is in the **Executive Office of the President**, often referred to as the West Wing. The heads of these agencies are appointed by the president and confirmed by the U.S. Senate, serve at the will of the president, are chosen for their loyalty to the president, and often become his or her close advisors. Examples of agencies in the Executive Office include the Office of Management and Budget, the National Security Council, the Council of Economic Advisers, and the Office of the White House Counsel.[28] This last office serves as the legal advisors to the presidency. The Office of the White House Counsel sometimes works in cooperation with—and sometimes in conflict with—the Office of Legal Counsel in the U.S. Department of Justice.[29]

The third type of agency is **public corporations**. These are government-operated enterprises that could be in the private sector. The heads of these agencies are also appointed by the president and confirmed by the Senate, are chosen for their business experience and expertise, and serve at the will of the president. Examples of this type of agency include Amtrak (government-owned passenger train service), the Tennessee Valley Authority (government-owned public utilities), and the U.S. Postal Service.[30] Notice that in other countries these services may be provided by private corporations. For example, in the Netherlands the post office is a private company not owned by the government.

Independent regulatory boards or commissions are the fourth type of federal agency. These agencies are headed by multi-member boards and commissions. The members of the controlling committees are appointed by the president and confirmed by the Senate, but the president cannot remove any individual board member or commissioner until his or her term of office expires. If there are seven commissioners, each might serve a seven-year term. Consequently, it may take years before the president can appoint a majority of the board or commission members and thus acquire political control of these agencies. Examples of this type of agency include the Federal Reserve Board, the Federal Communications Commission, the Securities and Exchange Commission, and the Nuclear Regulatory Commission. These boards and commissions regulate critical sectors of the economy and society, and when Congress created these agencies it decided that they needed to be allowed to use an incremental approach to policy making that would not be subject to immediate political pressures. The U.S. Supreme Court approved this type of agency structure in *Humphrey's Executor v. United States* (1935).

CONGRESSIONAL AND PRESIDENTIAL OVERSIGHT OF AGENCY ACTIONS

As noted earlier, Congress generally creates the federal agencies, and it also funds them. Agency heads often try to lobby Congress to pass legislation that supports their own agendas.[31] Agencies cannot promulgate rules or regulations unless specifically authorized by Congress. For example, the Supreme Court in *Food and Drug Administration v. Brown & Williamson Tobacco Corp.* (2000) said the Food and Drug Administration could not regulate the nicotine in cigarettes as a drug because Congress had not authorized such agency regulation. And Congress can overrule any agency decision merely by passing a new statute or by restricting the way that agencies can spend their money.

Congress also holds oversight hearings to determine if the agencies are properly following their congressional mandate. These hearings might be what are called "fire alarm" hearings, called only after some problem or scandal has become public. Or they might be "police patrol" events, which occur on a regular schedule even when there is no pending crisis.[32] In many ways, Congress writes the authorizing statutes for agencies in such a way as to maintain as much political control over agency decisions as possible, either directly or indirectly.[33]

The Freedom of Information Act and the Government in the Sunshine Act

As part of Congress's effort to make bureaucratic decision making more open, with greater participation from a variety of voices, it enacted three important laws that have increased government openness: the Freedom of Information Act of 1966 (FOIA), the Federal Advisory Committee Act of 1972, and the Government in the Sunshine Act of 1976. **The Freedom of Information Act** gives anyone the right to request federal agency records and requires agencies to release them unless they fall within one of nine exempt categories. The exemptions include classified records, internal agency personnel records, records exempted by other statutes, records that contain trade secrets and confidential commercial information, records that are privileged and inadmissible in court, certain records that might violate personal privacy, certain law enforcement records, and certain records that concern banking and oil regulation.[34] The **Federal Advisory Committee Act** requires committees that advise executive branch policy makers to disclose information about their membership and have open meetings.[35] The **Government in the Sunshine Act** only applies to multi-member agency boards and commissions. This act requires these agencies to open their meetings to the public except under ten circumstances, which are similar to the FOIA exceptions.[36]

Not surprisingly, all three of these acts have led to more litigation about the openness of agency decision-making processes. For example, in *Cheney v. United States District Court for the District of Columbia* (2004), the Supreme Court seemed to be saying that the president's assertion of executive privilege can overrule the information-sharing requirements of the Federal Advisory Committee Act. Controversies over these three acts continue. While President Obama pledged to make government decisions more transparent than his predecessor did, questions remain about exactly how open the government really is. As journalist James Ball concluded, "Evidence suggests that [Obama] administration officials have struggled to overturn the long-standing culture of secrecy in Washington."[37]

Presidents and Federal Agencies

The president's control over the federal bureaucracy is one of the most important sources of presidential power in the modern era.[38] Presidents appoint the top 2–3 percent of all agency personnel, and the president can remove most of these political appointees from their position for any reason. The Office of Management and Budget, which almost always acts to further the president's agenda, must approve all agency rules before they can go into force.

The president has the power to issue **executive orders** to the agencies, directing them to do certain things or to refrain from doing certain things.[39] These executive orders can sometimes be used to force reorganizations within agencies, thus increasing presidential control over agency decisions.[40] Presidents also negotiate with Congress to determine the amount of agency independence.[41] The president seems to use executive orders more often when Congress is controlled by the other political party.[42] But sometimes there seems to be coordination between Congress and the president when an executive order is issued.[43] These executive orders have the force of law, and agencies are supposed to follow them.[44]

Presidents can also issue signing statements when they sign congressional legislation into law, as discussed in Chapter 11. These signing statements are not technically a source of law but instead reflect the president's views about the intent and meaning of the new statute.[45] One purpose of these signing statements is to signal to the bureaucracy how the president would like federal agencies to interpret the new law.[46]

JUDICIAL OVERSIGHT OF FEDERAL AGENCIES

All agency decisions are subject to review by the courts to make sure that the agencies are acting constitutionally and are following the proper statutory processes and procedures. Thus, most administrative agencies employ a large number of lawyers.[47] In the 1960s and 1970s, the regulatory apparatus became more complex and agency decisions began affecting a much larger portion of our society. With this growth in the importance of agency decision making came an increase in judicial review of agency decisions. Congress also passed statutes that allowed citizen groups and others to challenge more and more agency decisions through the courts. At about the same time, the federal courts liberalized their standing requirements, which permitted more lawsuits to be filed concerning administrative decisions.[48] While lawsuits against the agencies in the 1930s and 1940s generally came from business interests on the right who felt that the agencies were moving too fast in the policy-making process, the so-called public interest suits in the 1970s came from groups on the left who felt that the agencies were moving too slowly.[49]

Agencies are certainly aware of the increased likelihood that their decisions will be challenged in court and have changed many of their practices accordingly. At times, the mere threat of a lawsuit will force an agency to change proposed rules.[50] For example, one study found that agencies were beginning to make more policy decisions through adjudications than through rule making, as it was harder for courts to review the adjudication decisions than it was for them to examine the policy choices made through the rule-making procedures.[51] Sometimes the effects of potential litigation on agency decision making are quite subtle. As one study of the bureaucracy has concluded, "The mere existence of the judiciary and the threat of litigation exert a powerful deterrent effect on the behavior of rulemaking bureaucracies. [. . .] Those writing rules have learned that when their work affects persons and groups with sufficient resources to sue, litigation is a distinct possibility. They also know that judges are not reluctant to obliterate years of work if the court is convinced that the law has been violated in some way."[52]

Court Deference to Agency Decisions

The courts clearly have a role in oversight of agency decision making. A key question then arises: how much deference should the courts give to agency decisions? From the 1940s until the early 1970s, the courts generally gave agency decisions a fair amount of deference. As political scientist Shep Melnick has noted,

"In the years immediately following 1937, the Court's newfound deference to Congress was nearly matched by its deference to administrative agencies."[53] In 1971, however, Judge David Bazelon of the U.S. Court of Appeals for the District of Columbia Circuit signaled a new era of judicial activism in the interactions between courts and agencies. (Recall that this court hears a very large number of appeals in administrative law cases.) In *Environmental Defense Fund v. Ruckelshaus* (1971), Judge Bazelon made the following statement:

> We stand on the threshold of a new era in the history of the long and fruitful collaboration of administrative agencies and reviewing courts. For many years, courts have treated administrative policy decisions with great deference, confining judicial attention primarily to matters of procedure. [. . .] Courts are increasingly asked to review administrative action that touches on fundamental personal interests in life, health, and liberty. These interests have always had a special claim to judicial protection, in comparison with the economic interests at stake in ratemaking or licensing proceedings.[54]

One of the things courts would now consider would be the breadth of participation in the notice and comment process. The courts would want to make sure that the agencies had considered all voices, not just those of the industries under regulation.[55] Agencies also had to respond fully to all reasonable criticisms of their proposals.[56] As the prominent scholar Martin Shapiro has argued, the courts were demanding a new agency process, one that made sure an agency "gathers all the facts, considers all alternatives and all the possible consequences of each, and chooses those policies with the highest probability of achieving agreed goals at least cost."[57] The role of the judge was to make sure that the agencies were following the law and the intent of Congress. As a judge on the U.S. Court of Appeals for the D.C. Circuit noted, "Our duty, in short, is to see that the legislative purposes heralded in the halls of Congress are not lost in the vast halls of the federal bureaucracy."[58]

Many conservatives attacked this new judicial activism in administrative law cases, claiming that the courts were unconstitutionally narrowing the inherent powers of the executive branch.[59] They also felt that liberal judges were intentionally thwarting the objectives of conservative presidents by improperly interfering in agency decisions.[60] Conservatives wanted more judicial deference to agency decisions in order to increase presidential power.[61]

Throughout the 1960s and 1970s, the Supreme Court generally avoided administrative law cases, thus allowing the U.S. courts of appeals to set policy in this area. Since the U.S. Court of Appeals for the D.C. Circuit heard so many appeals from administrative agencies, as we have seen, its rulings were especially important in administrative law. However, in 1984 the U.S. Supreme Court issued a ruling that dramatically changed the courts' approach to administrative decisions. In *Chevron v. Natural Resources Defense Council* (1984), the Supreme Court ordered the lower courts to give a great deal of deference to the agency's interpretation of the federal statutes they were responsible for implementing, thus returning to the earlier approach that had started in 1937. The majority in *Chevron* made the following clear statement of how much deference courts should give agencies:

> If the statute is silent or ambiguous with respect to the specific issue, the question for the court is whether the agency's answer is based on a permissible construction of the statute. [. . . A] court may not substitute its own construction of a statutory provision for a reasonable interpretation made by the administrator of an agency.[62]

Several academic studies that attempted to determine the extent to which the lower courts actually followed the *Chevron* decision came up with mixed results. Most studies found that right after *Chevron,* judicial deference to agency decisions increased for a while, but then it went down again a few years later.[63] This may be due to the fact that, in its own rulings, the Supreme Court often deviated from *Chevron* without much explanation.[64] But the *Chevron* standard remains: courts should give a great deal of deference to how agencies interpret their statutory authorization.

Recent research has come to the conclusion that the U.S. Supreme Court supports the agency position in litigation about 70 percent of the time.[65] A different study found that from 1989 to 2005 the most activist justice in terms of invalidating agency decisions was Justice Antonin Scalia. The most restraintist justice in this area was Justice Stephen Breyer.[66]

Adversarial Legalism

In the United States, the courts interact with administrative agencies far more frequently than in other countries. As comparative politics scholar Susan Rose-Ackerman has noted, "The United States rulemaking process is both more open to public participation and more constrained by law than it is in most other political systems; as a consequence, it is also more time-consuming and more subject to judicial challenge."[67]

The American approach to having courts so involved with agencies is called **adversarial legalism**, a term coined by Professor Robert Kagan to refer to "a mode of policymaking, implementation, and dispute resolution characterized by frequent resort to highly adversarial legal contestation."[68] Thus, the courts in the United States will routinely second-guess substantive decisions by agency experts. They will challenge the scientific models that agencies use as well as their data analysis. They will also question the agency's priorities. All of this is done in a context of litigants suing the agency.[69] This creates an environment for agency decision making that is very different from the one found in most other countries, in which judges never override the technical expertise of the administrative agencies charged with implementing policy. In fact, in most countries judicial review of agency decisions is quite unusual.

Another important point about adversarial legalism is that the courts provide an alternative forum for interests that did not win in the legislative branch or in the agency decision-making process.[70] Because the courts make decisions using legal reasoning and legal analysis, this new arena for competition forces the government to justify its decisions in legal terms. Thus, adversarial legalism compels a dialogue among various institutional decision makers as well as among various groups. Recall how the Governance as Dialogue approach presumes that policy making in this country is really a continuous inter-institutional conversation. The president, the Congress, the agencies, and the courts are all part of this critical conversation. Without judicial oversight of administrative agencies, the executive branch would not need to participate in this dialogue as much as it does now. In other words, without judicial oversight the executive branch could implement its policies without considering how other political actors would react to these decisions.

Adversarial legalism makes the United States different from almost any other country in the world and adds to the notion of American exceptionalism. Our courts are the most powerful in the world, and in many ways the most activist. Probably no other country uses litigation and judicial policy making to the extent that we do in the United States. As Professor Kagan has concluded, "The United States also remains unique in the extent to which courts, by wielding constitutional powers, have become intimately engaged in ongoing institutional reform efforts."[71]

THE FEDERAL COURTS VERSUS STATE AND LOCAL AGENCIES

The federal courts have spent a great deal of time reviewing the decisions of federal administrative agencies. However, the federal courts have also gotten involved in supervising state and local administrative agencies. Most of the courts' attention has been focused on schools, prisons, and the police, with federal judges directing how and to whom these state and local agencies must provide a variety of goods, services, and protections.[72]

The Courts and Local Schools

A fairly large number of U.S. Supreme Court decisions have dealt with the question of racial discrimination in the local public schools. *Brown v. Board of Education* (1954) said that public schools could not be segregated by race because separate was never equal. In *Swann v. Charlotte-Mecklenburg Board of Education* (1971), the Supreme Court decided that federal trial judges could order busing to achieve racial desegregation in public schools with a history of de jure racial discrimination. This was the case in the school district that figured in the lawsuit, as North Carolina had at one time required that the different races attend separate schools. This decision would wind up greatly increasing the role of federal judges in local school administration matters. However, in a case involving desegregation in the Detroit public schools, *Millikin v. Bradley* (1974), the Court ruled that federal judges could not order busing across district lines because the segregation in greater Detroit was de facto instead of de jure—it resulted from voluntary segregated housing patterns and not from discrimination required by law. The *Millikin* decision created some limits on the ability of federal trial judges to intervene in local school affairs, but federal oversight of school districts was still extensive: a fairly recent study found that more than six hundred school districts were subject to desegregation decrees from the courts.[73]

In *Parents Involved in Community Schools v. Seattle School District No. 1* (2007), the Supreme Court went even further, with the majority ruling that local schools could not use race as a factor in assigning students to specific school buildings. This case seemed to have the effect of further limiting the role of federal trial judges in the functioning of local schools.

The U.S. Supreme Court has gotten involved in other school-related issues besides racial discrimination. For example, in *Engel v. Vitale* (1962), the Court ruled that school officials could not require organized spoken prayer in public schools. In *Lee v. Weisman* (1992), the Court prohibited school officials from inviting clergy to say prayers at public school graduation ceremonies. The Supreme Court extended this prohibition on prayers in public schools to student-led prayers before high school football games in *Santa Fe Independent School District v. Doe* (2000). In *Plyer v. Doe* (1982), the Court ruled that schools could not refuse to educate children who were in the country illegally. And in *Tinker v. Des Moines Independent Community School District* (1969), the Supreme Court ruled that school officials had to protect students' freedom of speech. However, in a variety of later cases the Court gave school officials much greater latitude in order to preserve discipline and order. For example, school principals could censor a high school newspaper, as determined in *Hazelwood School District v. Kuhlmeier* (1988). Schools officials could search student backpacks and lockers without a **search warrant**, as the Court ruled in *New Jersey v. T.L.O.* (1985). Schools could even require random drug testing for all extracurricular activities, as the Court ruled in *Board of Education v. Earls* (2002). School officials went too far, however, when they ordered a strip search of a student for allegedly giving other students prescription and over-the-counter drugs, as the Court determined in *Safford Unified School District #1 v. Redding* (2009).

During the 1960s and 1970s, federal judges eventually got involved with a variety of other school-related issues, including the hiring and placement of teachers, language training, testing issues, discipline, sports facilities, and even the content of the curriculum.[74] They issued decisions concerning sites for new schools and forced governments to raise taxes to pay for them. For example, in Kansas City, Missouri, a federal judge ordered the construction of seventeen new school buildings and then ordered major renovations for fifty-five more at a total cost of over $1.5 billion.[75]

Apart from schools, federal judges also became involved in other institutions. As one example, they virtually took over day-to-day control of various state mental health institutions, starting with those in Alabama in 1972. By 1978, ten other states' facilities were operating under similar federal court orders.[76] In 2000, more than thirty state child welfare agencies were operating under court supervision and court order.[77] Judges in institutional reform cases often issue detailed injunctions that require the institutions to be supervised by the courts for years and even decades.[78]

Prison Reform Litigation

Perhaps one of the largest areas where courts took control over state administrative agencies occurred in the context of prison reform litigation. Until the 1960s, federal courts basically refused to hear cases that involved prisoners claiming that prison conditions violated their constitutional rights. This all changed with the Supreme Court's decision in *Cooper v. Pate* (1964). In this case, Thomas Cooper, a black Muslim, complained that Illinois prison officials had refused to allow him to purchase a copy of the Koran. The Supreme Court ruled in favor of the prisoner's rights. For the first time in history, a federal court had ordered a state prison official to rectify an agency policy.[79]

After this, a host of federal judges got deeply involved in the administration of state prisons. First, a federal judge essentially took control of the state prison system in Arkansas in 1969. Then federal constitutional cases brought by prisoners and their advocates spread quickly throughout the nation. By 1995, prisons in forty-one states plus the District of Columbia, Puerto Rico, and the U.S. Virgin Islands were under federal court orders. The entire correctional systems of at least ten states were basically under judicial control. Federal judges directed the prisons to come up with comprehensive plans for prison management, covering such diverse matters as "residence facilities, sanitation, food, clothing, medical care, discipline, staff hiring, libraries, work, and education."[80]

The quick pace at which judges ordered state prisons to change conditions for prisoners was remarkable. As two key scholars of prison reform litigation have noted, "Over the course of a single decade, the federal courts fashioned a complex set of judicially enforceable rules from constitutional literature, sociology, and their own perceptions of political morality."[81] In an attempt to greatly reduce the number of prisoner lawsuits, Congress passed the Prison Litigation Reform Act of 1996. This act made it much more difficult for new prison reform cases to be heard in the federal courts.

A key area of concern for federal judges was state prison overcrowding. Over the years, the federal courts had issued many rulings attempting to correct for overcrowding at state prisons. One of the most recent cases in this area went all the way to the U.S. Supreme Court. The Court ruled in *Brown v. Plata* (2011) that the California prison system had to release more than thirty thousand prisoners in order to alleviate unconstitutional overcrowding. Justice Kennedy's opinion in the 5–4 case described the California prison system as one that failed to deliver minimal care to prisoners with serious medical and mental health problems, thus producing needless suffering and even death.[82] In January 2013, Governor Edmund "Jerry" Brown of California argued that the state prisons should be free of federal court oversight and that the prisoner releases should be halted, even though the system had yet to meet the population goals put into place by federal judges. California was expected to spend $8.6 billion on its state prisons in 2013, the third-largest piece of the state's total budget, just behind spending on public schools and health care.[83]

The Courts and Local Agencies

A very important point about this massive wave of institutional reform litigation concerning local educational institutions, state mental health institutions, and state prisons is that, at least at first, the judicial orders were all supported by federal agency officials, professional public administration groups, and even the state officials who were being sued. Instead of the normal adversary process, in these suits it was usually all of these parties on one side versus the state legislature on the other. Most of these suits were perceived as an effective way to force state legislatures to find additional funding for these institutions. The administrators of these facilities were generally supportive of the judicial attention to their institutions because they had been begging for money for years prior to the lawsuits. They saw court orders as a way to get the money they needed from reluctant governors and state legislatures.[84]

This theme of using the courts to extract more money from state legislatures is also prevalent in litigation brought in state courts to force changes in municipal agency behavior. One recent study looked at the role of litigation in state courts in bringing about needed changes in the areas of police use of excessive force, local government sexual harassment policies, and improvements in playground safety. This research found that a combination of activist lawyer networks, professional public administrators, and concerned citizens was able to bring about enormous changes in the practices of local governmental agencies: "newly energized activist movements and liability lawyers forced agencies to face up to long-ignored problems of abuse and injury, and because managers came to recognize that these legal claims represented fundamental threats to their public and professional legitimacy."[85]

THE SUPREME COURT AND OTHER AGENCY ISSUES

There are a few more U.S. Supreme Court cases regarding administrative agencies that are of interest. The first is *Goldberg v. Kelly* (1970), which created the so-called due process revolution in administrative procedures.[86] In this case, welfare recipients in New York claimed that the state administrative agency had cut off their benefits without due process of law. The Supreme Court agreed, finding that welfare recipients had to have a hearing before the state agency could end their welfare benefits. This ruling had the wider effect of giving litigants a constitutional foundation to challenge the fairness of agency decisions, and it resulted in agencies having to create a myriad of administrative hearing procedures.[87]

Questions have also arisen about how Congress can act to overturn federal agency decisions, including the issue of the one-house legislative veto, which reached the Supreme Court in *Immigration and Naturalization Service v. Chadha* (1983), a case featured in previous chapters. The INS had moved to deport Jagdish Chadha, but the attorney general moved to suspend the deportation, as allowed by the legislation. Then the U.S. House of Representatives voted to override the attorney general's decision, raising the question of whether a single house of Congress could override a federal agency ruling. The Supreme Court said no, stating that Congress must overturn agency decisions by passing a normal statute, which the president has the power to veto. But as we have discussed before, even though the Supreme Court declared that legislative vetoes are unconstitutional, Congress has ignored the Court's ruling and continues to enact these one-house legislative vetoes.[88]

The next case involves the question of who can prosecute wrongdoing within the federal executive branch. The attorney general is the nation's chief law enforcement officer, but how can that official be expected to prosecute criminal behavior by the president or others in the federal government when the president can fire the attorney general at any time? During the Watergate scandal, the attorney general hired a special prosecutor to look into the alleged criminal activities in the White House (the terms *special prosecutor* and *independent counsel* are often used interchangeably). After Watergate, Congress enacted the Ethics in Government Act of 1978, which created the Office of the Independent Counsel to investigate any potential criminal activity at the top of the executive branch. The independent counsel was appointed by a special panel of federal judges and could be removed from office only "for good cause." President Ronald Reagan challenged the constitutionality of the Office of the Independent Counsel on the grounds that the president did not appoint this executive branch official, but the Supreme Court upheld the constitutionality of the Ethics in Government Act. In *Morrison v. Olson* (1988), the Court ruled that the Office of the Independent Counsel did not violate the constitutional principles of the separation of powers.[89] The temporary act was renewed several times, but Congress allowed it to lapse in 1999.

CHAPTER SUMMARY

This chapter examined the interactions between the courts and executive branch agencies, beginning with a look at agency rule making and adjudication and how American courts supervise many aspects of both these processes. The chapter discussed the various types of federal agencies and some of the trends in judicial oversight of their decisions. The chapter next explored the ways that Congress and the president oversee executive agencies, before examining various U.S. Supreme Court decisions regarding the decision-making processes in administrative agencies, including the question of how much deference the courts should give to an agency's interpretation of its authorizing statutes. The chapter then examined the role of the federal courts in supervising state and local institutions, including schools and prisons. Finally, the chapter concluded with a look at a few other Supreme Court cases that involve administrative agencies and their work.

For Further Reading

Clayton, Cornell W., ed. 1995. *Government Lawyers: The Federal Legal Bureaucracy and Presidential Politics.* Lawrence: University Press of Kansas.

Epp, Charles R. 2009. *Making Rights Real: Activists, Bureaucrats, and the Creation of the Legalistic State.* Chicago: University of Chicago Press.

Feeley, Malcolm M., and Edward Rubin. 1998. *Judicial Policy Making and the Modern State: How the Courts Reformed America's Prisons.* New York: Cambridge University Press.

Harringer, Katy J. 2000. *The Special Prosecutor in American Politics.* 2nd edition. Lawrence: University Press of Kansas.

Kagan, Robert A. 2001. *Adversarial Legalism: The American Way of Law.* Cambridge, MA: Harvard University Press.

Kerwin, Cornelius M., and Scott R. Furlong. 2010. *Rulemaking: How Government Agencies Write Law and Make Policy,* 4th ed. Washington, DC: CQ Press.

Melnick, R. Shep. 1983. *Regulation and the Courts: The Case of the Clean Air Act.* Washington, DC: Brookings Institution.

———. 1994. *Between the Lines: Interpreting Welfare Rights.* Washington, DC: Brookings Institution.

Schmidt, Patrick. 2005. *Lawyers and Regulation: The Politics of the Administrative Process.* Cambridge: Cambridge University Press.

Shapiro, Martin. 1988. *Who Guards the Guardians: Judicial Control of Administration.* Athens: University of Georgia Press.

Courts Beyond the United States

Although the courts in the United States can be quite complex and difficult for many Americans to understand, the situation becomes even more complicated when one considers how U.S. judges interact with their colleagues around the world. This relatively new phenomenon has led scholars to focus a fair amount of attention on comparative judicial studies and comparative judicial politics.[1] As legal issues and the law itself become more globalized, perhaps it is inevitable that judges in the United States will meet with judges abroad and read their decisions.[2] It may also be inevitable that U.S. judges will cite more and more international precedents in their rulings.[3] Whether American judges should cite international judicial decisions at all remains highly controversial, in part because of the clear differences between U.S. courts and the legal systems in other countries. This chapter begins with a few case studies that will show how the U.S. legal system is different from or similar to other national legal systems. Then it will look at how judges in the United States interact with law, courts, and judges in other societies.

COMMON LAW VERSUS CIVIL LAW COURTS: DIFFERENCES AND SIMILARITIES

The following four case studies highlight some of the differences and similarities between the common law and civil law legal systems.

The Amanda Knox Trial: An Italian Example

Along with her Italian former boyfriend, American college student Amanda Knox was convicted of the November 2007 murder and sexual assault of her roommate, British citizen Meredith Kercher, in Perugia, Italy. Knox and her Italian co-defendant were held in jail in Italy for over a year before the original trial began because, unlike in the United States, Italy has no bail system. In December 2009, Knox was sentenced to twenty-six years in prison and the boyfriend to twenty-five years in prison in a case that drew worldwide media attention. In a separate trial, a third defendant was sentenced to thirty years in prison for the murder, although on appeal his sentence was reduced to sixteen years.[4] Much information about the prosecutor's criminal investigation in the Knox case was leaked to the press before the original trial, which was heard by a panel of two professional judges and six lay judges (something close to jurors in American usage).[5]

Italy is a civil law country, with a legal system based in part on the Roman legal codes but in much larger part on the Napoleonic codes of France. Historically, Italy had been a mosaic of city-states and regional kingdoms. It was not until the enactment of the Civil Code of 1865 that Italy's law became unified.[6] The first comprehensive criminal code in Italy was not enacted until 1930. A brand-new criminal code was enacted in 1988. Recall that the central features of the civil law tradition include detailed codes of law, professional judges who are separate from the legal profession, investigative procedures controlled by the judges and the prosecutors together, reverence for the law professors who write the codes, and the inability of judges to make public policy decisions.[7]

Criminal law tends to differ rather widely from country to country. As scholar Marcus Dirk Dubber has argued, "Of all branches of law, criminal law historically has been the one most closely associated with [a nation's] sovereignty."[8] However, there are some commonalities in criminal law in countries that are part of the civil law tradition. For example, criminal trials follow the inquisitorial model. This means that the judges, the prosecutor, and even the defense attorney work together to find the truth in the case. Another way of explaining the differences between the adversary system used in the common law tradition and the inquisitorial system generally used in the civil law tradition is that in the inquisitorial model the judges can be actively involved in investigating the facts of the case, whereas in the adversarial system the role of the judge is primarily that of an impartial referee between the prosecution and the defense. The rights afforded to criminal defendants in civil law nations can be very different from those given to defendants in the United States. For instance, in many civil law countries the defendant has no right to remain silent during criminal investigations and trial proceedings. There is also no prohibition on double jeopardy. As scholar James Q. Whitman has noted, "Europeans have never cared as much about procedural protections as Americans."[9]

The Knox case helps to illustrate the fact that the differences between the civil law world and the common law world can be quite stark at times. One fundamental difference between the two families of legal systems is that traditionally in the civil law world the law is seen as a science: there is a single right answer to any legal question, and judges should all be able to agree on it. Thus, there are multiple judges at trial so that the system can discover the right legal conclusion. However, in the common law tradition, the law is seen as an art, and the system tolerates differing legal interpretations by different judges. Therefore, in the common law world there is one judge at trial and multiple judges on appellate courts, with dissenting opinions allowed in almost all appellate cases. Civil law societies tend to avoid dissenting opinions from their courts. The European Court of Justice, the highest court of the European Union, attempts to incorporate practices from both broad legal traditions.

After Knox and her Italian boyfriend spent more than four years in prison, their convictions were overturned by an appeals court in October 2011. In Italy, the first appeal involves what amounts to a trial de novo, unlike in the United States, where appeals only involve questions of law, not questions of fact. A **trial de novo** means that the appeals court starts over from scratch instead of adopting the facts found at trial, as American appellate courts do. Thus, the Italian appeals court, consisting of a new panel of two professional judges and six lay judges (in the appeals court, the lay judges had to have higher educational qualifications than was the case in the original trial), reexamined all the evidence in the case and reheard the testimony of all the witnesses. In large part because of questions about the trustworthiness of the DNA evidence used at the first trial, Knox and her former boyfriend were eventually acquitted by the appellate court.[10] However, Knox was convicted of the crime of slander (slander is a civil wrong in the United States but a criminal one in Italy) for various statements she made before and during the trial. The sentence from the Italian appellate court for that crime was prison time already served plus a substantial fine.

The prosecutor appealed the acquittals to the highest court in the country. In the United States prosecutors can almost never appeal a finding of not guilty. Surprisingly, the highest criminal appeals court in Italy overturned the acquittals in March 2013 and ordered a third trial in the case. This would not happen in the United States because of our notion of double jeopardy. Italian law does not allow the judges to compel Knox to return for the new trial, and her lawyers indicated that she has no plans to do so. It is expected that the new trial will occur at some point in 2014.[11]

The acquittal on the murder charges received worldwide media attention, with some British media outlets at first mistakenly reporting that the convictions had been upheld.[12] In general, it seemed that the American media were quite sympathetic to Knox, while the British media paid more attention to the victim's family and their loss. Immediately after her acquittal, Knox returned to her hometown, in the Seattle area. This case received so much publicity that she was even able to publish a book about her ordeal, entitled *Waiting to Be Heard.*[13]

Some American commentators have argued that Knox's initial conviction and the appeal of the acquittal came about because the prosecutor, the police, and the judges all needed to save face in a case that was based on fairly weak circumstantial evidence.[14] Many Americans seemed bewildered by the Italian legal system and its series of trials in this case. As the *New York Times* reported, "Many American news media outlets, which were largely sympathetic to the Knox family in their coverage, frequently portrayed the American as having been caught up in what was sometimes described as a medieval or barbaric legal system. Italian legal experts dismissed such accusations."[15]

Many have called for reforms in the Italian judicial system, including former Prime Minister Silvio Berlusconi, who has had his own run-ins with the law. In Italy, over 50 percent of criminal convictions are overturned or greatly modified on appeal.[16] As British journalist Tobias Jones wrote, "It's one of the many failings of Italian justice that it never delivers conclusive, door-slamming certainty."[17] An editorial from a British newspaper agrees, noting that in Italy, "one hearing simply opens the door to another, orchestrated by a media and a publishing frenzy."[18] Some have also argued that part of the problem with the Italian justice system is that judges and prosecutors are selected based on nepotism rather than on proven merit or competence.[19] As *Boston Globe* journalist Victor L. Simpson summarized it, the problem with the Italian criminal justice system is that "[i]t is a system where people cleared of serious crimes can have the threat of prison hanging over them for years, while powerful people such as Silvio Berlusconi, the former prime minister, can avoid jail sentences almost indefinitely by filing appeal after appeal until the statute of limitations runs out."[20] The multiple levels of appeals in the Italian system were designed to prevent the government from having too much power, as it did in the Fascist era, but one wonders if the Italian system has gone too far in preventing finality of judicial decisions.

Dominique Strauss-Kahn:
Criminal Arrests in the United States and in France

Another example that shows the differences between the civil law and common law legal systems is the arrest in New York City of former International Monetary Fund president Dominique Strauss-Kahn on charges of attempted rape after an incident involving a hotel maid in a Manhattan luxury hotel in May 2011. Strauss-Kahn was arrested on an airplane bound for Paris just before the flight could take off from a New York airport. Before his arrest, Strauss-Kahn was a leading contender to become the Socialist Party candidate for the presidency of France in 2012. He lived a lavish lifestyle that freely displayed his great wealth. His accuser was a thirty-two-year-old immigrant from the West African nation of Guinea who made a living working as a maid at the hotel. Thus, the case raised questions of class and race, among other issues. During the investigation of this alleged crime, the prosecutor found that the maid's story had too many holes in it to be taken to trial, and eventually the criminal charges against Strauss-Kahn were dropped and his house arrest in New York City was lifted. However, the maid did file a separate civil lawsuit against Strauss-Kahn, which was later settled out of court.[21] Recall that in the United States it is much easier to prove a civil case than a criminal case because the burden of proof is much lower than the standard of guilt beyond a reasonable doubt used in criminal proceedings.

This story helps illustrate some of the differences between the American (common law) and French (civil law) legal systems. Americans generally think that the French criminal justice system does not provide as many rights to accused criminals as does the U.S. system. For example, the French assume that the accused is guilty until proven innocent, the exact opposite of the American approach. However, this case may bring into question the assumption that the French criminal system is always harsher than the American one. Given American sensitivities about protecting victims of sexual crimes, the American media generally did not publish the name or photos of the accuser, although the French press did so immediately.[22]

The French were outraged that the media published photos of Strauss-Kahn in handcuffs following his arrest as part of the American and especially the New York City tradition of the **perp walk**, which is when the police parade the arrested criminal defendant in front of the media, often on the way into the jail or courthouse.[23] A commentary in *Vanity Fair* magazine pointed out, "Although Americans pride themselves on their 'innocent until proven guilty' mantra, the perp walk is an exercise in public shame and disgrace that stigmatizes the suspect no matter what the final outcome of the case. It's raw meat flung to the mob, a prejudicial incitement."[24] A former French justice minister called the images of Strauss-Kahn "incredibly brutal, violent, and cruel," a French senator called them an "appalling global lynching," and an American presidential hopeful from the Green Party concluded that the United States has a much more violent judicial system than France does.[25] While some Americans criticized the perp walk, most seemed to accept the practice as standard operating procedure among American police officials. Americans are used to seeing the perp walk on TV news as well as in fictional movies and television shows such as *Law & Order*. The *Vanity Fair* article continued, "The arrest of Dominique Strauss-Kahn [. . .] was conducted like an old-school bust in a TV cop drama, his removal from an Air France flight [. . .] packing the punch of a classic *Law & Order* opening."[26] In the summer of 2013, Strauss-Kahn was ordered to stand trial in France for his alleged involvement in a prostitution ring operating in both France and in the United States, charges unrelated to the New York City incident.[27]

Part of the reason for this difference in the reaction to the case on the two sides of the Atlantic is the fact that for largely historical reasons the French believe in equality of treatment in criminal law and treat all their accused the way they would treat upper-class defendants. The United States also believes in equality of treatment, but the American justice system treats all accused like lower-class defendants, stressing degradation of the accused and harsh punishments for those convicted of criminal behavior. As scholar James Q. Whitman explained, the difference is that "Europeans live with the memory of an age of social hierarchy and feel a corresponding horror at historically low-status punishments. [. . .] We [Americans] can revive old-style public shaming without feeling any European qualms [because] humiliating and degrading offenders, for us, does not smack of social hierarchy."[28] On the other hand, Whitman argued, "[c]ontemporary France and Germany are countries [. . .] with a deep commitment to the proposition that criminal offenders must not be degraded—that they must be accorded *respect and dignity*."[29] Thus, in France, "high-status punishments have slowly driven the low-status punishments out."[30]

The Strauss-Kahn arrest in New York City helps us to understand the different priorities in French and American criminal procedures. The American legal system attempted to protect the rights of the accuser, while the French civil system would have done much more to protect the rights of the accused in this particular case.

Geert Wilders: Freedom of Speech in the Netherlands

Despite these great differences between legal systems in Continental Europe and in the United States, in some ways these differences are becoming less pronounced. The criminal trials of Dutch parliamentarian Geert Wilders in 2010 and 2011 illustrate this convergence phenomenon. At the time, Wilders was the head of the right-wing nationalist Freedom Party in the Netherlands, which came in third in national elections in June 2010. Wilders had produced an incendiary anti-Muslim film entitled *Fitna,* had delivered many public speeches attacking Muslims, and had published a variety of newspaper articles in which he likened Islam to Nazism. He also demanded that the Koran be banned, comparing it to violent revolutionary literature from authoritarian rulers such as Hitler's *Mein Kampf*. Wilders had become the face of the anti-immigrant and anti-Muslim movements in Western Europe and was invited by various nationalist figures to give speeches in the United Kingdom, Germany, and other member countries of the European Union.

Wilders's criminal trial was initiated by a group of citizens who petitioned the Dutch justice ministry to prosecute him. In January 2010, a Dutch appeals court ordered prosecutors to file hate speech and group defamation charges against Wilders, even though the prosecutors felt the charges should not go forward.[31] In the fall of 2010, Wilders initially stood trial on five counts of hate speech, inciting racial and religious hatred, and group defamation, all crimes in the Netherlands. If he had been found guilty of all the charges, Wilders could have faced a potential one-year prison sentence and a stiff fine.

Generally, the Dutch pay very little attention to their courts. They assume that the judges will make the correct technocratic decision in any given case, as is often the assumption in the judicial systems of the civil law tradition. Wilders wanted publicity for his case, however, and so he argued that the original trial was a political farce and an assault on freedom of speech. He implied that the Dutch judges were political hacks. He accused the judges of making improper political comments during the trial, and he used Twitter to claim that "Dutch justice was like the mafia."[32] During the trial, one of the judges did make a number of critical comments about Wilders's right to remain silent during the proceeding. The initial trial was eventually dismissed because the judges in the case were deemed to be biased, and a new trial was ordered. In February 2011, the new trial began before a different panel of judges.

Wilders's accusations that the judges were politically motivated shocked the Dutch. As Rudy Andeweg, professor of Dutch politics in the Netherlands, said of the strange political nature of the trial, "[Wilders] is trying to turn the court into a podium for his political activities. He enjoys the attention. He wants a political trial but judges won't have that."[33] Stressing the traditional notion of the politically neutral nature of the Dutch justice system, Andeweg argued, "Judges will not give Wilders any special treatment. They just treat him as any other citizen, which is what it has to be."[34]

In June 2011, the three trial judges found Wilders not guilty on all counts because the charges violated constitutional free speech principles. In this way, the Dutch ruling was very similar to various rulings on free speech grounds handed down by the U.S. Supreme Court. The court ruled that "his public comments still fell within the limitations set by the law" because, according to the prosecutors in the case, "Mr. Wilders' comments were addressed to a religion (Islam) rather than to the people that practice it (Muslims), and could not therefore be seen as hate-mongering against a group."[35] However, as the *Economist* reported, the judges did find "Mr. Wilders' language to be 'rude and denigrating' and warned him that he walked 'on the edge of what is allowed'" by the Dutch criminal code.[36]

Since the Dutch court ruled in favor of free speech principles, even if on very narrow technical grounds, this case demonstrates that in some ways the U.S. common law system and the Continental European civil law system are converging, even if their fundamental approaches to the law are still quite different.[37] Americans often see judicial decisions in political terms, and they see the courts as the protectors of broad constitutional principles such as freedom of speech and expression. Traditionally, the Dutch have viewed their courts and their judges not as political actors and makers of public policy but as technocratic legal actors who decide narrow legal disputes. Using the notion of free speech to dismiss the criminal charges, the Dutch judges went outside the strict confines of the Dutch criminal code, in certain ways acting more like their American counterparts.

Because of the two Wilders trials, the Dutch criminal justice system received a great deal of media and public attention, a rarity in most civil law countries. The Dutch Ministry of Justice even established a special commission of experts to examine the procedural flaws in the original Wilders trial.[38] The Dutch courts attempted to maintain the justice system's traditional neutrality regarding the larger political questions in the cases. In the civil law world, courts and judges are rarely seen as political actors but instead are thought of as technocratic enforcers of society's properly enacted legal codes.

Humberto Leal Garcia Jr.: Capital Punishment and the Rights of Mexican Citizens

The last example involves Mexico (a civil law nation) and the American practice of the death penalty, used by many U.S. states and the federal government. (See Chapter 5 for more details on the process used in death penalty cases in the United States.) The death penalty remains a clear difference between the United States and almost all other industrialized democracies because except for Japan virtually all advanced societies have abolished the death penalty; for example, the abolition of the death penalty is a requirement for membership in the European Union. Few countries will extradite accused criminal defendants to the United States if they could face capital punishment here.[39] The use of the death penalty by the United States has created a great deal of controversy in our interactions with other countries, including with our southern neighbor, Mexico.

In July 2011, the state of Texas executed Humberto Leal Garcia Jr., a Mexican citizen convicted of the 1994 rape and murder of a teenage woman in Texas. The defendant was put to death despite requests from the government of Mexico, President Obama, the U.N. High Commissioner for Human Rights, and various other national and international officials that the execution be at least delayed. The concern of the Obama Administration was that Americans abroad would not receive proper treatment in the national courts of other nations unless our courts provided non-American defendants the rights afforded them under the U.N. Charter and the Vienna Convention on Consular Relations.

The international controversy surrounding the case had little to do with the evidence used to prove the rape and murder. Rather, it revolved around the fact that the defendant was never advised of his right to consult with officials at the Mexican consulate in Texas after his arrest. One question was whether a trial attorney supplied by the Mexican government would have done a better job in the case than the defendant's court-appointed lawyer. In 2004, the International Court of Justice (ICJ) in The Hague ruled that Garcia and a number of other foreign nationals on death row in the United States deserved review and reconsideration of their cases because of local authorities' failure to allow the defendants to contact officials at their national embassies or consulates. In 2005, President George W. Bush, a former governor of Texas, told state officials in Texas that they needed to comply with the international court's ruling, specifically in the Garcia case. In 2008, the U.S. Supreme Court rejected by a 5–4 vote a request to stay Garcia's execution; it also ruled that the United States needed to comply with the ICJ ruling, but that the president alone could not order the states to follow the international court's directive without congressional approval. The U.S. Supreme Court ruled that Congress needed to enact legislation to effect such compliance, but the federal legislative branch failed to act before the July 7, 2011, execution date. Governor Rick Perry of Texas refused to delay the execution, telling the press that "he did not view the matter through the lens of reciprocal international obligations."[40] After the execution, the Mexican government sent a note of formal protest to the U.S. State Department.[41]

This case highlights the fact that American courts cannot make their decisions in a vacuum in our quickly globalizing world. American courts generally follow many principles of international law, and at times they must even consider the rulings of foreign courts. It is important at this point to make a distinction between international law and foreign law. **International law** has its source in treaties and the decisions of supranational courts such as the International Court of Justice. The United States has been very hesitant to sign any treaties or join any international institutions that would render the U.S. Constitution inferior to international law. On the other hand, **foreign law** means the legal decisions of the courts of other nation-states.[42] Some justices on the U.S. Supreme Court look to the judicial rulings of other nations as persuasive precedent on a variety of issues, while other justices refuse to consider the rulings of courts outside the United States.[43] This death penalty case study shows that there are limits on the extent to which American courts will abide by principles of international law.

USING INTERNATIONAL PRECEDENTS IN THE U.S. COURTS

Are American judges remaining isolated in their decision making, or is the American judiciary becoming part of an international and global community of judges?

Litigation is becoming more globalized and internationalized, which is forcing judges around the world to pay much more attention to the decisions of their international colleagues.[44] As legal disputes cross national boundaries more and more, judges must rule on legal questions that involve multiple countries and multiple courts. For example, when two international corporations sign a contract in another country, is that contract enforceable in American courts? What should an American court do when the courts of two different countries come to opposite conclusions on child custody issues? What about patent and copyright issues that cross national borders? And, as the previous death penalty example illustrated, when must American judges consider principles of international law?

Contacts and interactions among judges have greatly increased throughout the world. Today, judges are no longer isolated within their own countries; they are meeting and appreciating judges from other courts from around the globe as well as reading their judicial opinions. Scholars of comparative judicial politics refer to this as **judicial comity**, which means that more and more judges are giving deference to the rulings and reasoning of their international colleagues because all judges internationally share a certain respect for the rule of law. They also respect other courts and their judges, not just as sources of law in disputes with international implications but also as "co-equals in the global task of judging."[45] As one American judge has phrased it, in today's world there must be "an ongoing dialogue between the adjudicative bodies of the world community."[46] The question facing judges around the world, in the words of Stephen Breyer before he joined the U.S. Supreme Court, is how to "help the world's legal systems work together, in harmony, rather than at cross purposes."[47]

Around the globe, judges are struggling with whether and under what circumstances to cite international precedents in their own decisions. In her book *Constitutional Engagement in a Transnational Era,* comparative judicial politics scholar Vicki G. Jackson argues that there are three main approaches to this issue. Some courts, such as those interpreting the 1997 South African Constitution and the Canadian Charter of Rights and Freedoms of 1982, are purposely internationalist in their use of international or transnational sources of law. Some judges, such as Justice Antonin Scalia and Judge Richard A. Posner (to be discussed in more detail below), are clearly resistant to using international precedents because they believe that only legal norms that have been adopted in this country should be considered in interpreting our laws.[48] Others, including Justices Anthony F. Kennedy and Stephen G. Breyer, periodically engage with transnational sources of law when they feel that other courts have already considered similar legal problems and proposed solutions that might work in another legal context.

It has become much easier for judges to find international sources of law and international precedents because most legal opinions from around the world are now easily available on the Internet, and many courts are now translating their decisions into English.[49] Thus, judges across the globe are reading more decisions from abroad, but they are also beginning to think of themselves as part of a global judicial community. This phenomenon leads us to ask whether U.S. judges are part of this broader international judicial community or remain unique decision makers in a legal system that has its foundations in the notion of American exceptionalism. American laws and courts are certainly different from those found elsewhere. Does that mean that American judges should not pay any attention to the decisions made by their colleagues abroad?

The U.S. Supreme Court and Non-American Court Decisions

Judges outside the United States have long cited U.S. Supreme Court decisions when those are applicable to the disputes they face.[50] Because our system of justice is based on the English common law system, early in our history U.S. judges would frequently cite British precedents, and American judges continue to cite old English rulings in certain circumstances.[51] However, when U.S. courts today cite the decisions of foreign courts, an enormous controversy often follows.

A recent example of this controversy was Justice Kennedy's majority opinion in *Lawrence v. Texas* (2003), when the Supreme Court struck down a state law prohibiting homosexual sodomy. Writing for the majority, Justice Kennedy noted that the European Court of Human Rights, based in Strasbourg, France, had already declared such anti-sodomy laws to be invalid in all of the forty-five countries that had agreed to follow the decisions of that court. While not required to do so, many other countries have also begun to incorporate the rulings of the European Court of Human Rights into their national legal systems.[52] In *Lawrence v. Texas*, Justice Kennedy noted that the right to engage in consensual homosexual sexual conduct "has been accepted as an integral part of human freedom in many other countries."[53]

Justice Scalia objected strenuously to the use of foreign judicial precedents in the *Lawrence v. Texas* decision. Writing for the dissent, Justice Scalia noted that constitutional rights in the United States do not "spring into existence, as the Court seems to believe, because foreign nations decriminalize conduct."[54] Quoting Justice Clarence Thomas's statements in a previous case, Justice Scalia also objected in the *Lawrence* decision to "imposing foreign moods, fads, or fashions on Americans."[55]

The debate continued in *Roper v. Simmons* (2005), where the Court declared in an opinion written by Justice Kennedy that executing juveniles was unconstitutional. In this case, Justice Kennedy noted, "Our determination that the death penalty is disproportionate punishment for offenders under age 18 finds confirmation in the stark reality that the United States is the only country in the world that continues to give official sanction to the juvenile death penalty. [. . . In prior rulings], the Court has referred to the laws of other countries and to international authorities as instructive for its interpretation of the Eighth Amendment's prohibition of 'cruel and unusual punishments.'"[56] He continued, "It does not lessen our fidelity to the Constitution or our pride in its origins to acknowledge that the express affirmation of certain fundamental rights by other nations and peoples simply underscores the centrality of those same rights within our own heritage of freedom."[57]

Not surprisingly, Justice Scalia saw things differently, arguing in his dissent in the *Roper* case, "The basic premise of the Court's argument—that American law should conform to the laws of the rest of the world—ought to be rejected out of hand. [. . .] In many significant respects the laws of most other countries differ from our law."[58] Scalia also noted, "To invoke alien law when it agrees with one's own thinking, and ignore it otherwise, is not reasoned decisionmaking, but sophistry."[59] He concluded, "What these foreign sources affirm [. . .] is the Justices' own notion of how the world ought to be, and their diktat that it shall be so henceforth in America."[60] Justice Scalia was even blunter in *Printz v. United States* (1997), a case dealing with federalism issues, when he wrote, "We think comparative analysis inappropriate to the task of interpreting a constitution, though it was of course quite relevant to the task of writing one."[61]

Judge Richard A. Posner of the U.S. Court of Appeals for the Seventh Circuit agrees that American judges should refrain from citing international precedent. "Another objection to our nascent judicial cosmopolitanism is that foreign decisions emerge from complex social, political, cultural, and historical backgrounds of which Supreme Court Justices, like other American judges and lawyers, are largely ignorant," he has written.[62] "Citing foreign decisions is best understood as an effort to mystify the adjudicative process and disguise the political decisions that are the core of the Supreme Court's constitutional output."[63]

Other justices besides Kennedy have also developed a habit of referring to international sources of law when they find those international judicial precedents to be helpful or even persuasive. In fact, this practice has been somewhat common in American history. In his study on this issue, political scientist Stephen A. Simon has found that "[o]f the 80 justices who have served on the Court since 1870 for any substantial time, almost half (37) have written at least one opinion employing foreign law."[64] As Justice Breyer has noted on this issue, the "willingness to consider foreign judicial views in comparable cases is not surprising in a Nation that from its birth has given a 'decent respect to the opinions of mankind.'"[65] Judge Shirley S. Abrahamson, a former chief justice of the Wisconsin Supreme Court, agreed: "[W]hen courts from around the world have written well-reasoned and provocative opinions in support of a position at odds with our familiar American views, we would do well to read carefully and take notes."[66] Even Justice Sandra Day O'Connor in her dissent in *Roper* noted, "Over the course of nearly half a century, the Court has consistently referred to foreign and international law as relevant to its assessment of evolving standards of decency."[67] Justice Sonia Sotomayor has commented, "International law and foreign law will be very important in the decision of how to think about the unsettled issues in our own legal system," particularly "as a source of ideas, informing our understanding of our own constitutional rights."[68] Justices Ruth Bader Ginsburg, David Souter, John Paul Stevens, and Elena Kagan also have been known to support citing international sources of law in American court opinions.

Thus, the debate among American judges about the wisdom of citing international sources of law continues. The potential consequences are broad. As scholar Melissa A. Waters has so carefully argued, "With their battling opinions in *Lawrence* and *Roper*, the Justices begin in earnest a debate that has been brewing among them for some time regarding the proper relationship between U.S. courts and foreign and international law. The central question underlying the growing judicial debate is this: To what extent, if at all, should U.S. courts engage in the rich international judicial dialogue (particularly with regard to constitutional issues) that is taking place among foreign and international courts around the world?"[69]

Conservative Opposition to the
Use of International Precedent

This controversy over the proper uses of international sources of law can be found in the broader American public as well as among the judiciary. Generally conservatives in the United States oppose allowing American courts to cite international judicial opinions, while liberals generally see no harm in this practice. Liberals note that the U.S. Supreme Court has been citing international sources of law since the end of the eighteenth century.[70]

The Federalist Society (as previously noted, an organization of conservative judges, law professors, and law students who want to encourage more conservative rulings from American courts) has taken the lead in the legal community in opposing the use of foreign and international sources of law in American courts. One of the group's main concerns is the protection of American sovereignty at all costs. Many of these individuals believe that the United States should be able to pick and choose which international organizations it joins, which treaties it ratifies, which international agreements it follows, and which military actions require international support. The most important principle in their view of the world is American self-determination. Thus, they believe that both international law and foreign law should be irrelevant in the American judicial system because nothing can be superior to the U.S. Constitution as a source of law in the United States.[71] In other words, since the United States is an exceptional country, which by definition should have exceptional laws, it is not appropriate to apply European, Canadian, or other foreign precedents to domestic judicial decision making.[72] Former attorney general Edwin Meese has stated that American judges who cite international and foreign sources of law are simply looking for a result that American legal traditions will not justify.[73]

Congress has gotten involved in this debate. For example, following the Supreme Court's decision in the *Roper* case, fifty-four conservative congressmen sponsored a resolution condemning the use of foreign sources in U.S. Supreme Court decisions.[74] In 2004, the House passed the Reaffirming American Independence Resolution, which provided that American judicial decisions should not be based on "judgments, laws or pronouncements of foreign institutions" unless they supported an originalist interpretation of the U.S. Constitution. The bill died in the U.S. Senate. In 2005, two U.S. senators introduced the Constitution Restoration Act of 2005, which called for the impeachment of any U.S. judge who cited any foreign source of law except English common law in force in 1789. This bill never became law.[75]

Representative Steve King, a conservative Republican from Iowa, was so upset that he conducted a study of the Supreme Court justices' international travel, noting that between 1998 and 2003 the justices took a total of ninety-three foreign trips, a number of which he severely criticized.[76] Former House majority leader Tom DeLay (R-Tex.) was especially critical of justices who cited international precedents, and he made Justice Kennedy the target for his attacks. Representative DeLay declared on a Fox radio show, "We've got Justice Kennedy writing decisions based upon international law, not the Constitution of the United States. That's just outrageous."[77] Some conservatives were so angry with Justice Kennedy for citing international precedent that they have called for his impeachment.[78] Several U.S. senators have asserted that citing international cases should be an impeachable offense for any U.S. federal judge.[79]

Because so many conservatives were upset that the U.S. Supreme Court was citing international legal sources, the Subcommittee on the Constitution of the U.S. House Judiciary Committee held hearings on the issue in July 2005. Many witnesses who were sympathetic to the views of the religious right and other social conservatives testified that allowing U.S. judges to cite international precedents would harm U.S. sovereignty and undermine the unique place of the American government on the world stage. They attacked the use of foreign sources of law in the Supreme Court's decision in *Lawrence v. Texas* (striking down anti-sodomy laws), *Roper v. Simmons* (outlawing the death penalty for juvenile defendants), and the 2003 decision of the Massachusetts Supreme Judicial Court declaring a right to same-sex marriage in the state (*Goodridge v. Department of Public Health*). The Massachusetts decision had relied heavily on a similar decision by the Supreme Court of Canada declaring a right to same-sex marriage in that country.[80] The chair of the Subcommittee on the Constitution explained why social conservatives were so unhappy with these judges: "By looking to and relying on the decisions of foreign courts in the interpretation of the Constitution of the United States, the judiciary not only is undermining the vision of our Founding Fathers but is chipping away at the core principles on which the country was founded, chipping away at our Nation's sovereignty and independence."[81]

In 2006, the U.S. Congress went even further in its attempt to prevent the federal courts from using international sources of law. The issue concerned the legal rights of accused terrorists then being held by U.S. military authorities at Guantanamo Bay in Cuba. President George W. Bush had declared that these individuals were "enemy combatants," with no legal rights under U.S. or international law.[82] In a series of rulings, the U.S. Supreme Court had disagreed with President Bush and the U.S. Congress on this issue.[83] In the Military Commissions Act of 2006,

Congress prohibited federal judges from consulting international or foreign sources of law when interpreting Common Article 3 of the Geneva Conventions on the treatment of prisoners of war, leaving the interpretation solely to the president. The act also attempted to strip the courts of the right to hear habeas corpus appeals from the Guantanamo Bay detainees. The Supreme Court eventually declared these provisions to be unconstitutional in *Boumediene v. Bush* (2008).

In December 2011, the U.S. House Judiciary Committee's Subcommittee on the Constitution again held hearings on the issue of the use of foreign precedents in U.S. judicial opinions. The chair of the subcommittee started off the hearing with this statement: "[M]odern foreign law cannot tell us anything relevant about the original meaning of our Constitution."[84] One of the key tenets of the Tea Party movement is that the American government must be restored to the constitutional principles articulated by the Founding Fathers.[85] The subcommittee chair concluded, "At its core, the issue is whether Americans will remain a sovereign, self-governing people or whether we will be governed by an elite caste of judges, imposing rules based on the supposed preferences of the so-called international community."[86] The chair of the House Judiciary Committee added his own views on the issue when he said, "Reliance on foreign law exacerbates judicial activism and empowers judges to impose their own policy preferences from the bench. Judges who rely on foreign law can pick and choose the sources of foreign law that reinforce their own personal or political biases."[87]

Among those concerned that state judges might use foreign sources of law in their decisions, a movement has emerged to pass state laws prohibiting such actions. State legislators seem especially worried that Muslim legal principles and practices (known as sharia) might find their way into state judicial decisions in family law and other areas. As of March 2012, twenty-four states were considering legislation forbidding judges from using international sources of law; such laws had already been enacted in the states of Louisiana, Arizona, and Tennessee. Oklahoma passed a ballot measure outlawing the use of sharia in the state courts, but a federal judge blocked implementation of the law. The Kansas legislature also passed a law banning the use of sharia in that state. The American Bar Association, among other groups, has condemned these measures, but it is not clear whether the courts will declare any or all of these laws to be unconstitutional.[88]

INTERACTIONS AMONG U.S. JUDGES AND FOREIGN JUDGES

Another reason for the apparent globalization of the judiciary is the great deal of contact taking place between American judges and judges from abroad. Some of this contact occurs through formal meetings of international judges, but much of it remains highly informal and decentralized. Formal meetings of judges from around the world are occurring with increasing frequency. For example, as early as 1995 twenty-five countries in the Western Hemisphere formed the Organization of Supreme Courts of the Americas, which held conferences where judges from the various counties could meet one another. Also in 1995, delegates from Australia, New Zealand, Ireland, India, the United States, Canada, and Great Britain attended the First Worldwide Common Law Judiciary Conference. In 1997, the Second Worldwide Common Law Judiciary Conference was held in May in Washington, D.C., at which representatives of the countries of Israel, Singapore, and South Africa joined the seven countries that had participated in the first conference. In 1998 Justices O'Connor, Breyer, Ginsburg, and Kennedy went to Luxembourg City to meet with their counterparts on the European Court of Justice (ECJ). In April 2000, a delegation from the ECJ went to Washington, D.C., to meet with U.S. Supreme Court justices. Prior to 2000, Justice O'Connor led several delegations of Supreme Court justices to meet with their counterparts in France, Germany, England, and India.[89] During their summer break, several of the justices have been known to teach short courses at law schools abroad.

Linda Greenhouse, who covered the Supreme Court for many years for the *New York Times*, noted in 2003 that many of the justices were beginning to think of themselves as part of an international judicial community. As Greenhouse wrote then, "Extensive foreign travel has made both Justice Kennedy and Justice O'Connor more alert to how their peers on other constitutional courts see similar issues. Justices have always traveled, teaching or taking part in seminars. But these are trips with a difference. [. . .] It is not surprising that the justices have begun to see themselves as participants in a worldwide constitutional conversation."[90]

Informal Contact Among Judges Around the World

Judges around the world also maintain contact with each other in less formal ways. With the use of email or other electronic means, communication has become much easier. As Claire L'Heureux-Dube, a former justice of the Canadian Supreme Court, notes, "Judges often discuss common problems at international judges' conferences, by e-mail, and over the telephone. [. . .] Close interactions are now becoming commonplace. I know that the friendships I have developed with judges from countries like the United States, Zimbabwe, South Africa, and Israel, to name just a few, have enabled me to discuss and correspond with them about decisions of our court and theirs, and about issues that cross national boundaries."[91]

Many American judges agree with the need for judges around the globe to have more personal contact with each other. In a 2002 speech, Chief Justice William Rehnquist urged all American judges to participate in international judicial exchanges because it is "important for judges and legal communities of different nations to exchange views, share information and learn to better understand one another and our legal systems."[92] Justice Breyer feels so strongly about the need for judges to learn about their international colleagues that he co-edited a book entitled *Judges in Contemporary Democracy: An International Conversation.*[93] In this effort, Justice Breyer and Judge Robert Badinter, the former president of the Constitutional Council of France, brought together leading judges and legal scholars from around the world to discuss and debate the role of the judge in a modern democracy.[94]

More-Formal Meetings Among Judges Around the World

Some of these meetings among international judges occur under the leadership of federal judges themselves. Chief Justice Rehnquist and the U.S. Judicial Conference created the Committee on International Judicial Relations in 1993. The purpose of this committee of federal judges is to encourage exchanges and training programs between U.S. judges and foreign judges. At the request of this committee, the Administrative Office of the Federal Courts created a publication entitled *The Federal Court System in the United States: An Introduction for Judges and Judicial Administrators in Other Countries.* The Administrative Office also provides staffing and other support services for the Committee on International Judicial Relations.

The justices of the Supreme Court have regular meetings with their counterparts on the European Court of Justice, the German Federal Constitutional Court, the French Conseil d'Etat, the new Supreme Court of the United Kingdom (and before that its predecessors), the Indian Supreme Court, the Supreme Court of Canada, and the Supreme Court of Mexico, among others.[95] The Supreme Court of the United States employs a rotating judicial fellow each year, and one of the duties of this individual is to explain the U.S. judicial system to a wide variety of international visitors. The U.S. Department of State has an international visitors program, which brings many judges and other judicial officials to the United States for visits. The U.S. Agency for International Development, an agency of the State Department, has a Rule of Law division that encourages exchanges and other contacts between U.S. judges and judges outside the United States. Other federal judicial agencies are facilitating these contacts today as well, but it is very difficult to get aggregate data on how many international judges visit the United States or on how many American judges visit judges in other countries.

The education and research agency for the federal judiciary, the Federal Judicial Center (FJC), established in 1967, is one of the key institutions of the U.S. federal judiciary that provides educational assistance to international judges. The International Judicial Relations Office was created in 1992 and coordinates the FJC's programming for international judges, lawyers, and government officials. In 2011, the Federal Judicial Center held 55 briefings for 553 judges, court officials, and attorneys from 49 different countries. In 2011, it also hosted 12 visiting judicial fellows from Brazil, Bulgaria, China, Japan, Kosovo, South Korea, Sri Lanka, and Togo for longer research stays at the Federal Judicial Center.[96] The previous year, 2010, the FJC hosted 65 briefings for 649 judges and others from 76 different countries;[97] in 2009 the numbers were 46 briefings for 448 judges and others from 75 different countries and territories.[98]

Efforts have come from the American Bar Association as well. For example, the ABA Central and Eastern European Law Initiative (CEELI) was established in 1990 after the fall of the Berlin Wall and has sent American judges to various central and eastern European countries to assist with law reform, codification efforts, and judicial training.[99] Starting in 2007, this initiative was consolidated into the American Bar Association's Rule of Law Initiative, although CEELI retains an independent office in Prague. Today, the ABA's Rule of Law Initiative maintains legal reform programs in more than forty countries around the world; it now has more than four hundred professional staffers and a multitude of volunteer lawyers and judges. Their work is aimed primarily at assisting judicial reform in emerging democracies and focuses on the following areas: access to justice and human rights, anti-corruption and public integrity, criminal law reform and anti–human trafficking, judicial reform, legal education reform and civil education, legal profession reform, and women's rights.

Law schools and other university-based groups have invited international judges to conferences in order to talk about their common problems and concerns.[100] For example, Brandeis University hosts the Brandeis Institute for International Judges. The National Center for State Courts, headquartered in Williamsburg, Virginia, provides assistance to state judges who wish to travel abroad and to international judges who wish to visit or study our various state judiciaries. The National Judicial College in Reno, Nevada, also provides some assistance to those who would like to visit international judiciaries.

Contact between American judges and international judges is increasing significantly, but these interactions remain mostly ad hoc and decentralized, many initiated by the judges themselves through various electronic media. Still, their existence means that a global judicial community is emerging. As scholar Melissa A. Waters has noted, "'Face-to-face' contact among the world's judges is increasingly frequent and takes a variety of forms—from international judicial conferences, to exchanges of judicial delegations among U.S., European and Latin American courts, to judicial participation in rule of law and law reform programs around the world. Although it is difficult to measure the influence of this most informal kind of judicial communication, it has undoubtedly played a significant role in creating an environment in which transnational judicial dialogue can flourish."[101] Among the benefits of these interactions for judges both in the United States and elsewhere are "[a] heightened appreciation for the talents and professionalism of their foreign counterparts, as well as greater awareness of the degree to which judges worldwide encounter similar legal issues in their work."[102] Scholar Anne Marie Slaughter agrees: "All these visits and exchanges and seminars have multiple functions. They certainly serve to educate and cross-fertilize. They broaden the perspectives of the participating judges. [. . .] But perhaps most important, they socialize their members as participants in a common global judicial enterprise."[103]

ADVERSARIAL LEGALISM AND GOVERNANCE AS DIALOGUE

The American legal system is very different from the world's other legal systems. In some ways, we share a great many things with other common law nations. Our judges interpret multiple sources of law, they are neutral arbiters of an adversarial system, and their main purpose is to find justice in any given case before them. However, even within the common law family, the American legal system is unique. One huge difference is the fact that the American legal system is grounded in adversarial legalism. Issues that would be settled in the legislative or executive branches in other countries end up in American courts. Our courts are not only the most powerful in the world but also among the most activist. Judges in the American system of government have a much more important role in policy making than their colleagues around the globe.

Another thing that makes American courts unique is the fact that policy in our country is created through a continuous dialogue among various institutions and political voices, a process known as Governance as Dialogue. This ongoing inter-institutional conversation among the president, Congress, administrative agencies, the states, and the courts gives the courts a place at the table in almost all policy making. The fact that our judges are selected through political processes makes our judges both legal actors and political actors. Therefore, it should be no surprise that the United States is the founding home of the academic study of judicial politics.

CHAPTER SUMMARY

This chapter explored some of the similarities and differences between American courts and courts abroad, beginning with a look at several case studies demonstrating how American courts handle issues differently than their colleagues in Italy, France, the Netherlands, and Mexico; the last of these reveals the extent to which American courts will apply international law principles in their deliberations. The chapter then turned to the issue of American courts using foreign law and international law in their judicial decision making. Liberals generally support such consultation of foreign legal sources, while conservatives generally oppose the practice. It then examined several U.S. Supreme Court decisions using foreign law. The chapter ended with a look at both formal and informal ways that American judges come into contact with their colleagues on courts around the world.

For Further Reading

Badinter, Robert, and Stephen Breyer, eds. 2004. *Judges in Contemporary Democracy: An International Conversation.* New York: New York University Press.

Barak, Aharon. 2006. *The Judge in a Democracy.* Princeton, NJ: Princeton University Press.

Epp, Charles. 1998. *The Rights Revolution: Lawyers, Activists, and Supreme Courts in Comparative Perspective.* Chicago: University of Chicago Press.

Jacob, Herbert, Erhard Blankenburg, Herbert M. Kritzer, Doris Marie Provine, and Joseph Sanders, eds. 1996. *Courts, Law, and Politics in a Comparative Perspective.* New Haven, CT: Yale University Press.

Maveety, Nancy. 2009. "Comparative Judicial Studies." In Mark C. Miller, ed., *Exploring Judicial Politics.* New York: Oxford University Press.

Russell, Peter H., and David M. O'Brien, eds. 2001. *Judicial Independence in the Age of Democracy: Critical Perspectives from Around the World.* Charlottesville: University Press of Virginia.

Shapiro, Martin. 1981. *Courts: A Comparative and Political Analysis.* Chicago: University of Chicago Press.

Sweet, Alec Stone. 2000. *Governing with Judges: Constitutional Politics in Europe.* New York: Oxford University Press.

———. 2004. *The Judicial Construction of Europe.* New York: Oxford University Press.

Tate, C. Neal, and Torbjorn Vallinder, eds. 1995. *The Global Expansion of Judicial Power.* New York: New York University Press.

Conclusion

Having read this book, you now know much more about the role and functions of courts in the United States. You have also realized that courts cannot be studied in a vacuum because the American judiciary is part of a much larger governmental system. The courts are legal institutions, where judges use legal reasoning and precedent to help them with their decisions. Law has its own language, and "thinking like a lawyer" means in part that lawyers share this unique approach to the use of language. Because the judicial system in the United States is an adversary system, the role of lawyers is to advance the best interests of their clients both inside and outside the courthouse. American courts, however, are also political institutions. The decisions that judges make, both individually and collectively, in all types of courts can have profound political effects in our society. In addition, all of our judges are chosen through political selection processes, thus ensuring that the judiciary is fully aware of the political consequences of its actions. In reading this book, you have thought much more about the judiciary and the notion of judicial politics in the broader universe of American government.

In the United States, courts and judges are clearly influenced by the actions of other political actors, and, in turn, the judiciary influences the decisions of those actors. The American public, the media, interest groups, legislators, executives, and bureaucratic officials all pay a great deal of attention to the decisions of American courts. In other countries, the courts are sometimes considered merely technocratic bodies and receive little notice because their decisions are seen as only affecting the parties before them. Many textbooks about government and politics in various foreign countries do not even mention the courts because they are not seen as relevant for students of politics in those societies. American government textbooks, however, cannot ignore the courts because judicial politics are so important for a full understanding of how our political system actually works.

Because the courts are so important as both political and legal decision makers in the United States, many political actors are quite willing to criticize, ignore, and sometimes even attempt to circumvent the rulings of American judges. There have also been times when interest groups or others have attempted to punish the courts for unpopular decisions. So while the relationships between the courts and other political and societal actors in the United States are typically positive and mutually respectful, these relationships can also become strained and tense. Recall that French philosopher Alexis de Tocqueville in the early 1800s said that all political questions in the United States eventually become legal ones, and all legal questions eventually become political ones. Tocqueville also said that lawyers were the American aristocracy, in part because of the role that lawyers play in all of our governmental institutions. The incrementalist approach taken by lawyers and judges in the United States affects the decision-making styles of nearly all governmental institutions in our nation.

In some ways, judicial politics in the United States is the same as it is in other countries, but in other ways it is very different. One key difference is the sheer power of our courts and judges, in large part because all regular courts in this country have the power of judicial review, that is, the ability to declare the actions of the president, the Congress, the bureaucracy, or the states to be unconstitutional. Judges differ in their judicial philosophies—that is, in how they will use their power of judicial review—but it remains a fact that the courts' right to determine the constitutionality of the actions of other political actors makes our courts one of the most powerful judiciaries in the world. Judges in all common law countries generally have more power than their counterparts in civil law countries because in the common law tradition law is judge-made, but American courts are more powerful than almost any other common law judiciary. Being at the top of our judicial hierarchy, the U.S. Supreme Court is at the pinnacle of judicial power in a world where judges and their decisions are becoming more important all over the globe.

Another difference lies in the federalism tradition in the United States, which means that we maintain two separate court systems (state and federal) with overlapping jurisdictions that share the same geographical space. Throughout the United States we often have state and federal courts sitting side by side hearing similar types of cases, which can make our courts very confusing, especially to non-Americans. Many other federal systems instead have created a single unified court system, such as the one used by our neighbors in Canada.

In the United States, we have a great deal of tolerance for the law being different from place to place in our country. Each state supreme court can interpret its state constitution as it pleases, as long as those interpretations do not conflict with the federal Constitution. Thus, each state can have very different laws and practices—we see that in how differently same-sex marriage has been treated by the different states. We also tolerate differences in federal law across the country. Because the U.S. Supreme Court declines to hear around 98 percent of the appeals presented to it, the U.S. courts of appeals become the main source of interpretation regarding federal law in our country. The different federal circuit courts often come to conflicting understandings of the requirements of federal law. While the Supreme Court of the United States might issue a ruling that would create a uniform legal rule that applies throughout the nation, it is under no obligation to do so. Therefore, federal law might be very different in the courts under the jurisdiction of the U.S. Court of Appeals for the Fourth Circuit than it is in the Ninth Circuit, for example. Many other countries would find that flexibility in the law to be chaotic, dangerous, and frankly unimaginable.

The relationships between our courts and other governmental institutions are uniquely American, although one could certainly study legislative-judicial interactions or executive-judicial relationships in other countries. At the federal level in the United States, the relationship among the governmental institutions has shifted over time. At times the president may be dominant in the relationship, while at other times Congress may hold the upper hand. The courts partner with other governmental actors depending on the circumstances, the issues at hand, and the era. For example, during the 1950s and 1960s, the Congress, the Supreme Court, and the president all took various actions to advance civil rights in this country. It seemed as though all the federal institutions were aligned in wanting to change the way our society treated minority citizens, especially African Americans. During other periods, it has seemed as though the courts are acting as referees in disputes between Congress and the president. This was certainly true when the Supreme Court limited President Truman's power after he seized striking steel mills during the Korean War, a move that was not authorized by Congress. At still other times—for example, when considering the legal rights of detainees held at Guantanamo Bay—the courts were the dissenting voice when Congress and the president were in agreement. Sometimes the courts give a great deal of deference to the decisions of bureaucratic officials, but at other times judges have rejected agency interpretations of statutes and other laws.

Since most state judges have to go through the election process to get their seats on the bench but federal judges have life terms, these two types of judges may have different relationships with their counterparts in the other branches of government. Some state judges may work in concert with their executive and legislative branch colleagues, while other state judges may find themselves in conflict with these state officials. The relationships between federal judges and various state officials may also be contentious, such as when federal judges order state prisons to reduce overcrowding or when federal judges get involved with local education decisions. Some federal judges are now challenging state bans on same-sex marriage while others are striking down state and local gun control laws, all of which has created a great deal of consternation among state officials.

In most other countries, judges are chosen because of merit and not through a politically based selection system. The civil law tradition values expertise among judges, and individuals may be chosen to become judges because of their test scores. Even in societies such as the United Kingdom and Canada, the judicial selection systems do not seem to privilege political considerations over merit considerations. Many judges around the world worry that the American judicial selection processes will exclude people who do not have the proper political connections or group support from becoming a judge. Although Americans may complain that their judges are too political, there is very little impetus to change our politically based judicial selection systems.

The study of judicial politics remains a mostly American endeavor among academics, though comparative judicial politics is a growing field. Scholars of judicial politics generally find their home in political science departments, rather than among law school faculty or in other disciplines. Scholars in other countries tend to study law or politics, but not both. When I meet judges from around the world, they are usually surprised that a political scientist is interested in their work. Law professors throughout the world are generally more concerned with legal doctrine than they are with the political, historical, and social forces that help produce those legal doctrines. Scholars of judicial politics, however, are much more concerned about the intersection of law and politics, as this book has demonstrated. There are some very good Canadian judicial politics scholars, and judicial politics is beginning to receive more attention in countries such as South Africa and Israel, where the courts have begun to make more politically sensitive legal decisions. For the most part, however, most judicial scholars around the world were educated in the United States and continue to teach in the United States. Given the unique mixture of law and politics in this country, it is perhaps not surprising that most judicial politics academics focus most of their efforts on judicial politics in the American context.

One of the key intellectual foundations of this book is the Governance as Dialogue concept. You will recall that the Governance as Dialogue movement argues that the meanings of the U.S. Constitution and the state constitutions evolve through a series of conversations among various political actors. The movement arose in part as a reaction against a notion of judicial supremacy taught by some law professors in the United States. In Canada, the Governance as Dialogue movement is a reaction against notions of legislative supremacy, often popular among academics in that country. Among Governance as Dialogue scholars, the courts are not seen as having a monopoly on constitutional interpretation because the other governmental institutions and other political actors are free to offer their constitutional interpretations as well. The courts clearly have a voice at the table, but the views of Congress, the president, bureaucratic officials, and state officials count too. At times, the other political actors have taken steps to curb the influence of the courts in the inter-institutional dialogue, but at other times they have acted to enhance the voice of the judiciary in this debate. Some have argued that the Governance as Dialogue approach makes the law too amorphous, too vague, and too indeterminate, while others counter that this concept helps us to understand more about the reality of constitutional decision making in the U.S. context. The courts are an important player in this conversation, but not the only voice in the dialogue.

The Governance as Dialogue approach also implies that the roles of courts and judges in the United States are constantly changing. The courts have faced many challenges in the past, and they may face additional challenges in the future. One major issue courts are dealing with today, and could continue to encounter, is resource constraints, especially because courts are dependent on legislatures for their annual budgets. As state governments and the federal government seek various spending cuts, the courts may be forced to tighten their budgets as well. For example, the federal courts had to reduce their spending significantly because of the sequester cuts that Congress enacted in March 2013. Since most judicial spending is for personnel costs, courts in the future may find themselves having to function with fewer judges or fewer staff as budgets get tighter and tighter. Judges want to invest in better technologies for case filings and case management, but they may not have the budget resources to do so. Court administrators are also worried about security issues, but enhanced security for judges and other courthouse personnel means that more financial resources are required.

Judges are concerned that the American public is beginning to perceive their decisions as based purely on political considerations. Judges always stress that their rulings are based on legal reasoning and the specific facts of the case before them, and that only in the rarest of cases do judges arrive at different decisions because of their diverging ideologies or worldviews. Judges often feel that interest groups and other political actors make too big a deal of the political differences among judges. However, since American judges are chosen through political methods, it is impossible to take all politics out of judicial decisions. In fact, we have already seen an increase in political fights among interest groups over confirmation of lower federal court judges, as well as an increase in the time and money spent on state judicial elections. As state judicial elections become more competitive and more expensive, they may receive more attention among the general public. These trends are probably here to stay, although the nature of judicial politics in the United States is subject to change as the society changes and evolves. Groups such as the American Judicature Society are advocating more merit-based selection systems, and perhaps someday a number of the states will opt for a different selection method for their state judges.

One trend that is certain to continue is the fact that judges from around the world are better able to read each other's opinions and to communicate directly with each other. Judges are no longer isolated in their own countries, since modern communications have allowed them to reach out to their colleagues abroad. Legal issues are also undergoing globalization, compelling judges to consider the law and legal rulings in other countries when deciding issues before them. As contact grows among judges around the world, there will be more professional relationships among judges from different legal systems and traditions, and more and more courts are translating their decisions into English. As judges everywhere become increasingly familiar with the work of judges in other countries, the study of judicial politics must change accordingly and become more global in scope.

GLOSSARY

Actus reus is a Latin term meaning the prohibited criminal act.

Adjudication is the procedure used by bureaucratic agencies to enforce their rules through a process presided over by an administrative law judge. It resembles a trial for a civil lawsuit.

Administrative law cases require the courts to review the decisions made by governmental bureaucratic agencies to make sure that these decisions follow the proper processes and procedures.

An **administrative law judge** is an employee of an agency and hears disputes between individuals, groups, or others and that agency's personnel.

The **administrative leader** of the Supreme Court hires the other officers of the Court and indirectly all Supreme Court employees. He or she also manages the certiorari conference and the conference on the merits at the Court. The chief justice fills this role automatically because of his title and position on the Court.

The **Administrative Office of the United States Courts** provides research, administrative, legal, financial, management, program, and information technology services to the federal judiciary. Its employees also serve as staff for the Judicial Conference of the United States.

The **Administrative Procedures Act**, enacted by Congress in 1946, spells out the necessary steps in the federal agency rule-making process in order to bring some uniformity to federal agency decision making.

In the **adversary system** in the common law tradition, lawyers protect the best interests of their clients and present their clients' best case to the court. The judge serves as an unbiased, neutral decision maker in the clash between the lawyers representing each side.

Adversarial legalism is a mode of policy making, implementation, and dispute resolution characterized by frequent resort to highly adversarial legal contestation in the courts.

An **advisory opinion** is a court's opinion on the constitutionality of legislation before that legislation goes into effect.

Alternative dispute resolution (ADR) is a collective term used to describe various procedures for settling a dispute without using the courts. Most forms of ADR are

325

not binding and involve referral of the case to a neutral third party such as an arbitrator, mediator, or rent-a-judge.

The **American Constitution Society for Law and Policy**, created at Georgetown Law School in 2001, is the contemporary liberal alternative to the conservative Federalist Society. It is a group of liberal law professors, law students, judges, and others who want to encourage courts to make liberal rulings.

Amicus curiae briefs are formal "friend of the court" briefs, often used by interest groups and others in order to try to lobby the Supreme Court. They can be filed at the certiorari stage and at the merits stage.

An **answer** is filed by the defendant in a civil lawsuit explaining the defendant's view of the issues in the dispute.

Appellate courts are where the appeals are filed.

Appellate jurisdiction means that cases reach the appellate courts through an appeal from a lower court.

Arbitration is a form of alternative dispute resolution that involves a neutral third party listening to both sides of the conflict. Unlike mediation, however, both parties must agree in advance that they will abide by the arbitrator's decisions.

Arraignment is where an arrested individual appears before a judge to learn the formal criminal charges against him or her.

An **arrest warrant** will be issued by a judge when he or she feels there is probable cause that the suspect has committed a crime.

Article II judges usually sit on specialized federal courts and have limited terms of office. The appointment process differs from Article III judges.

Article III judges serve on the regular federal courts. They are appointed by the president and confirmed by the U.S. Senate for life terms.

The **Articles of Confederation** laid out the first system of government in the United States, after the Revolution and before the ratification of the Constitution of 1789. This confederal system of government divided power between the national government and the states, but the states were considered supreme, with limited power given to the central government.

Associates at large law firms are new lawyers, usually right out of law school, and often from the best law schools in the country. These associates usually work six or seven years before they have the opportunity to be promoted to partner.

The **attitudinal model** of judicial decision making assumes that judges act in a purely ideological fashion, unconstrained by any other forces.

Bail is money a criminal defendant has to provide to the court to guarantee his or her attendance at trial.

Bankruptcy courts are the special federal courts that hear all bankruptcy cases. These Article II courts are attached to the regular U.S. district courts.

Bankruptcy judges are appointed by the majority of the regular federal judges who sit on the U.S. District Court. They serve fourteen-year terms on the specialized bankruptcy courts.

The **behavioral revolution** in political science meant that, instead of looking at institutional rules and structures, political scientists began to examine political behavior at the individual level of analysis.

A **bench trial** occurs when there is no jury present. The judge is responsible at trial for both questions of fact and questions of law.

A **bifurcated jury** system is required by the U.S. Supreme Court in death penalty cases. The first jury decides guilt or innocence, and the second jury decides whether the sentence should be death or life imprisonment. These two juries are usually made up of the same individuals, but they hear different evidence in each stage of the proceedings.

Billable hours are how large law firms determine how to bill their clients for their lawyers' time. Most lawyers at large firms bill in six- or twelve-minute increments.

Binding precedent means that lower court judges must follow the rulings of higher courts in their court hierarchy.

In a **blue slip** procedure, when a judicial nominee's name is sent to the Senate Judiciary Committee, the chairman automatically sends a blue sheet of paper to the home state senators asking for their endorsement of the candidate. If a home state senator fails to return the blue slip, then traditionally the chairman will not schedule confirmation hearings for that nominee.

The **briefs on the merits** at the U.S. Supreme Court argue how the Court should decide the case.

Burden of proof means the level of evidence that the plaintiff in a civil case (or the prosecutor in a criminal case) must prove in order to win the case.

A **bureaucracy** is any large, complex organization where employees work in a hierarchy and are charged with the performance of specific tasks.

Bureaucrats are executive branch employees.

Cabinet-level departments are federal agencies headed by a secretary (or, for the Department of Justice, the attorney general) who serves in the president's cabinet.

The **case method** as taught in U.S. law schools means that students almost exclusively read and study appellate court decisions.

Cause lawyers use the courts to bring about social change and for other political purposes. They may or may not be concerned about the needs of their specific clients.

Challenges for cause are when a judge determines that a potential juror cannot be impartial and releases that person from the jury pool.

A **charge bargain** occurs when the prosecutor and the defense attorney in a criminal case reach a plea bargain agreement where the prosecutor agrees to reduce the charges against the defendant in exchange for the defendant's guilty plea.

The **chief judge** on the U.S. Court of Appeals is the most senior judge on the circuit court who has been on the court for at least one year and who is under the age of sixty-five when the vacancy occurs. The chief judge has unique administrative responsibilities on the circuit court and within the broader judicial hierarchy.

Civil cases in the United States involve wrongs between individuals broadly defined.

The **civil law** family of legal systems of Continental Europe are based on the Roman and Napoleonic written legal codes. France, Spain, and Germany are probably the most notable contemporary models.

Class action lawsuits are lawsuits brought on behalf of a named plaintiff and all others in similar situations. These lawsuits consolidate many potential civil cases into one comprehensive lawsuit.

Clear and convincing evidence is a higher burden of proof than a preponderance of the evidence and is required for some civil cases.

Clinical programs in law schools are where law students supervised by a faculty member provide legal services to those who cannot otherwise afford such services.

Cloture is the process for ending a filibuster in the U.S. Senate. Under current Senate rules, it takes sixty votes to invoke cloture and end a filibuster.

Coercion is a remedy in a civil lawsuit. It means that the liable defendant is ordered to do something, such as pay back child support payments or rehire an employee who was wrongfully terminated.

Collusive cases are those in which there is no actual dispute. Federal courts cannot hear these cases under the Constitution's Article III case and controversy requirement.

Commercial law usually involves alleged violations of the Uniform Commercial Code and other laws regulating banking, sales, and other commercial practices.

The **common law** family of legal systems originated in England and is based on judge-made court decisions and precedent rather than on codified written laws, as in some other legal traditions.

Common law judicial rulings are not based on a specific written source of law, but nevertheless these judicial rulings have the force of law themselves. When there is no applicable source of law, the judge can make a decision based on the needs of justice.

In a **community of practice**, lawyers' professional norms and choices are greatly influenced by the other practitioners with whom they interact on a daily basis.

Compensatory damages are monetary remedies in a civil lawsuit for harm that can be counted or at least given a monetary value; such as lost wages and medical bills. Although much more difficult to calculate, "pain and suffering" are also remedied by compensatory damages.

In the **complaint,** the plaintiff in a civil case must explain the nature of the dispute and note the remedies being sought.

Compliance means that lower court judges follow the law and precedent as determined by the courts above them. Compliance can also be used to mean the general willingness of citizens to follow the law or the willingness of various actors to follow a ruling of the Supreme Court.

A **concurrence** is an opinion of an appellate court that agrees with the majority outcome, but for different reasons.

A **confederal system** means that there is a division of power between the national government and the regional governments, with the regional governments being supreme.

The **conference on certiorari** at the U.S. Supreme Court is the meeting where the justices vote on whether to accept or reject a petition for a writ of certiorari. It takes four votes for the Court to accept a petition for a writ of certiorari.

The **conference on the merits** at the U.S. Supreme Court is the meeting of the justices after oral arguments where the cases are discussed and a preliminary vote is taken based only on the outcome of the case.

Constitutional interpretation cases are those in which the courts interpret the U.S. Constitution or the various state constitutions.

A **contingency fee** is charged mostly by personal injury lawyers and means that the lawyers do not charge up front for their legal services, but instead take a percentage of any monetary awards they earn for their clients. Normally, this is one-third of the money the client receives from a case settlement or a judgment of a court in a civil lawsuit.

A **contract** is a legally enforceable agreement between two or more people or corporations that creates an obligation to do or not to do a particular thing.

Court-appointed attorneys are private lawyers paid by the state to handle certain criminal cases for the poor. The pay for these court-appointed attorneys varies greatly from state to state.

Court stripping is when the Congress enacts legislation to prevent the federal courts from hearing certain types of cases or specific cases. The Exceptions Clause in the U.S. Constitution seems to give Congress the ability to restrict the jurisdiction of the federal courts, but this power has been rarely used, and it remains an open question whether such court stripping actions would be declared unconstitutional by the courts.

The **courthouse community** is the term for the situation where prosecutors, criminal defense lawyers, and judges work together over a long period of time and develop a great deal of professional loyalty to each other.

A **crime** is a wrong against society. The courts are the only institution with the power to punish criminals in our country.

The **criminal defendant** is the individual accused of the crime.

Cue theory states that since the justices are so busy with the other aspects of their duties, they must find some shorthand method for processing the huge volume of petitions for writs of certiorari.

The **decision recall proposal** suggested by Theodore Roosevelt would have allowed the voters to overturn any court decision that declared a statute to be unconstitutional.

In a **default judgment**, the plaintiff in a civil case receives the remedies requested, without further deliberation by the court.

The **defendant** is the party against whom a civil lawsuit is brought. A criminal defendant is the individual accused of a crime.

A **deposition** can be part of the discovery process in a civil case and is where the lawyers question potential witnesses in the case under oath.

Deterrence is a goal of criminal sentencing. A severe sentence is given in the hope that it will deter others from committing crimes in the first place.

Diffuse support for the courts means a broad level of support of the judiciary without regard to any specific judicial decision.

A **directed verdict** in a civil lawsuit means that the plaintiff has not presented enough evidence at trial to meet the burden of proof of a preponderance of evidence.

The **discovery** process in a civil lawsuit allows both sides to learn more information about the lawsuit and the issues it presents.

A **discretionary docket** means that an appellate court such as the U.S. Supreme Court can decide which appeals to hear and which ones to reject.

The **discuss list** at the U.S. Supreme Court includes all the cases that the justices will discuss at their certiorari conference.

The **dissenting opinion** from an appellate court reflects the preferred outcome of the minority of judges and by definition the minority's reasoning.

Empirical research looks at what is, in contrast to normative studies, which propose what ought to be.

An *en banc* review at the U.S. courts of appeals means that the case will be reheard by the entire membership of the circuit, or by a significant portion of the membership in the largest courts, such as the U.S. Court of Appeals for the Ninth Circuit.

Equity partners are partners in large law firms whose salary is a share of the firm's annual profits.

In **ex parte communications**, only one party to a dispute is part of a conversation with a decision maker in the dispute, such as a judge or a mediator.

The **exclusionary rule** means that any evidence seized illegally by the police during a criminal investigation cannot be used at trial.

The **Executive Office of the President** is an umbrella term for a specific category of federal agency. These agencies house the closest advisors to the president.

Executive orders are issued by the president to federal agencies, directing them to do certain things or to refrain from doing certain things.

Executive privilege means that the president has the right to withhold certain information from the other branches of government because of the need for confidentiality in the internal workings of the White House or because of national security issues.

An **explicit plea bargain** in a criminal case is where the prosecutor and the defense actually communicate with each other about the deal.

Family law civil cases can involve issues of divorce, child custody, adoption, and child support.

The **Federal Advisory Committee Act** requires that committees that advise executive branch policy makers disclose information about their membership and have open meetings.

Federal agency rules and regulations have the force of law, and they often fill in the details of federal statutes.

The **Federal Judicial Center** is a federal judicial branch agency that provides training and research for the federal judiciary in a wide range of areas, including court administration, case management, budget and finance, human resources, and court technology.

Federal jurisdiction refers to the authority of a federal court to hear a particular case. A case cannot be heard in federal court unless it meets at least one of the four tests for federal jurisdiction listed in federal statutes.

Federal magistrate judges assist regular federal judges in many U.S. district courts, mostly with highly complex litigation. They are selected by a vote of the majority of the regular judges assigned to the district and serve an eight-year term.

The **Federal Sentencing Guidelines** are used by federal trial judges to help them determine appropriate criminal sentences in any specific case. They take into account the severity of the crime committed and the past behavior of the defendant.

Federal statutes are laws enacted by the U.S. Congress and either signed into law by the president or allowed to become law without his signature under certain circumstances.

Federalism is the division of power between the national government and the regional governments (in the United States, these are the states), with the national government being supreme.

The **Federalist Papers** were written by Alexander Hamilton, James Madison, and John Jay to persuade the states to ratify the U.S. Constitution.

The **Federalist Society,** established in the early 1980s, is a group of conservative lawyers, law students, law professors, and judges who advocate for conservative rulings from the federal courts.

A **felony** is a serious crime, usually punishable by at least one year in prison.

A **filibuster** means that unhappy U.S. senators can talk a bill or a nomination to death. Under current Senate rules, it takes sixty votes to invoke cloture and end debate on the question. In December 2013, the Senate changed its rules so that filibusters are no longer allowed for presidential nominees for executive branch positions or for nominees to fill seats on U.S. district courts or the U.S. courts of appeals.

Foreign law means the legal decisions of the courts of other nation-states. It is very different from the term *international law.*

The **Freedom of Information Act** gives anyone the right to request federal agency records and requires agencies to release them unless they fall within one of the nine exempt categories.

The **freshman effect** means that a new U.S. Supreme Court justice often experiences a period of uncertainty at the beginning of his or her service on the highest court. The new justice's early decisions may not reflect his or her later views.

General deterrence is a goal of criminal sentencing. The hope is that strong criminal sentences will deter potential criminals before they commit a crime.

General jurisdiction courts can hear a wide variety of criminal, civil, and administrative law cases. All of the regular federal courts and many state courts are courts of general jurisdiction.

The **Governance as Dialogue movement** holds that the Supreme Court is not the last word on interpreting the Constitution but instead is part of a continuing interinstitutional conversation.

The **Government in the Sunshine Act** only applies to multi-member agency boards and commissions. The act requires these agencies to open their meetings to the public except under ten circumstances, which are similar to the Freedom of Information Act exceptions.

A **grand jury** is convened by a prosecutor to determine whether there is enough evidence for a case to proceed to trial. A grand jury is required by the U.S. Constitution to bring an indictment of a criminal defendant before a federal criminal trial can proceed. Most states also use the grand jury process, although it is not constitutionally required. A grand jury can occur at various stages of the criminal justice process.

Habeas corpus literally means "produce the body." A writ of habeas corpus generally is a judicial order from a federal court forcing law enforcement authorities to produce a prisoner they are holding and to justify the prisoner's continued confinement. The writ of habeas corpus has been used by military prisoners, by state prison inmates objecting to their living conditions, by detainees at Guantanamo Bay, and in death penalty cases, among others.

Historical institutionalism is a model of judicial decision making that defines political institutions broadly and focuses on changes in institutions over time. Historical institutionalists usually do not examine only one institution or process at a set point in time but rather tend to look at politics as a very complex and complicated set of processes and institutions that vary over time and that interact in interesting and unexpected ways.

A **holding** is the legal doctrine that the majority opinion articulates for a case, or a concise statement of the precedent the ruling has created.

Impeachment is the process for removing federal judges from the bench. The U.S. Constitution provides that federal judges can be removed from office when a majority of the U.S. House of Representatives votes for articles of impeachment. Then the U.S. Senate holds a trial, and it takes a two-thirds vote of the Senate to remove the judge from office.

Implementation of a court policy or precedent means putting the policy into practice.

An **implicit plea bargain** means that the criminal defendant pleads guilty without any direct communication with the prosecutor or the judge in the case.

Incapacitation is a goal of criminal sentencing and means that a prison sentence will protect society from a dangerous individual.

Incorporation is the procedure used to apply the Bill of Rights to the states through the Fourteenth Amendment. Incorporation was done in a piecemeal fashion by the U.S. Supreme Court over an extended period of time starting after World War II.

Independent regulatory boards or commissions are a category of federal agency. The members of these boards or commissions are appointed by the president and confirmed by the Senate, but the president cannot remove any individual board member or commissioner until his or her term of office expires.

The **indictment** is handed down by a grand jury and lists the formal charges against the criminal defendant. The trial is limited to the charges listed in the indictment.

Individual deterrence is a goal of criminal sentencing. Imprisoning an individual prevents him or her from committing another crime during the prison term.

In-house lawyers are employees of a corporation, not an independent private law firm. They do the legal work of the organization that is not handled by outside law firms.

An **injunction** is a remedy in a civil lawsuit and prevents someone from taking an action.

The **intellectual leader** of the Supreme Court has the ability to persuade his or her fellow justices to follow a preferred approach to specific legal questions. This role may or may not be filled by the chief justice.

International law has its source in treaties and the decisions of supranational courts such as the International Court of Justice. The United States has been very hesitant to sign any treaties or join any international institutions that would render the U.S. Constitution inferior to international law. This is very different from *foreign law,* which means the decisions of national courts outside the United States.

An **interrogatory** can be part of the discovery process in a civil lawsuit and means that each party may present written questions to the other side, which must be answered in writing.

A **judge's sentence bargain** is a type of plea bargain in a criminal case where the judge suggests a possible sentence if the defendant pleads guilty.

The **judgment** states the legal remedies that are available to the winning party after having won a civil case.

A **judgment notwithstanding the verdict** can be issued by a judge in a civil case if the defendant can convince the judge that the jury verdict violates the law. It in effect overturns the jury's verdict in the case.

Judicial accountability means that judges' decisions should reflect the will of the voters because courts are making important public policy decisions.

Judicial activism occurs whenever courts declare something to be unconstitutional. Judicial activists tend to interpret the U.S. Constitution as a living and changing document that needs to be reinterpreted as the society evolves. Judicial activists see making public policy as a natural part of the purpose of the courts in our nation. Activist judges are quite willing to declare actions of other political actors to be unconstitutional.

Judicial comity means that more and more judges are giving deference to the rulings and reasoning of their international colleagues because all judges internationally share a certain respect for the rule of law.

The **Judicial Conference of the United States** is the committee that voices the collective views of the federal judiciary to the outside world. In other words, it is the policymaking arm for all federal courts. It is chaired by the chief justice of the United States.

Judicial independence means that courts must be able to make their decisions without interference from the other branches and without fear that other political actors will directly retaliate against judges because of their legal decisions.

Judicial politics is the study of the political processes by which courts are constituted and legal decisions are made and implemented.

Judicial restraint occurs whenever a court upholds the constitutionality of the actions of other governmental actors. Restraintists are uncomfortable with judges' immense power of judicial review. Restraintists tend to believe that the Constitution should be interpreted only as the Framers intended. Judicial restraintists do not believe that the courts should be policy makers but instead should make only purely legal decisions such as the courts in the United Kingdom do. Restraintists do not often exercise their power of judicial review, thus deferring to the decisions of the elected branches of government.

Judicial review is the power of the courts to determine the constitutionality of the actions of other political actors such as Congress, the president, the bureaucracy, or the states.

Jurisdiction means the power or authority of a court to hear a certain type of case. Jurisdiction can be vertical, meaning that a lower court must decide a case before a higher court can review that decision. Jurisdiction can also be horizontal, meaning that some courts can only hear cases regarding certain subject matters.

A **jurisprudential regime** is a key precedent or set of related precedents affecting how the Supreme Court justices arrive at decisions in a particular legal area.

A **jury** usually consists of twelve lay people. In most criminal cases it must make a unanimous decision.

Jury instructions are given by the judge in a trial in order to help the jury in their deliberations. These instructions help the jurors understand the legal issues in the case. Jury instructions are often suggested by the lawyers on each side, or there may be boilerplate instructions used repeatedly in a specific jurisdiction.

Jury nullification refers to when juries refuse to convict a criminal defendant because they feel that the law in question is unjust or because they feel that it would be unjust to enforce the law in the specific circumstances of the case.

The **jury pool** is the broad group from which potential jurors will be chosen.

Juvenile courts are special courts designed to handle issues of juvenile delinquency and neglect.

A **juvenile offense** is a criminal action that leads to a finding of juvenile delinquency in a juvenile court. The offense may or may not be a crime for adults.

Large law firms are usually defined as ones that employ at least fifty lawyers. Some boutique law firms that specialize in particular areas of the law may be quite small but function in ways similar to large law firms.

Law can be defined as the principles and regulations established by a government or other authority and applicable to a people, whether by legislation or by custom, enforced by judicial decision. Laws are rules that are enforced and sanctioned by the authority of government.

Law clerks at the U.S. Supreme Court work for a specific justice for one year and are recent law school graduates who finished at or near the top of their law school classes at some of the most prestigious law schools in the country. They have usually spent a year clerking for a U.S. court of appeals judge before coming to the Supreme Court.

The **legal model** of judicial decision making assumes that judges make their decisions purely on the basis of legal analysis and legal reasoning.

Legal realism is a philosophy that claims that judges have a great deal of discretion in their decision making and that political factors do influence how a judge rules in a case. A famous statement of the legal realists is that "the law is what the judges say it is."

The **Legal Services Corporation**, established as part of the Great Society and War on Poverty programs enacted during Lyndon Johnson's presidency in the 1960s, hires government-sponsored lawyers to help serve the poor in civil proceedings.

Limited jurisdiction courts can only hear cases regarding certain prescribed subject matters.

Litigation means appearing in court during a trial.

Litigators are lawyers who actually appear in court.

The **living Constitution theory** means that the Constitution is a living and changing document that judges should interpret and reinterpret with a modern eye. Thus, constitutional interpretation must evolve as the society evolves.

The **majority opinion** of an appellate court reflects the majority outcome and the majority reasoning among the judges. The majority opinion states who wins and who loses, but its reasoning becomes the precedent from the case.

A **mandatory docket** means that an appellate court must hear every appeal filed with it.

Mandatory sentences are an approach to criminal sentencing in which the legislature mandates a specific sentence or a mandatory minimum sentence for someone convicted of a specific crime.

Mediation is a form of alternative dispute resolution. The parties to the dispute agree to have a neutral third party help them find a negotiated solution to the problem. The mediator hears both sides of the conflict and then suggests a compromise solution.

Medical examinations may be required during the discovery phase of a trial, meaning that the parties may have to give the other side reports from physicians' examinations of them.

Mens rea is a Latin term, referring to the required criminal intent for a crime.

A **misdemeanor** is a less serious criminal offense that carries a sentence of less than a year in jail.

The **Missouri Plan** is a judicial selection method whereby the governor appoints a merit selection commission to evaluate the qualifications of applicants for vacant judgeships. The commission then forwards three names to the governor for each judicial opening, and the governor chooses one to appoint as judge. After a set number of years, usually seven to ten, the appointed judge must face the voters in a retention election.

A **moot** case, in a legal context, means a case where there is no dispute because the controversy has already been resolved. Thus; the case cannot be heard by the federal courts.

Natural law theories generally hold that there are universal rules and norms that supersede laws created by individuals.

The **new institutionalist model** of judicial decision making explores how institutional cultures, structures, rules, and norms constrain the choices and actions of judges. The new institutionalism thus combines the interests of traditionalist scholars in studying formal institutional rules and structures with the focus of behavioralist scholars on examining the actions of individual political actors.

In **nonpartisan elections,** the party label for the candidates does not appear on the general election ballot for judicial elections. However, in many states candidates for the general election are chosen through partisan conventions or primaries.

Normative research proposes what ought to be, in contrast to empirical studies, which look at what is.

Norms are less formal than laws and are the shared rules of conduct that specify how people ought to think and act.

One-shotters are parties that deal with the legal system quite infrequently. They might be a business or an organization, but they are most likely to be individuals. They usually do not have a regular relationship with a lawyer, and they pursue a short-term litigation strategy.

Oral arguments before appellate courts are designed to clarify the arguments made in the written briefs on the merits.

Ordinances are what local laws are often called.

Originalism is the belief that the Constitution should be interpreted as the Framers intended. It is somewhat similar to an approach that says that the words of the Constitution should be read literally.

Original jurisdiction means that the case originates in appellate courts instead of in a trial court.

Paralegals are individuals without law degrees who do legal research and other work for the lawyers at large law firms.

In **partisan elections**, candidates from both political parties run against each other for election to the bench for fairly short terms of office. The party membership of each candidate appears directly on the ballot.

Patronage in the judicial selection context means that home state U.S. senators can reward loyal supporters by having the president appoint them to the federal bench.

Peremptory challenges are used when lawyers on either side in a case wish to excuse a potential juror without giving a reason.

A **perp walk** is when the police parade an arrested criminal defendant in front of the media, often on the way into the jail or courthouse.

Persuasive precedent means that judges may, but are not required to, borrow the reasoning used by judges on roughly equivalent courts.

The **plaintiff** is the party who files a civil lawsuit.

A **plea bargain** means that a criminal defendant pleads guilty in exchange for an expected lesser sentence for the crime.

Pleadings is the collective term for the complaint and the answer in a civil case.

A **plurality opinion** of an appellate court does not get a majority vote on the court but may become the controlling precedent of the court under certain rare circumstances.

Political questions are cases that the federal courts will not hear because the disputes are better handled by a different branch of government.

Politics is generally the allocation of power and resources in a society. According to one famous political scientist, "Politics is who gets what, when, and how."

Positive law theories often argue that law should reflect the will of a majority in a society.

Precedent is the articulation of legal principles in a historical succession of judicial decisions. In other words, prior judicial decisions are used to help determine future legal cases. Binding precedent can be thought of as precedent in a vertical sense, while persuasive precedent can be considered horizontal precedent.

Preemption of state laws means that under the U.S. Constitution's Supremacy Clause the federal law preempts enforcement of any contrary state laws.

A **preliminary hearing** as part of the criminal justice process allows the judge to make sure that the police have not arrested the wrong person.

Preponderance of the evidence is the normal burden of proof in a civil case and means that the plaintiff must prove the case by tipping the scales of justice in one direction.

Presidential executive orders direct executive branch agencies in the permanent federal bureaucracy to do certain things or to refrain from doing certain things.

Principal agent theory states that the lower courts should act as the agents of the higher courts and follow the precedents of their superiors.

Probate law means the rules regarding how property passes to another after a person's death.

Pro bono means that lawyers provide their services for free or at reduced rates to certain low-income clients.

Production of documents is part of the discovery phase of a trial and means that each side's lawyers have the right to review relevant documents in the case.

A **profession** is an occupation with (1) specific requirements for formal training and learning, (2) admission to practice by licensing, and (3) a unique code of ethics and a system to discipline its members for violation of the ethical codes.

Property law cases involve real property or personal property issues.

The **prosecutor** is the lawyer in a criminal court case who represents the interests of the society and argues against the defendant.

A **prosecutor sentence bargain** is a type of plea bargain in a criminal case where the prosecutor agrees to recommend a reduced sentence to the judge in exchange for a guilty plea from the defendant.

Public corporations are government-operated enterprises that could be in the private sector.

Public defenders are government-paid criminal defense attorneys for the poor.

Punitive damages are remedies in a civil lawsuit that are paid to the successful plaintiff and are intended to modify the behavior of the defendant and all potential future defendants.

Questions of fact are the main focus of trial courts. If there is a jury present, the jury's sole responsibility is to determine questions of fact. When focusing on questions of fact, trial courts are only concerned about the specific case before them.

Questions of law are the focus of appellate courts. These are issues that will arise in future cases. The court's answer to a question of law, and especially the reasoning for that answer, is what is known as precedent.

Racial or ethnic profiling means that the police will target or stop an individual based primarily on his or her race or ethnicity rather than because of any individualized suspicion.

Rainmaking means bringing new business into law firms.

Rational choice institutionalism is a model of judicial decision making that has its roots in economics and formal modeling analysis. In rational choice models, the political actors are assumed to be acting rationally and institutions are assumed to be seeking the most efficient decision-making processes.

A **recess appointment** is when the president makes a temporary appointment to a federal agency or to the federal courts when the Senate is not in formal session.

Recusal occurs when a judge disqualifies himself or herself from a case if there might be a perception that the judge could not be impartial.

Regime politics theory is the idea that the Supreme Court is a willing partner in the governing coalition, including the president and Congress, that controls politics and policy.

Regulations are the decisions of bureaucratic agencies that have the force of law and fill in the details of federal statutes. Regulations are also known as *agency rules*.

Rehabilitation is a goal of criminal sentencing and means changing the individual so that he or she can become a useful member of society when punishment ends.

Remedies are what a plaintiff in a civil suit is asking the court to provide.

"Rent-a-judge" is a form of alternative dispute resolution in which lawyers or former judges agree to hear both sides and then suggest a decision based on the law.

A **repeat player** has already had a great deal of litigation experience and anticipates having further repeated contact with the courts. Repeat players may be corporations, governmental organizations, or interest groups.

Restitution is a remedy in a civil lawsuit and means that the plaintiff is made whole.

Retribution is a goal of criminal sentencing and focuses on a form of societal revenge, where the convicted criminal defendant gets the punishment the members of the society feel is appropriate.

Ripe refers to a case filed at an appropriate time. A case that is not ripe is one that has been filed too early.

Role theory is the idea that an individual may make very different decisions as a judge than in other roles, such as legislator or president.

Rules or regulations mean the whole or part of an agency statement of general or particular applicability and future effect designed to implement, interpret, or proscribe law or policy.

Salient is the term used by political scientists to describe issues that are widely known by the public and reported on by the media.

A **search warrant** is issued by a judge to the police when the judge is convinced there is probable cause to believe that a crime has been committed.

Senatorial courtesy means that U.S. senators must approve the nomination for any federal judicial nominees from their state.

A **senior judge** is someone who is technically retired from the bench but who continues to hear cases, although with a reduced caseload. The seat held by a senior judge is technically vacant, and the president can nominate someone to fill this seat on the bench.

Separation of powers means that governmental power is divided into distinct and separate functions, known as the executive, legislative, and judicial branches of government. Under the traditional notion of separation of powers, each branch of government has its own distinct job to do.

Service of process means that the plaintiff in a civil lawsuit must notify the defendant of the lawsuit and give the defendant a copy of the complaint according to the local court rules.

Sins of commission mean that the defendant has committed a prohibited criminal act.

Sins of omission mean that the defendant has not done something that is required by law.

Small group theory holds that group variables influence a judge to behave differently than he or she would alone.

The **social leader** makes sure that everyone in a group remains happy in their job and maintains good relationships with the others in the group.

Sociological institutionalism is a model of judicial decision making that has its roots in sociology, anthropology, and cultural studies. It stresses the idea of institutional cultures and norms.

Sociological theories of law argue that law represents a reflection of the values, mores, and culture of the society that produces it.

The **Socratic method** as used in U.S. law schools means that the professor calls on a student without prior warning and asks the student about the facts of the case and the reasoning behind the court's ruling. The professor then continues to ask hypothetical questions regarding the application of the court's reasoning, often taking the student to logical extremes.

The **solicitor general** is the lawyer for the federal executive branch in cases before the Supreme Court of the United States. The Office of the Solicitor General must also approve all appeals of any cases involving the federal government.

Standing means that the person bringing the lawsuit is the right party in the case and has actual harm, as the courts have defined the case and controversy requirement of Article III of the Constitution.

Stare decisis is a Latin term meaning "let the ruling stand." It is often used as a synonym for *precedent*.

Statutory interpretation cases occur when courts interpret state or federal statutes and no constitutional issues are presented in the case. The courts clear up any ambiguities in the statute. These decisions are fairly easy for legislatures to overturn by merely enacting a new statute.

Strategic models of judicial decision making assume that judges are both legal actors and ideological actors who act within the institutional constraints of the judiciary but also strategically anticipate the reactions of others in their decision-making processes.

Summer associates are law students who work for large law firms over the summer months.

The **Supremacy Clause** in the U.S. Constitution makes the federal sources of law superior to the state sources of law.

The **task leader** is the person in a group who makes sure the group gets its work done.

Thinking like a lawyer means speaking, writing, and reading like a lawyer or a judge, that is, learning legal reasoning and analysis, and developing a distinct legal professional identity.

"Three strikes and you're out" laws are a form of mandatory criminal sentence that generally call for life sentences without parole for people convicted of three violent felonies or perhaps just three felonies of any type.

Torts are civil wrongs where a person's behavior has unfairly caused someone else to suffer loss or harm.

Tort reform refers to efforts to make it more difficult for plaintiffs to win money damage awards in civil lawsuits or perhaps even to prevent them from filing suit in the first place.

Traditionalist scholars in political science are most interested in examining the formal structures and rules that are the foundation of political and governmental institutions.

Treaties are agreements between nations that are negotiated by the president and ratified by a two-thirds vote of the U.S. Senate.

Trial courts are the courts of first instance where cases and litigants enter the court system. American trials are public events, open to the press and to the general public. In the United States, trial courts in both the federal and state systems usually use a single judge to hear a case.

A **trial de novo** means that the appeals court in a foreign country starts over from scratch instead of adopting the facts found at trial, as American appellate courts do.

The term **two hemispheres of the law** refers to the fact that the work of lawyers in large law firms is quite different from the work of lawyers in smaller firms. The two hemispheres are divided by the wealth of the clients, the income of the lawyers, and the intellectual difficulty of the lawyers' work.

A **unitary system** is where all power is centralized in the national government. Local or regional governments have almost no power in a unitary system.

The **United States Sentencing Commission** recommends federal sentencing guidelines to Congress, which must then enact these suggestions into law.

Venue means the geographical area over which the court has the authority or jurisdiction to hear cases.

The **verdict** in a case is the decision about what facts drive the legal outcome for the dispute. The verdict announces who wins and who loses.

Voir dire is when the lawyers on both sides of a case and the judge get to question potential jurors individually to determine if there is any reason why they should not be allowed to serve on the jury.

Voter roll-off is a phenomenon in which voters vote in some races on a ballot but do not vote in others on the same ballot. This is especially a problem in low-information judicial elections.

A petition for a **writ of certiorari** is the formal written request for the U.S. Supreme Court to hear the case.

NOTES

Chapter 1: Functions of Courts,
Basics of Legal Analysis, and Sources of Law

1. See, e.g., C. Neal Tate and Torbjorn Vallinder, eds., *The Global Expansion of Judicial Power* (New York: New York University Press, 1995).

2. Robert A. Kagan, "American Courts and the Policy Dialogue: The Role of Adversarial Legalism," in Mark C. Miller and Jeb Barnes, eds., *Making Policy, Making Law: An Interbranch Perspective* (Washington, DC: Georgetown University Press, 2004), 24.

3. Martin Shapiro and Alec Stone, "The New Constitutional Politics of Europe," *Comparative Political Studies* 26 (1994): 397–420.

4. Martin Shapiro, "The United States," in C. Neal Tate and Torbjorn Vallinder, eds., *The Global Expansion of Judicial Power* (New York: New York University Press, 1995), 43.

5. Gillian K. Hadfield and Barry R. Weingast, "Law Without the State: Legal Attributes and the Coordination of Decentralized Collective Punishment," *Journal of Law and Courts* 1 (2013): 3–34.

6. Sheryl L. Grna, Jane C. Ollenburger, and Mark Nicholas, *The Social Context of Law,* 2nd ed. (Upper Saddle River, NJ: Prentice Hall, 2002), 14.

7. Elizabeth Mertz, *The Language of Law School: Learning to Think like a Lawyer* (New York: Oxford University Press, 2007), 3.

8. Lief H. Carter and Thomas F. Burke, *Reason in Law*, 8th ed. (New York: Longman, 2010), 8.

9. David B. Brinkerhoff, Lynn K. White, and Suzanne Trager Ortega, *Essentials of Sociology,* 3rd ed. (Minneapolis: West Publishing, 1995), 39.

10. Sanford Levinson, "Foreword," in Lief H. Carter and Thomas F. Burke, eds., *Reason in Law*, 8th ed. (New York: Longman, 2010), viii.

11. Harold D. Lasswell, *Politics: Who Gets What, When, How* (Ann Arbor: University of Michigan Press, 1936).

12. David Easton, *The Political System: An Inquiry into the State of Political Science* (New York: Knopf, 1953), 126.

13. Keith E. Whittington, R. Daniel Kelemen, and Gregory A. Caldeira, "The Study of Law and Politics," in Keith E. Whittington, R. Daniel Kelemen, and Gregory A. Caldeira, eds., *The Oxford Handbook of Law and Politics* (New York: Oxford University Press, 2008), 3.

14. Ibid., 9.

15. Walter F. Murphy, C. Herman Pritchett, Lee Epstein, and Jack Knight, *Courts, Judges, and Politics: An Introduction to the Judicial Process,* 6th ed. (New York: McGraw-Hill, 2005), 3.

16. Herbert Jacob, "Introduction," in Herbert Jacob, Erhard Blankenburg, Herbert M. Kritzer, Doris Marie Provine, and Joseph Sanders, eds., *Courts, Law, and Politics in a Comparative Perspective* (New Haven: Yale University Press, 1996), 1.

17. Donald P. Kommers, "American Courts and Democracy: A Comparative Perspective," in Kermit L. Hall and Kevin T. McGuire, eds., *The Judicial Branch* (New York: Oxford University Press, 2005), 200–201.

18. Twenty-five of the fifty-two signers of the Declaration of Independence were lawyers, as were thirty-one of the fifty-five members of the Continental Congress. Esther Lucile Brown, *Lawyers, Law Schools, and the Public Service* (New York: Russell Sage Foundation, 1948), 17.

19. Mark C. Miller, *The High Priests of American Politics: The Role of Lawyers in American Political Institutions* (Knoxville: University of Tennessee Press, 1995).

20. Sandra Day O'Connor, "Foreword," in Norman Gross, ed., *America's Lawyer-Presidents: From Law Office to Oval Office* (Evanston, IL: Northwestern University Press, 2004), ix.

21. Norman Gross, "Introduction," in Norman Gross, ed., *America's Lawyer-Presidents: From Law Office to Oval Office* (Evanston, IL: Northwestern University Press, 2004), xv.

22. See Robert A. Kagan, *Adversarial Legalism: The American Way of Law* (Cambridge, MA: Harvard University Press, 2001).

23. Alexis de Tocqueville, *Democracy in America*, trans. George Lawrence (New York: Harper and Row, 1966), 99.

24. Frederick Schauer, *Thinking Like a Lawyer: A New Introduction to Legal Reasoning* (Cambridge, MA: Harvard University Press, 2009), 103–106.

25. H. Patrick Glenn, *Legal Traditions of the World* (New York: Oxford University Press, 2000).

26. Tom Ginsburg, *Judicial Review in New Democracies: Constitutional Courts in Asian Cases* (Cambridge: Cambridge University Press, 2003).

27. Murphy et al., *Courts, Judges, and Politics*, 7.

28. Schauer, *Thinking Like a Lawyer*, 107.

29. Murphy et al., *Courts, Judges, and Politics*, 5.

30. Ibid., 7.

31. See, e.g., James V. Calvi and Susan Coleman, *American Law and Legal Systems*, 7th ed. (Boston: Longman, 2012), 6–7.

32. Richard A. Posner, *How Judges Think* (Cambridge, MA: Harvard University Press, 2008), 232.

33. See, e.g., Laurence Tribe, "Clarence Thomas and 'Natural Law,'" *New York Times,* July 15, 1991.

34. Calvi and Coleman, *American Law and Legal Systems,* 7.

35. Graham G. Dodds, *Take Up Your Pen: Unilateral Presidential Directives in American Politics* (Philadelphia: University of Pennsylvania Press, 2013).

36. Lyn Ragsdale, *Presidential Politics* (Boston: Houghton Mifflin, 1993), 74–75.

37. Carter and Burke, *Reason in Law.*

38. Lawrence Baum, "The Future of the Judicial Branch: Courts and Democracy in the Twenty-First Century," in Kermit L. Hall and Kevin T. McGuire, eds., *The Judicial Branch* (New York: Oxford University Press, 2005), 517.

39. C. Herman Pritchett, "The Development of Judicial Research," in Joel Grossman and Joseph Tanenhaus, eds., *Frontiers of Judicial Research* (New York: Wiley, 1969), 42.

40. Quoted in Barbara A. Perry, *The Priestly Tribe: The Supreme Court's Image in the American Mind* (Westport, CT: Praeger, 1999), 48.

41. T. R. Van Geel, *Understanding Supreme Court Opinions,* 6th ed. (New York: Pearson Longman, 2009), 48.

42. William Haltom, *Reporting on the Courts: How the Mass Media Cover Judicial Actions* (Chicago: Nelson-Hall, 1998), 30.

43. Mertz, *The Language of Law School,* 4.

44. Schauer, *Thinking Like a Lawyer,* 13.

45. William M. Sullivan, Anne Colby, Judith Welch Wegner, Lloyd Bond, and Lee S. Shulman, *Educating Lawyers: Preparation for the Profession of Law* (San Francisco: Wiley, 2007).

46. Stephen G. Breyer, "Judicial Independence in the United States," *St. Louis University Law Review* 40 (1996): 989–996.

47. Gregory A. Caldeira and James L. Gibson, "The Etiology of Public Support for the Supreme Court," *American Journal of Political Science* 36 (1992): 635–664, at 659.

48. James L. Gibson and Gregory A. Caldeira, *Citizens, Courts, and Confirmations: Positivity Theory and the Judgments of the American People* (Princeton, NJ: Princeton University Press, 2009), 122.

49. Kommers, "American Courts and Democracy," 200–201.

50. Tate and Vallinder, eds., *The Global Expansion of Judicial Power.*

51. Herbert M. Kritzer, "Courts, Justice, and Politics in England," in Herbert Jacob, Erhard Blankenburg, Herbert M. Kritzer, Doris Marie Provine, and Joseph Sanders, eds., *Courts, Law, and Politics in a Comparative Perspective* (New Haven, CT: Yale University Press, 1996), 82.

52. Peter H. Russell and David M. O'Brien, eds., *Judicial Independence in the Age of Democracy: Critical Perspectives from Around the World* (Charlottesville: University Press of Virginia, 2001).

53. Stephen Breyer, *Making Democracy Work: A Judge's View* (New York: Alfred A. Knopf, 2010), 3.

54. Erhard Blankenburg, "Changes in Political Regimes and Continuity of the Rule of Law in Germany," in Herbert Jacob, Erhard Blankenburg, Herbert M. Kritzer, Doris Marie Provine, and Joseph Sanders, eds., *Courts, Law, and Politics in a Comparative Perspective* (New Haven: Yale University Press, 1996).

55. See Mark Tushnet, *Weak Courts, Strong Rights: Judicial Review and Social Welfare Rights in Comparative Constitutional Law* (Princeton, NJ: Princeton University Press, 2009).

56. Lawrence A. Cunningham, *Contracts in the Real World: Stories of Popular Contracts and Why They Matter* (New York: Cambridge University Press, 2012), 5.

57. See Charles R. Epp, *Making Rights Real: Activists, Bureaucrats, and the Creation of the Legalistic State* (Chicago: University of Chicago Press, 2009).

58. Jeb Barnes, *Dust-up: Asbestos Litigation and the Failure of Commonsense Policy Reform* (Washington, DC: Georgetown University Press, 2011), 12–13.

59. Martha A. Derthick, *Up in Smoke: From Legislation to Litigation in Tobacco Politics,* 2nd ed. (Washington, DC: CQ Press, 2005).

60. Lynn Mather, "The Fired Football Coach (Or, How Trial Courts Make Policy)," in Lee Epstein, ed., *Contemplating Courts* (Washington, DC: CQ Press, 1995).

61. Jeb Barnes, "Adversarial Legalism, the Rise of Judicial Policymaking, and the Separation-of-Powers Doctrine," in Mark C. Miller and Jeb Barnes, eds., *Making Policy, Making Law: An Interbranch Perspective* (Washington, DC: Georgetown University Press, 2004).

62. Koen Lenerts, "Constitutionalism and the Many Faces of Federalism," *American Journal of Comparative Law* 38 (1990): 205–264.

63. Baum, "The Future of the Judicial Branch," 517.

64. Barnes, "Adversarial Legalism."

65. Richard E. Neustadt, *Presidential Power: The Politics of Leadership from FDR to Carter* (New York: Wiley, 1980), 26.

66. Daniel Halberstam, "Comparative Federalism and the Role of the Judiciary," in Keith E. Whittington, R. Daniel Kelemen, and Gregory A. Caldeira, eds., *The Oxford Handbook of Law and Politics* (New York: Oxford University Press, 2008).

67. Robert A. Katzmann, *Courts and Congress* (Washington, DC: Brookings Institution Press, 1997), 1.

68. Tocqueville, *Democracy in America,* 103–104.

69. Antonin Scalia, *A Matter of Interpretation: Federal Courts and the Law* (Princeton, NJ: Princeton University Press, 1997).

70. Robert W. Bennett and Lawrence B. Solum, *Constitutional Originalism: A Debate* (Ithaca, NY: Cornell University Press, 2011), vii.

71. Edwin Meese III, speech before the D.C. Chapter of the Federalist Society Lawyers Division, November 15, 1985, reprinted in Steven G. Calabresi, ed., *Originalism: A Quarter-Century of Debate* (Washington, DC: Regnery, 2007), 74.

72. Ibid., 79.

73. Steven G. Calabresi, "A Critical Introduction to the Originalism Debate," in Steven G. Calabresi, ed., *Originalism: A Quarter-Century of Debate* (Washington, DC: Regnery, 2007), 4.

74. Antonin Scalia, "Foreword," in Steven G. Calabresi, ed., *Originalism: A Quarter-Century of Debate* (Washington, DC: Regnery, 2007), 43.

75. Jeffrey Toobin, "Heavyweight: How Ruth Bader Ginsburg Has Moved the Supreme Court," *New Yorker,* March 8, 2013, 41.

76. Antonin Scalia, remarks at Woodrow Wilson International Center for Scholars, March 14, 2005, excerpted in George McKenna and Stanley Feingold, eds., *Taking Sides: Clashing Views on Political Issues*, 18th ed. (New York: McGraw-Hill, 2013), 93.

77. Antonin Scalia and Amy Gutmann, *A Matter of Interpretation: Federal Courts and the Law* (Princeton, NJ: Princeton University Press, 1998).

78. Scalia, remarks at Woodrow Wilson Center, 95.

79. Antonin Scalia, William Howard Taft Constitutional Law Lecture, University of Cincinnati, September 16, 1988, reprinted in David M. O'Brien, ed., *Judges on Judging: Views from the Bench,* 3rd ed. (Washington, DC: CQ Press, 2009), 203.

80. William J. Brennan Jr., speech to the Text and Teaching Symposium at Georgetown University, October 12, 1985, reprinted in Steven G. Calabresi, ed., *Originalism: A Quarter-Century of Debate* (Washington, DC: Regnery, 2007), 58–61.

81. Thurgood Marshall, remarks at the annual seminar of the San Francisco Patent and Trademark Law Association, May 16, 1987, reprinted in David M. O'Brien, ed., *Judges on Judging: Views from the Bench,* 3rd ed. (Washington, DC: CQ Press, 2009), 207–208.

82. *Trop v. Dulles*, 356 U.S. 86 at 101 (1958).

83. *Atkins v. Virginia,* 536 U.S. 304 at 321 (2002).

84. *Roper v. Simmons,* 543 U.S. 551 at 561 (2005).

85. *Roper v. Simmons,* 543 U.S. 551 at 587 (2005) (Stevens, J., concurring).

86. Breyer, *Making Democracy Work*, 75.

87. Ibid., 80.

88. Richard A. Posner, *How Judges Think* (Cambridge, MA: Harvard University Press, 2008), 230.

89. Kermit Roosevelt III, *The Myth of Judicial Activism: Making Sense of Supreme Court Decisions* (New Haven: Yale University Press, 2008), 16.

90. Brian Z. Tamanaha, "How an Instrumental View of Law Corrodes the Rule of Law," *DePaul Law Review* 56 (2007): 469–505, at 490.

91. See, e.g., Frank B. Cross, *The Failed Promise of Originalism* (Stanford, CA: Stanford University Press, 2013).

92. See, e.g., Glenn A. Phelps and John B. Gates, "The Myth of Jurisprudence: Interpretive Theory in the Constitutional Opinions of Justices Rehnquist and Brennan," *Santa Clara Law Review* 31 (1991): 567–596; John B. Gates and Glenn A. Phelps, "Intentionalism in Constitutional Opinions," *Political Research Quarterly* 49 (1996): 245–261.

93. Lawrence Baum, *The Puzzle of Judicial Behavior* (Ann Arbor: University of Michigan Press, 1997), 75.

94. Roosevelt, *The Myth of Judicial Activism*.

95. Stefanie A. Lindquist and Frank B. Cross, *Measuring Judicial Activism* (New York: Oxford University Press, 2009), 1.

96. William G. Ross, *A Muted Fury: Populists, Progressives, and Labor Unions Confront the Courts, 1890–1937* (Princeton, NJ: Princeton University Press, 1994).

97. Lucas A. Powe Jr., *The Warren Court and American Politics* (Cambridge, MA: Belknap Press, 2000).

98. See, e.g., Herman Schwartz, ed., *The Rehnquist Court: Judicial Activism on the Right* (New York: Hill and Wang, 2002).

99. Thomas Keck, *The Most Activist Supreme Court in History: The Road to Modern Judicial Conservatism* (Chicago: University of Chicago Press, 2004).

100. David G. Savage, "GOP Lawyers See Tilt to Activist High Court," *Los Angeles Times,* April 1, 2012.

101. Adam Cohen, "Psst . . . Justice Scalia . . . You Know, You're an Activist Judge Too," *New York Times,* April 19, 2005.

102. Theda Skocpol and Vanessa Williamson, *The Tea Party and the Remaking of Republican Conservatism* (New York: Oxford University Press, 2012), 48.

103. Ibid., 52.

104. Roy B. Flemming, B. Dan Wood, and John Bohte, "Attention to Issues in a System of Separated Powers: The Macrodynamics of American Policy Agendas," *Journal of Politics* 61 (1999): 76–108, at 104.

105. Jonathan D. Casper, "The Supreme Court and National Policy Making," *American Political Science Review* 70 (1976): 50–63, at 62.

106. Ruth Bader Ginsburg, "Communicating and Commenting on the Court's Work," *Georgetown Law Journal* 83 (1995): 2119–2129, at 2125.

107. Robert H. Jackson, *The Supreme Court in the American System of Government* (Cambridge, MA: Harvard University Press, 1955), 2.

108. Quoted in Mark C. Miller, *The View of the Courts from the Hill: Interactions Between Congress and the Federal Judiciary* (Charlottesville: University of Virginia Press, 2009), 8.

Chapter 2: Structure of Courts in the United States

1. Lawrence Baum, *American Courts: Process and Policy,* 7th ed. (Boston: Wadsworth, 2013), 29–30.

2. Thomas G. Walker, *Eligible for Execution: The Story of the Daryl Atkins Case* (Washington, DC: CQ Press, 2008).

3. Jeffrey Abramson, *We, the Jury: The Jury System and the Ideal of Democracy* (Cambridge, MA: Harvard University Press, 2000), 90–104.

4. Steven Shavell, "The Appeals Process as a Means of Error Correction," *Journal of Legal Studies* 24 (1995): 379–426.

5. Nicole L. Waters, Shauna M. Strickland, and Brian J. Ostrom, "State Trial Courts: Achieving Justice in Civil Litigation," in Mark C. Miller, ed., *Exploring Judicial Politics* (New York: Oxford University Press, 2009), 85.

6. See, e.g., Joseph A. Ranney, "'This New and Beautiful Organism': The Evolution of American Federalism in Three State Supreme Courts," *Marquette Law Review* 87 (2003): 253–296.

7. Oliver Wendell Holmes, *Collected Legal Papers* (New York: Harcourt, Brace, 1920), 295–296.

8. Wendy L. Martinek, "Appellate Workhorses of the Federal Judiciary: The U.S. Court of Appeals," in Mark C. Miller, ed., *Exploring Judicial Politics* (New York: Oxford University Press, 2009), 126–127.

9. Baum, *American Courts,* 260.

10. Anna Law, *The Immigration Battle in American Courts* (New York: Cambridge University Press, 2010).

11. Deborah J. Barrow and Thomas G. Walker, *A Court Divided: The Fifth Circuit Courts of Appeals and the Politics of Judicial Reform* (New Haven, CT: Yale University Press, 1988).

12. David E. Klein, *Making Law in the United States Courts of Appeals* (New York: Cambridge University Press, 2002).

13. Virginia A. Hettinger and Stefanie A. Lindquist, "Decision Making in the U.S. Courts of Appeals: The Determinants of Reversal on Appeal," in Kevin T. McGuire, ed., *New Directions in Judicial Politics* (New York: Routledge, 2012).

14. Virginia A. Hettinger, Stefanie A. Lindquist, and Wendy L. Martinek, *Judging on a Collegial Court: Influences on Federal Appellate Decision Making* (Charlottesville: University of Virginia Press, 2006).

15. Micheal W. Giles, Thomas G. Walker, and Christopher Zorn, "Setting a Judicial Agenda: The Decision to Grant En Banc Review in the U.S. Courts of Appeals," *Journal of Politics* 68 (2006): 852–866, at 853.

16. Paul D. Carrington, Daniel J. Meador, and Maurice Rosenberg, *Justice on Appeal* (St. Paul: West Publishing, 1976).

17. Martinek, "Appellate Workhorses of the Federal Judiciary," 127.

18. See, e.g., Jeffrey A. Segal, Donald R. Songer, and Charles M. Cameron, "Decision Making on the U.S. Courts of Appeals," in Lee Epstein, ed., *Contemplating Courts* (Washington, DC: CQ Press, 1995); Donald R. Songer, Reginald S. Sheehan, and Susan B. Haire, *Continuity and Change on the United States Courts of Appeals* (Ann Arbor: University of Michigan Press, 2000); Law, *The Immigration Battle in American Courts.*

19. See, e.g., C. Herman Pritchett, *The Roosevelt Court: A Study in Judicial Politics and Values, 1937–1947* (New York: Macmillan, 1948).

20. Barbara Perry, *The Priestly Tribe: The Supreme Court's Image in the American Mind* (Westport, CT: Praeger, 1999).

21. Lawrence Baum, *The Supreme Court,* 10th ed. (Washington, DC: CQ Press, 2010).

22. Frank Cross, "Judicial Independence," in Keith E. Whittington, R. Daniel Kelemen, and Gregory A. Caldeira, eds., *The Oxford Handbook of Law and Politics* (New York: Oxford University Press, 2008), 558.

23. Richard L. Pacelle Jr., "The Dynamics and Determinants of Agenda Change in the Rehnquist Court," in Lee Epstein, ed., *Contemplating Courts* (Washington, DC: CQ Press, 1995).

24. Lawrence Baum, *Specializing the Courts* (Chicago: University of Chicago Press, 2011), 194.

25. Ibid., 149–150.

26. Ibid., 82.

27. See ibid., 68–71; Jonathan Lurie, *Pursuing Military Justice: The History of the United States Court of Appeals for the Armed Forces, 1951–1980* (Princeton, NJ: Princeton University Press, 1998).

28. Waters, Strickland, and Ostrom, "State Trial Courts," 83–84.

29. G. Alan Tarr, *Without Fear or Favor: Judicial Independence and Judicial Accountability in the States* (Stanford, CA: Stanford University Press, 2012), 79.

30. See, e.g., Baum, *Specializing the Courts.*

31. Baum, *American Courts,* 38.

32. Robert W. Tobin, *Creating the Judicial Branch: The Unfinished Reform* (Williamsburg, VA: National Center for State Courts, 1999).

33. Baum, *American Courts,* 38.

34. Jack Sullivan, "Reigning Supreme: Clerk-Magistrates, with Lifetime Tenure and No Mandatory Retirement Age, Rule the Roost in Massachusetts Courthouses," *Commonwealth Magazine,* April 12, 2011.

35. Andrea Estes and Thomas Farragher, "Ex-Probation Chief, 2 Aides Indicted in Hiring Scandal: Accused of Rigging Selection Process for Job Applicants," *Boston Globe,* February 24, 2012.

36. Christopher P. Manfredi, *The Supreme Court and Juvenile Justice* (Lawrence: University Press of Kansas, 1998), 24.

37. Ibid., 93–94.

38. Steven M. Cox, John J. Conrad, and Jennifer M. Allen, *Juvenile Justice: A Guide to Theory and Practice* (New York: McGraw-Hill, 2003), 102–103.

39. Waters, Strickland, and Ostrom, "State Trial Courts," 86.

40. Ibid., 85.

41. *Hortonville Joint School District No. 1. v. Hortonville Education Association,* 426 U.S. 482, 488 (1976).

42. Tarr, *Without Fear or Favor,* 106.

43. *Murdock v. City of Memphis,* 20 Wall. 590 (1875).

44. Tarr, *Without Fear or Favor,* 107.

45. See, e.g., Paul Brace and Kellie Sims Butler, "New Perspectives for the Comparative Study of the Judiciary: The State Supreme Court Project," *Justice System Journal* 22 (2001): 243–262.

46. Neal Devins and Nicole Mansker, "Public Opinion and State Supreme Courts," *University of Pennsylvania Journal of Constitutional Law* 13 (2010): 455–509, at 456–457.

47. Louis Fisher and Katt J. Harringer, *American Constitutional Law,* 9th ed. (Durham, NC: Carolina Academic Press, 2011), 21.

48. Tarr, *Without Fear or Favor,* 80.

49. Neal Devins, "How State Supreme Courts Take Consequences into Account: Toward a State-Centered Understanding of State Constitutionalism," *Stanford Law Review* 62 (2010): 1629–1653, at 1636.

50. Helen Hershkoff, "State Courts and the 'Passive Virtues': Rethinking the Judicial-Function," *Harvard Law Review* 114 (2001): 1833–1941.

51. Anthony DePalma, "Canadian Court Rules Quebec Cannot Secede on Its Own," *New York Times,* August 21, 1998.

52. Tarr, *Without Fear or Favor,* 24.

53. Mel A. Topf, *A Doubtful and Perilous Experiment: Advisory Opinions, State Constitutions, and Judicial Supremacy* (New York: Oxford University Press, 2011).

Chapter 3: Judicial Selection

1. Bruce Peabody, "Introduction," in Bruce Peabody, ed., *The Politics of Judicial Independence: Courts, Politics, and the Public* (Baltimore: Johns Hopkins University Press, 2011), 13.

2. See William H. Rehnquist, *Grand Inquests: The Historic Impeachments of Justice Samuel Chase and President Andrew Johnson* (New York: William Morrow, 1992).

3. Richard E. Ellis, *The Jeffersonian Crisis: Courts and Politics in the Young Republic* (New York: Oxford University Press, 1971), 69–75.

4. Walter Murphy, *Congress and the Court* (Chicago: University of Chicago Press, 1962), 14.

5. Richard L. Pacelle Jr., *The Role of the Supreme Court in American Politics: The Least Dangerous Branch?* (Boulder: Westview Press, 2002), 96.

6. Charles G. Geyh, *When Courts and Congress Collide: The Struggle for Control of America's Judicial System* (Ann Arbor: University of Michigan Press, 2006), 54.

7. See, e.g., Aman L. McLeod, "Differences in State Judicial Selection," in Mark C. Miller, ed., *Exploring Judicial Politics* (New York: Oxford University Press, 2009).

8. Jed Handelsman Shugerman, "The Twist of Long Terms: Judicial Elections, Role Fidelity, and American Tort Law," *Georgetown Law Journal* 98 (2010): 1349–1413.

9. Roy Schotland, "Judicial Campaign Finance Could Work," *National Law Journal,* November 23, 1998, A21.

10. See Amy Steigerwalt, *Battle over the Bench: Senators, Interest Groups, and Lower Court Nominations* (Charlottesville: University of Virginia Press, 2010), 70, 221.

11. Joel B. Grossman, *Lawyers and Judges: The ABA and the Politics of Judicial Selection* (New York: Wiley, 1965).

12. Henry A. Abraham, "Beneficial Advice or Presumptuous Veto? The ABA's Committee on Federal Judiciary Revisited," in *Judicial Selection: Merit, Ideology, and Politics* (Washington, DC: National Legal Center for the Public Interest, 1990).

13. Richard L. Vining Jr., Amy Steigerwalt, and Susan Navarro Smelcer, "Bias and the Bar: Evaluating the ABA Ratings of Federal Judicial Nominees," paper presented at the annual meeting of the Midwest Political Science Association, Chicago, April 2–5, 2009.

14. Steigerwalt, *Battle over the Bench*, 70, 221.

15. Vining, Steigerwalt, and Smelcer, "Bias and the Bar."

16. William G. Ross, "Participation by the Public in the Federal Judicial Selection Process," *Vanderbilt Law Review* 43 (1990): 1–84, at 36–39.

17. Abraham, "Beneficial Advice or Presumptuous Veto?"

18. Robert S. Greenberger and David S. Cloud, "Bush to Weaken ABA Role on Nominees," *Wall Street Journal*, March 19, 2001, B11.

19. Charlie Savage, "Ratings Shrink President's List for Judgeships," *New York Times*, November 22, 2011.

20. Lee Epstein and Jeffrey A. Segal, *Advice and Consent: The Politics of Judicial Appointments* (New York: Oxford University Press, 2005), 88.

21. Steigerwalt, *Battle over the Bench*, 70.

22. Ibid., 98.

23. Paul M. Collins Jr. and Lori A. Ringhand, *Supreme Court Confirmation Hearings and Constitutional Change* (New York: Cambridge University Press, 2013).

24. Steigerwalt, *Battle over the Bench*, 221.

25. Ibid., 73.

26. Sheldon Goldman, *Picking Federal Judges: Lower Court Selection from Roosevelt Through Reagan* (New Haven, CT: Yale University Press, 1997), 10.

27. Brannon P. Denning, "The 'Blue Slip': Enforcing the Norms of the Judicial Confirmation Process," *William and Mary Bill of Rights Journal* 10 (2001): 75–102.

28. Joseph Harris, *The Advice and Consent of the Senate* (Berkeley: University of California Press, 1953).

29. Wendy L. Martinek, "Appellate Workhorses of the Federal Judiciary," in Mark C. Miller, ed., *Exploring Judicial Politics* (New York: Oxford University Press, 2009), 138.

30. Elliot E. Slotnick, "Reforms in Judicial Selection: Will They Affect the Senate's Role?" *Judicature* 64 (1980): 60, 69–73.

31. Steigerwalt, *Battle over the Bench*, 61.

32. Benjamin Wittes, *Confirmation Wars: Preserving Independent Courts in Angry Times* (Lanham, MD: Rowman and Littlefield, 2006), 155–156.

33. Matt Viser, "Senators Can Still Block Nominations Without Filibuster," *Boston Globe*, November 29, 2013.

34. Goldman, *Picking Federal Judges,* 359.

35. Nancy Scherer, *Scoring Points: Politicians, Activists, and the Lower Federal Court Appointment Process* (Stanford, CA: Stanford University Press, 2005), 144–146.

36. Steve Tetreault, "Reid Seeks to Bypass Heller on Federal Judge Nominee," *Las Vegas Review-Journal,* April 25, 2012.

37. Lauren Cohen Bell, *Warring Factions: Interest Groups, Money, and the New Politics of Senate Confirmation* (Columbus: Ohio State University Press, 2002), 102.

38. Steigerwalt, *Battle over the Bench,* 74.

39. Norman J. Ornstein, "Extortion Is Legal in the Senate: It's Called 'the Hold,'" *Roll Call,* July 29, 1999, 1–7.

40. Richard S. Beth and Stanley Bach, *Filibusters and Cloture in the Senate,* CRS Report RI30360 (Washington, DC: Congressional Research Service, 2003).

41. See, e.g., Barbara Sinclair, *The Transformation of the U.S. Senate* (Baltimore: Johns Hopkins University Press, 1989).

42. See, e.g., Sarah A. Binder, *Minority Rights, Majority Rule: Partisanship and the Development of Congress* (New York: Cambridge University Press, 1997).

43. See David Nather, "Race Against the Nuclear Clock," *Congressional Quarterly Weekly Report,* May 30, 2005, 1440–1443.

44. Lisa R. McElroy and John Cannan, "Obama's Second Term and the Federal Courts," *Judicature* 96 (2012): 99–107.

45. Joanna Anderson, "For Second Time, Senate GOP Blocks Halligan Vote," *CQ Weekly Report,* March 11, 2013.

46. Philip Rucker, "Obama Remolds Federal Bench," *Washington Post,* March 4, 2013.

47. "Democracy Returns to the Senate" (editorial), *New York Times,* November 22, 2013.

48. Charlie Savage, "Obama Nominates Two Lawyers for the Federal Appeals Court in Washington," *New York Times,* June 12, 2012.

49. Jennifer Bendery, "Judicial Vacancies Skyrocket During President Obama's First Term," *Huffington Post,* December 2, 2012.

50. Ibid.

51. Matt Viser, "As Obama, Senate Collide, Courts Caught Short," *Boston Globe,* March 10, 2013.

52. Rucker, "Obama Remolds Federal Bench."

53. Bill Mears, "Obama Judicial Nominees Likely to Reignite Controversy," CNN .com, January 4, 2013.

54. Rucker, "Obama Remolds Federal Bench."

55. John Roberts, *2012 Year-End Report on the Federal Judiciary* (Washington, DC: U.S. Supreme Court, 2012).

56. Ibid., 9–10.

57. "Judges Needed for Federal Courts: President Obama and the Senate Must Make Filling the Judiciary a Paramount Priority" (editorial), *New York Times,* December 13, 2012.

58. Quoted in Viser, "As Obama, Senate Collide, Courts Caught Short."

59. Jeffrey Toobin, *The Oath: The Obama White House and the Supreme Court* (New York: Doubleday, 2012), 27–28.

60. Anderson, "For Second Time, Senate GOP Blocks Halligan Vote."

61. Jeremy W. Peters, "Senate Confirms a Judge, but Rancor Remains," *New York Times,* May 23, 2013.

62. Viser, "As Obama, Senate Collide, Courts Caught Short."

63. Ibid.

64. "Advise and Consent" (editorial), *New York Times,* June 5, 2013.

65. "Blocked by GOP, Obama Withdraws Court Nomination," *Boston Globe,* March 23, 2013.

66. Jeremy W. Peters, "Obama Pushes His Choice for Position on Appeals Court," *New York Times,* April 9, 2013.

67. Peters, "Senate Confirms a Judge."

68. Michael D. Shear and Jeremy W. Peters, "Judicial Picks Set the Stage for a Battle in the Senate," *New York Times,* June 4, 2013.

69. Jeremy W. Peters, "Republican Effort to Unpack the Court," *New York Times,* April 11, 2013.

70. Charlie Savage, "Despite Filibuster Limits, a Door Remains Open to Block Judge Nominees," *New York Times,* November 28, 2013.

71. Quoted in John Anthony Maltese, *The Selling of Supreme Court Nominees* (Baltimore: Johns Hopkins University Press, 1995), 121.

72. Slotnick, "Reforms in Judicial Selection."

73. Goldman, *Picking Federal Judges.*

74. C. K. Rowland and Robert A. Carp, *Politics and Judgment in Federal District Courts* (Lawrence: University Press of Kansas, 1996).

75. Nancy Scherer, *Scoring Points: Politicians, Activists, and the Lower Federal Court Appointment Process* (Stanford, CA: Stanford University Press, 2005), 6.

76. Jo Mannies, "Clinton Goes on Attack Here: Bush Blasted on Thomas and Lack of Strategy on Jobs," *St. Louis Post-Dispatch,* August 1, 1992.

77. Scherer, *Scoring Points,* 136–139.

78. Ibid., 149.

79. Ibid., 49.

80. See Neal D. McFeeley, *Appointment of Judges: The Johnson Presidency* (Austin: University of Texas Press, 1987), 26.

81. Harry A. Chernoff, Christopher M. Kelly, and John R. Kroger, "The Politics of Crime," *Harvard Journal on Legislation* 33 (1996): 527–579.

82. Timothy B. Tomasi and Jess A. Velona, "All the President's Men? A Study of Ronald Reagan's Appointments to the U.S. Courts of Appeals," *Columbia Law Review* 87 (1987): 766–793.

83. Maltese, *The Selling of Supreme Court Nominees,* 121–122.

84. Sarah A. Binder and Forrest Maltzman, "Advice and Consent: The Politics of Confirming Federal Judges," in Lawrence C. Dodd and Bruce I. Oppenheimer, eds., *Congress Reconsidered,* 10th ed. (Thousand Oaks, CA: CQ Press, 2013).

85. Michael Avery and Danielle McLaughlin, *The Federalist Society: How Conservatives Took the Law Back from Liberals* (Nashville, TN: Vanderbilt University Press, 2013), 3.

86. Charlie Savage, "Liberal Legal Group Is Following New Administration's Path to Power," *New York Times,* December 10, 2008.

87. Avery and McLaughlin, *The Federalist Society,* 3–4.

88. Alan Neff, *The United States District Judge Nominating Commissions: Their Members, Procedures, and Candidates* (Chicago: American Judicature Society, 1981).

89. McElroy and Cannan, "Obama's Second Term and the Federal Courts."

90. Alliance for Justice, *The State of the Judiciary: Judicial Selection During the Remainder of President Obama's First Term* (Washington, DC: Alliance for Justice, 2012), 9.

91. Charlie Savage, "Obama Lags on Judicial Picks, Limiting His Mark on Courts," *New York Times,* August 17, 2012.

92. Carrie Johnson, "Obama Gets High Marks for Diversifying the Bench," National Public Radio, August 1, 2011.

93. Rucker, "Obama Remolds Federal Bench."

94. McElroy and Cannan, "Obama's Second Term and the Federal Courts," 99.

95. Michael Comiskey, *Seeking Justices: The Judging of Supreme Court Nominees* (Lawrence: University Press of Kansas, 2004), 66–67.

96. Maltese, *The Selling of Supreme Court Nominees,* 72–74.

97. Ibid., 12–19.

98. Kevin J. McMahon, *Nixon's Court: His Challenge to Judicial Liberalism and Its Political Consequences* (Chicago: University of Chicago Press, 2011), 115.

99. Comiskey, *Seeking Justices,* 8.

100. Christopher L. Eisgruber, *The Next Justice: Repairing the Supreme Court Appointments Process* (Princeton, NJ: Princeton University Press, 2007), 127.

101. Linda Greenhouse, *Becoming Justice Blackmun: Harry Blackmun's Supreme Court Journey* (New York: Times Books, 2006).

102. Epstein and Segal, *Advice and Consent,* 85.

103. Maltese, *The Selling of Supreme Court Nominees,* 137–138.

104. Lauren Cohen Bell, "In Their Own Interest: Pressure Groups in the Federal Judicial Selection Process," in Mark C. Miller, ed., *Exploring Judicial Politics* (New York: Oxford University Press, 2009), 36.

105. Steigerwalt, *Battle over the Bench,* 120.

106. Comiskey, *Seeking Justices,* 105.

107. Quoted in Maltese, *The Selling of Supreme Court Nominees,* 8–9.

108. David A. Yalof, "Filling the Bench," in Keith E. Whittington, R. Daniel Kelemen, and Gregory A. Caldeira, eds., *The Oxford Handbook of Law and Politics* (New York: Oxford University Press, 2008), 469.

109. Ed Gillespie, "Judging Obama's Nominee," *Washington Post,* May 20, 2009.

110. James L. Gibson and Gregory A. Caldeira, *Citizens, Courts, and Confirmations: Positivity Theory and the Judgments of the American People* (Princeton, NJ: Princeton University Press, 2009), 63.

111. David Stout, "Alito Is Sworn In as Justice After 58–42 Vote to Confirm Him," *New York Times,* January 31, 2006.

112. Maura Reynolds, "A Stark Division in Vote for Alito," *Los Angeles Times,* February 1, 2006, A2.

113. Lawrence Baum, *American Courts: Process and Policy,* 7th ed. (Boston: Wadsworth, 2013), 98.

114. Lawrence Baum, *The Supreme Court,* 10th ed. (Washington, DC: CQ Press, 2010), 30.

115. Quoted in Joan Biskupic, "Ginsburg: Court Needs Another Woman," *USA Today,* May 5, 2009.

116. Quoted in Matt Sedensky, "Justice Questions Way Court Nominees Are Grilled," Associated Press, May 14, 2010.

117. G. Alan Tarr, *Understanding State Constitutions* (Princeton, NJ: Princeton University Press, 1998), 18–19.

118. Laura Langer and Teena Wilhelm, "State Supreme Courts as Policymakers: Are They Loved?" in Mark C. Miller, ed., *Exploring Judicial Politics* (New York: Oxford University Press, 2009), 112.

119. See, e.g., McLeod, "Differences in State Judicial Selection."

120. Daniel R. Pinello, *The Impact of Judicial-Selection Method on State Supreme Court Policy: Innovation, Reaction, and Atrophy* (Westport, CT: Greenwood Press, 1995), 40.

121. James V. Calvi and Susan Coleman, *American Law and Legal Systems,* 7th ed. (Boston: Longman, 2012), 67.

122. Matthew J. Streb, "Partisan Involvement in Partisan and Nonpartisan Trial Court Elections," in Matthew J. Streb, ed., *Running for Judge: The Rising Political, Financial, and Legal Stakes of Judicial Elections* (New York: New York University Press, 2007), 102.

123. Toobin, *The Oath,* 211.

124. Langer and Wilhelm, "State Supreme Courts as Policymakers," 112.

125. John Felice, John Kilwein, and Elliot Slotnick, "Judicial Reform in Ohio," in Anthony Champagne and Judith Haydel, eds., *Judicial Reform in the States* (Lanham, MD: University Press of America, 1993).

126. McLeod, "Differences in State Judicial Selection," 28–29.

127. Doug McMurdo, "Voters Reject Changing Judge Selection," *Las Vegas Review-Journal,* November 3, 2010.

128. G. Alan Tarr, *Without Fear or Favor: Judicial Independence and Judicial Accountability in the States* (Stanford, CA: Stanford University Press, 2012), 69–70.

129. Toobin, *The Oath,* 212.

130. Chris W. Bonneau and Melinda Gann Hall, *In Defense of Judicial Elections* (New York: Routledge, 2009), 3.

131. Schotland, "Judicial Campaign Finance Could Work."

132. Dan Eggen, "Special-Interest Spending Surges," *Washington Post*, August 16, 2010.

133. See Bonneau and Hall, *In Defense of Judicial Elections*, 1.

134. Gibson and Caldeira, *Citizens, Courts, and Confirmations*, 19.

135. Morgan Smith, "Lawyers Biggest Donors to Judicial Elections," *Texas Tribune*, February 2, 2010.

136. Lawrence Baum and David Klein, "Voter Responses to High-Visibility Judicial Campaigns," in Matthew J. Streb, ed., *Running for Judge: The Rising Political, Financial, and Legal Stakes of Judicial Elections* (New York: New York University Press, 2007), 140.

137. David Pozen, "Are Judicial Elections Democracy-Enhancing?" in Charles Gardner Geyh, *What's Law Got to Do with It? What Judges Do, Why They Do It, and What's at Stake* (Stanford, CA: Stanford University Press, 2011), 271.

138. Keith J. Bybee, *All Judges Are Political, Except When They Are Not* (Stanford, CA: Stanford University Press, 2010), 7.

139. Chris W. Bonneau, "Electoral Verdicts: Incumbent Defeats in State Supreme Courts," *American Politics Research* 33 (2005): 818–841, at 834.

140. Larry Aspin, "Judicial Retention Election Trends 1964–2006," *Judicature* 90 (2007): 208–213, at 210.

141. Paul Brace and Kellie Sims Butler, "New Perspectives for the Comparative Study of the Judiciary: The State Supreme Court Project," *Justice System Journal* 22 (2001): 243–262.

142. David E. Pozen, "The Irony of Judicial Elections," *Columbia Law Review* 108 (2008): 265–330, at 307.

143. Joanna M. Shepherd, "Are Appointed Judges Strategic Too?" *Duke Law Journal* 58 (2009): 1589–1626, at 1602.

144. Richard B. Saphire and Paul Moke, "The Ideologies of Judicial Selection: Empiricism and the Transformation of the Judicial Selection Debate," *University of Toledo Law Review* 39 (2008): 551–590, at 568.

145. Melinda Gann Hall, "On the Cataclysm of Judicial Elections and Other Popular Antidemocratic Myths," in Charles Gardner Geyh, ed., *What's Law Got to Do with It? What Judges Do, Why They Do It, and What's at Stake* (Stanford, CA: Stanford University Press, 2011), 231.

146. Matthew J. Streb, "How Judicial Elections Are like Other Elections and What That Means for the Rule of Law," in Charles Gardner Geyh, *What's Law Got to Do with It? What Judges Do, Why They Do It, and What's at Stake* (Stanford, CA: Stanford University Press, 2011), 199.

147. Todd S. Purdum, "Rose Bird, Once California's Chief Justice, Is Dead at 63," *New York Times*, December 6, 1999.

148. Grant Schulte, "Iowans Dismiss Three Justices," *Des Moines Register,* November 3, 2010.

149. Toobin, *The Oath,* 212–213.

150. "Politics, Principle, and an Attack on the Courts" (editorial), *New York Times,* September 24, 2012.

151. Ryan J. Foley, "Voters Retain Iowa Justice Who Backed Gay Marriage," *Connecticut News-Times,* November 7, 2012.

152. "A Battle for Florida's Courts" (editorial), *New York Times,* July 31, 2012.

153. See, e.g., Sherrilyn A. Ifill, "Through the Lens of Diversity: The Fight for Judicial Elections After *Republican Party of Minnesota v. White,*" *Michigan Journal of Race and Law* 10 (2004): 55–99, at 93.

154. Bonneau and Hall, *In Defense of Judicial Elections.*

155. Eggen, "Special-Interest Spending Surges."

156. C. Feldman, "A State Constitutional Remedy to the Sale of Justice in Texas Courts," *South Texas Law Review* 41 (2000): 1415–1421.

157. Neal Devins and Nicole Mansker, "Public Opinion and State Supreme Courts," *University of Pennsylvania Journal of Constitutional Law* 13 (2010): 455–509, at 495.

158. Quoted in Eggen, "Special-Interest Spending Surges."

159. Deborah Goldberg, Sarah Samis, Edwin Bender, and Rachel Weiss, *The New Politics of Judicial Elections 2004* (Washington, DC: Justice at Stake Campaign, 2005).

160. Morgan Smith, "Lawyers Biggest Donors to Judicial Elections," *Texas Tribune,* February 2, 2010.

161. Damon M. Cann and Jeff Yates, "Homegrown Institutional Legitimacy: Assessing Citizens' Diffuse Support for State Courts," *American Politics Research* 36 (2008): 297–329; James L. Gibson, "Challenges to the Impartiality of State Supreme Courts: Legitimacy Theory and 'New Style' Judicial Campaigns," *American Political Science Review* 102 (2008): 59–75.

162. Quoted in Eggen, "Special-Interest Spending Surges."

163. Cann and Yates, "Homegrown Institutional Legitimacy," 313.

164. Melinda Gann Hall, "State Supreme Courts in American Democracy: Probing the Myths of Judicial Reform," *American Political Science Review* 95 (2001): 315–330, at 318.

165. Philip L. Dubois, *From Ballot to Bench: Judicial Elections and the Quest for Accountability* (Austin: University of Texas Press, 1980), 67.

166. Brian F. Schaffner and Jennifer Segal Diascro, "Judicial Elections in the News," in Matthew J. Streb, ed., *Running for Judge: The Rising Political, Financial, and Legal Stakes of Judicial Elections* (New York: New York University Press, 2007), 119.

167. Lawrence Baum, "Judicial Elections and Judicial Independence: The Voter's Perspective," *Ohio State Law Journal* 64 (2003): 13–42, at 19–20.

168. Bonneau and Hall, *In Defense of Judicial Elections,* 2.

169. Ibid., 14.

170. Frank Cross, "Judicial Independence," in Keith E. Whittington, R. Daniel Kelemen, and Gregory A. Caldeira, eds., *The Oxford Handbook of Law and Politics* (New York: Oxford University Press, 2008), 570–571.

171. Frank B. Cross, "Thoughts on Goldilocks and Judicial Independence," *Ohio State Law Journal* 64 (2003): 195–219.

172. Melinda Gann Hall, "Voluntary Retirements from State Supreme Courts: Assessing Democratic Pressures to Relinquish the Bench," *Journal of Politics* 63 (2001): 1112–1140.

173. James L. Gibson, *Electing Judges: The Surprising Effects of Campaigning on Judicial Legitimacy* (Chicago: University of Chicago Press, 2012).

174. Tarr, *Without Fear or Favor,* 84–87.

175. Rachel P. Caufield, "The Changing Tone of Judicial Election Campaigns as a Result of *White,*" in Matthew J. Streb, ed., *Running for Judge: The Rising Political, Financial, and Legal Stakes of Judicial Elections* (New York: New York University Press, 2007), 39.

176. Roy A. Schotland, "Comment: Judicial Independence and Accountability," *Law and Contemporary Problems* 61 (1998): 149–155.

177. Schaffner and Diascro, "Judicial Elections in the News," 116.

178. Hall, "On the Cataclysm of Judicial Elections," 231.

179. Richard L. Hasen, "First Amendment Limits on Regulating Judicial Campaigns," in Matthew J. Streb, ed., *Running for Judge: The Rising Political, Financial, and Legal Stakes of Judicial Elections* (New York: New York University Press, 2007), 30.

180. See Laurence Leamer, *The Price of Justice: A True Story of Greed and Corruption* (New York: Times Books, 2013).

181. See, e.g., "Justice Not for Sale" (editorial), *New York Times,* March 3, 2009.

182. James Sample, Adam Skaggs, Jonathan Blitzer, and Linda Casey, *The New Politics of Judicial Elections, 2000–2009: Decades of Change* (Washington, DC: Justice at Stake, 2010), 61.

183. Alexander Polikoff, "So How Did We Get into This Mess? Observations on the Legitimacy of Citizens United," *Northwestern University Law Review Colloquy* 105 (2011): 203–227, at 222.

Chapter 4: The Legal Profession

1. Richard L. Abel, *American Lawyers* (New York: Oxford University Press, 1989), 3.

2. Alexis de Tocqueville, *Democracy in America,* trans. George Lawrence (New York: Harper and Row, 1966).

3. William M. Sullivan, Anne Colby, Judith Welch Wegner, Lloyd Bond, and Lee S. Shulman, *Educating Lawyers: Preparations for the Profession of Law* (San Francisco: Wiley, 2007), 1.

4. See, e.g., Lynn Mather, "Bringing the Lawyers Back In," in Mark C. Miller, ed., *Exploring Judicial Politics* (New York: Oxford University Press, 2009).

5. Frances Kahn Zemans and Victor G. Rosenblum, *The Making of a Public Profession* (Chicago: American Bar Foundation, 1981), 1.

6. See, e.g., Conrad S. Ciccotello, C. Terry Grant, and Mark Dickie, "Will Consult for Food! Rethinking Barriers to Professional Entry in the Information Age," *American Business Law Journal* 40 (2003): 905–939, at 909; Clifford Winston, Robert W. Crandall, and Vikram Maheshri, *First Thing We Do, Let's Deregulate All the Lawyers* (Washington, DC: Brookings Institution, 2011).

7. Gerald L. Geison, ed., *Professions and Professional Ideologies in America* (Chapel Hill, NC: University of North Carolina Press, 1983).

8. Mark C. Miller, *The High Priests of American Politics: The Role of Lawyers in American Political Institutions* (Knoxville: University of Tennessee Press, 1995), 18.

9. Sullivan et al., *Educating Lawyers*, 2.

10. Winston, Crandall, and Maheshri, *First Thing We Do*, 3.

11. Ibid.

12. Ibid., 3.

13. Brian Z. Tamanaha, *Failing Law Schools* (Chicago: University of Chicago Press, 2012), 176.

14. Lawrence Baum, *American Courts: Process and Policy*, 7th ed. (Boston: Wadsworth, 2013), 54.

15. Winston, Crandall, and Maheshri, *First Thing We Do*, 5.

16. Carole Silver, "Internationalizing U.S. Legal Education: A Report on the Education of Transnational Lawyers," *Cardozo Journal of International and Comparative Law* 14 (2006): 143–175.

17. Catherine Ho, "Law School Applications Continue to Slide," *Washington Post*, June 2, 2013.

18. Ethan Bronner, "Law Schools' Applications Fall as Cost Rise and Jobs Are Cut," *New York Times*, January 31, 2013.

19. Tamanaha, *Failing Law Schools*, 85.

20. Steven J. Harper, *The Lawyer Bubble: A Profession in Crisis* (New York: Basic Books, 2013).

21. Baum, *American Courts*, 55.

22. Sullivan et al., *Educating Lawyers*, 3.

23. Geison, ed., *Professions and Professional Ideologies*.

24. Miller, *The High Priests of American Politics*.

25. Magali Sarfatti Larson, *The Rise of Professionalism: A Sociological Analysis* (Berkeley: University of California Press, 1977), 229.

26. Abel, *American Lawyers*, 5.

27. Sullivan et al., *Educating Lawyers*, 4.

28. Ibid., 5.

29. See, e.g., Paul Wice, *Judges and Lawyers: The Human Side of Justice* (New York: Harper Collins, 1991), 9.

30. Sullivan et al., *Educating Lawyers,* 47–86.

31. Sally F. Goldfarb and Edward A. Adams, *Inside the Law Schools,* 5th ed. (New York: Plume, 1991), 13.

32. Steven E. Barkan, *Law and Society: An Introduction* (Upper Saddle River, NJ: Pearson, 2009), 259.

33. Abel, *American Lawyers,* 212.

34. David Bryden, "What Do Law Students Learn? A Pilot Study," *Journal of Legal Education* 34 (1984): 479–506, at 500.

35. Adam Liptak, "Law Scholarship's Lackluster Reviews," *New York Times,* October 21, 2013.

36. Jess Bravin, "Justice Kennedy on Law School, Blogging, and Popular Culture," *Wall Street Journal,* October 10, 2013.

37. Tamar Lewin, "Task Force Backs Changes in Legal Education System," *New York Times,* September 20, 2013.

38. Daniel B. Rodriguez and Samuel Estreicher, "Make Law Schools Earn a Third Year," *New York Times,* January 18, 2013.

39. Ibid.

40. Peter Lattman, "N.Y.U. Law Plans Overhaul of Students' Third Year," *New York Times,* October 17, 2012.

41. Ibid.

42. Ethan Bronner, "No Lawyer for 100 Country Miles, So One Rural State Offers Pay," *New York Times,* April 9, 2013.

43. Lincoln Caplan, "An Existential Crisis for Law Schools," *New York Times,* July 14, 2012.

44. David Segal, "Is Law School a Losing Game?" *New York Times,* January 8, 2011.

45. Harper, *The Lawyer Bubble,* 4.

46. See, e.g., Tamanaha, *Failing Law Schools,* 109.

47. Lawrence E. Mitchell, "Law School Is Worth the Money," *New York Times,* November 28, 2012.

48. Ibid.

49. Baum, *American Courts,* 55–57.

50. Abel, *American Lawyers,* 6.

51. Richard H. Sander and E. Douglass Williams, "Why Are There So Many Lawyers? Perspective on a Turbulent Market," *Law and Social Inquiry* 14 (1989): 431–479.

52. Sullivan et al., *Educating Lawyers,* 1.

53. Baum, *American Courts,* 57.

54. Abel, *American Lawyers,* 6.

55. Baum, *American Courts,* 58.

56. Ronit Dinovitzer, Bryant Garth, Richard Sander, Joyce Sterling, and Gita Wilder, *After the JD: The First Results of a National Study of Legal Careers* (Chicago: NALP Foundation for Law Career Research and Education and the American Bar Foundation, 2004).

57. Ronit Dinovitzer, Robert Nelson, Gabriele Plickert, Rebecca Sandefur, and Joyce Sterling, *After the JD II: Second Results from a National Study of Legal Careers* (Chicago: American Bar Foundation and NALP, 2010), 18.

58. Mather, "Bringing the Lawyers Back In," 57.

59. Dinovitzer et al., *After the JD II*, 18.

60. Mather, "Bringing the Lawyers Back In," 57.

61. Dinovitzer et al., *After the JD II*, 15.

62. Susan Smith Blakely, *Best Friends at the Bar: The New Balance for Today's Woman Lawyer* (New York: Wolters Kluwer, 2012).

63. See, e.g., John M. Golden, "The Supreme Court as 'Prime Percolator': A Prescription for Appellate Review of Questions in Patent Law," *UCLA Law Review* 56 (2009): 657–724.

64. Abel, *American Lawyers*, 182.

65. Baum, *American Courts*, 60.

66. Karen Sloan, "Billing Blues," *National Law Journal*, December 10, 2010, 10.

67. Mather, "Bringing the Lawyers Back In," 56.

68. Marc Galanter and Thomas Palay, *Tournament of Lawyers: The Transformation of the Big Law Firm* (Chicago: University of Chicago Press, 1994).

69. Mather, "Bringing the Lawyers Back In," 57.

70. Galanter and Palay, *Tournament of Lawyers*.

71. Harper, *The Lawyer Bubble*, 57–66.

72. Jennifer L. Pierce, *Gender Trials: Emotional Lives in Contemporary Law Firms* (Berkeley: University of California Press, 1996).

73. See, e.g., Lynn Mather, Craig A. McEwen, and Richard J. Maiman, *Divorce Lawyers at Work: Variety of Professionalism in Practice* (New York: Oxford University Press, 2001).

74. John Heinz and Edward Laumann, *Chicago Lawyers: The Social Structure of the Bar* (New York: Russell Sage Foundation and American Bar Foundation, 1982). This study was updated in John P. Heinz, Robert L. Nelson, Rebecca L. Sandefur, and Edward O. Laumann, *Urban Lawyers: The New Social Structure of the Bar* (Chicago: University of Chicago Press, 2005).

75. Abel, *American Lawyers*, 166.

76. Clara N. Carson, *The Lawyer Statistical Report: The U.S. Legal Profession in 2000* (Chicago: American Bar Foundation, 2004).

77. Abel, *American Lawyers*, 167.

78. Baum, *American Courts*, 63.

79. Tamanaha, *Failing Law Schools*, 59.

80. John G. Roberts Jr., *2006 Year-End Report on the Federal Judiciary* (Washington, DC: Supreme Court of the United States, 2007).

81. Richard Susskind, *Tomorrow's Lawyers: An Introduction to Your Future* (New York: Oxford University Press, 2013).

82. See, e.g., Mather, "Bringing the Lawyers Back In," 50.

83. Ibid., 50–56.

84. Mather, McEwen, and Maiman, *Divorce Lawyers at Work*.

85. Mary C. Vogel, *Coercion to Compromise: Plea Bargaining, the Courts, and the Making of Political Authority* (New York: Oxford University Press, 2007).

86. Leslie C. Levin and Lynn Mather, eds., *Lawyers in Practice: Ethical Decision Making in Context* (Chicago: University of Chicago Press, 2012).

87. Stephen Daniels and Joanne Martin, "Plaintiffs' Lawyers and the Tension Between Professional Norms and the Need to Generate Business," in Leslie C. Levin and Lynn Mather, eds., *Lawyers in Practice: Ethical Decision Making in Context* (Chicago: University of Chicago Press, 2012), 111.

88. Abel, *American Lawyers*, 119.

89. Stuart A. Scheingold and Austin Sarat, *Something to Believe In: Politics, Professionalism, and Cause Lawyering* (Stanford, CA: Stanford University Press, 2004).

90. Deborah L. Rhode, *Access to Justice* (New York: Oxford University Press, 2004).

91. Amy Bach, *Ordinary Injustice: How America Holds Court* (New York: Metropolitan Books, 2009), 12–32.

92. Welsh S. White, *Litigating in the Shadow of Death: Defense Attorneys in Capital Cases* (Ann Arbor: University of Michigan Press, 2006).

93. Donald Robertson, "Pro Bono as a Professional Legacy," *Law in Context* 19 (2001): 97–126, at 108.

94. Ethan Bronner, "Right to Lawyer Can Be an Empty Promise for the Poor," *New York Times*, March 16, 2013.

95. Corey S. Shdaimah, "Legal Services Lawyers: When Conceptions of Lawyering and Values Clash," in Leslie C. Levin and Lynn Mather, eds., *Lawyers in Practice: Ethical Decision Making in Context* (Chicago: University of Chicago Press, 2012), 317.

96. Corey S. Shdaimah, *Negotiating Justice: Progressive Lawyering, Low-Income Clients, and the Quest for Social Change* (New York: New York University Press, 2011).

97. John Kilwein, "The Decline of the Legal Services Corporation: 'It's Ideological, Stupid!'" in Francis Regan, ed., *The Transformation of Legal Aid: Comparative and Historical Studies* (New York: Oxford University Press, 1999).

98. Robert Granfield and Lynn Mather, "Pro Bono, the Public Good, and the Legal Profession: An Introduction," in Robert Granfield and Lynn Mather, eds., *Private Lawyers and the Public Interest: The Evolving Role of Pro Bono in the Legal Profession* (New York: Oxford University Press, 2009), 7.

99. Rebecca L. Sandefur, "Lawyers' Pro Bono Service and Market-Reliant Legal Aid," in Robert Granfield and Lynn Mather, eds., *Private Lawyers and the Public Interest: The Evolving Role of Pro Bono in the Legal Profession* (New York: Oxford University Press, 2009), 95.

100. Richard L. Abel, "State, Market, Philanthropy, and Self-Help as Legal Services Delivery Methods," in Robert Granfield and Lynn Mather, eds., *Private Lawyers and the Public Interest: The Evolving Role of Pro Bono in the Legal Profession* (New York: Oxford University Press, 2009), 305.

101. Granfield and Mather, "Pro Bono, the Public Good, and the Legal Profession," 8.

102. Deborah L. Rhode, *Pro Bono in Principle and Practice* (Stanford, CA: Stanford University Press, 2005).

103. Abel, "State, Market, Philanthropy, and Self-Help," 296.

104. Ibid.

105. Cynthia Adcock, "Shaped by Educational, Professional, and Social Crises: The History of Law Student Pro Bono Service," in Robert Granfield and Lynn Mather, eds., *Private Lawyers and the Public Interest: The Evolving Role of Pro Bono in the Legal Profession* (New York: Oxford University Press, 2009).

106. Tamanaha, *Failing Law Schools,* 59.

107. Steven A. Boutcher, "The Institutionalization of Pro Bono in Large Law Firms: Trends and Variation Across the AmLaw 200," in Robert Granfield and Lynn Mather, eds., *Private Lawyers and the Public Interest: The Evolving Role of Pro Bono in the Legal Profession* (New York: Oxford University Press, 2009), 138–139.

108. Abel, "State, Market, Philanthropy, and Self-Help," 297.

109. Ethan Bronner, "At Stanford Law School, a Unique Clinic Offers Training in Religious-Liberty Cases," *New York Times,* January 22, 2013.

110. Abel, *American Lawyers,* 172.

111. Ibid.

112. Wice, *Judges and Lawyers,* 52.

113. Ibid., 56.

114. Ibid.

115. Adam Liptak, "Politicians in Robes? Not Exactly, But . . . ," *New York Times,* November 27, 2012.

116. Lee Epstein, William M. Landes, and Richard A. Posner, *The Behavior of Federal Judges: A Theoretical and Empirical Study of Rational Choice* (Cambridge, MA: Harvard University Press, 2013).

117. Cass R. Sunstein, David Schkade, Lisa M. Ellman, and Andres Sawicki, *Are Judges Political? An Empirical Analysis of the Federal Judiciary* (Washington, DC: Brookings Institution, 2006).

118. Alliance for Justice, *The State of the Judiciary: Judicial Selection During the Remainder of President Obama's First Term* (Washington, DC: Alliance for Justice, 2012), 18.

119. Susan L. Goldberg, "Judicial Socialization: An Empirical Study," *Journal of Contemporary Law* 11 (1985): 423–451, at 425.

120. Baum, *American Courts,* 133.

121. Robert Carp and Russell Wheeler, "Sink or Swim—Socialization of a Federal Judge," *Journal of Public Law* 21 (1972): 359–393.

122. Wice, *Judges and Lawyers,* 203.

123. Baum, *American Courts,* 133.

124. See Sheldon Goldman, Elliot Slotnick, and Sara Schiavoni, "Obama's Judiciary at Midterm: The Confirmation Drama Continues," *Judicature* 96 (2001): 296–297.

125. Baum, *American Courts,* 125.

126. Malia Reddick, Michael J. Nelson, and Rachel Paine Caufield, "Racial and Gender Diversity on State Courts: An AJS Study," *Judges' Journal* 48 (2009): 28–33.

127. Ibid.

128. Baum, *American Courts,* 129.

129. See, e.g., David W. Allen and Diane E. Wall, "Role Orientations and Women State Supreme Court Justices," *Judicature* 77 (1993): 156, 159–165.

130. See, e.g., Adam B. Cox and Thomas J. Miles, "Judging the Voting Rights Act," *Columbia Law Review* 108 (2008): 1–54; Pat K. Chew and Robert E. Kelly, "Myth of the Color-Blind Judge: An Empirical Analysis of Racial Harassment Cases," *Washington University Law Review* 86 (2009): 1117–1166.

131. Frank B. Cross, *Decision Making in the U.S. Courts of Appeals* (Stanford, CA: Stanford University Press, 2007), 75.

132. See, e.g., Jennifer L. Peresie, "Female Judges Matter: Gender and Collegial Decisionmaking in the Federal Appellate Courts," *Yale Law Journal* 114 (2005): 1759–1790; Christina L. Boyd, Lee Epstein, and Andrew D. Martin, "Untangling the Causal Effects of Sex on Judging," *American Journal of Political Science* 54 (2010): 389–411.

133. Cross, *Decision Making in the U.S. Courts of Appeals,* 75.

134. Quoted in Brian Lamb, Susan Swain, and Mark Farkas, eds., *The Supreme Court: A C-SPAN Book Featuring the Justices in Their Own Words* (New York: Public Affairs, 2010), 185.

135. Ibid., 295.

136. Neil A. Lewis, "Debate on Whether Female Judges Decide Differently Arises Anew," *New York Times,* June 3, 2009.

137. Quoted in Joan Biskupic, "Ginsburg: Court Needs Another Woman," *USA Today,* May 5, 2009.

138. Jeffrey Toobin, "Heavyweight: How Ruth Bader Ginsburg Has Moved the Supreme Court," *New Yorker,* March 8, 2013, 42–43.

139. Linda Greenhouse, *Becoming Justice Blackmun: Harry Blackmun's Supreme Court Journey* (New York: Times Books, 2005).

140. Debra Cassens Weiss, "Kagan Reveals Affinity for Action Heroes, Weekend Plans to Shoot Antelope with Scalia," *ABA Journal,* October 22, 2012.

Chapter 5: Trial Courts: Criminal Cases

1. Thomas H. Cohen and Tracey Kyckelhahn, *Felony Defendants in Large Urban Counties, 2006* (Washington, DC: Bureau of Justice Statistics, U.S. Department of Justice, 2010).

2. Lawrence Baum, *American Courts: Process and Policy,* 7th ed. (Boston: Wadsworth, 2013), 162–163.

3. Julie Scelfo, "'Quite Unprecedented': Former U.S. Attorney Mary Jo White Explains Why the Firing of Eight Federal Prosecutors Could Threaten the Historic Independence of Federal Law-Enforcement Officials," *Newsweek,* March 15, 2007.

4. James Q. Whitman, *Harsh Justice: Criminal Punishment and the Widening Divide Between America and Europe* (New York: Oxford University Press, 2003), 3.

5. Peter Baldwin, *The Narcissism of Minor Differences: How America and Europe Are Alike* (New York: Oxford University Press, 2009), 76.

6. Charles Ogletree, Robert J. Smith, and Johanna Wald, "Coloring Punishment: Implicit Social Cognition and Criminal Justice," in Justin D. Levinson and Robert J. Smith, eds., *Implicit Racial Bias Across the Law* (New York: Cambridge University Press, 2012), 45.

7. Whitman, *Harsh Justice,* 196–197.

8. Bureau of Justice Statistics, *Criminal Victimization in the United States, 2007* (Washington, DC: U.S. Department of Justice, 2010).

9. Joan Petersilia, *Racial Disparities in the Criminal Justice System* (Santa Monica, CA: Rand Corporation, 1983), 45.

10. Ibid.

11. Joseph A. Goldstein, "Police Discretion Not to Invoke the Criminal Process: Low-Visibility Decisions in the Administration of Justice," *Yale Law Journal* 69 (1960): 543–594, at 543.

12. Wesley G. Skogan, "Criminal Justice and the Police," in Keith E. Whittington, R. Daniel Kelemen, and Gregory A. Caldeira, eds., *The Oxford Handbook of Law and Politics* (New York: Oxford University Press, 2008), 615.

13. See, e.g., Wayne R. LaFave, "The Police and Non-Enforcement of the Law—Part II," *Wisconsin Law Review,* 1962, 179–239.

14. Jerome H. Skolnick, *Justice Without Trial: Law Enforcement in Democratic Society* (New York: Wiley, 1966).

15. Jeannine Bell, *Policing Hatred: Law Enforcement, Civil Rights, and Hate Crime* (New York: New York University Press, 2002).

16. See, e.g., Sara R. Benson, "Failure to Arrest: A Pilot Study of Police Response to Domestic Violence in Rural Illinois," *American University Journal of Gender, Social Policy, and the Law* 17 (2009): 685–704.

17. Bell, *Policing Hatred,* 120.

18. Leland Ware, "Prohibiting Racial Profiling: The ACLU's Orchestration of the Missouri Legislation," *St. Louis University Public Law Review* 22 (2003): 59–72.

19. Bell, *Policing Hatred,* 9.

20. Lisa J. McIntyre, *The Public Defender: The Practice of Law in the Shadows of Repute* (Chicago: University of Chicago Press, 1987).

21. Sheryl J. Grana, Jane C. Ollenburger, and Mark Nicholas, *The Social Context of Law,* 2nd ed. (Upper Saddle River, NJ: Pearson, 2002), 174.

22. Jeffrey Abramson, *We, the Jury: The Jury System and the Ideal of Democracy* (Cambridge, MA: Harvard University Press, 2000), 3–4.

23. Ibid., 61.

24. See, e.g., Gary J. Simson, "Jury Nullification in the American System: A Skeptical View," *Texas Law Review* 54 (1976): 488–506.

25. Abramson, *We, the Jury,* 6.

26. Robert G. Boatright, "The Politics of Jury Reform," in Mark C. Miller, ed., *Exploring Judicial Politics* (New York: Oxford University Press, 2009), 66.

27. Stephen J. Adler, *The Jury: Disorder in the Court* (New York: Doubleday, 1994), 218.

28. Boatright, "The Politics of Jury Reform."

29. *Batson v. Kentucky,* 476 U.S. 86 (1986); *J.E.B. v. Alabama ex rel. T.B.,* 511 U.S. 127 (1994).

30. Adler, *The Jury,* 5.

31. G. Alan Tarr, *Judicial Process and Judicial Policymaking,* 3rd ed. (Belmont, CA: Wadsworth, 2003), 199.

32. John F. Pfaff, "The Future of Appellate Sentencing Review: Booker in the States," *Marquette Law Review* 93 (2009): 683–715.

33. Douglas F. Fries, "The Federal Sentencing Guidelines Weight-Loss Plan: Just How Mandatory Are the 'Advisory' Guidelines After *United States v. Booker?*" *Case Western Reserve Law Review* 55 (2005): 1097–1124.

34. Adam Liptak, "Court Weighs Revisions in Cocaine-Case Sentences," *New York Times,* April 17, 2012.

35. Charles Doyle, *Federal Mandatory Minimum Sentencing Statutes* (Washington, DC: Congressional Research Service, 2007).

36. Richard A. Oppel Jr., "Sentencing Shift Gives New Leverage to Prosecutors," *New York Times,* September 25, 2011.

37. Baum, *American Courts,* 189.

38. David Bjerk, "Making the Crime Fit the Penalty: The Role of Prosecutorial Discretion Under Mandatory Minimum Sentencing," *Journal of Law and Economics* 48 (2005): 591–625.

39. *Ewing v. California,* 538 U.S. 11, at 28 (2003).

40. *Ewing v. California,* 538 U.S. 11, at 33 (2003) (Stevens, J. dissenting).

41. Glen Johnson and Brian R. Ballou, "Deval Patrick Signs Repeat Offender Crime Bill in Private State House Ceremony," *Boston Globe,* August 2, 2012.

42. Mary E. Vogel, *Coercion to Compromise: Plea Bargaining, the Courts, and the Making of Political Authority* (New York: Oxford University Press, 2007).

43. George Fisher, *The Triumph of Plea Bargaining: A History of Plea Bargaining in America* (Stanford, CA: Stanford University Press, 2003), 6.

44. Baum, *American Courts,* 165.

45. Arthur I. Rosett and Donald R. Cressey, *Justice by Consent: Plea Bargaining in the American Courthouse* (Philadelphia: Lippincott, 1976).

46. See Lynn Mather, Craig A. McEwen, and Richard J. Maiman, *Divorce Lawyers at Work: Variety of Professionalism in Practice* (New York: Oxford University Press, 2001).

47. Baum, *American Courts,* 167.

48. David Sudnow, "Normal Crimes: Sociological Features of the Penal Code in a Public Defender's Office," *Social Problems* 12 (1965): 255–276.

49. Peter F. Nardulli, *The Courtroom Elite: An Organizational Perspective on Criminal Justice* (Cambridge, MA: Ballinger, 1978), 68.

50. Steven E. Barkan, *Law and Society: An Introduction* (Upper Saddle River, NJ: Pearson, 2009), 273.

51. Baum, *American Courts,* 167.

52. Tarr, *Judicial Process and Judicial Policymaking,* 186.

53. Fisher, *The Triumph of Plea Bargaining,* 208.

54. Bach, *Ordinary Injustice,* 115.

55. Nardulli, *The Courtroom Elite,* 68.

56. McIntyre, *The Public Defender,* 153.

57. Malcolm Feeley, *The Process Is the Punishment: Handling Cases in a Lower Criminal Court,* rev. ed. (New York: Russell Sage Foundation, 1992).

58. Amy Bach, *Ordinary Injustice: How America Holds Court* (New York: Metropolitan Books, 2009), 109.

59. Kenneth Jost, *Plea Bargaining,* CQ Researcher (Washington, DC: CQ Press, 1999), 115–133.

60. Barkan, *Law and Society,* 275.

61. "Plea Deal Rejected in Aurora Shooting," Associated Press, March 28, 2013.

62. Leonard Downie Jr., *Justice Denied: The Case for Reform of the Courts* (Baltimore: Penguin, 1972).

63. Fisher, *The Triumph of Plea Bargaining,* 2.

64. Tarr, *Judicial Process and Judicial Policymaking,* 189–190.

65. Fisher, *The Triumph of Plea Bargaining,* 1.

66. Vogel, *Coercion to Compromise,* vii.

67. Michelle Janaye Nealy, "Maryland Legislators Vote in Favor of Eliminating Death Penalty," *Boston Globe,* March 16, 2013.

68. Katharine Q. Seelye, "New Hampshire Nears Repeal of Death Penalty," *New York Times,* March 12, 2014.

69. Jurow, "New Data on the Effect of a 'Death Qualified' Jury."

70. Thomas G. Walker, *Eligible for Execution: The Story of the Daryl Atkins Case* (Washington, DC: CQ Press, 2009).

71. Justin J. Wert, *Habeas Corpus in America: The Politics of Individual Rights* (Lawrence: University Press of Kansas, 2011), 194.

72. Jeffrey Crouch, *The Presidential Pardon Power* (Lawrence: University Press of Kansas, 2009).

73. Robert M. Bohm, *Deathquest: An Introduction to the Theory and Practice of Capital Punishment in the United States* (Cincinnati, OH: Anderson. 2007).

74. Austin Sarat, *Mercy on Trial: What It Means to Stop an Execution* (Princeton, NJ: Princeton University Press, 2005), 4–5.

75. Welsh S. White, *Litigating in the Shadow of Death: Defense Attorneys in Capital Cases* (Ann Arbor: University of Michigan Press, 2006), 5.

76. Sarat, *Mercy on Trial,* 9–10.

77. Grana, Ollenburger, and Nicholas, *The Social Context of Law,* 189.

78. David C. Baldus, George Woodworth, and Charles A. Pulaski, *Equal Justice and the Death Penalty: A Legal and Empirical Analysis* (Boston: Northeastern University Press, 1990); Donald R. Songer and Isaac Unah, "The Effect of Race, Gender, and Location on Prosecutorial Decisions to Seek the Death Penalty in South Carolina," *South Carolina Law Review* 58 (2006): 161–205.

79. Barkan, *Law and Society,* 162.

80. Raymond Paternoster, *Capital Punishment in America* (New York: Lexington Books, 1991), 183.

81. Suzanne Samuels, *Law, Politics, and Society* (Boston: Houghton Mifflin, 2006), 276.

82. Ogletree, Smith, and Wald, "Coloring Punishment," 46.

83. Samuels, *Law, Politics, and Society,* 276.

84. Ronald H. Weich and Carlos T. Angulo, *Justice on Trial: Racial Disparities in the American Criminal Justice System* (Washington, DC: National Leadership Conference on Civil Rights, 2000).

85. Patricia Y. Warren and Amy Farrell, "The Environmental Context of Racial Profiling," *Annals of the American Academy of Political and Social Science* 623 (2009): 52–63, at 52.

86. See, e.g., Rod K. Brunson and Jody Miller, "Young Black Men and Urban Policing in the United States," *British Journal of Criminology* 46 (2005): 613–640; Patricia Y. Warren, Donald Tomaskovic-Devey, Matthew Zingraff, William Smith, and Marcinda Mason, "Driving While Black: Bias Processes and Racial Disparity in Police Stops," *Criminology* 4 (2006): 709–737.

87. Ronald Weitzer and Steven Tuch, "Race and Perceptions of Police Misconduct," *Social Problems* 51 (2004): 305–325.

88. Ogletree, Smith, and Wald, "Coloring Punishment."

89. David S. Kirk, "The Neighborhood Context of Racial and Ethnic Disparities in Arrest," *Demography* 45 (2008): 55–77.

90. Dorothy E. Roberts, "Constructing a Criminal Justice System Free of Racial Bias: An Abolitionist Framework," *Columbia Human Rights Law Review* 39 (2007): 261–285.

91. Samuel R. Sommers and Phoebe C. Ellsworth, "Race in the Courtroom: Perceptions of Guilt and Dispositional Attributions," *Personality and Social Psychology Bulletin* 26 (2000): 1367–1379.

92. David B. Mustard, "Racial, Ethnic, and Gender Disparities in Sentencing: Evidence from the U.S. Federal Courts," *Journal of Law and Economics* 64 (2001): 285–314.

93. Tara L. Mitchell, Ryann M. Haw, Jeffrey E. Pfeifer, and Christian A. Meissner, "Racial Bias in Mock Juror Decision-Making: A Meta-Analytic Review of Defendant Treatment," *Law and Human Behavior* 29 (2005): 621–637.

Chapter 6: Trial Courts: Civil Cases

1. Lawrence Baum, *American Courts: Process and Policy,* 7th ed. (Boston: Wadsworth, 2013), 201.

2. Thomas F. Burke, *Lawyers, Lawsuits, and Legal Rights: The Battle over Litigation in American Society* (Berkeley: University of California Press, 2002), 25.

3. Lawrence A. Cunningham, *Contracts in the Real World: Stories of Popular Contracts and Why They Matter* (New York: Cambridge University Press, 2012), 5.

4. Sean Farhang, *The Litigation State: Public Regulation and Private Lawsuits in the U.S.* (Princeton, NJ: Princeton University Press, 2010).

5. See, e.g., Austin Sarat and Stuart Scheingold, eds., *Cause Lawyering: Political Commitments and Professional Responsibilities* (New York: Oxford University Press, 1998); Austin Sarat and Stuart Scheingold, eds., *Cause Lawyers and Social Movements* (Stanford, CA: Stanford University Press, 2006).

6. See, e.g., William M. Tabb and Elaine W. Shoben, *Remedies in a Nutshell* (St. Paul, MN: Thomson/West, 2005).

7. See William Haltom and Michael McCann, *Distorting the Law: Politics, Media, and the Litigation Crisis* (Chicago: University of Chicago Press, 2004), 183–190; Lief H. Carter and Thomas F. Burke, *Reason in Law,* 8th ed. (New York: Longman, 2010), 139–140.

8. Gerald M. Stern, *The Buffalo Creek Disaster* (New York: Vintage Books, 1976).

9. Jonathan Harr, *A Civil Action* (New York: Vintage Books, 1995).

10. Burke, *Lawyers, Lawsuits, and Legal Rights.*

11. See, e.g., Douglas Laycock, *Modern American Remedies: Cases and Materials,* 4th ed. (New York: Aspen, 2010).

12. Corey S. Shdaimah, "Legal Services Lawyers: When Conceptions of Lawyering and Values Clash," in Leslie C. Levin and Lynn Mather, eds., *Lawyers in Practice: Ethical Decision Making in Context* (Chicago: University of Chicago Press, 2012), 317.

13. Deborah Rhode, *Access to Justice* (New York: Oxford University Press, 2004), 26.

14. Reynolds Holding, "Discovery, It Turns Out, Is the Better Part of Judgments," *San Francisco Chronicle,* October 11, 1998.

15. Jonathan Harr, *A Civil Action* (New York: Vintage, 1996).

16. Baum, *American Courts,* 204.

17. Ibid., 204.

18. Robert G. Boatright, "The Politics of Jury Reform," in Mark C. Miller, ed., *Exploring Judicial Politics* (New York: Oxford University Press, 2009).

19. Valerie P. Hans and Neil Vidmar, *Judging the Jury* (Cambridge, MA: Perseus, 1986), 31.

20. Stephen J. Adler, *The Jury: Disorder in the Courts* (New York: Doubleday, 1994), 146.

21. Ibid., 173.

22. Alexis de Tocqueville, *Democracy in America,* trans. George Lawrence (New York: Harper and Row, 1966), 274.

23. Ibid., 275.

24. *Exxon Shipping Co. v. Baker*, 554 U.S. 471 at 509 (2008).

25. Baum, *American Courts*, 205.

26. Daniel A. Crane, "Optimizing Private Antitrust Enforcement," *Vanderbilt Law Review* 63 (2010): 675–723.

27. Hans and Vidmar, *Judging the Jury*, 31.

28. Jeffrey Abramson, *We, the Jury: The Jury System and the Ideal of Democracy* (Cambridge, MA: Harvard University Press, 2000), 1.

29. John Gastil, E. Pierre Deess, Philip J. Weiser, and Cindy Simmons, *The Jury and Democracy: How Jury Deliberation Promotes Civil Engagement and Political Participation* (New York: Oxford University Press, 2010), 4.

30. Boatright, "The Politics of Jury Reform," 67.

31. Gastil et al., *The Jury and Democracy*.

32. Adler, *The Jury*, xiii.

33. Abramson, *We, the Jury*, 1.

34. Hans and Vidmar, *Judging the Jury*, 49.

35. *Taylor v. Louisiana*, 419 U.S. 522 (1975).

36. Boatright, "The Politics of Jury Reform," 66–67.

37. Ibid., 68.

38. Ibid., 74.

39. Thomas King Kistler and Terrence R. Nealon, "Juror Note-Taking in Civil Trials: An Idea Whose Time Has Come," *Pennsylvania Bar Association Civil Litigation Update* 5 (2002): 1, 11–18.

40. Robert G. Boatright, *Improving Citizen Response to Jury Summonses* (Chicago: American Judicature Society, 1998).

41. Robert G. Boatright and Beth Murphy, "Behind Closed Doors: Assisting Jurors with Their Deliberations," *Judicature* 83 (1999): 52–58.

42. G. Alan Tarr, *Without Fear or Favor: Judicial Independence and Judicial Accountability in the States* (Stanford, CA: Stanford University Press, 2012), 79–80.

43. Michael Avery and Danielle McLaughlin, *The Federalist Society: How Conservatives Took the Law Back from Liberals* (Nashville, TN: Vanderbilt University Press, 2013), 79.

44. Ibid., 82.

45. David M. Engel, "The Oven Bird's Song: Insiders, Outsiders, and Personal Injuries in an American Community," in Sheldon Goldman and Austin Sarat, eds., *American Court Systems: Readings in Judicial Process and Behavior,* 2nd ed. (New York: Longman, 1989).

46. Abramson, *We, the Jury*, 4.

47. Rhode, *Access to Justice*, 39–40.

48. Quoted in Gail Russell Chaddock, "Emerging Supporter of Harriet Miers: Businesses," *Christian Science Monitor,* October 12, 2005, 4.

49. Stuart Taylor Jr. and Evan Thomas, "Civil Wars," *Newsweek,* December 15, 2003, 44.

50. Quoted in Rhode, *Access to Justice,* 26.

51. Quoted in ibid., 26.

52. Quoted in ibid., 27.

53. Avery and McLaughlin, *The Federalist Society,* 77–80.

54. "Excessive Litigation's Impact on America's Global Competitiveness," Hearings Before the Subcommittee on the Constitution and Civil Justice of the U.S. House Judiciary Committee, March 5, 2013.

55. Brett Coughlin, "House Judiciary Approves Tort Reform," *Politico,* February 16, 2011.

56. Thomas Koenig and Michael Rustad, "His and Her Tort Reform: Gender Injustice in Disguise," *Washington Law Review* 70 (1995): 1–88.

57. Stephen Daniels and Joanne Martin, *Civil Juries and the Politics of Reform* (Evanston, IL: Northwestern University Press, 1995).

58. Valerie P. Hans, *Business on Trial: The Civil Jury and Corporate Responsibility* (New Haven, CT: Yale University Press, 2000).

59. Haltom and McCann, *Distorting the Law.*

60. Marc Galanter, "Real World Torts: An Antidote to Anecdote," *Maryland Law Review* 55 (1996): 1093–1160.

61. Herbert M. Kritzer and Susan S. Silbey, eds., *In Litigation Do the "Haves" Still Come Out Ahead?* (Stanford, CA: Stanford University Press, 2003), 7.

62. Susan Silbey and Austin Sarat, "Dispute Processing in Law and Legal Scholarship: From Institutional Critique to the Reconstruction of Judicial Subject," *University of Denver Law Review* 66 (1989): 437–498.

63. Christine Harrington, *Shadow Justice: The Ideology and Institutionalization of Alternatives to Court* (Westport, CT: Greenwood Press, 1985).

64. Joel Auerback, *Justice Without Law?* (New York: Oxford University Press, 1983).

65. Burke, *Lawyers, Lawsuits, and Legal Rights,* 35–36.

66. Marc Galanter, "Why the 'Haves' Come Out Ahead: Speculations on the Limits of Legal Change," *Law and Society Review* 9 (1974): 95–160.

67. Kritzer and Silbey, eds., *In Litigation Do the "Haves" Still Come Out Ahead?* 4–5.

68. Ibid.

69. Donald R. Songer, Reginald S. Sheehan, and Susan Brodie Haire, "Do the 'Haves' Come Out Ahead over Time? Applying Galanter's Framework to Decisions of the U.S. Courts of Appeals, 1925–1988," in Herbert M. Kritzer and Susan S. Silbey, eds., *In Litigation Do the "Haves" Still Come Out Ahead?* (Stanford, CA: Stanford University Press, 2003), 85.

70. Kritzer and Silbey, eds., *In Litigation Do the "Haves" Still Come Out Ahead?* 5.

71. Ibid., 6.

72. Songer, Sheehan, and Haire, "Do the 'Haves' Come Out Ahead," 85.

73. Ibid., 99.

74. Herbert M. Kritzer, *The Justice Broker: Lawyers and Ordinary Litigation* (New York: Oxford University Press, 1990), 57–59.

75. Stephen Daniels and Joanne Martin, "Plaintiffs' Lawyers and the Tension Between Professional Norms and the Need to Generate Business," in Leslie C. Levin and Lynn Mather, eds., *Lawyers in Practice: Ethical Decision Making in Context* (Chicago: University of Chicago Press, 2012).

Chapter 7: The Appellate Court Process

1. Wendy L. Martinek, "Appellate Workhorses of the Federal Judiciary: The U.S. Courts of Appeals," in Mark C. Miller, ed., *Exploring Judicial Politics* (New York: Oxford University Press, 2009), 126–127.

2. H. W. Perry Jr., *Deciding to Decide: Agenda Setting in the United States Supreme Court* (Cambridge, MA: Harvard University Press, 1991), 24–25.

3. *Murdock v. City of Memphis,* 20 Wall. 590 (1875).

4. Artemus Ward, "Sorcerers' Apprentices: U.S. Supreme Court Law Clerks," in Mark C. Miller, ed., *Exploring Judicial Politics* (New York: Oxford University Press, 2009), 162.

5. Artemus Ward and David L. Weiden, *Sorcerers' Apprentices: Law Clerks at the U.S. Supreme Court* (New York: New York University Press, 2006).

6. Ward, "Sorcerers' Apprentices," 162.

7. Brian Lamb, Susan Swain, and Mark Farkas, eds., *The Supreme Court: A C-Span Book Featuring the Justices in Their Own Words* (New York: Public Affairs, 2010), 151.

8. Perry, *Deciding to Decide,* 67–69.

9. Noah Feldman, *Scorpions: The Battles and Triumphs of FDR's Great Supreme Court Justices* (New York: Twelve, 2010).

10. Perry, *Deciding to Decide.*

11. Lawrence Baum, *The Supreme Court,* 11th ed. (Washington, DC: CQ Press, 2013), 90–95.

12. Perry, *Deciding to Decide,* 118.

13. Joseph Tanenhaus, Marvin Schick, Matthew Muraskin, and Daniel Rosen, "The Supreme Court's Certiorari Jurisdiction: Cue Theory," in Glendon Schubert, ed., *Judicial Decision Making* (New York: Free Press, 1963), 118.

14. Perry, *Deciding to Decide,* 115.

15. Tanenhaus et al., "The Supreme Court's Certiorari Jurisdiction," 130.

16. See, e.g., S. Sidney Ulmer, William Hintze, and Louise Kirklosky, "The Decision to Grant or Deny Certiorari: Further Consideration of Cue Theory," *Law and Society Review* 6 (1972): 637–644; Doris Marie Provine, *Case Selection in the United States Supreme Court* (Chicago: University of Chicago Press, 1980).

17. Richard L. Pacelle Jr., *The Transformation of the Supreme Court's Agenda: From the New Deal to the Reagan Administration* (Boulder, CO: Westview Press, 1991).

18. Provine, *Case Selection in the United States Supreme Court.*

19. Perry, *Deciding to Decide,* 125.

20. Gregory A. Caldeira and John R. Wright, "Organized Interests and Agenda Setting in the U.S. Supreme Court," *American Political Science Review* 82 (1988): 1109–1127; Gregory A. Caldeira and John R. Wright, "*Amicus Curiae* Before the Supreme Court: Who Participates, When and How Much," *Journal of Politics* 52 (1990): 782–806.

21. Quoted in Baum, *The Supreme Court,* 95.

22. Kevin T. McGuire, Georg Vanberg, Charles E. Smith Jr., and Gregory A. Caldeira, "Measuring Policy Content on the U.S. Supreme Court," *Journal of Politics* 71 (2009): 1305–1321, at 1307.

23. Baum, *The Supreme Court,* 93.

24. William H. Rehnquist, *The Supreme Court: How It Was, How It Is* (New York: William Morrow, 1987), 127.

25. "Confirmation Hearings on the Nominations of Thomas Perrelli, Nominee to Be Associate Attorney General of the United States, and Elena Kagan, Nominee to Be Solicitor General of the United States," Senate Judiciary Committee, 111th Congress, 1st Session, February 10, 2009.

26. Perry, *Deciding to Decide.*

27. Quoted in Lamb, Swain, and Farkas, eds., *The Supreme Court,* 13.

28. Perry, *Deciding to Decide,* 251.

29. Quoted in Lamb, Swain, and Farkas, eds., *The Supreme Court,* 126–127.

30. Perry, *Deciding to Decide,* 119.

31. Gregory A. Caldeira and John R. Wright, "Organized Interests and Agenda Setting in the U.S. Supreme Court," *American Political Science Review* 82 (1988): 1109–1127; Caldeira and Wright, "*Amicus Curiae* Before the Supreme Court."

32. Lincoln Caplan, *The Tenth Justice: The Solicitor General and the Rule of Law* (New York: Alfred A. Knopf, 1987); Rebecca Mae Salokar, *The Solicitor General: The Politics of Law* (Philadelphia: Temple University Press, 1992).

33. Lawrence Baum, *The Puzzle of Judicial Behavior* (Ann Arbor: University of Michigan Press, 1997), 81.

34. David R. Stras, "The Supreme Court's Gatekeepers: The Role of Law Clerks in the Certiorari Process," *Texas Law Review* 85 (2007): 947–997, at 981.

35. Perry, *Deciding to Decide,* 170.

36. Ibid., 174.

37. Adam Liptak, "Bucking a Trend, Supreme Court Justices Reject Video Coverage," *New York Times,* February 19, 2013.

38. Joanna Anderson, "Judiciary Panel OKs Bill Urging High Court TV," *CQ Weekly,* February 13, 2012.

39. Liptak, "Bucking a Trend."

40. Walter Pincus, "The Case for Keeping Cameras Out of the Supreme Court," *Washington Post,* March 29, 2013.

41. Jeffrey A. Segal and Harold J. Spaeth, *The Supreme Court and the Attitudinal Model Revisited* (New York: Cambridge University Press, 2002), 280.

42. David W. Rohde and Harold J. Spaeth, *Supreme Court Decision-Making* (San Francisco: Freeman, 1976), 153.

43. Ryan C. Black, Timothy R. Johnson, and Justin Wedeking, *Arguments and Coalition Formation on the U.S. Supreme Court: A Deliberate Dialogue* (Ann Arbor: University of Michigan Press, 2012).

44. Ibid., 6–9.

45. William H. Rehnquist, *The Supreme Court,* rev. ed. (New York: Vintage, 2001), 243.

46. Quoted in Jan Crawford Greenburg, "Interview with Chief Justice Roberts," *Nightline,* ABC News, November 15, 2006.

47. Paul J. Wahlbeck, "Strategy and Constraints on Supreme Court Opinion Assignments," *University of Pennsylvania Law Review* 154 (2006): 1729–1755.

48. Jan Crawford, "Roberts Switched Views to Uphold Health Care Law," CBS News, July 1, 2012.

49. Baum, *The Supreme Court,* 132.

50. Quoted in ibid., 131.

51. Linda Greenhouse, "Down the Memory Hole," *New York Times,* October 2, 2009.

52. See Bernard Schwartz, *Decision: How the Supreme Court Decides Cases* (New York: Oxford University Press, 1996).

53. See, e.g., Todd C. Peppers and Artemus Ward, eds., *In Chambers: Stories of Supreme Court Law Clerks and Their Justices* (Charlottesville: University of Virginia Press, 2012).

54. Ward, "Sorcerers' Apprentices," 152.

55. Todd C. Peppers and Christopher Zorn, "Law Clerk Influence on Supreme Court Decision Making: An Empirical Assessment," *DePaul Law Review* 58 (2008): 51–77.

56. Baum, *The Supreme Court,* 16.

57. Cory Ditslear and Lawrence Baum, "Selection of Law Clerks and Polarization in the U.S. Supreme Court," *Journal of Politics* 63 (2001): 869–885.

58. Charles Lane, "Former Clerks' Signing Bonuses Rival Salaries on the High Court," *Washington Post,* May 15, 2006.

59. Baum, *The Supreme Court,* 16.

60. Quoted in Lamb, Swain, and Farkas, eds., *The Supreme Court,* 153.

61. Ward, "Sorcerers' Apprentices," 152.

62. Todd C. Peppers, *Courtiers of the Marble Palace: The Rise and Influence of the Supreme Court Law Clerk* (Stanford, CA: Stanford University Press, 2006), 17.

63. Bob Woodward and Scott Armstrong, *The Brethren: Inside the Supreme Court* (New York: Simon and Schuster, 1979).

64. Edward Lazarus, *Closed Chambers: The First Eyewitness Account of the Epic Struggles Inside the Supreme Court* (New York: Times Books, 1998).

65. Barbara A. Perry, *The Priestly Tribe: The Supreme Court's Image in the American Mind* (Westport, CT: Praeger, 1999), 76.

66. Ibid., 94.

67. Sam Baker, "Supreme Court Healthcare Ruling Leaks Have DC Buzzing: Who Is the Culprit?" *The Hill*, July 4, 2012; Dylan Byers, "Who Leaked the Supreme Court Story?" *Politico*, July 3, 2012.

68. Harvey Rishikof and Barbara A. Perry, "Separateness but Interdependence, Autonomy but Reciprocity: A First Look at Federal Judges' Appearances Before Legislative Committees," *Mercer Law Review* 46 (1995): 667–676.

69. Christopher R. Benson, "A Renewed Call for Diversity Among Supreme Court Clerks: How a Diverse Body of Clerks Can Aid the High Court as an Institution," *Harvard BlackLetter Law Journal* 23 (2007): 23–54.

70. Peppers, *Courtiers of the Marble Palace*, 20–23.

71. Ibid., 24.

72. Tony Mauro, "Rehnquist: Diversity a Grad Pool Function," *USA Today*, December 8, 1998.

73. Todd Ruger, "Statistics Show No Progress in Federal Law Clerk Diversity," *National Law Journal*, May 2, 2012.

74. Tony Mauro, "Corps of Clerks Lacking in Diversity," *USA Today*, March 13, 1998; Tony Mauro, "Only 1 New High Court Clerk Is a Minority," *USA Today*, September 10, 1998.

75. "Protest Outside High Court," *New York Times*, October 6, 1998.

76. See, e.g., Robert M. Agostisi and Brian P. Corrigan, "Do as We Say or Do as We Do: How the Supreme Court Law Clerk Controversy Reveals a Lack of Accountability at the High Court," *Hofstra Labor and Employment Law Journal* 18 (2001): 625–658; Randall Kennedy, "The Clerkship Question and the Court," *American Lawyer*, April 1999, 114–115; Laura Gatland, "A Clerkship for White Males Only," *Student Lawyer*, October 1999, 34–39.

77. Joan Biskupic, "In Testimony, Justices Defend Court's Hiring Practices," *Washington Post*, March 11, 1999; Joan Biskupic, "Two Justices Defend Lack of Minority Court Clerks," *Washington Post*, March 16, 2000.

78. Linda Greenhouse, "Women Suddenly Scarce Among Justices' Clerks," *New York Times*, August 30, 2006.

79. Christopher P. Banks, *Judicial Politics in the D.C. Circuit Court* (Baltimore: Johns Hopkins University Press, 1999), 97.

80. Martinek, "Appellate Workhorses of the Federal Judiciary," 130.

81. Virginia A. Hettinger, Stefanie A. Lindquist, and Wendy L. Martinek, *Judging on a Collegial Court: Influences on Federal Appellate Decision Making* (Charlottesville: University of Virginia Press, 2006), 36.

82. David E. Klein, *Making Law in the United States Courts of Appeals* (New York: Cambridge University Press, 2002), 34.

83. Malia Reddick and Sara C. Benesh, "Norm Violation by the Lower Courts in the Treatment of Supreme Court Precedent: A Research Framework," *Justice System Journal* 21 (2000): 117–142.

84. Frank B. Cross, *Decision Making in the U.S. Courts of Appeals* (Stanford, CA: Stanford University Press, 2007), 228.

85. Hettinger, Lindquist, and Martinek, *Judging on a Collegial Court,* 53.

86. Shelley Murphy and Sarah Schweitzer, "A Bulger Win as Trial Judge Is Removed," *Boston Globe,* March 15, 2013.

87. Darryl Van Dutch, "Senior Judge Ranks Close Vacancy Gap," *National Law Journal,* July 22, 1996.

88. Hettinger, Lindquist, and Martinek, *Judging on a Collegial Court,* 54.

89. Martinek, "Appellate Workhorses of the Federal Judiciary," 137.

90. Hettinger, Lindquist, and Martinek, *Judging on a Collegial Court,* 35.

91. Cross, *Decision Making in the U.S. Courts of Appeals,* 160.

92. Ibid., 163.

93. Scott A. Comparato, Scott D. McClurg, and Shane A. Gleason, "Patterns of Policy Making Across State Supreme Courts," in Kevin McGuire, ed., *New Directions in Judicial Politics* (New York: Routledge, 2012), 110.

94. See, e.g., Louis Fisher and Katy J. Harringer, *American Constitutional Law,* 9th ed. (Durham, NC: Carolina Academic Press, 2011), 215–225.

95. Bradley Canon and Charles Johnson, *Judicial Policies: Implementation and Impact,* 2nd ed. (Washington, DC: CQ Press, 1998).

96. Baum, *The Supreme Court,* 190.

97. Cross, *Decision Making in the U.S. Courts of Appeals,* 99–100.

98. Richard A. Posner, *How Judges Think* (Cambridge, MA: Harvard University Press, 2008), 71.

99. Evan H. Caminker, "Why Must Inferior Courts Obey Supreme Court Precedents?" *Stanford Law Review* 46 (1994): 817–873.

100. Canon and Johnson, *Judicial Policies,* 92–114.

101. G. Alan Tarr, *Judicial Impact and State Supreme Courts* (Lexington, MA: Lexington Books, 1977).

102. David R. Manwaring, "The Impact of *Mapp v. Ohio,*" in David H. Everson, ed., *The Supreme Court as Policy-Maker,* 2nd ed. (Carbondale, IL: Public Affairs Research Bureau, 1968).

103. Reddick and Benesh, "Norm Violation by the Lower Courts in the Treatment of Supreme Court Precedent."

104. Sara C. Benesh and Wendy L. Martinek, "Lower Court Compliance with Precedent," in Kevin McGuire, ed., *New Directions in Judicial Politics* (New York: Routledge, 2012), 261.

105. *Burnet v. Coronado Oil and Gas Company,* 285 U.S. 293, 406 (1932).

106. Comparato, McClurg, and Gleason, "Patterns of Policy Making Across State Supreme Courts," 119.

107. Jennifer K. Luse, Geoffrey McGovern, Wendy L. Martinek, and Sara C. Benesh, "'Such Inferior Courts . . . ': Compliance by Circuits with Jurisprudential Regimes," *American Politics Research* 37 (2009): 75–106.

Chapter 8: Studying Decision Making on Appellate Courts

1. Michael A. Bailey and Forrest Maltzman, *The Constrained Court: Law, Politics, and the Decisions Justices Make* (Princeton, NJ: Princeton University Press, 2011), 5.

2. Walter F. Murphy, C. Herman Pritchett, and Lee Epstein, *Courts, Judges, and Politics: An Introduction to the Judicial Process* (Boston: McGraw-Hill, 2002), 13.

3. Oliver Wendell Holmes Jr., *The Common Law* (Boston: Little, Brown, 1881), 1.

4. Quoted in Christopher Wolfe, *Judicial Activism: Bulwark of Freedom or Precarious Security?* (Lanham, MD: Rowman and Littlefield, 1997), 30.

5. Richard A. Posner, *How Judges Think* (Cambridge, MA: Harvard University Press, 2008), 41.

6. Ibid.

7. Bailey and Maltzman, *The Constrained Court*, 2.

8. Richard L. Pacelle Jr., Brett W. Curry, and Bryan W. Marshall, *Decision Making by the Modern Supreme Court* (New York: Cambridge University Press, 2011), 2.

9. R. A. W. Rhodes, Sarah A. Binder, and Bert A. Rockman, eds., *The Oxford Handbook of Political Institutions* (New York: Oxford University Press, 2006), xii.

10. See C. Herman Pritchett, *The Roosevelt Court: A Study in Judicial Politics and Values, 1937–1947* (New York: Macmillan, 1948); C. Herman Pritchett, *Civil Liberties and the Vinson Court* (Chicago: University of Chicago Press, 1954); C. Herman Pritchett, *Congress Versus the Supreme Court, 1957–60* (Minneapolis: University of Minnesota Press, 1961).

11. Bailey and Maltzman, *The Constrained Court*, 5.

12. Forrest Maltzman, James F. Spriggs II, and Paul J. Wahlbeck, *Crafting Law on the Supreme Court: The Collegial Game* (New York: Cambridge University Press, 2000), 11–12.

13. Jeffrey Segal and Harold Spaeth, *The Supreme Court and the Attitudinal Model Revisited* (New York: Cambridge University Press, 2002).

14. Lawrence Baum, *Judges and Their Audiences: A Perspective on Judicial Behavior* (Princeton, NJ: Princeton University Press, 2006), 5.

15. Ibid., 7.

16. Bailey and Maltzman, *The Constrained Court*, 5.

17. Ibid., 1–2.

18. Pacelle, Curry, and Marshall, *Decision Making by the Modern Supreme Court*, 2.

19. Frank B. Cross, "Law Is Politics," in Charles Gardner Geyh, ed., *What's Law Got to Do with It: What Judges Do, Why They Do It, and What's at Stake* (Stanford, CA: Stanford University Press, 2011), 92.

20. Quoted in Adam Liptak, "Roberts Sets Off Debate on Judicial Experience," *New York Times,* February 16, 2009.

21. Judge Richard Posner, however, supports the idea that judges are ideological beings. Posner, *How Judges Think*, 93–121.

22. Adam Liptak, "Approval Rating for Justices Hits Just 44% in New Poll," *New York Times,* June 7, 2012.

23. Sheryl Gay Stolberg and Dalia Sussman, "Gay Marriage Seen as Issue for the States," *New York Times,* June 7, 2013.

24. Bailey and Maltzman, *The Constrained Court,* 154.

25. James L. Gibson, "From Simplicity to Complexity: The Development of Theory in the Study of Judicial Behavior," *Journal of Political Behavior* 5 (1983): 7–49, at 9.

26. See, e.g., Rogers Smith, "Political Jurisprudence: The New Institutionalism and the Future of Public Law," *American Political Science Review* 82 (1988): 89–108.

27. John M. Carey, "Parchment, Equilibria and Institutions," *Comparative Political Studies* 33 (2000): 735–761, at 735.

28. Douglas C. North, *Institutions, Institutional Change and Economic Performance* (New York: Cambridge University Press, 1990), 30.

29. Kim A. Shepsle, "Rational Choice Institutionalism," in R. A. W. Rhodes, Sarah A. Binder, and Bert A. Rockman, eds., *The Oxford Handbook of Political Institutions* (New York: Oxford University Press, 2006).

30. Rhodes, Binder, and Rockman, eds., *The Oxford Handbook of Political Institutions,* xiii.

31. Peter A. Hall and Rosemary C. R. Taylor, "Political Science and the Three New Institutionalisms," *Political Studies* 44 (1996): 936–957, at 947.

32. Ibid.

33. Ibid., 938.

34. Rhodes, Binder, and Rockman, eds., *The Oxford Handbook of Political Institutions,* xv.

35. Lee Epstein and Jack Knight, *The Choices Justices Make* (Washington, DC: CQ Press, 1998), 12.

36. Walter F. Murphy, *Elements of Judicial Strategy* (Chicago: University of Chicago Press, 1964).

37. See Maltzman, Spriggs, and Wahlbeck, *Crafting Law on the Supreme Court.*

38. Epstein and Knight, *The Choices Justices Make,* 1–9.

39. See ibid.

40. Ibid., 145.

41. Pacelle, Curry, and Marshall, *Decision Making by the Modern Supreme Court,* 48.

42. Linda Greenhouse, "A Justice in Chief," *New York Times,* June 28, 2012.

43. Robert Barnes and Del Quentin Wilber, "Chief Justice John Roberts's Health-Care Ruling Gets Plenty Second-Guessing," *Washington Post,* June 29, 2012.

44. Greenhouse, "A Justice in Chief."

45. Baum, *Judges and Their Audiences.*

46. Eileen Braman, *Law, Politics, and Perception: How Policy Preferences Influence Legal Reasoning* (Charlottesville: University of Virginia Press, 2009), 4.

47. Pacelle, Curry, and Marshall, *Decision Making by the Modern Supreme Court.*

48. Ibid., 201.

49. Mark J. Richards and Herbert M. Kritzer, "Jurisprudential Regimes in Supreme Court Decision Making," *American Political Science Review* 96 (2002): 305–320, at 308.

50. Lawrence Baum, "Law and Policy: More and Less Than a Dichotomy," in Charles Gardner Geyh, ed., *What's Law Got to Do with It: What Judges Do, Why They Do It, and What's at Stake* (Stanford, CA: Stanford University Press, 2011), 77.

51. Justice Frank Sullivan Jr. of the Indiana Supreme Court, quoted in Charles Gardner Geyh, ed., *What's Law Got to Do with It: What Judges Do, Why They Do It, and What's at Stake* (Stanford, CA: Stanford University Press, 2011), 328.

52. Judge Nancy Vaidik of the Indiana Court of Appeals, quoted in Geyh, ed., *What's Law Got to Do with It,* 333.

53. U.S. District Court Judge Sarah Evans Barker, quoted in Geyh, ed., *What's Law Got to Do with It,* 337.

54. See, e.g., Mark A. Graber, "Legal, Strategic or Legal Strategy: Deciding to Decide During the Civil War and Reconstruction," in Ronald Kahn and Ken I. Kersch, eds., *The Supreme Court and American Political Development* (Lawrence: University Press of Kansas, 2006), 59.

55. See, e.g., Richards and Kritzer, "Jurisprudential Regimes in Supreme Court Decision Making."

56. Lawrence M. Friedman, "Judge the Judges: Some Remarks on the Way Judges Think and the Way Judges Act," in John N. Drobak, ed., *Norms and the Law* (New York: Cambridge University Press, 2006), 149 (emphasis in original).

57. Posner, *How Judges Think,* 61.

58. *Roper v. Simmons,* 543 U.S. 551 at 607 (2005).

59. *Gonzales v. Raich,* 545 U.S. 1 at 57 (2005).

60. *Griswold v. Connecticut,* 381 U.S. 479 at 527 (1965).

61. *Lawrence v. Texas,* 539 U.S. 558 at 605 (2003).

62. Quoted in Linda Greenhouse, "Justice Weighs Desire v. Duty (Duty Prevails)," *New York Times,* August 25, 2005.

63. Quoted in Jeffrey Rosen, "The Dissenter," *New York Times Magazine,* September 23, 2007.

64. S. Sidney Ulmer, *Courts as Small and Not So Small Groups* (New York: General Learning, 1971), 1.

65. William H. Rehnquist, *The Supreme Court* (New York: Alfred A. Knopf, 2001), 222.

66. Noah Feldman, *Scorpions: The Battles and Triumphs of FDR's Great Supreme Court Justices* (New York: Twelve, 2010).

67. Barbara A. Perry, *The Priestly Tribe: The Supreme Court's Image in the American Mind* (Westport, CT: Praeger, 1999), 1–2.

68. Murphy, *Elements of Judicial Strategy,* 83.

69. David J. Danelski and Jeanne C. Danelski, "Leadership in the Warren Court," in Sheldon Goldman and Austin Sarat, eds., *American Court Systems: Reading in Judicial Process and Behavior,* 2nd ed. (New York: Longman, 1989).

70. Linda Greenhouse, *Becoming Justice Blackmun: Harry Blackmun's Supreme Court Journey* (New York: Times Books, 2006).

71. Joan Biskupic, *Sandra Day O'Connor: How the First Woman on the Supreme Court Became Its Most Influential Justice* (New York: HarperCollins, 2006).

72. Ibid.

73. Timothy M. Hagle, "'Freshman Effects' for Supreme Court Justices," *American Journal of Political Science* 37 (1993): 1142–1157.

74. Virginia A. Hettinger, Stefanie A. Lindquist, and Wendy L. Martinek, "Acclimation Effects on the United States Courts of Appeals," *Social Science Quarterly* 84 (2003): 792–810.

75. See, e.g., Lawrence Baum, *American Courts: Process and Policy,* 6th ed. (Boston: Houghton Mifflin, 2008), 278–281.

76. Virginia A. Hettinger, Stefanie A. Lindquist, and Wendy L. Martinek, *Judging on a Collegial Court: Influences on Federal Appellate Decision Making* (Charlottesville: University of Virginia Press, 2006).

77. Ibid., 33.

78. Posner, *How Judges Think,* 31.

79. See, e.g., Richard L. Revesz, "Environmental Regulation, Ideology, and the D.C. Circuit," *Virginia Law Review* 83 (1997): 1717–1772; Frank B. Cross and Emerson H. Tiller, "Judicial Partisanship and Obedience to Legal Doctrine: Whistleblowing on the Federal Courts of Appeals," *Yale Law Journal* 107 (1998): 2155–2176.

80. Harry T. Edwards, "The Effects of Collegiality on Judicial Decision Making," *University of Pennsylvania Law Review* 151 (2003): 1639–1690.

81. Frank B. Cross, *Decision Making in the U.S. Courts of Appeals* (Stanford, CA: Stanford University Press, 2007), 177.

82. See, e.g., Anna Law, *The Immigration Battle in American Courts* (New York: Cambridge University Press, 2010).

83. Sara C. Benesh and Wendy L. Martinek, "Lower Court Compliance with Precedent," in Kevin McGuire, ed., *New Directions in Judicial Politics* (New York: Routledge, 2012), 263.

84. Wendy L. Martinek, "Appellate Workhorses of the Federal Judiciary: The U.S. Courts of Appeals," in Mark C. Miller, ed., *Exploring Judicial Politics* (New York: Oxford University Press, 2009), 136.

85. Donald R. Songer and Susan Reid, "Policy Change on the U.S. Courts of Appeals: Exploring the Contribution of the Legal and Democratic Subcultures," paper presented at the annual meeting of the American Political Science Association, September 1–3, 1989.

86. Donald R. Songer, Jeffrey A. Segal, and Charles M. Cameron, "The Hierarchy of Justice: Testing a Principal-Agent Model of Supreme Court–Circuit Court Interactions," *American Journal of Political Science* 38 (1994): 673–696.

87. See, e.g., Anna Malia Reddick, "The Applicability of Legal and Attitudinal Models to the Treatment of Precedent in the Courts of Appeals," Ph.D. dissertation,

Michigan State University, 1997; Sara C. Benesh, *The U.S. Courts of Appeals and the Law of Confession: Perspectives on the Hierarchy of Justice* (New York: LFB Scholarly Publishing, 2002).

88. Pacelle, Curry, and Marshall, *Decision Making by the Modern Supreme Court,* 11.

89. Martinek, "Appellate Workhorses of the Federal Judiciary," 136.

90. David E. Klein, *Making Law in the United States Courts of Appeals* (New York: Cambridge University Press, 2002), 122.

91. Ibid., 135.

92. Cross, *Decision Making in the U.S. Courts of Appeals,* 99–100.

93. Robert A. Dahl, "Decision-Making in a Democracy: The Supreme Court as a National Policy-Maker," *Journal of Public Law* 6 (1957): 279–295.

94. Thomas M. Keck, "Party Politics or Judicial Independence? The Regime Politics Literature Hits the Law Schools," *Law and Social Inquiry* 32 (2007): 511–544, at 512.

95. Dahl, "Decision-Making in a Democracy," 285.

96. Keck, "Party Politics or Judicial Independence?" 515.

97. Ibid., 513.

98. Howard Gillman, "Regime Politics, Jurisprudential Regimes, and Unenumerated Rights," *University of Pennsylvania Journal of Constitutional Law* 9 (2006): 107–119, at 107.

99. Cornell W. Clayton and J. Mitchell Pickerill, "The Politics of Criminal Justice: How the New Right Regime Shaped the Rehnquist Court's Criminal Justice Jurisprudence," *Georgetown Law Journal* 94 (2006): 1385–1425, at 1391.

100. Gerald N. Rosenberg, *The Hollow Hope: Can Courts Bring About Social Change?* (Chicago: University of Chicago Press, 1991).

101. Terri Peretti, *In Defense of a Political Court* (Princeton, NJ: Princeton University Press, 1999), 100.

102. Robert McCloskey, *The American Supreme Court* (Chicago: University of Chicago Press, 1960), 23.

103. Bailey and Maltzman, *The Constrained Court,* 83.

104. Jonathan D. Casper, "The Supreme Court and National Policy Making," *American Political Science Review* 70 (1976): 50–63, at 62.

105. Keck, "Party Politics or Judicial Independence?," 517.

106. Richards and Kritzer, "Jurisprudential Regimes in Supreme Court Decision Making."

107. McCloskey, *The American Supreme Court,* 20.

108. Roy B. Flemming, B. Dan Wood, and John Bohte, "Attention to Issues in a System of Separated Powers: The Macrodynamics of American Policy Agendas," *Journal of Politics* 61 (1999): 76–108, at 104.

109. Casper, "The Supreme Court and National Policy Making," 62.

110. Ruth Bader Ginsburg, "Communicating and Commenting on the Court's Work," *Georgetown Law Journal* 83 (1995): 2119–2129, at 2125.

111. Robert H. Jackson, *The Supreme Court in the American System of Government* (Cambridge, MA: Harvard University Press, 1955), 2.

112. Alexander M. Bickel, *The Least Dangerous Branch: The Supreme Court at the Bar of Politics* (Indianapolis, IN: Bobbs-Merrill, 1962).

113. Louis Fisher, *Constitutional Dialogues: Interpretation as Political Process* (Princeton: Princeton University Press, 1988).

114. Louis Fisher, "Judicial Finality or an Ongoing Colloquy?" in Mark C. Miller and Jeb Barnes, eds., *Making Policy, Making Law: An Interbranch Perspective* (Washington, DC: Georgetown University Press, 2004), 153.

Chapter 9: Public Opinion, Interest Groups, the Media, and the Courts

1. Philip B. Kurland, "'The Cult of the Robe' and the Jaworski Case," *Washington Post*, June 23, 1974.

2. Alexis de Tocqueville, *Democracy in America*, trans. George Lawrence (New York: Harper and Row, 1966), 150.

3. Jeffery J. Mondak and Shannon Ishiyama Smithey, "The Dynamics of Public Support for the Supreme Court," *Journal of Politics* 59 (1997): 1114–1142.

4. Sara C. Benesh, "Judicial Elections: Directions in the Study of Institutional Legitimacy," *Judicature* 96 (2013): 204–208, 205.

5. Ibid.

6. James L. Gibson, *Electing Judges: The Surprising Effects of Campaigning on Judicial Legitimacy* (Chicago: University of Chicago Press, 2012), 5.

7. James L. Gibson and Gregory A. Caldeira, *Citizens, Courts, and Confirmations: Positivity Theory and the Judgments of the American People* (Princeton, NJ: Princeton University Press, 2009), 42.

8. Quoted in Brian Lamb, Susan Swain, and Mark Farkas, eds., *The Supreme Court: A C-SPAN Book Featuring the Justices in Their Own Words* (New York: Public Affairs, 2010), 167.

9. James L. Gibson and Gregory A. Caldeira, "The Etiology of Public Support for the Supreme Court," *American Journal of Political Science* 36 (1992): 635–664, at 658.

10. James Bryce, *The American Commonwealth,* 2nd ed., vol. 1 (London: Macmillan, 1891).

11. Walter Murphy, *Congress and the Court* (Chicago: University of Chicago Press, 1962).

12. Jeffrey A. Segal, Harold J. Spaeth, and Sara C. Benesh, *The Supreme Court in the American Legal System* (New York: Cambridge University Press, 2005), 17.

13. Walter Murphy, *Elements of Judicial Strategy* (Chicago: University of Chicago Press, 1964), 16.

14. Barbara A. Perry, *The Priestly Tribe: The Supreme Court's Image in the American Mind* (Westport, CT: Praeger, 1999).

15. Ibid., 2.

16. See, e.g., Arthur Miller, "Some Pervasive Myths About the U.S. Supreme Court," *St. Louis University Law Journal* 10 (1965): 153–189; Gibson and Caldeira, *Citizens, Courts, and Confirmations,* 44.

17. Robert J. Hume, "Legitimacy, Yes: But at What Cost?" *Judicature* 96 (2013): 209–212.

18. Gibson and Caldeira, *Citizens, Courts, and Confirmations,* 44.

19. Adam Liptak and Allison Kopicki, "Approval Rating for Justices Hits Just 44% in New Poll," *New York Times,* June 7, 2012.

20. Adam Liptak and Allison Kopicki, "Public's Opinion of Supreme Court Drops After Health Care Law Decision," *New York Times,* July 18, 2012.

21. Sheryl Gay Stolberg and Dalia Sussman, "Gay Marriage Seen as Issue for the States," *New York Times,* June 7, 2013.

22. Ibid.

23. Lawrence Baum, *Judges and Their Audiences: A Perspective on Judicial Behavior* (Princeton, NJ: Princeton University Press, 2006), 155.

24. See, e.g., Michael W. Giles, Bethany Blackstone, and Richard L. Vining, "The Supreme Court in American Democracy: Unraveling the Linkages Between Public Opinion and Judicial Decision Making," *Journal of Politics* 70 (2008): 293–306.

25. Michael J. Klarman, *From Jim Crow to Civil Rights: The Supreme Court and the Struggle for Racial Equality* (New York: Oxford University Press, 2004), 6.

26. Quoted in R. W. Apple, "Justices Are People," *New York Times,* April 10, 1989.

27. Thomas Marshall, *Public Opinion and the Supreme Court* (New York: Unwin Hyman, 1989).

28. Quoted in Linda Greenhouse, "Public Opinion and the Supreme Court: The Puzzling Case of Abortion," *Daedalus, the Journal of the American Academy of Arts and Sciences* 141 (2012): 69–82, at 72.

29. See, e.g., David Adamany and Joel Grossman, "Support for the Supreme Court as a National Policy Maker," *Law and Policy Quarterly* 5 (1983): 405–437.

30. Kevin T. McGuire and James A. Stimson, "The Least Dangerous Branch Revisited: New Evidence on Supreme Court Responsiveness to Public Preferences," *Journal of Politics* 66 (2004): 1018–1035, at 1019.

31. Richard A. Posner, *How Judges Think* (Cambridge, MA: Harvard University Press, 2008), 14.

32. See, e.g., Jeffrey A. Segal and Harold J. Spaeth, *The Supreme Court and the Attitudinal Model Revisited* (Cambridge: Cambridge University Press, 2002).

33. Christopher J. Casillas, Peter K. Enns, and Patrick C. Wohlfarth, "How Public Opinion Constrains the U.S. Supreme Court," *American Journal of Political Science* 55 (2011): 74–88, at 75.

34. Isaac Unah and Ange-Marie Hancock, "U.S. Supreme Court Decision Making, Case Salience, and the Attitudinal Model," *Law and Policy* 28 (2006): 295–320.

35. Forrest Maltzman, James F. Spriggs II, and Paul J. Wahlbeck, *Crafting Law on the Supreme Court: The Collegial Game* (New York: Cambridge University Press, 2000).

36. Elliot E. Slotnick and Jennifer A. Segal, *Television News and the Supreme Court* (New York: Cambridge University Press, 1998), 81.

37. Casillas, Enns, and Wohlfarth, "How Public Opinion Constrains the U.S. Supreme Court," 81.

38. See, e.g., Robert H. Durr, Andrew D. Martin, and Christina Wolbrecht, "Ideological Divergence and Public Support for the Supreme Court," *American Journal of Political Science* 44 (2000): 768–776.

39. See, e.g., Robert A. Dahl, "Decision-Making in a Democracy: The Supreme Court as a National Policy-Maker," *Journal of Public Law* 6 (1957): 279–295.

40. Charles H. Franklin and Liane Kosaki, "The Republican Schoolmaster: The Supreme Court, Public Opinion and Abortion," *American Political Science Review* 83 (1989): 751–772.

41. See, e.g., Danette Brickman and David A. M. Peterson, "Public Opinion Reaction to Repeated Events: Citizen Response to Multiple Supreme Court Abortion Decisions," *Political Behavior* 28 (2006): 87–112; Franklin and Kosaki, "The Republican Schoolmaster."

42. Christopher Wlezien and Malcolm L. Goggin, "The Courts, Interest Groups, and Public Opinion About Abortion," *Political Behavior* 15 (1993): 381–405.

43. Timothy R. Johnson and Andrew D. Martin, "The Public's Conditional Response to Supreme Court Decisions," *American Political Science Review* 92 (1998): 299–309.

44. Brickman and Peterson, "Public Opinion Reaction to Repeated Events," 107.

45. Johnson and Martin, "The Public's Conditional Response to Supreme Court Decisions."

46. Michael A. Unger, "After the Supreme Word: The Effect of *McCreary County v. ACLU* (2005) and *Van Orden v. Perry* (2005) on Support for Public Displays of the Ten Commandments," *American Politics Research* 36 (2008): 750–775.

47. James W. Stoutenborough, Donald P. Haider-Markel, and Mahalley D. Allen, "Reassessing the Impact of Supreme Court Decisions on Public Opinion: Gay Civil Rights Cases," *Political Research Quarterly* 59 (2006): 419–433.

48. David Pozen, "Are Judicial Elections Democracy-Enhancing?" in Charles Gardner Geyh, ed., *What's Law Got to Do with It? What Judges Do, Why They Do It, and What's at Stake* (Stanford, CA: Stanford University Press, 2011), 271.

49. Thomas M. Keck, "Beyond Backlash: Assessing the Impact of Judicial Decisions on LGBT Rights," *Law and Society Review* 43 (2009): 151–185, at 162.

50. Johnson and Martin, "The Public's Conditional Response to Supreme Court Decisions," *American Political Science Review* 92 (2009): 299–309, at 299.

51. Neal Devins and Nicole Mansker, "Public Opinion and State Supreme Courts," *University of Pennsylvania Journal of Constitutional Law* 13 (2010): 455–509, at 456.

52. Grant Schulte, "Iowans Dismiss Three Justices," *Des Moines Register,* November 3, 2010.

53. Devins and Mansker, "Public Opinion and State Supreme Courts."

54. Paul Brace and Melinda Gann Hall, "Studying Courts Comparatively: The View from the American States," *Political Research Quarterly* 48 (1995): 5–29.

55. Gregory A. Huber and Sanford C. Gordon, "Accountability and Coercion: Is Justice Blind When It Runs for Office?" *American Journal of Political Science* 48 (2004): 247–263.

56. See, e.g., Lee Epstein, "Electoral Benefits: The Assault on the Assaulters of Judicial Elections," *Judicature* 96 (2013): 218–222.

57. Quoted in Paul Riedinger, "The Politics of Judging," *American Bar Association Journal* 73 (1997): 52–81, at 58.

58. See, e.g., T. R. Tyler, *Why People Obey the Law* (New Haven, CT: Yale University Press, 1990); James P. Wenzel, Shaun Bowler, and David J. Lanoue, "The Sources of Public Confidence in State Courts: Experience and Institutions," *American Politics Research* 31 (2003): 191–211.

59. Sara C. Benesh, "Understanding Public Confidence in American Courts," *Journal of Politics* 68 (2006): 697–707.

60. Gibson, *Electing Judges.*

61. Benesh, "Understanding Public Confidence in American Courts."

62. Christine A. Kelleher and Jennifer Wolak, "Explaining Public Confidence in the Branches of State Government," *Political Research Quarterly* 60 (2007): 707–721.

63. Ibid., 715.

64. Ibid., 718.

65. See Kay Lehman Schlozman and John T. Tierney, *Organized Interests and American Democracy* (New York: Harper and Row, 1986).

66. Gregory A. Caldeira and John R. Wright, "*Amicus Curiae* Before the Supreme Court: Who Participates, When and How Much," *Journal of Politics* 52 (1990): 782–806.

67. Paul M. Collins Jr., "Interest Groups and Their Influence on Judicial Policy," in Kevin T. McGuire, ed., *New Directions in Judicial Politics* (New York: Routledge, 2012).

68. Baum, *Judges and Their Audiences,* 119.

69. See, e.g., Welsh S. White, *Litigating in the Shadow of Death: Defense Attorneys in Capital Cases* (Ann Arbor: University of Michigan Press, 2006).

70. Karen O'Connor, "Lobbying the Justices or Lobbying for Justice? The Role of Organized Interests in the Judicial Process," in Paul S. Herrnson, Ronald G. Shaiko, and Clyde Wilcox, *The Interest Group Connection: Electioneering, Lobbying, and Policymaking in Washington* (Washington, DC: CQ Press, 2005), 328–329.

71. Collins, "Interest Groups and Their Influence on Judicial Policy," 223.

72. Carl Tobias, "Standing to Intervene," *Wisconsin Law Review,* 1991, 415–463.

73. Michael Rustad and Thomas Koenig, "The Supreme Court and Junk Social Science: Selective Distortion in Amicus Briefs," *North Carolina Law Review* 72 (1993): 91–162.

74. Joseph Kearney and Thomas Merrill, "The Influence of Amicus Curiae Briefs on the Supreme Court," *University of Pennsylvania Law Review* 148 (2000): 743–854.

75. Lee Epstein and Jack Knight, "Mapping Out the Strategic Terrain: The Informational Role of Amici Curiae," in Cornell W. Clayton and Howard Gillman, eds.,

Supreme Court Decision Making: New Institutionalist Approaches (Chicago: University of Chicago Press, 1999), 225.

76. Paul M. Collins Jr., *Friends of the Court: Interest Groups and Judicial Decision Making* (New York: Oxford University Press, 2008), 47.

77. Collins, "Interest Groups and Their Influence on Judicial Policy," 225–226.

78. Ibid., 227–228.

79. Ibid., 229, 237.

80. Alia Beard Rau, "Court's Review of SB 1070 Provokes Dozens of Briefs," *Arizona Republic,* April 21, 2012.

81. Greg Stohr, "Record Number of Amicus Briefs Filed in Health Care Cases," Bloomberg News, March 15, 2012.

82. James F. Spriggs II and Paul J. Wahlbeck, "Amicus Curiae and the Role of Information in the Supreme Court," *Political Research Quarterly* 50 (1997): 365–386.

83. See, e.g., Ryan J. Owens and Lee Epstein, "Amici Curiae During the Rehnquist Years," *Judicature* 89 (2005): 127–132.

84. Kearney and Merrill, "The Influence of Amicus Curiae Briefs on the Supreme Court."

85. Kelly J. Lynch, "Best Friends? Supreme Court Law Clerks on Effective Amicus Curiae Briefs," *Journal of Law and Politics* 20 (2004): 33–75.

86. Paul M. Collins Jr. and Wendy L. Martinek, "Friends of the Circuits: Interest Group Influence on Decision Making in the U.S. Courts of Appeals," *Social Science Quarterly* 91 (2010): 397–414.

87. Scott A. Comparto, *Amici Curiae and Strategic Behavior in State Supreme Courts* (Westport, CT: Praeger, 2003).

88. Donald R. Songer, Ashlyn Kuersten, and Erin Kaheny, "Why the Haves Don't Always Come Out Ahead: Repeat Players Meet Amici Curiae for the Disadvantaged," *Political Research Quarterly* 53 (2000): 537–556.

89. Stephen Breyer, "The Interdependence of Science and Law," *Judicature* 82 (1998): 24–27, at 26.

90. Casillas, Enns, and Wohlfarth, "How Public Opinion Constrains the U.S. Supreme Court."

91. Lauren Cohen Bell, "In Their Own Interest: Pressure Groups in the Federal Judicial Selection Process," in Mark C. Miller, ed., *Exploring Judicial Politics* (New York: Oxford University Press, 2009), 36.

92. David M. O'Brien, *Storm Center: The Supreme Court in American Politics*, 3rd ed. (New York: W. W. Norton, 1993).

93. Nancy Scherer, *Scoring Points: Politicians, Activists, and the Lower Federal Court Appointment Process* (Stanford, CA: Stanford University Press, 2005), 136–139.

94. Nancy Scherer, Brandon L. Bartels, and Amy Steigerwalt, "Sounding the Fire Alarm: The Role of Interest Groups in the Lower Federal Court Confirmation Process," *Journal of Politics* 70 (2008): 1026–1039.

95. Gibson, *Electing Judges,* 2.

96. Stephen J. Ware, "Money, Politics, and Judicial Decisions: A Case Study of Arbitration Law in Alabama," *Journal of Law and Politics* 15 (1999): 645–686, at 656.

97. G. Alan Tarr, *Without Fear or Favor: Judicial Independence and Judicial Accountability in the States* (Stanford, CA: Stanford University Press, 2012), 79–80.

98. Quoted in Clive S. Thomas, Michael L. Boyer, and Ronald J. Hrebenar, "Interest Groups and State Court Elections: A New Era and Its Challenges," *Judicature* 87 (2003): 135–149, at 137.

99. Dan Eggen, "Special-Interest Spending Surges in State Supreme Court Campaigns," *Washington Post,* August 16, 2010.

100. Deborah Goldberg, "Interest Group Participation in Judicial Elections," in Matthew J. Streb, ed., *Running for Judge: The Rising Political, Financial, and Legal Stakes of Judicial Elections* (New York: New York University Press, 2007), 78–79.

101. Adam Skaggs, Maria de Silva, Linda Casey, and Charles Hall, *The New Politics of Judicial Elections 2009–2010* (Washington, DC: Justice at Stake Campaign, 2011).

102. Rorie L. Solberg and Eric N. Waltenburg, "Why Do Interest Groups Engage the Judiciary? Policy Wishes and Structural Needs," *Social Science Quarterly* 87 (2006): 558–572, at 570.

103. See, e.g., Hume, "Legitimacy, Yes: But at What Cost?"

104. Donald P. Haider-Markel, Mahalley D. Allen, and Morgen Johansen, "Understanding Variations in Media Coverage of U.S. Supreme Court Decisions: Comparing Media Outlets in Their Coverage of *Lawrence v. Texas*," *Harvard International Journal of Press/Politics* 11 (2006): 64–85, at 64.

105. See, e.g., Dorothy A. Bowles and Rebekah V. Bromley, "Newsmagazine Coverage of the Supreme Court During the Reagan Administration," *Journalism Quarterly* 69 (1992): 948–959; Richard Davis, "Lifting the Shroud: News Media Portrayal of the U.S. Supreme Court," *Communications and the Law* 9 (1987): 43–58; Michael Solimine, "Newsmagazine Coverage of the Supreme Court," *Journalism Quarterly* 57 (1980): 661–663.

106. Richard Davis and Vincent J. Strickler, "The Invisible Dance: The Supreme Court and the Press," *Perspectives on Political Science* 29, no. 9 (2000): 85–92, at 85.

107. Perry, *The Priestly Tribe*, 39.

108. Joe Mathewson, *The Supreme Court and the Press: The Indisputable Conflict* (Evanston, IL: Northwestern University Press), xv.

109. Davis and Strickler, "The Invisible Dance," 85.

110. Perry, *The Priestly Tribe*, 2.

111. Richard Davis, *Justices and Journalists: The U.S. Supreme Court and the Media* (New York: Cambridge University Press, 2011), 31.

112. See, e.g., William Haltom, *Reporting on the Courts: How the Mass Media Cover Judicial Actions* (Chicago: Nelson-Hall, 1998).

113. Davis, *Justices and Journalists*, 7.

114. Davis and Strickler, "The Invisible Dance," 87.

115. Perry, *The Priestly Tribe*, 39.

116. Richard Davis, *Decisions and Images: The Supreme Court and the Press* (Englewood Cliffs, NJ: Prentice Hall, 1994).

117. Quoted in Slotnick and Segal, *Television News and the Supreme Court,* 29.

118. Davis, *Justices and Journalists,* 192–193.

119. Florian Sauvageau, David Schneiderman, and David Taras, *The Last Word: Media Coverage of the Supreme Court of Canada* (Vancouver: University of British Columbia Press, 2006), 2–3.

120. Ibid., 200.

121. Ibid., 210.

122. Ibid.

123. Adam Liptak, "Politicians in Robes? Not Exactly, But . . . ," *New York Times,* November 27, 2012.

124. See, e.g., Davis, *Justices and Journalists.*

125. Lyle Denniston, *The Reporter and the Law: Techniques of Covering the Courts* (New York: Hastings House, 1980), xvii.

126. Quoted in Haltom, *Reporting on the Courts,* 107.

127. Baum, *Judges and Their Audiences,* 139.

128. Davis, *Justices and Journalists,* 12.

129. Baum, *Judges and Their Audiences,* 142.

130. Ibid., 141.

131. Davis, *Decisions and Images.*

132. Haider-Markel, Allen, and Johansen, "Understanding Variations in Media Coverage of U.S. Supreme Court Decisions," 64.

133. Haltom, *Reporting on the Courts,* 92.

134. See, e.g., Roy B. Flemming, B. Dan Wood, and John Bohte, "Attention to Issues in a System of Separated Powers: The Macrodynamics of American Policy Agendas," *Journal of Politics* 61 (1999): 76–108.

135. Roy B. Flemming, John Bohte, and B. Dan Wood, "One Voice Among Many: The Supreme Court's Influence on Attentiveness to Issues in the United States, 1947–92," *American Journal of Political Science* 41 (1997): 1224–1250, at 1247.

136. Haltom, *Reporting on the Courts,* 60.

137. Slotnick and Segal, *Television News and the Supreme Court,* 185.

138. Baum, *Judges and Their Audiences,* 143.

139. Haider-Markel, Allen, and Johansen, "Understanding Variations in Media Coverage of U.S. Supreme Court Decisions," 82.

140. Herbert M. Kritzer and Robert E. Drechsel, "Local News of Civil Litigation: All the Litigation News That's Fit to Print or Broadcast," *Judicature* 96 (2012): 16–22.

141. Clyde Brown and Herbert Waltzer, "Lobbying the Press: 'Talk to the People Who Talk to America,'" in Allan J. Cigler and Burdett A. Loomis, eds., *Interest Group Politics,* 6th ed. (Washington, DC: CQ Press, 2002), 253.

142. Davis and Strickler, "The Invisible Dance," 88.

143. See, e.g., Gregory A. Caldeira, "Neither the Purse Nor the Sword: Dynamics of Confidence in the U.S. Supreme Court," *American Political Science Review* 80 (1986): 1209–1226.

144. Slotnick and Segal, *Television News and the Supreme Court*, 6.

145. D. A. Graber, *Mass Media and American Politics*, 3rd ed. (Washington, DC: Congressional Quarterly, 1989).

146. Davis, *Justices and Journalists*, 30.

147. Haltom, *Reporting on the Courts*, 201.

148. William Haltom and Michael McCann, *Distorting the Law: Politics, Media, and the Litigation Crisis* (Chicago: University of Chicago Press, 2004).

149. Brian F. Schaffner and Jennifer Segal Diascro, "Judicial Elections in the News," in Matthew J. Streb, ed., *Running for Judge: The Rising Political, Financial, and Legal Stakes of Judicial Elections* (New York: New York University Press, 2007), 119.

150. Haltom, *Reporting on the Courts*, 128.

151. Quoted in ibid., 126.

152. Devins and Mansker, "Public Opinion and State Supreme Courts," 457.

153. Mathewson, *The Supreme Court and the Press*, 371.

154. Quoted in ibid., 372.

Chapter 10: Legislatures and the Courts

1. See, e.g., Jeb Barnes, *Overruled? Legislative Overrides, Pluralism, and Court-Congress Relations in a Age of Statutes* (Stanford, CA: Stanford University Press, 2004); George I. Lovell, *Legislative Deferrals: Statutory Ambiguity, Judicial Power, and American Democracy* (New York: Cambridge University Press, 2003).

2. See, e.g., Howard Gillman, "How Political Parties Can Use the Courts to Advance Their Agendas: Federal Courts in the United States, 1875–1891," *American Political Science Review* 96 (2002): 511–524.

3. Lori Hausegger and Lawrence Baum, "Inviting Congressional Action: A Study of Supreme Court Motivations in Statutory Interpretation," *American Journal of Political Science* 43 (1999): 162–185.

4. Michael A. Bailey and Forrest Maltzman, "Gridlocks and the Supreme Court: Understanding the Relationship Between the Supreme Court, the President, and the Congress," in Kevin T. McGuire, ed., *New Directions in Judicial Politics* (New York: Routledge, 2012).

5. Lovell, *Legislative Deferrals*, xix–xx.

6. J. Mitchell Pickerill, *Constitutional Deliberation in Congress: The Impact of Judicial Review in a Separated System* (Durham, NC: Duke University Press, 2004), 130.

7. Maurice S. Culp, "A Survey of the Proposals to Limit or Deny the Power of Judicial Review by the Supreme Court of the United States," *Indiana Law Journal* 4 (1929): 386–398.

8. Richard E. Ellis, *The Jeffersonian Crisis: Courts and Politics in the Young Republic* (New York: Oxford University Press, 1971).

9. Ross K. Baker, *Strangers on a Hill: Congress and the Court* (New York: W. W. Norton, 2007).

10. Charles Geyh, "The Choreography of Courts-Congress Conflicts," in Bruce Peabody, ed., *The Politics of Judicial Independence: Courts, Politics, and the Public* (Baltimore: Johns Hopkins University Press, 2011).

11. Quoted in Mark C. Miller, *The View of the Courts from the Hill: Interactions Between Congress and the Federal Judiciary* (Charlottesville: University of Virginia Press, 2009), 17.

12. See, e.g., Ryan J. Owens, Justin Wedeking, and Patrick C. Wohlfarth, "How the Supreme Court Alters Opinion Language to Evade Congressional Review," *Journal of Law and Courts* 1 (2013): 35–59.

13. See, e.g., Cornell Clayton and Howard Gillman, eds., *Supreme Court Decision-Making: New Institutionalist Approaches* (Chicago: University of Chicago Press, 1999); Howard Gillman and Cornell Clayton, eds., *The Supreme Court in American Politics: New Institutionalist Interpretations* (Lawrence: University Press of Kansas, 1999).

14. Mark Tushnet, *In the Balance: Law and Politics on the Roberts Court* (New York: W. W. Norton, 2013), xiii.

15. Quoted in Miller, *The View of the Courts from the Hill,* 78.

16. Roger H. Davidson and Walter J. Oleszek, *Congress and Its Members*, 9th ed. (Washington, DC: CQ Press, 2004), 350.

17. Robert A. Katzmann, ed., *Judges and Legislators: Toward Institutional Comity* (Washington, DC: Brookings Institution, 1988), 7.

18. David G. Savage, "GOP Lawyers See Tilt to Activist High Court," *Los Angeles Times,* April 1, 2012.

19. Ibid.

20. Quoted in Kathleen Hennessey, "Obama and the Supreme Court," *Los Angeles Times,* April 6, 2012.

21. Laura Langer and Teena Wilhelm, "State Supreme Courts as Policymakers: Are They Loved?" in Mark C. Miller, ed., *Exploring Judicial Politics* (New York: Oxford University Press, 2009), 110.

22. G. Alan Tarr, *Without Fear or Favor: Judicial Independence and Judicial Accountability in the States* (Stanford, CA: Stanford University Press, 2012), 79–80.

23. Administrative Office of the U.S. Courts, *The Third Branch*, October 2010.

24. Quoted in ibid.

25. Quoted in ibid.

26. John G. Roberts Jr., *2007 Year-End Report on the Federal Judiciary* (Washington, DC: Supreme Court of the United States, 2008), 5.

27. Harvey Rishikof and Barbara A. Perry, "Separateness but Interdependence, Autonomy but Reciprocity: A First Look at Federal Judges' Appearances Before Legislative Committees," *Mercer Law Review* 46 (1995): 667–676.

28. Tom Schoenberg and Andrew Zajac, "Sequestration Hits the Law as Courts Keep Bankers' Hours," Bloomberg.com, March 8, 2013.

29. Ibid.

30. "Federal Defenders Face Deep Budget Cuts; Warn of Delays in Justice System," *Washington Post,* March 24, 2013.

31. Adam Liptak, "Budget Cuts Imperil Federal Court System, Roberts Says," *New York Times,* December 31, 2013.

32. John G. Roberts Jr., *2013 Year-End Report on the Federal Judiciary* (Washington, DC: Supreme Court of the United States, 2014), 5.

33. Ibid., 3.

34. See, e.g., Travis Andersen, "SJC Chief Justice Applauds Emergency Funds for Courts," *Boston Globe,* October 14, 2011.

35. See, e.g., Thomas G. Walker and Deborah J. Barrow, "Funding the Federal Judiciary: The Congressional Connection," *Judicature* 69 (1985): 43–50; Eugenia Froedge Toma, "Congressional Influence and the Supreme Court: The Budget as a Signaling Device," *Journal of Legal Studies* 20 (1991): 131–146; Barbara A. Perry, *The Priestly Tribe: The Supreme Court's Image in the American Mind* (Westport, CT: Praeger, 1999).

36. See, e.g., "The Feeblest Branch: An Underfunded Court System Weakens the Economy as Well as Access to Justice," *Economist,* October 1, 2011.

37. John G. Roberts Jr., *2007 Year-End Report on the Federal Judiciary* (Washington, DC: Supreme Court of the United States, 2008), 6.

38. John G. Roberts Jr., *2008 Year-End Report on the Federal Judiciary* (Washington, DC: Supreme Court of the United States, 2009), 7.

39. Ibid., 8.

40. Toma, "Congressional Influence and the Supreme Court," at 146.

41. John R. Schmidhauser and Larry L. Berg, *The Supreme Court and Congress: Conflict and Interaction 1945–1968* (New York: Free Press, 1972), 9.

42. Quoted in Ruth Marcus, "Boot the Bench: There's New Ferocity in Talk of Firing Activist Judges," *Washington Post*, April 11, 2005.

43. Quoted in Rick Klein, "DeLay Apologized for Blaming Federal Judges in Schiavo Case, but House Leader Calls for Probe of 'Judicial Activism,'" *Boston Globe*, April 14, 2005.

44. American Bar Association, "ABA President Robinson: The State Court Funding Crisis Is a Threat to Our System of Justice," *ABA Now,* February 7, 2012, available at www.abanow.org/2012/02/aba-president-robinson-the-state-court-funding-crisis-is -a-threat-to-our-justice-system.

45. National Center for State Courts, *Survey of Judicial Salaries* (Williamsburg, VA: National Center for State Courts, 2012).

46. William Glaberson, "Pay Frozen, More New York Judges Leave Bench," *New York Times,* July 4, 2011.

47. Peter Schworm, "Senate OK's Pay Raise for Judges," *Boston Globe,* May 25, 2013.

48. Schmidhauser and Berg, *The Supreme Court and Congress,* 29.

49. Deborah J. Barrow and Thomas G. Walker, *A Court Divided: The Fifth Circuit Court of Appeals and the Politics of Judicial Reform* (New Haven, CT: Yale University Press, 1988).

50. See, e.g., Martin Kasindorf, "The Court Conservatives Love to Hate," *USA Today,* February 7, 2003; Carl Tobias, "Should the Ninth Circuit Be Split? Congress Considers Dividing the Appellate Court," *Washington Times,* December 30, 2005; Amy Fagan, "House Panel OKs Provision to Divide the 9th Circuit Court," *Washington Times,* November 4, 2005.

51. See, e.g., Louis Fisher and Katy J. Harringer, *American Constitutional Law,* 9th ed. (Durham, NC: Carolina Academic Press, 2011), 215–225.

52. Neal Devins, "Party Polarization and Judicial Review: Lessons from the Affordable Care Act," *Northwestern University Law Review* 106 (2012): 1838.

53. Adam Liptak, "In Congress's Paralysis, a Mightier Supreme Court," *New York Times,* August 21, 2012.

54. "Congress Can Right High Court's Errors" (editorial), *New York Times,* March 2, 1992.

55. Richard Barnes, "Over Ginsburg's Dissent, Court Limits Bias Suits," *Washington Post,* May 30, 2007.

56. See Stephen G. Bragnaw and Mark C. Miller, "The City of Boerne: Two Tales from One City," in Mark C. Miller and Jeb Barnes, eds., *Making Policy, Making Law: An Interbranch Perspective* (Washington, DC: Georgetown University Press, 2004).

57. See, e.g., Robert Dahl, "Decision-Making in a Democracy: The Supreme Court as a National Policy-Maker," *Journal of Public Law* 6 (1957): 279–295; Joseph Ignagni and James Meernik, "Explaining Congressional Attempts to Reverse Supreme Court Decisions," *Political Research Quarterly* 47 (1994): 353–371.

58. See, e.g., Mark C. Miller, "Conflicts Between the Massachusetts Supreme Judicial Court and the Legislature: Campaign Finance Reform and Same-Sex Marriage," *Pierce Law Review* 4 (2006): 279–316.

59. *Citizens United v. Federal Election Commission,* 130 S. Ct. 876, at 904 (2010).

60. Adam Liptak, "Court Declines to Revisit Its *Citizens United* Decision," *New York Times,* June 25, 2012.

61. Bert Brandenburg and Amy Kay, *Crusading Against the Courts: The New Mission to Weaken the Role of the Courts in Protecting Our Religious Liberties* (Washington, DC: Justice at Stake, 2007), 16–17.

62. Grant Schulte, "Iowans Dismiss Three Justices," *Des Moines Register,* November 3, 2010.

63. Edward Keynes and Randall K. Miller, *The Court vs. Congress: Prayer, Busing, and Abortion* (Durham, NC: Duke University Press, 1989).

64. William G. Ross, *A Muted Fury: Populists, Progressives, and Labor Unions Confront the Courts, 1890–1937* (Princeton, NJ: Princeton University Press, 1994).

65. Edwin Meese III and Rhett DeHart, "Reining in the Federal Judiciary," *Judicature* 80 (1997): 178–183.

66. Jon Kyl, "Restoring Popular Control of the Constitution: The Case for Jurisdiction-Stripping Legislation," report from the U.S. Senate Republican Policy Committee, September 28, 2004.

67. Keynes and Miller, *The Court vs. Congress.*

68. *Ex Parte McCardle,* 74 U.S. 506 at 514 (1869).

69. *United States v. Klein,* 80 U.S. 128 at 146–147 (1872).

70. *National Mutual Insurance v. Tidewater Transfer Co.,* 337 U.S. 582 at 655 (1949) (Frankfurter, J., dissenting).

71. *Glidden Co. v. Zdanok,* 370 U.S. 530 at 606 (1962) (Douglas, J., dissenting).

72. See, e.g., Lee Epstein and Thomas G. Walker, *Constitutional Law for a Changing America: Institutional Powers and Constraints* (Washington, DC: CQ Press, 2007), 97; Charles G. Geyh, *When Courts and Congress Collide: The Struggle for Control of America's Judicial System* (Ann Arbor: University of Michigan Press, 2006), 67; Barry Friedman, "The Birth of an Academic Obsession: The History of the Countermajoritarian Difficulty," *Yale Law Journal* 112 (2002): 153–259.

73. Ross, *A Muted Fury,* 8.

74. Laurence Tribe, *American Constitutional Law,* 3rd ed. (New York: Foundation Press, 2000), 1:273 (emphasis in original).

75. William French Smith, "Letter of Attorney General William French Smith to Senate Judiciary Chairman Strom Thurmond on S. 1742," May 6, 1982, 97th Cong., 2nd Sess., *Congressional Record* 128, daily ed. (May 6), S4727–S4730.

76. Mary C. Porter and G. Alan Tarr, eds., *State Supreme Courts in State and Nation* (New Haven, CT: Yale University Press, 1988), 41.

77. Mel A. Topf, *A Doubtful and Perilous Experiment: Advisory Opinions, State Constitutions, and Judicial Supremacy* (New York: Oxford University Press, 2011).

78. Opinions of the Justices of the SJC to the Senate, 440 Mass. 1201; 802 N.E.2d 565 (2004).

79. Laura Langer, *Judicial Review in State Supreme Courts: A Comparative Study* (Albany: State University of New York Press, 2002), 37.

80. Miller, "Conflicts Between the Massachusetts Supreme Judicial Court and the Legislature."

81. Christopher Berry, "The Impact of School Finance Judgments on State Fiscal Policy," in Martin R. West and Paul E. Peterson, eds., *School Money Trials: The Legal Pursuit of Educational Adequacy* (Washington, DC: Brookings Institution Press, 2007), 213.

82. Matthew H. Bosworth, *Courts as Catalysts: State Supreme Courts and Public School Finance Equity* (Albany: State University of New York Press, 2001).

83. Pamela Ferdinand, "Education Funding Issue Colors New England Fall; Changes in Tax Code, Redistribution of Revenue Go Against the Grain of Many Yankee Residents," *Washington Post,* October 18, 1998.

84. Tarr, *Without Fear or Favor,* 79–80.

85. Chris W. Bonneau and Melinda Gann Hall, *In Defense of Judicial Elections* (New York: Routledge, 2009), 66; Joanna M. Shepherd, "Money, Politics, and Impartial Justice," *Duke Law Journal* 58 (2009): 623–685, at 644.

86. Daniel R. Pinello, *The Impact of Judicial Selection Method on State Supreme Court Policy: Innovation, Reaction, Atrophy* (Westport, CT: Greenwood, 1995).

87. Miller, "Conflicts Between the Massachusetts Supreme Judicial Court and the Legislature."

88. Mark C. Miller, *The High Priests of American Politics: The Role of Lawyers in American Political Institutions* (Knoxville: University of Tennessee Press, 1995), 101.

89. Ibid.

90. Tarr, *Without Fear or Favor,* 94.

91. Miller, *The High Priests of American Politics,* 102.

92. Ibid., 103.

93. Langer and Wilhelm, "State Supreme Courts as Policymakers," 111.

94. Ibid., 117–121.

95. Kevin T. McGuire, "Public Opinion, Religion, and Constraints on Judicial Behavior," in Kevin T. McGuire, ed., *New Directions in Judicial Politics* (New York: Routledge, 2012), 249.

96. Tarr, *Without Fear or Favor,* 174–175.

97. Abbe R. Gluck, "The States as Laboratories of Statutory Interpretation: Methodological Consensus and the New Modified Textualism," *Yale Law Journal* 119 (2010): 1750–1862.

Chapter 11: Executives and the Courts

1. Gerald N. Rosenberg, "Judicial Independence and the Reality of Political Power," *Review of Politics* 54 (1992): 369–398.

2. Robert Scigliano, *The Supreme Court and the Presidency* (New York: Free Press, 1971).

3. Sen. James Jackson of Georgia, as quoted in Walter Murphy, *Congress and the Court* (Chicago: University of Chicago Press, 1962), 9.

4. Sen. Stevens Thompson Mason of Virginia, as quoted in Walter F. Murphy, C. Herman Pritchett, Lee Epstein, and Jack Knight, *Courts, Judges, and Politics: An Introduction to the Judicial Process,* 6th ed. (Boston: McGraw-Hill, 2006), 9.

5. Charles G. Geyh, *When Courts and Congress Collide: The Struggle for Control of America's Judicial System* (Ann Arbor: University of Michigan Press, 2006), 53.

6. C. Herman Pritchett, *Congress Versus the Supreme Court, 1957–60* (Minneapolis: University of Minnesota Press, 1961), 6.

7. Quoted in James F. Simon, *In His Own Image: The Supreme Court in Richard Nixon's America* (New York: David McKay, 1973), 10.

8. Letter to Mrs. John Adams, September 11, 1804, in Thomas Jefferson, *Writings* (New York: Library of America, 1984), 11:50.

9. *Marbury v. Madison,* 1 Cranch 137 at 177 (1803).

10. Murphy, *Congress and the Court,* 26.

11. Robert McCloskey, *The American Supreme Court,* 2nd ed. (Chicago: University of Chicago Press, 1994), 42.

12. See Robert V. Remini, *The Legacy of Andrew Jackson: Essays on Democracy, Indian Removal, and Slavery* (Baton Rouge: Louisiana State University Press, 1988), 70.

13. See, e.g., Murphy, *Congress and the Court,* 26; Richard E. Ellis, *The Union at Risk: Jacksonian Democracy, States' Rights, and the Nullification Crisis* (New York: Oxford University Press, 1987), 31.

14. Quoted in Murphy et al., *Courts, Judges, and Politics,* 358–359.

15. Remini, *The Legacy of Andrew Jackson,* 24–31.

16. Arthur M. Schlesinger Jr., *The Age of Jackson* (Boston: Little, Brown, 1953), 485.

17. Keith E. Whittington, *Political Foundations of Judicial Supremacy: The Presidency, the Supreme Court, and Constitutional Leadership in U.S. History* (Princeton, NJ: Princeton University Press, 2007), 34–35.

18. Quoted in Murphy et al., *Courts, Judges, and Politics,* 359.

19. Brian McGinity, *Lincoln and the Court* (Cambridge, MA: Harvard University Press, 2008).

20. Quoted in Scigliano, *The Supreme Court,* 23.

21. David M. O'Brien, *Storm Center: The Supreme Court in American Politics*, 7th ed. (New York: W. W. Norton, 2005), 348.

22. See, e.g., C. Herman Pritchett, *The Roosevelt Court: A Study in Judicial Politics and Values, 1937–1947* (New York: Macmillan, 1948); Murphy, *Congress and the Court.*

23. William G. Ross, *A Muted Fury: Populists, Progressives, and Labor Unions Confront the Courts, 1890–1937* (Princeton, NJ: Princeton University Press, 1994), 1.

24. Howard Gillman, review of *A Muted Fury* by William G. Ross, *Journal of Interdisciplinary History* 26 (1996): 736–737.

25. Ross, *A Muted Fury.*

26. Donald Grier Stephenson, *Campaigns and the Court: The U.S. Supreme Court in Presidential Elections* (New York: Columbia University Press, 1999).

27. Ross, *A Muted Fury,* 131

28. Quoted in ibid., 148.

29. Stephenson, *Campaigns and the Courts,* 129.

30. Ross, *A Muted Fury,* 151.

31. Quoted in Murphy, *Congress and the Court,* 50.

32. Stephenson, *Campaigns and the Courts*, 131.

33. Richard L. Pacelle Jr., *The Transformation of the Supreme Court's Agenda: From the New Deal to the Reagan Administration* (Boulder, CO: Westview Press, 1991), 50.

34. Geyh, *When Courts and Congress Collide,* 109.

35. Lucas A. Powe Jr., *The Warren Court and American Politics* (Cambridge, MA: Belknap Press, 2000), 61.

36. Robert McCloskey, *The Modern Supreme Court* (Cambridge, MA: Harvard University Press, 1972), 359.

37. Kevin J. McMahon, *Nixon's Court: His Challenge to Judicial Liberalism and Its Political Consequences* (Chicago: University of Chicago Press, 2011), 3.

38. Quoted in ibid., 42.

39. Ibid., 38.

40. Ibid., 3.

41. Stephenson, *Campaigns and the Courts*, 201–204.

42. Richard Davis, *Justices and Journalists: The U.S. Supreme Court and the Media* (New York: Cambridge University Press, 2011), 8.

43. Adam Liptak and Michael D. Shear, "Republicans Turn Judicial Power into a Campaign Issue," *New York Times,* October 23, 2011.

44. Quoted in ibid.

45. Quoted in ibid.

46. Quoted in Robert Barnes, "Alito Dissents on Obama Critique of Court Decision," *Washington Post,* January 28, 2010.

47. Kathleen Hennessey, "Obama and the Supreme Court," *Los Angeles Times,* April 6, 2012.

48. Barnes, "Alito Dissents."

49. Quoted in David G. Savage, "Retired Justice Assails Decision," *Los Angeles Times,* May 31, 2012.

50. "Obama Remarks on Health Care and the Supreme Court," Associated Press, April 5, 2012.

51. Anne Gearan, "Obama Setting Up Supreme Court as Campaign Issue," Associated Press, April 5, 2012.

52. David G. Savage, "GOP Lawyers See Tilt to Activist High Court," *Los Angeles Times,* April 1, 2012.

53. Hennessey, "Obama and the Supreme Court."

54. Sheryl Gay Stolberg, "Future of an Aging Court Raises Stakes of Presidential Vote," *New York Times,* June 27, 2012.

55. Charlie Savage, "Recess Appointments Ruling to Be Appealed," *New York Times,* March 12, 2013.

56. Joanna Anderson, "For Second Time, Senate GOP Blocks Halligan Vote," *CQ Weekly Report,* March 11, 2013, 462.

57. "Executive Overreach: The President's Unprecedented 'Recess' Appointments," Hearings Before the U.S. House Judiciary Committee, February 15, 2012.

58. Charlie Savage and Steven Greenhouse, "Court Rejects Obama Move to Fill Posts," *New York Times,* January 26, 2013.

59. Ibid.

60. Richard L. Pacelle Jr., *Between Law and Politics: The Solicitor General and the Structuring of Race, Gender, and Reproductive Rights Policy* (College Station: Texas A&M University Press, 2003).

61. Ryan C. Black and Ryan J. Owens, *The Solicitor General and the United States Supreme Court: Executive Branch Influence and Judicial Decisions* (New York: Cambridge University Press, 2012).

62. Rebecca Mae Salokar, *The Solicitor General: The Politics of Law* (Philadelphia: Temple University Press, 1992).

63. Timothy R. Johnson, "The Supreme Court, the Solicitor General, and the Separation of Powers," *American Politics Research* 31 (2003): 426–451.

64. Marc Galanter, "Why the 'Haves' Come Out Ahead: Speculations on the Limits of Legal Change," *Law and Society Review* 9 (1974): 95–160.

65. Kevin McGuire, *The Supreme Court Bar: Legal Elites in the Washington Community* (Charlottesville: University of Virginia Press, 1993).

66. Joseph Kearney and Thomas Merrill, "The Influence of Amicus Curiae Briefs on the Supreme Court," *University of Pennsylvania Law Review* 148 (2000): 743–854.

67. O'Brien, *Storm Center,* 266.

68. Lawrence Baum, *The Supreme Court,* 8th ed. (Washington, DC: CQ Press, 2004), 100.

69. Lawrence Baum, *American Courts: Process and Policy,* 5th ed. (Boston: Houghton Mifflin, 2001), 262.

70. Lee Epstein, Jeffrey A. Segal, Harold J. Spaeth, and Thomas G. Walker, *The Supreme Court Compendium: Data, Decisions, and Developments,* 4th ed. (Washington, DC: CQ Press, 2007).

71. Black and Owens, *The Solicitor General and the United States Supreme Court,* 25–26; McGuire, *The Supreme Court Bar.*

72. Black and Owens, *The Solicitor General and the United States Supreme Court,* 5.

73. James F. Spriggs II and Paul J. Wahlbeck, "Amicus Curiae and the Role of Information in the Supreme Court," *Political Research Quarterly* 50 (1997): 365–386.

74. H. W. Perry Jr., *Deciding to Decide: Agenda Setting in the United States Supreme Court* (Cambridge, MA: Harvard University Press, 1991), 132.

75. Lincoln Caplan, *The Tenth Justice: The Solicitor General and the Rule of Law* (New York: Alfred A. Knopf, 1987).

76. Black and Owens, *The Solicitor General and the United States Supreme Court,* 136–137.

77. Patrick C. Wohlfarth, "The Tenth Justice? Consequences of Politicization in the Solicitor General's Office," *Journal of Politics* 70 (2009): 224–237.

78. Peter N. Ubertaccio III, "The Solicitor General: Learned in the Law and Politics," in Mark C. Miller, ed., *Exploring Judicial Politics* (New York: Oxford University Press, 2009), 140.

79. Mike Eckel, "Gay Marriage: Judge Overturns DOMA, Stepping Up Pressure on Supreme Court," *Christian Science Monitor,* May 25, 2012.

80. Warren Richey, "Appeals Court Strikes Down DOMA: Tradition Doesn't Justify Unequal Treatment," *Christian Science Monitor,* May 31, 2012.

81. Charlie Savage, "Justice Dept. Won't Contest Benefits Case," *New York Times,* February 18, 2012.

82. Graham G. Dodds, *Take Up Your Pen: Unilateral Presidential Directives in American Politics* (Philadelphia: University of Pennsylvania Press, 2013), 249.

83. Ronald A. Cass and Peter L. Strauss, "The Last Word? The Constitutional Implications of Presidential Signing Statements: The Presidential Signing Statements Controversy," *William and Mary Bill of Rights Journal* 16 (2007): 11–25.

84. President George W. Bush's aggressive use of signing statements was highly controversial. According to law professor Neal Devins, "The Bush White House used signing statements to advance its vision of a strong presidency-voicing constitutional objections to legislation impinging on presidential power, especially the President's power as Commander in Chief." Neal Devins, "The Last Word? The Constitutional Implications of Presidential Signing Statements: Signing Statements and Divided Government," *William and Mary Bill of Rights Journal* 16 (2007): 63–79, at 66.

85. Chad Thompson, "Comment: Presidential Signing Statements: The Big Impact of a Little Known Presidential Tool," *University of Toledo Law Review* 39 (2007): 185–208.

86. Banks Miller, "Describing the State Solicitors General," *Judicature* 93 (2010): 238–246.

87. Matthew H. Bosworth, *Courts as Catalysts: State Supreme Courts and Public School Finance Equity* (Albany: State University of New York Press, 2001), 39.

88. "A Battle for Florida's Courts" (editorial), *New York Times,* July 31, 2012.

89. "Politics, Principle, and an Attack on the Courts" (editorial), *New York Times,* September 24, 2012.

90. Tom Schoenberg and Andrew Zajac, "Sequestration Hits the Law as Courts Keep Bankers' Hours," Bloomberg.com, March 8, 2013.

91. Jerry Markon and Alice Crites, "As Governor, Mitt Romney Backtracked on Promised Reforms in Appointing Judges," *Washington Post,* May 30, 2012.

92. Monica Davey, "Fueled by Protests, Angry Wisconsin Voters Show Up to Fight," *New York Times,* April 2011.

93. Patrick Marley, "State Board Declares Prosser Winner," *Milwaukie Journal Sentinel,* May 23, 2011.

94. Monica Davey and Jeff Zeleny, "Walker Survives Wisconsin Recall Vote," *New York Times,* June 5, 2012.

95. Kevin T. McGuire, "Public Opinion, Religion, and Constraints on Judicial Behavior," in Kevin T. McGuire, ed., *New Directions in Judicial Politics* (New York: Routledge, 2012), 249.

96. Jeffrey Crouch, *The Presidential Pardon Power* (Lawrence: University Press of Kansas, 2009), 26.

97. Nancy Kassop, "The Presidency and the Courts," in Lori Cox Han, ed., *New Directions in the American Presidency* (New York: Routledge, 2011), 112.

98. Lawrence Baum, *Judges and Their Audiences: A Perspective on Judicial Behavior* (Princeton, NJ: Princeton University Press, 2006), 64–65.

99. Linda Greenhouse, "For Justices, Another Day on Detainees," *New York Times,* December 3, 2007.

100. See Louis Fisher, "The Federal Courts and Terrorism," in Mark C. Miller, ed., *Exploring Judicial Politics* (New York: Oxford University Press, 2009).

101. See Mark C. Miller, *The View of the Courts from the Hill: Interactions Between Congress and the Federal Judiciary* (Charlottesville: University of Virginia Press, 2009).

Chapter 12: Courts and Governmental Bureaucracies

1. See, e.g., Kenneth J. Meier, *Politics and the Bureaucracy: Policymaking in the Fourth Branch of Government* (Monterey, CA: Brooks/Cole, 1987).

2. Donald R. Kettl, "Public Bureaucracies," in R. A. W. Rhodes, Sarah A. Binder, and Bert A. Rockman, eds., *The Oxford Handbook of Political Institutions* (New York: Oxford University Press, 2006), 367–368.

3. Charles T. Goodsell, *The Case for Bureaucracy: A Public Administration Polemic,* 4th ed. (Washington, DC: CQ Press, 2004).

4. See Cornelius M. Kerwin, *Rulemaking: How Government Agencies Write Law and Make Policy,* 2nd ed. (Washington, DC: CQ Press, 1999), 2.

5. Ernest Gellhorn and Ronald M. Levin, *Administrative Law and Process in a Nutshell* (St. Paul, MN: West Publishing, 1997), 237.

6. Kerwin, *Rulemaking,* 51.

7. Cornelius M. Kerwin and Scott R. Furlong, *Rulemaking: How Government Agencies Write Law and Make Policy,* 4th ed. (Washington, DC: CQ Press, 2011).

8. R. Shep Melnick, "Courts and Agencies," in Mark C. Miller and Jeb Barnes, eds., *Making Policy, Making Law: An Interbranch Perspective* (Washington, DC: Georgetown University Press, 2004), 89.

9. Ibid., 90.

10. Gellhorn and Levin, *Administrative Law and Process in a Nutshell,* 1.

11. Meier, *Politics and the Bureaucracy,* 151.

12. Kerwin and Furlong, *Rulemaking,* 46–47.

13. Ibid., 49.

14. Martin Shapiro, "APA: Past, Present, and Future," *Virginia Law Review* 72 (1986): 447–492.

15. See, e.g., "Note: Oversight and Insight: Legislative Review of Agencies and Lessons from the States," *Harvard Law Review* 121 (2007): 613–636.

16. Kerwin, *Rulemaking,* 53.

17. R. Shep Melnick, *Regulation and the Courts: The Case of the Clean Air Act* (Washington, DC: Brookings Institution, 1983), 10.

18. Kerwin, *Rulemaking,* 232.

19. Ibid., 56.

20. Susan Rose-Ackerman, "Law and Regulation," in Keith E. Whittington, R. Daniel Kelemen, and Gregory A. Caldeira, eds., *The Oxford Handbook of Law and Politics* (New York: Oxford University Press, 2008), 583.

21. Melnick, *Regulation and the Courts,* 10.

22. Wendy L. Martinek, "Appellate Workhorses of the Federal Judiciary: The U.S. Courts of Appeals," in Mark C. Miller, ed., *Exploring Judicial Politics* (New York: Oxford University Press, 2009), 131.

23. Lawrence Baum, *American Courts: Process and Policy,* 7th ed. (Boston: Wadsworth, 2013), 35.

24. Anna Law, *The Immigration Battle in American Courts* (New York: Cambridge University Press, 2010).

25. Melnick, "Courts and Agencies," 91.

26. Baum, *American Courts,* 33.

27. Andrew Rudalevige, "The President and the Cabinet," in Michael Nelson, ed., *The Presidency and the Political System* (Washington, DC: CQ Press, 2006), 541–542.

28. Justin S. Vaughn and Jose D. Villalobos, "White House Staff," in Lori Cox Han, ed., *New Directions in the American Presidency* (New York: Routledge, 2011).

29. Nancy Kassop, "The View from the President," in Mark C. Miller and Jeb Barnes, eds., *Making Policy, Making Law: An Interbranch Perspective* (Washington, DC: Georgetown University Press, 2004), 78.

30. Meier, *Politics and the Bureaucracy,* 25–26.

31. Daniel P. Carpenter, *The Forging of Bureaucratic Autonomy: Representation, Networks, and Policy Innovation in Executive Agencies, 1862–1928* (Princeton, NJ: Princeton University Press, 2001).

32. Matthew McCubbins and Thomas Schwartz, "Congressional Oversight Overlooked: Police Patrols Versus Fire Alarms," *American Journal of Political Science* 28 (1987): 165–179.

33. David Epstein and Sharyn O'Halloran, *Delegating Powers: A Transaction Cost Politics Approach to Policy Making Under Separation of Powers* (New York: Cambridge University Press, 1999).

34. Margaret B. Kwoka, "The Freedom of Information Act Trial," *American University Law Review* 61 (2011): 217–279, at 222–223.

35. Howard Gillman, Mark A. Graber, and Keith E. Whittington, *American Constitutionalism,* vol. 1, *Structures of Government* (New York: Oxford University Press, 2013), 708.

36. Jennifer A. Bensch, "Government in the Sunshine Act: Seventeen Years Later: Has Government Let the Sun Shine In?" *George Washington Law Review* 61 (1993): 1475–1514.

37. James Ball, "Government Still Not Open, Analysis Shows," *Boston Globe,* August 4, 2012.

38. David E. Lewis, "Presidents and the Bureaucracy: Management Imperatives in a Separation of Powers System," in Michael Nelson, ed., *The Presidency and the Political System* (Washington, DC: CQ Press, 2006), 410.

39. Graham G. Dodds, *Take Up Your Pen: Unilateral Presidential Directives in American Politics* (Philadelphia: University of Pennsylvania Press, 2013).

40. B. Dan Wood and Richard W. Waterman, "The Dynamics of Political Control of the Bureaucracy," *American Political Science Review* 85 (1991): 801–828.

41. David E. Lewis, *Presidents and the Politics of Agency Design: Political Insulation in the United States Government Bureaucracy, 1946–1997* (Stanford, CA: Stanford University Press, 2003).

42. David Shafie, "The Presidency and Domestic Policy," in Lori Cox Han, ed., *New Directions in the American Presidency* (New York: Routledge, 2011), 174.

43. Brandon Rottinghaus, "The Presidency and Congress," in Lori Cox Han, ed., *New Directions in the American Presidency* (New York: Routledge, 2011), 93–94.

44. Ibid.

45. According to scholar John F. Cooney, "Signing statements have no legal force and effect. They have the same legal significance as a presidential speech, a radio address, or an answer to a question at a press conference—none at all." John F. Cooney, "Presidential Signing Statements II," *Administrative and Regulatory Law News* 32 (2007): 5–6.

46. Neal Devins, "The Last Word? The Constitutional Implications of Presidential Signing Statements: Signing Statements and Divided Government," *William and Mary Bill of Rights Journal* 16 (2007): 63–79.

47. Cornell W. Clayton, ed., *Government Lawyers: The Federal Legal Bureaucracy and Presidential Politics* (Lawrence: University Press of Kansas, 1995).

48. Melnick, *Regulation and the Courts,* 10.

49. Melnick, "Courts and Agencies," 93.

50. See, e.g., Rosemary O'Leary, *Environmental Change: Federal Courts and the EPA* (Philadelphia: Temple University Press, 1993).

51. Emerson H. Tiller and Pablo T. Spiller, "Strategic Instruments: Legal Structure and Political Games in Administrative Law," *Journal of Law, Economics, and Organization* 15 (1999): 349–377.

52. Kerwin and Furlong, *Rulemaking,* 249.

53. Melnick, "Courts and Agencies," 91.

54. *Environmental Defense Fund v. Ruckelshaus,* 439 F.2d 584 at 597–598 (D.C. Circuit, 1971).

55. Richard Stewart, "Reformation of American Administrative Law," *Harvard Law Review* 88 (1975): 1667–1813, at 1712.

56. Melnick, "Courts and Agencies," 94.

57. Martin Shapiro, *Who Guards the Guardians: Judicial Control of Administration* (Athens: University of Georgia Press, 1988), 15.

58. *Calvert Cliffs Coordinating Committee v. AEC,* 449 F.2d 1109, at 1111 (D.C. Circuit, 1971).

59. Jeremy Rabkin, *Judicial Compulsions* (New York: Basic Books, 1989).

60. Cornell W. Clayton, "Separate Branches, Separate Politics: Judicial Enforcement of Congressional Intent," *Political Science Quarterly* 109 (1994): 843–873.

61. Stefanie A. Lindquist and Frank B. Cross, *Measuring Judicial Activism* (New York: Oxford University Press, 2009), 90.

62. *Chevron v. Natural Resources Defense Council,* 467 U.S. 837, at 843–844 (1984).

63. See, e.g., Peter Schuck and E. Donald Elliot, "To the Chevron Station: An Empirical Study of Federal Administrative Law," *Duke Law Journal* 1990, 984–1077; Aaron Avila, "Application of the Chevron Doctrine in the D.C. Circuit," *New York University Environmental Law Journal* 8 (2000): 398–436.

64. Melnick, "Courts and Agencies," 96.

65. Lindquist and Cross, *Measuring Judicial Activism,* 91.

66. Thomas J. Miles and Cass R. Sunstein, "Do Judges Make Regulatory Policy? An Empirical Investigation of Chevron," *University of Chicago Law Review* 73 (2006): 823–882.

67. Rose-Ackerman, "Law and Regulation," 576.

68. Robert A. Kagan, "American Courts and the Policy Dialogue: The Role of Adversarial Legalism," in Mark C. Miller and Jeb Barnes, eds., *Making Policy, Making Law: An Interbranch Perspective* (Washington, DC: Georgetown University Press, 2004), 14.

69. Ibid., 17.

70. Ibid.

71. Ibid., 24.

72. Melnick, "Courts and Agencies," 97.

73. Ross Sandler and David Shoenbrod, *Democracy by Decree: What Happens When Courts Run Government* (New Haven, CT: Yale University Press, 2003), 4.

74. Melnick, "Courts and Agencies," 98.

75. Charles R. Wise and Rosemary O'Leary, "Breaking Up Is Hard to Do: The Dissolution of Judicial Supervision of Public Services," *Public Administration Review* 63 (2003): 177–191.

76. Gerald Frug, "Judicial Power of the Purse," *Pennsylvania Law Review* 126 (1978): 715–794, at 718.

77. Sandler and Shoenbrod, *Democracy by Decree,* 122.

78. Melnick, "Courts and Agencies," 99.

79. Malcolm M. Feeley and Edward L. Rubin, *Judicial Policy Making and the Modern State: How Courts Reformed America's Prisons* (New York: Cambridge University Press, 1998).

80. Kagan, "American Courts and the Policy Dialogue," 23.

81. Feeley and Rubin, *Judicial Policy Making and the Modern State,* 14.

82. Adam Liptak, "Justices, 5–4, Tell California to Cut Prisoner Population," *New York Times,* May 23, 2011.

83. Jennifer Medina, "California Sheds Prisoners but Grapples with Courts," *New York Times,* November 21, 2013.

84. Melnick, "Courts and Agencies," 100.

85. Charles R. Epp, *Making Rights Real: Activists, Bureaucrats, and the Creation of the Legalistic State* (Chicago: University of Chicago Press, 2009), 1–2.

86. Charles R. Epp, *Making Rights Real: Activists, Bureaucrats, and the Creation of the Legalistic State* (Chicago: University of Chicago Press, 2009), 1–2.

87. Charles R. Epp, *Making Rights Real: Activists, Bureaucrats, and the Creation of the Legalistic State* (Chicago: University of Chicago Press, 2009), 1–2.

88. Ibid.

89. Ibid.

Chapter 13: Courts Beyond the United States

1. See, e.g., C. Neal Tate and Torbjorn Vallinder, eds., *The Global Expansion of Judicial Power* (New York: New York University Press, 1995); Nancy Maveety, "Comparative Judicial Studies," in Mark C. Miller, ed., *Exploring Judicial Politics* (New York: Oxford University Press, 2009); Vicki G. Jackson, *Constitutional Engagement in a Transnational Era* (New York: Oxford University Press, 2010); Mary L. Volcansek and John F. Stack Jr., eds., *Courts Crossing Borders: Blurring the Lines of Sovereignty* (Durham, NC: Carolina Academic Press, 2005).

2. Anne-Marie Slaughter, "Judicial Globalization," *Virginia Journal of International Law* 40 (2000): 1103–1124.

3. Melissa A. Waters, "Mediating Norms and Identity: The Role of Transnational Judicial Dialogue in Creating and Enforcing International Law," *Georgetown Law Journal* 93 (2005): 487–574.

4. Elisabetta Povoledo, "Amanda Knox Freed After Appeal in Italian Court," *New York Times,* October 3, 2011.

5. "Kercher Murder Case: A Revolving Door" (editorial), *Guardian* (London), October 4, 2011.

6. Konrad Zweigert and Hein Kötz, *Introduction to Comparative Law* (Oxford: Clarendon Press, 1998), 104–105.

7. H. Patrick Glenn, *Legal Traditions of the World: Sustainable Diversity in Law* (New York: Oxford University Press, 2000), 125–126.

8. Markus Dirk Dubber, "Comparative Criminal Law," in Mathias Reimann and Reinhard Zimmerman, eds., *The Oxford Handbook of Comparative Law* (New York: Oxford University Press, 2006), 1288.

9. James Q. Whitman, *Harsh Justice: Criminal Punishment and the Widening Divide Between America and Europe* (New York: Oxford University Press, 2003), 202.

10. John Hooper and Tom Kington, "Amanda Knox Case Overturned on Lack of Motive and Forensic Errors, Juror Says," *Guardian* (London), October 4, 2011.

11. Frances D'Emilio, "Italian Court Orders a New Trial for Knox," *Boston Globe,* March 27, 2013.

12. Charlie Beckett, "Amanda Knox Mistake Exposes the Media's Guilty Secret," *Guardian* (London), October 4, 2011.

13. Amanda Knox, *Waiting to Be Heard: A Memoir* (New York: HarperCollins, 2013).

14. Douglas Preston, "Amanda Knox: Victim of Italian Code Which Puts Saving Face Before Justice," *Guardian* (London), October 4, 2011.

15. Povoledo, "Amanda Knox Freed After Appeal in Italian Court."

16. Preston, "Amanda Knox."

17. Tobias Jones, "Amanda Knox Case Is Typical of Italy's Inconclusive Justice," *Guardian* (London), October 4, 2011.

18. "Kercher Murder Case: A Revolving Door."

19. Jones, "Amanda Knox Case Is Typical of Italy's Inconclusive Justice."

20. Victor L. Simpson, "Knox Decision Puts Italian Justice System Under Scrutiny," *Boston Globe,* March 28, 2013.

21. Russ Buettner, "Strauss-Kahn, Hotel Housekeeper Settle Civil Suit," *Boston Globe,* December 11, 2012.

22. Adam Cohen, "Rush to Misjudgment?" *Time,* July 18, 2011.

23. "That Guilty Look," *Economist,* July 9, 2011, 48.

24. James Wolcott, "Pepe Le Perp," *Vanity Fair,* August 2011, 58.

25. Quoted in "That Guilty Look," 48.

26. Wolcott, "Pepe Le Perp," 56.

27. Scott Sayare, "France Orders Strauss-Kahn to Stand Trial," *New York Times,* July 27, 2013.

28. Whitman, *Harsh Justice,* 11.

29. Ibid., 8 (italics in original).

30. Ibid., 10.

31. Lisanne Groen and Martijn Stronks, *Entangled Rights of Freedom: Freedom of Speech, Freedom of Religion, and the Non-Discrimination Principle in the Dutch Wilders Case* (The Hague: Eleven International Publishing, 2010), 9, 110–114.

32. Ian Traynor, "Geert Wilders Hate Speech Trial Collapses in Netherlands," *Guardian* (London), October 22, 2010.

33. Quoted in Bruce Mutsvairo, "Geert Wilders Hate Speech Trial to Resume in Netherlands," *Christian Science Monitor,* October 5, 2010.

34. Quoted in ibid.

35. Ibid.

36. "Not a Hater, Say the Judges," *Economist,* June 23, 2011.

37. Ugo Mattei and Luca G. Pes, "Civil Law and Common Law: Toward Convergence?" in Keith E. Whittington, R. Daniel Kelemen, and Gregory A. Caldeira, eds., *The Oxford Handbook of Law and Politics* (New York: Oxford University Press, 2008).

38. Ned May, "Judicial Bias in the Geert Wilders Trial," *Guardian* (London), January 21, 2011.

39. Waters, "Mediating Norms and Identity."

40. Adam Liptak, "Texas Is Pressed to Spare Mexican Citizen on Death Row," *New York Times*, June 27, 2011.

41. "Despite U.S. Pleas, Texas Executes Mexican Killer," Associated Press, July 7, 2011.

42. Michael Avery and Danielle McLaughlin, *The Federalist Society: How Conservatives Took the Law Back from Liberals* (Nashville, TN: Vanderbilt University Press, 2013), 197.

43. See, e.g., Stephen A. Simon, "The Supreme Court's Use of Foreign Law in Constitutional Rights Cases," *Journal of Law and Courts* 2 (2013): 279–301.

44. "The global economy creates increasingly global litigation. When products can have their components manufactured in three different countries, be assembled in a fourth, and be marketed and distributed in five or six others, the number of potential fora for resolving disputes multiplies rapidly, leading litigants to battle as fiercely over jurisdiction and choice of forum as over the merits." Slaughter, "Judicial Globalization," 1112.

45. Ibid., 1113.

46. *In the Matter of the Application of Euromepa, S.A.*, 51 F.3d 1095, at 1101 (2d Cir. 1995).

47. *Howe v. Goldcorp Investments Ltd.*, 946 F.2d 944, at 950 (1st Cir. 1991). Quoted in Slaughter, "Judicial Globalization," 1113.

48. Vicki G. Jackson, *Constitutional Engagement in a Transnational Era* (New York: Oxford University Press, 2010), 8.

49. Ibid., 5–6.

50. George A. Billias, *American Constitutionalism Heard Round the World, 1776–1989: A Global Perspective* (New York: New York University Press, 2010); Anne-Marie Slaughter, *A New World Order* (Princeton, NJ: Princeton University Press, 2004), 71.

51. Slaughter, *A New World Order*, 71.

52. Slaughter, "Judicial Globalization," 1110–1111.

53. *Texas v. Lawrence*, 539 U.S. 558 at 573 (2003).

54. *Texas v. Lawrence*, 539 U.S. at 598 (Scalia, J., dissenting).

55. *Texas v. Lawrence*, 539 U.S. at 598 (Scalia, J., dissenting) (quoting *Foster v. Florida*, 537 U.S. 990, 990 [2002] [Thomas, J., concurring in denial of certiorari]).

56. *Roper v. Simmons*, 543 U.S. at 575 (2005).

57. *Roper v. Simmons*, 543 U.S. at 578 (2005).

58. *Roper v. Simmons*, 543 U.S. at 624 (2005) (Scalia, J., dissenting).

59. *Roper v. Simmons*, 543 U.S. at 627 (2005) (Scalia, J., dissenting).

60. *Roper v. Simmons*, 543 U.S. at 627 (2005) (Scalia, J., dissenting).

61. *Printz v. United States*, 521 U.S. 898 at 921 n. 11 (1997).

62. Richard A. Posner, "Foreword: A Political Court," *Harvard Law Review* 119 (2005): 31–103, at 86.

63. Ibid., 89.

64. See, e.g., Stephen A. Simon, "The Supreme Court's Use of Foreign Law in Constitutional Rights Cases," *Journal of Law and Courts* 2 (2013): 279–301, at 287.

65. *Knight v. Florida,* 120 S. Ct. 459, at 464 (1999).

66. Shirley S. Abrahamson and Michael J. Fischer, "All the World's a Courtroom: Judging in the New Millennium," *Hofstra Law Review* 26 (1997): 276–293, at 284.

67. *Roper v. Simmons,* 543 U.S. at 604 (2005) (O'Connor, J., dissenting).

68. Quoted in U.S. House, Committee on the Judiciary, Subcommittee on the Constitution, "Judicial Reliance on Foreign Law: Hearing Before the Subcommittee on the Constitution of the House Judiciary Committee," 112th Cong., 1st Sess., December 14, 2011, 2.

69. Waters, "Mediating Norms and Identity," 488–489.

70. Steven G. Calabresi and Stephanie Dotson Zimdahl, "The Supreme Court and Foreign Sources of Law: Two Hundred Years of Practice and the Juvenile Death Penalty Decision," *William and Mary Law Review* 47 (2005): 743–909. The authors surveyed Supreme Court decisions from 1789 to 2005 to examine the extent to which foreign law was cited.

71. Avery and McLaughlin, *The Federalist Society,* 170–171.

72. Steven Calabresi, "'A Shining City on the Hill': American Exceptionalism and the Supreme Court's Practice of Relying on Foreign Law," *Boston University Law Review* 86 (2006): 1335–1416.

73. Edwin Meese III, "The Double Standard in Judicial Selection," *University of Richmond Law Review* 41 (2007): 369–377, at 376.

74. Jeffrey Toobin, *The Nine: Inside the Secret World of the Supreme Court* (New York: Doubleday, 2007), 198.

75. Avery and McLaughlin, *The Federalist Society,* 189.

76. Toobin, *The Nine,* 198.

77. Quoted in ibid.

78. See, e.g., Jason DeParle, "In Battle to Pick Next Justice, Right Says Avoid a Kennedy," *New York Times,* June 27, 2005; Toobin, *The Nine,* 198–199.

79. See "Confirmation Hearing on the Nomination of John G. Roberts, Jr. to Be Chief Justice of the United States, Hearing Before the Senate Committee on the Judiciary," 109th Cong. 293 (2005) (statement of Sen. Tom Coburn).

80. Mark C. Miller, *The View of the Courts from the Hill: Interactions Between Congress and the Federal Judiciary* (Charlottesville: University of Virginia Press, 2009), 141.

81. U.S. House, Committee on the Judiciary, Subcommittee on the Constitution, "House Resolution on the Appropriate Role of Foreign Judgments in the Interpretation of the Constitution of the United States: Hearing Before the Subcommittee on the Constitution of the House Judiciary Committee," 109th Cong., 1st Sess., July 19, 2005.

82. Louis Fisher, "The Federal Courts and Terrorism," in Mark C. Miller, ed., *Exploring Judicial Politics* (New York: Oxford University Press, 2009).

83. See *Hamdi v. Rumsfeld,* 542 U.S. 507 (2004); *Rasul v. Bush,* 542 U.S. 466 (2004); *Hamdan v. Rumsfeld,* 126 S.Ct. 2749 (2006).

84. U.S. House, Committee on the Judiciary, Subcommittee on the Constitution, "Judicial Reliance on Foreign Law: Hearing Before the Subcommittee on the Constitution of the House Judiciary Committee," 112th Cong., 1st Sess., December 14, 2011, 1.

85. Theda Skocpol and Vanessa Williamson, *The Tea Party and the Remaking of Republican Conservatism* (New York: Oxford University Press, 2012), 48.

86. "Judicial Reliance on Foreign Law," 3.

87. Ibid., 5.

88. Matt Sedensky, "Bids to Ban Foreign Laws Being Pushed in 24 States," *Boston Globe*, March 3, 2012.

89. Slaughter, *A New World Order*, 96.

90. Linda Greenhouse, "Ideas and Trends: Evolving Opinions: Heartfelt Words from the Rehnquist Court," *New York Times*, July 6, 2006.

91. Claire L'Heureux-Dube, "The Importance of Dialogue: Globalization and the International Impact of the Rehnquist Court," *Tulsa Law Journal* 34 (1998): 15–38, at 26.

92. Quoted in Slaughter, *A New World Order*, 66.

93. Stephen Breyer and Robert Badinter, eds., *Judges in Contemporary Democracy: An International Conversation* (New York: New York University Press, 2004).

94. In a similar vein, the former president of the Supreme Court of Israel has also written a book on this subject. Aharon Barak, *The Judge in a Democracy* (Princeton, NJ: Princeton University Press, 2006).

95. Slaughter, *A New World Order*, 65.

96. Federal Judicial Center Annual Report 2011, 12.

97. Ibid., 13.

98. Ibid., 12.

99. As Judge Shirley Abrahamson, former chief justice of the Wisconsin Supreme Court, has noted, "The American Bar Association's Central and East European Law Initiative ('CEELI') has, with the support of the federal government, dispatched scholars, practitioners, and judges into former Soviet countries to review constitutional drafts and help formulate laws, especially in the economic sphere. A vast array of scholarly writings and statutory models pertaining to the organization of the legal profession, legal education, and commercial, environmental, and criminal law has been proffered to post-Communist legislators, judges, lawyers, and legal educators." Abrahamson and Fischer, "All the World's a Courtroom," at 279–280.

100. Slaughter, "Judicial Globalization," 122.

101. Waters, "Mediating Norms and Identity," 495–496.

102. Mark C. Rahdert, "Comparative Constitutional Advocacy," *American University Law Review* 56 (2007): 553–665, at 608.

103. Slaughter, *A New World Order*, 99.

TABLE OF CASES

INDEX